# THE
# EARLY CHRISTIANS

Selected and Edited from all the
Sources of the First Centuries

by

## Eberhard Arnold

**BAKER BOOK HOUSE**
Grand Rapids, Michigan

Paperback edition issued 1979 by
Baker Book House
with permission of copyright owners

ISBN: 0-8010-0142-0

Library of Congress Catalog Card Number: 70-115839

Originally published in 1926 as
*Die ersten Christen nach dem Tode der Apostel*
by the Hochweg Verlag in Berlin together with
the Eberhard Arnold Verlag in Sannerz and Leipzig

Translated and edited by the Society of Brothers
at Rifton, New York

PHOTOLITHOPRINTED BY CUSHING - MALLOY, INC.
ANN ARBOR, MICHIGAN, UNITED STATES OF AMERICA
1 9 7 9

# CONTENTS

Foreword                                                                                  vii

Preface to the English Edition                                                            ix

Introduction and Survey, I.&S.                                                            I

Sources of the First Centuries

State, Society, and Martyrs, S.S.&M.                                                      59
Christian Self-Portraits, C.S.P.                                                          95
Confession of Faith and Scriptures, C.F.&S.                                              127
Lord's Sayings, The Teaching of the Twelve Apostles,
     and Letters, L.S.T.A.&L.                                                            171
Meetings and Worship, M.&W.                                                              217
Proclamation and Prophecy, P.&P.                                                         261

Annotations, Explanations, and Supplementary Sources

To Introduction and Survey, I.&S.                                                        315
To State, Society, and Martyrs, S.S.&M.                                                  335
To Christian Self-Portraits, C.S.P.                                                      343
To Confession of Faith and Scriptures, C.F.&S.                                           348
To Lord's Sayings, The Teaching of the Twelve
     Apostles, and Letters, L.S.T.A.&L.                                                  365
To Meetings and Worship, M.&W.                                                           387
To Proclamation and Prophecy, P.&P.                                                      399

Indexes and Selected Bibliographies

Topical Index                                                                            413
Index of Names and Writings with Dates                                                   432
Selected Bibliography, German Edition                                                    452
Selected Bibliography, English Edition                                                   462
Symbols Used in This Book                                                                 468

( ) boldface parentheses will be used in numbering the individual selections of early Christian source material and their corresponding annotations.

[ ] square brackets indicate editorial additions.

⟨ ⟩ angular brackets indicate insertions in the English edition by the translators. English reference books cited within these brackets are for the purpose of additional reading only. Our translations are from the German, which in turn was often from the original Hebrew, Greek, or Latin.

# FOREWORD

This compilation of excerpts from the sources of early Christianity differs from former collections in that it is not organized according to dates or persons but rather as to topics. The dominant topic is the transforming power of the Spirit, which made the first Christians both rebels and reformers. This principle of election came from Arnold's own experience in the Nazi time, when the great imperative was to defy the demonic powers and to show forth the transforming power of love and devotion. The primary emphasis in the choice of material is not martyrology, but to learn what sustained the martyrs. The answer is the new birth in the Spirit, which springs from and includes beliefs with respect to Christ, what He was, what He said, what He enjoined. But Arnold is not interested in the difference between modalism and adoptionism. The index does not contain the names of Sabellius and Cerinthus. Piety and conduct are set forth in hymns, prayers, and poetry. Social concerns appear in the excerpts on property, war, and peace. Attention is paid to the faith of the uninstructed. A number of excerpts are from the New Testament Apocrypha.

The selection here given will speak to Christians who are living under conditions parallel to those of the early Church. Today Christian reformers are subject to torture and assassination. We in this country are called upon at times to resist and at times to collaborate with our government. We need guidance as to which. The early Christians also had to make choices between conformity and nonconformity. These excerpts will both inform and inspire.

Roland H. Bainton

# PREFACE TO THE ENGLISH EDITION

With the publication of this volume we wish these early Christian testimonies to speak to our time. A way of life that can be lived today results from the early Christian spirit, which is so close in power and in truth to New Testament Christianity. That this life could become reality was the faith and experience which influenced the selection of source material by the editor, Eberhard Arnold, and his little Christian community in Germany known as the Bruderhof. Today the same faith and experience in the communities of the Bru derhof or Hutterian Society of Brothers made us decide to translate the original work and to publish it in English.

We are not unaware of the important discoveries and the research done since the completion of the German edition. Yet for the general reader we know of no other collection of early Christian sources undertaken with the same purpose and point of view. Our chief concern for the English edition has been to keep the original message of the book intact. This message can best be described by quoting what Eberhard Arnold himself wrote at the beginning of the annotations:

> We have not attempted to go into scholarly discussion on theological opinions or on the results of earlier or later research. This would have to be done elsewhere. With this book we want to render simple and objective help to those who have earnest questions and concerns so that they might begin to grasp the Christ-witness in past centuries just as it was given to men in those times.

The conclusions and results of scholarship and research, however, especially in the last decades, have been fully taken into consideration. Without taking sides, we have tried to highlight all the trends which led from a living faith to a practical life of love in trust and loyalty under Christ's direction. Among other factors that bear out the authenticity of these early Christian testimonies is their simultaneous quotation by many different ancient sources.

Above all, however, the express purpose of this source book should be kept in mind: to point to faith in God, to the witness of the Living Christ, and to the working of the Holy Spirit among the gathered believers everywhere throughout the centuries.

And in a letter to his father:

Most of all I want to thank you for the very warm and kind way you have accepted my work and the dedication in my book. As you could see from my last letter, I was well aware that a certain degree of inner kinship with Tertullian, Gottfried Arnold, Sören Kierkegaard, and Leo Tolstoi in my book would not please you in some ways, but you thought rightly that I can't do otherwise, and that even in striving toward a greater objectivity I still can't deny my personal enthusiasm for the truth as I see it in the history of the early Christians. Therefore, if I take a distance from myself, as it were, if I look at my own convictions as an observer, so to speak, I must admit that the selection of the material and the evaluation of this early time is to a large extent determined by a personal conviction which I find confirmed in this "old" Christianity. On the other hand, though, you will allow that I have honestly tried to consider the answers to the deepest questions, the fulfillment of the innermost longing, and the final result of the moderating direction which had already begun in the emerging institutional Church and which comes to terms with the State and the world.

Plans for a second German edition were not realized. From the beginning of the Bruderhof (the Hutterian Society of Brothers), the witness of a daily life of brotherhood in radical discipleship of full community always came first, before any written (or spoken) witness. This order of priority had determined the book's character and delayed further publishing. A brief account of the editor's life and the community's history may help the reader to understand our book and its point of view.

Eberhard Arnold studied theology, philosophy, and education at the universities of Breslau, Halle, and Erlangen in Germany, receiving his doctorate from Erlangen in 1909. He and his fiancée, Emmy von Hollander, had by then already broken with the State Church and with both of their families in deciding for a believers' Church and for believers' baptism. After their marriage he wrote and lectured in Leipzig, Halle, and Berlin. In 1916 he became literary director of the Furche Press in Berlin and editor of the monthly *Die Furche*.

In their seeking for full Christian discipleship, Eberhard and Emmy Arnold were influenced by the search for social justice in the early German Youth Movement; by the communal life of the sixteenth-century Anabaptists, in particular the Hutterian Brothers; and by the faith in the coming Kingdom of God represented by Johann Christoph Blumhardt and his son Christoph. In 1920 at Sannerz in Hesse, out of a burning desire to practice the clear demands of the Sermon on the Mount, the Arnolds with their five children and a few others began a communal life finding its inspiration and strength in the spirit and power of the early Christians.

The coming of new members to the household led to the purchase of a farm in a very poor region of the Rhön mountains in 1927. The community was now called a "Bruderhof" out of respect for the radicalism of the early Hutterian communities. In 1930, during Eberhard Arnold's visit of nearly a year to the present-day Hutterian communities in North America, he and his Bruderhof were fully incorporated into the Hutterian Church.

The next few years brought increasing difficulties with the rising power of Hitler. On November 22, 1935, Eberhard failed to recover from a serious leg operation. His death was a tragic blow to our struggling community life.

The German Bruderhof was soon closed by the Nazis. Our people were all allowed to enter England and continue community life as the Hutterian Society of Brothers until the war drove us to Paraguay in 1940. The move to the United States began in1954. For us it is a miracle that fifty years after the beginning in Sannerz we can still try to live this life of primitive Christian community.

*Douglas A. Moody*

# INTRODUCTION AND SURVEY [1]

ESUS BROUGHT fresh news to the world. It is news about a totally different order, news that implies judgment and complete reversal for the life of the present world-age. His news concerns the reign of God that must come to put an end to the present time, the time of man. Without God our age sinks down into hollowness and coldness of heart, into stubbornness and self-delusion. In Jesus the revelation of the Father's love was manifest. Love wants to conquer and rule everything which once belonged to it. Jesus calls, urging a divided mankind to sit together at one table, God's table, which has enough places for all. He invites men to a Meal of Fellowship and fetches His guests from the roadsides and skid rows. The future age comes as God's banquet, God's wedding-feast, God's reign of unity. It is a question of God becoming Lord again over His creation, and in it He shall consummate the victory of His Spirit of unity and love.

[1] The superior figures throughout this section point to the annotations, explanations, and supplementary sources at the back of the book. See further pp. 314 and 315.

Jesus called to God as to our Father[2] that His primal will
should alone prevail on this earth, that His age of the future
in which He alone rules should draw near. His Being, His
Name, shall at last be hallowed and honored because He
alone is worthy. Then God becomes liberation from all the evil
of the present world, from its wickedness and from its death,
from Satan, the evil one now ruling. God grants forgiveness
of sin by making manifest His power and His love. This saves
and protects men from the hour of temptation, the hour of
crisis for the whole world. This is how God conquers the earth,
with the burden of its historical development and the necessity of man's daily nourishment.

However, the dark powers of godlessness pervade the world
as it is today so strongly that they can be conquered only in the
last stronghold of the Enemy's might, in death itself. So Jesus
calls men to His heroic way of an utterly ignominious death.
The catastrophe of the final battle must be provoked, for Satan
with all his demonic powers can be driven out in no other way.
Death on the cross is the decisive act. This death makes Jesus
the sole leader on the new way that reflects the coming time
of God. It makes Him the sole captain in the great battle
which shall consummate the victory.

The gulf between the two deadly hostile camps is the gulf
between the present and the future, between the age of the
world we now live in and the coming epoch of history. Therefore the heroism of Jesus is untimely, hostile in every way to the
spirit of the age. For His way manifests itself by subjecting
every aspect and every condition of life in the present to the
coming goal of the future. God's time is in the future; yet it
has been made known now. Its essence and nature and power
became person in Jesus, became history in Him, clearly stated
in His words and victoriously fought out in His life and deeds.
It is in this Messiah of God alone that God's future is present.

The new future puts an end to all powers, legal systems, and property laws now in force. The coming Kingdom is revealed even now as the unity of all-powerful love in God and therefore as a life of surrendered brotherhood among men. Jesus proclaimed and brought nothing but God, nothing but His coming rule and order. He founded neither Churches nor sects. His life belonged to greater things. Pointing toward the ultimate goal, He gave the direction. He brought God's magnet which determines the way by taking its bearings from the pole of the future.

Jesus called men to a practical way of loving brotherhood. It is the only way in keeping with the expectation of that which is coming. It alone leads to men, it alone breaks down the barriers erected by the covetous will to possess, because it is the way of a love determined to give itself to all men. The Sermon on the Mount[3] depicts the liberating power of God's love wherever this love rules supreme. In sending out His disciples and ambassadors, Jesus gave them their actual work assignment, without which no one can go on His way as He did:[4] in word and in deed we are to stand for the imminence of the Kingdom. Authority is given to overcome diseases and demonic powers. Opposition to the order of the present world epoch and insistence on the task at hand demand complete abandonment of all possessions and an incessantly itinerant life. Readiness in the fierce battle of spirits to become a target for people's hatred and finally to be killed in action is the hallmark of His mission.

After Jesus had been killed, the first and decisive victim, a small band of His disciples represented this message in Jerusalem with new power from the Spirit:[5] He who was shamefully executed is and remains the coming Ruler in the future time of God. He who was dead has come alive again. The present age of the world is nearing its end. We are faced with the greatest turn in the history of the earth and in the order of creation that ever was and ever will be. Jesus will appear a second time in glory and authority. Then God's rule will be made secure over the whole earth.

The reality of the message embodied in the primitive Church was demonstrated by the working of powers that belong to the future world epoch. Men were transformed and made new. The strength to die inherent in Jesus' sacrifice led men heroically to accept the way of martyrdom, and more, it gave them assurance of victory over the demonic powers behind all malice, wickedness, and disease. The strength to rise again of Him who rose to life through the Spirit exploded in an utterly new attitude to life—love tó one's brother and love to one's enemy—in a divine justice that bears the mark of the coming Kingdom. Through this new Spirit, property was abolished in the primitive Church. Material possessions were given in to the Church, handed over to the ambassadors and to the poor of the Church. The band of followers, as a community believing in the Messiah, became a brotherhood through the presence and power of the Spirit.

This was their immense task: to challenge the people of Israel in the face of imminent catastrophe and more, to shake the whole of mankind out of its sleep in the face of certain destruction so that all men might be prepared for the coming of the Kingdom. People from depressed and mean circumstances suddenly knew that their new faith was the determining factor, the moment of decision for the history of humankind. For this tremendous certainty, the primitive Church gained the strength she needed daily in the writings of the Jewish Law and the Jewish Prophets; in the symbol of faith given by the prophet John and by Jesus himself, the witness of holy surrender to death in the watery grave; in their communal meals celebrated to proclaim the death of Jesus; and in the common calling upon God and the Name of Jesus. All the words and stories of Jesus and all this that they demanded were told over and over again, so that it is in the primitive Church that the original sources for the Gospels and the New Testament are to be found.

"Lord, come!" was their ancient cry of faith and infinite longing, preserved in the original Aramaic from this early time of first love. He who was executed and buried was not dead. He drew near as the Living One, the Sovereign. That the Messiah Jesus rose from the dead and that God's Kingdom will break in at His second coming was the message of His first followers, one of whom was Peter, who was leading the Church at Jerusalem at the time of its founding.

Friends of Stephen, their first martyr, took this very same message from Jerusalem to Antioch. As a consequence, this nearby metropolis of Greek culture led the way in the work of the apostles, even before Ephesus in Asia Minor, or Corinth, or Rome. It was here that their enemies coined the name "Christians" for the "people of the Christ." The striking aptness of this name, so well suited to distinguish those who belong to the Messianic future of the Christ, surely did not remain unnoticed. From Antioch, Paul and Barnabas were sent to the Gentiles, apostles by the Spirit who was leading and deciding in the Church. Were they the first new apostles after the original circle of twelve?

Paul's witness, his avowal of the Cross and the resurrection, of the freedom and unity of the Holy Spirit, had a very powerful influence in the Church. The work of Paul extended over a considerable part of the known world. It was Paul who, under the leadership of Jerusalem, instituted a standard of life and behavior that united both Jewish and Gentile Christians.[6] The barring of sexual license, the rejection of association with idols as demonic, and the repudiation of the use of blood for food constituted the practical unity between Jews and Gentiles; this unity was of great significance because it was an expression of powerful victory over the rule of demons, now struck to the core and exposed as the rule of impurity, idolatry, and blood-lust. The Acts of the Apostles contains the charter of this agreement.

No definite year marks the boundary between the earliest period, led by the primitive Church and the apostles, and the following time of transition with which this book is concerned. The extinction of the primitive Jewish-Christian Church at the time of the destruction of Jerusalem and Judea in the year 70 gives us the closest approximation to a boundary date between the two periods. James, for over thirty years trusted leader of the Jerusalem Church, and its two most fruitful apostles Paul and Peter, had suffered martyrdom and death a few years before that date. The sources collected in this book speak of the time following the death of James and the end of Jerusalem and the martyrdom of the apostles Paul and Peter.

The witness of the primitive Church in Jerusalem and of the original apostles permeated very strongly the period that concerns us here. During this period, the continuity in the Spirit with the original movement that sprang from Jesus was evident in the retention of certain fundamental elements of the Jerusalem Church. These were: the message proclaimed by the apostles, the accounts written down by them about their own work, the ancient Jewish writings, the new book of the New Testament, and above all, the apostles' determined stand against the pagan spirit of the existing order. This strong influence of the primitive Church is all the more striking because the first Church (and with it early Jewish Christianity) perished in the merciless massacres of the two wars waged by Rome against the Jews, in the years 70 and 135, and in the persecutions and martyrdoms brought about by a Jewry turned fanatical as a result of these wars.[7] This humanly speaking final extermination and annihilation corresponds to the equally annihilating death by execution that ended the life of Jesus.

Not until the cataclysm of judgment is past, can God's new order break in with all its splendor; death must come before resurrection, the resurrection of the flesh; the promise of a future millennium is linked to the prophecy of judgment, a prophecy that attacks the prevailing order and conditions of mankind at their roots. All this springs from the original message passed on by the very first Church. The tension is between future and present, God and demons, selfish possessive will and the loving, giving will of God; between the present order of the State, which assumes absolute power with its economic pressures, and God's coming rule of love and justice. The tension is between two antagonistic forces sharply provoking each other. The present world-age is doomed, in fact the Messiah who is to come has already overpowered its champion and leader—this is the new accomplished fact of the suprahistorical revolution as the primitive Church handed it down to the next generation. Jesus rose from the dead: too late did the Prince of Death realize that his power was conclusively broken.[8]

From the time of the primitive Church and from Paul's time the Cross is and remains the one and only proclamation.[9] Christians shall know only one way, that of being nailed to His Cross with Christ.[10] Only dying His death with Him leads to resurrection and to the Kingdom. No wonder then that Celsus the antichristian was amazed how the tree and the resurrection from the tree was so much in evidence among the Christians,[11] and that the pagan satirist Lucian expressed his surprise that one who was hung on the cross in Palestine could have introduced this death as a new mystery, that the mystery of dying with him on the cross should have been the essence of his bequest.[12] The early Christians, then, used to stretch out their hands to imitate the extended arms on the Cross, a symbol of triumph frequently used in those times.

N THIS CERTAINTY of victory, the Christians who were gathered for the Lord's Supper heard the alarmed question of Satan and Death, "Who is He that robs us of our power?" They answered with the exultant shout of victory, "Here is Christ, the Crucified!"[13] The proclamation of Christ's death meant the "doing" of His resurrection at this meal, letting this decisive event become reality, letting life be transformed and given a new shape. His resurrection is the supreme fact. The victorious power of His whole life on earth culminates in His suffering and dying and rising again, in His ascent to the Throne, and in His second coming in the future. For that which Christ has done He does again and again in His Church. His victory is perfected. Terrified, the Devil must give up his own. The dragon with seven heads is slain. The evil venom is destroyed.[14]

The Church therefore sings the praise of Him who became man, who suffered and died and rose again and overpowered the realm of the Underworld when He descended into Hades. He is "the Strong," "the Mighty," "the Immortal."[15] He comes in person, He comes to His Church, escorted by the hosts of His angel princes. Now the Heavens are opened to the believers. They see and hear the choir of singing angels. His coming to the Church in the power of the Spirit, here and now, makes Christ's first historical coming and His second, future appearance a certainty. In trembling awe the Church experiences her Lord and Sovereign as a guest: "Now He has appeared among us!"[16] Some see Him sitting in person at the table to share their Meal. The celebration of the Lord's Supper is for them a foretaste of the Wedding Feast belonging to the future.

The Spirit has descended upon them. Grace has entered into the believers. Their fellowship is consummated. The powers of God's Spirit penetrate the gathered Church. Gripped by the Spirit, filled with the Spirit, they have become one with Christ. In Him they are merged as into a new person other than themselves. Only by actually becoming one with the Crucified can those who are tied to the Cross withstand the lures of this storm-tossed world and the violent passions of this age, just as Ulysses, tied to the mast of his ship, sailed past the Sirens unscathed.

The trials of all Greek heroes cannot match the intensity of this majestic battle between the spirits. By becoming one with the Christ triumphant, early Christian life becomes a soldier's life, sure of victory over the greatest Enemy of all time in the bitter struggle with the dark powers of this world-age. No murderous weapons, no amulets, no magic spells or rites are of use in this war. Nor will men look to water, oil, salt, incense, burning lamps, sounding, ringing brass, or even to the outward sign of the Cross for that mighty victory over the demonic powers, as long as they truly believe in the Name of Jesus, the power of His Spirit, His actual life in history, and His suprahistorical victory. Whenever the believers found unity in their meetings, especially when they celebrated their bath of immersion and their "Meal of the Lord" and "Lovemeal," the power of Christ's presence was indisputable: sick bodies were healed, demons were driven out, sins were forgiven, life and resurrection became certainty, men were freed from all their weaknesses and turned away from their past wrongs.

The holy nature of the bath of immersion and of the Meal required no ecclesiastical forms at that time. Outwardly, baptism was much more like a simple bath and the Meal of fellowship more like an ordinary mealtime than either was like a Church rite.[17] The Apostolic Confession or Rule of Faith, the readings from Jewish prophetic writings and from the Lord's Sayings and the Gospels, the pronouncements made by Spirit-filled witnesses, the united calling upon Christ, the offering of prayers and gifts, and the hymns sung in praise of God's deeds and those of Christ—these marked *man's* expression of his experience in the gathered Church. God responded with the coming of the Spirit, the coming of the Christ.

The gifts presented in devotion[18] reflected the surrendered gratitude of the community. The firstfruits of all crops and earnings, "much or little," were contributed even by those who had nothing, and who had to suffer privation in order to be able to make these offerings of gratitude and love. The visible thanks-offering of food used at the common Meal, to which bread and wine belonged as a solemn crowning, was united with the surrender of hearts and the offering of prayers. As fruit, fowl, flowers, grapes, wine and bread, and all the other gifts were brought to the table by all those assembled, the leader of the meeting received these gifts from them. They washed their hands. The festive elements for the Lord's Supper were separated from the rest; the loaves were placed on the table in three or five rows; wine was poured into the cup. At times it was mixed with water.[19] During the Meal the believers partook of all foods, thanking and praising God for all they ate.[20]

In this manner the Lovemeal was originally linked with the Lord's Supper of bread and wine. This "Meal of Thanksgiving" or "Meal of Offerings," whose gifts were used straightaway to feed the poor and the prophets and apostles, has no parallel in any other religion. Irenaeus still taught that these offerings of thanks and praise to God are the only true and just sacrifice.[21] The antichristian Celsus criticized the Christians for offering and eating firstlings and tree-fruits, bread and wine at their Meals and at the same time rejecting blood sacrifices as demonic.[22] Whereas pagans and Jews destroyed their sacrifices for God, the Christians used their offerings for the work that had to be done and for the service of the poor. The food offered at the Meal was taken even to those who were absent because of sickness or imprisonment, to strengthen them.[23]

Through the Spirit of Christ, the love of God is translated into divine service of love to men. Whoever serves the poor, the destitute, the downtrodden, serves Christ himself, for God is near to them. To be loved by God means to love God and to love one's neighbor: community with God becomes community with one another. And so out of the expectation of the coming Kingdom, life in the Church and service in the Church take shape. Faith in that which is coming unites the believers in one common will and brings about brotherhood. This forming of a bond of unity in common dedication is the positive result of opposition to the present world-age.

Such uniting in the Spirit needs no set forms. In early times the elders, overseers, and deacons, who were needed even in the first period for the individual Church communities, while retaining the manifold diversity of their allotted tasks, were subject to the free gifts of grace given by the Holy Spirit. Although this unity was brought to the communities by the apostles and prophets in their tireless travels from place to place and strengthened by them, the consciousness of being one was created solely by the one God, the one Lord, the one Spirit, by one faith, one baptism, one ensouled body given to all.

Through the Spirit that determined it, this oneness wrought equality, an equality that has its roots and its being in God alone. Just as man's lost condition and neediness, his alienation from God, does away with all differences, so the Spirit bestows His divine gift the same for all: equality and totality. Man gripped by God can understand all present inequalities only as a powerful incentive to become brotherly in perfect love. The early Christians were "brothers" and "sisters," because they were all of them—in unity of purpose and through the one same Spirit—"consecrated ones," "saints," "elect," and "believers." The same neediness, guilt, and smallness made them all "poor," a name frequently used for them in the very early times because their belief in the one God and their attitude to temporal goods was looked upon as poverty.[24]

Because the early Christians recognized their equality in poverty and in grace, their message was simple and determined. It reached the most depraved criminal as well as the most uneducated rustic, laborer, or slave. It called each one to full healing while to the deepest mind it gave ultimate revelation. The unveiling of God's mysteries is a gift bestowed in straightforward clarity. Jesus Christ is the revelation of God. By disclosing His nature He is the physician for the sick as well as for the sinners.

Whoever receives His Spirit and becomes a new man by virtue of the second birth is free, confident, open, serene, radiant, and seeing, invested with a power which makes feasible what is most difficult and impracticable and impossible.[25] In his longing for those old times, Origen calls out:[26]

> Oh, that the Lord Jesus would lay His hands upon our eyes, too, so that we too begin to look not at the visible but at the invisible! Oh, that He would open our eyes, too, to see not the things of the present but the things of the future! Oh, that He would unveil to us too that vision of the heart by which God is perceived in the Spirit through Him, the Lord Jesus Christ.

The Christians of that time were "worshipers of God," "worshipers of the Word"; gripped by the Spirit in their innermost being, they received their bearings from the future. Their faith saw the depths of God, and therefore it was the source of their strength to do the "impossible."

Even the pagan quoted by Macarius Magnes saw that this was what the Church demanded: "He alone who has faith as a grain of mustard seed, the faith that has the power to do the impossible, can be counted among this brotherhood of believers."[27]

UCH WAS THE EQUALITY achieved in everyone by faith that from the very beginning every believer who stepped out of the baptismal bath was considered altogether pure and holy. The antichristian Porphyry was appalled that a man covered with guilt and evil should stand purified by one single washing, that a glutton and fornicator, an adulterer, drunkard, thief, pederast, poisoner, or a man vile, wicked, and filthy in other ways should simply be baptized, call upon the Name of Christ, and with this be freed so easily, casting off such enormous guilt as lightly as a snake sheds its skin. "All he has to do is to believe and be baptized."[28] About this forgiveness and complete removal of guilt, Justin, assured of victory, gives the answer: Only he who has truly ceased to sin shall receive baptism.[29] Whoever is baptized must keep the seal pure and inviolate.[30] Such an incredible practical demand and expectance of total change was possible only by faith in the power of the blowing, living Spirit, who descends on the water whenever the bath of baptism is taken and makes it a bath of rebirth, a symbol of life and purity, a symbol of transformation and renewal.

The severity of what was demanded and expected in the early Church resulted in the practice that anyone who desired baptism was, whenever possible, initiated individually in the Spirit-given character and the ethical and social commitment of the new way. In the course of this instruction he was told everything about the witness to be given concerning God and Christ. The *Teaching of the Twelve Apostles,* the only unabridged text in this book, contains early second century baptismal instruction of this kind.[31] With such thorough work it was both expected and possible for the teacher, himself equipped with the Spirit, to answer for those asking for baptism with his personal authority. Under these conditions it was only after the middle of the second century that there could be any question of infant baptism. It is certain that at the beginning there was no infant baptism.[32] With baptism stood or fell the conviction of the first Christians that through their faith in the Holy Spirit they were the Church of the believers and saints, the Church that could forgive every sin because in it every sin was overcome. Many came to the Christians, impressed by the possibility of a totally new way of living, and seeking a power that would save them from their unworthy lives.[33]

More and more warriors and soldiers of the Spirit were sworn to the "symbol" of the "military oath" through the baptismal bath and the simultaneous "confession" of the truth. They were bound by that "mystery" to the sober service of Christ and the simplicity of His divine works. In the water, the believer had buried his entire former life with all its ties and involvements. Plunged so deeply into Christ the Crucified that the water could be likened to the blood of Christ, the believer accepted as his own the cutting-off by the Cross of all demon powers ruling this world-age and the victory of the Cross over them; henceforth he lived in the strength and the future of the Risen One. Each one who made this break broke with the entire status quo and was thereby committed to live and to die for the cause he embraced in such a consecration unto death. The new time invaded the old world with a company of fighters pledged to die, a triumphal march of truth and power.

Celsus launched bitter attacks against the wool-workers, cobblers, and tanners who accosted young people and womenfolk in the absence of their elders or teachers. He accused them of persuading their "victims" with wonderful words to leave parents and teachers in order to learn what is good from them, the handworkers, in their workshops or in the women's apartments. Celsus actually admits that they often achieved their purpose.[34] The sharp break made through baptism involved the Christian fighters of that time in such grave conflicts with their relatives that households were dissolved, whole families were split, engagements annulled, and marriages destroyed.

Indeed during this first period, these fighters, hated by all the world, were recruited from the lower middle class, from the ranks of freed slaves (artisans and laborers), and from among the domestic and industrial slaves so numerous at that time.

At the beginning of our period it was exceptional for members of the upper classes to join the Christian communities; toward the end of the first century their number increased gradually, and they came in considerable numbers only after the second century. The actual spreading of the movement during the period covered by this book was almost exclusively limited to the hard-working people. The way membership was made up was reflected in the value the Church set upon work. Everybody was expected to earn his living. Everybody's work was expected to produce enough to allow his love to help others in want. All had to work, for all had to make offerings in order that all might live. It followed that the Church had to provide jobs for any who really wanted to work. This obligation to provide work shows to what extent the Christian communities of that time shared their work and goods.[35] Whoever was not willing to do the work he was capable of—whoever "made his Christianity a business proposition"—was not tolerated in the communities. "An idler can never be a believer."[36]

The freedom for each one to exercise his will to work and the possibility of employing his capacities were the practical substructure for all acts of love and charity. Self-determination, that freedom so clearly recognized in the right to work, gave an entirely voluntary character to all social work done by the early Christians in support of those in need. It is therefore all the more indicative of the Spirit ruling in the Church that, even according to Hermas, the wealthy could be fitted into the building of the Church, along with the others, only after they had stripped themselves of their wealth for the sake of their poor brothers.[37] Still in his time, wealth, deadly dangerous to the owner, had to be made serviceable to the public by being given away. In agreement with natural law, with the origin and destiny of creation, it was taught that, like light, air, and soil, all goods are the common property of all men.

Love that ultimately surrenders all and everything was so much the hallmark by which Christians were recognized that the decline of this love was considered tantamount to the loss of the Spirit of Christ.[38] Urged by this love, many sold themselves into slavery or went to debtors' prison for the sake of others. Nothing was too costly for the Christians when the common interest of the surrendered brotherhood was at stake, so that they developed an incredible activity in the works of love.[39]

Everything the Church owned at that time actually belonged to the poor. Their affairs were the business of the Church. Every meeting served to support bereft women and children, the sick, and the destitute.[40] The basic feature of the movement, the spirit of boundless voluntary giving, was more essential than its fruit, the communal form of life and the rejection of private property. In the primitive Church the spontaneity of genuine love merged private property into communism of love. The same urge of love later made Christian women of rank give away their property and become beggars. The pagans deplored the fact that instead of commanding respect by means of their wealth these women became truly pitiful creatures, who knocked at doors of houses much less respected than their own had been.[41] To enable them to help others, the Christians took the hardest privations upon themselves,[42] without limiting their works of love to their fellow believers. Julian, the antichristian Emperor, had to admit that "the godless Galileans feed our poor in addition to their own."[43]

For the Christians, property sprang from the primordial crime of man: it was the result of sin. However necessary property might be for the general order of the present demonic epoch, the Christians could not cling to it. The private larder or storeroom had to be put at the disposal of guests and wanderers just as much as the common treasury.[44] Nor could anybody evade the Church's obligation to extend hospitality. This was one way in which each Church community reached out far beyond its own circle.

But in other ways too the communities helped their brothers in different places. In very early times Rome already enjoyed the highest esteem in all Christian circles because she "presided in works of love." The rich capital city was able to display the greatest activity in sending help in all directions, whereas on the other hand the poorer Jerusalem had to accept support from all the Churches in order to meet her heavy obligations toward the many pilgrims that thronged Jerusalem. In her own circle the relatively small Church at Rome gave regular support to fifteen hundred distressed persons in the year 250.[45]

However, in even the smallest Church community the overseer had to be a friend of the poor,[46] and there had to be at least one widow responsible to see to it, day and night, that no sick or needy person was neglected.[47] To inquire into and locate poverty and to impress on the rich the need to do their utmost was the deacons' service, which was combined with the service at table.[48] Nor was it an excuse for any other Christian that he had not learned to do this service or was unable to perform this task.[49] Everybody was expected to seek out, street by street, the poorest dwellings of strangers, with the result that the Christians spent more money in the streets than the followers of other religions spent in their temples.[50] Working for the destitute was, then, what distinguished the first Christians.

Every fellowman was equally respected because he was a brother equally judged and equally called. The result was equality and fellowship in all things, the same rights, the same obligation to work, and the same opportunities in life for all, leading to a general preference for a simple standard of living. Even those who were cared for by the Church, the Spirit-bearers and leaders in the truth, could expect no more than the simplest daily fare of the poor. The mutual respect among Christians at that time bore fruit in a "socialistic" solidarity, which has its roots in that love which is based on the belief in the equal birth of all men.

The rank afforded by property and profession in the present world-age is repugnant to and incompatible with such fellowship and simplicity. For that reason alone, the early Christians had an aversion to any high government office of judicial authority and to commissions in the army.[51] This aversion is explained more clearly and precisely by the fact that the Christians found it impossible to take responsibility for any penalty or imprisonment, any disfranchisement, any judgment over life or death, or the execution of any death sentence pronounced by martial or criminal courts. Because they were connected with demonic idolatry and immorality, several other trades and professions were out of the question or highly dubious, with the result that a Christian had to be prepared at any time to give up his occupation. The unemployment resulting from such a renunciation and the ensuing threat of hunger was to be no more frightening than the violent death of martyrdom.[52]

Underlying all these practical consequences was the unity of word and deed. A pattern of daily life that was in keeping with the deeds and historic facts proclaimed by the Christians was bound to emerge. What struck and astounded the outside observer most was the extent to which poverty was overcome in the vicinity of the communities. This was achieved by their voluntary work of love, which had nothing to do with the more or less compulsory social welfare of the State.

An equally tangible change in the conditions prevailing among men was achieved by putting into practice strict monogamy, absolute faithfulness in marriage, and chastity before marriage. In the beginning this came to expression most clearly in regard to the brothers serving in responsible positions, of whom it was demanded that they have only one wife. The foundation for Christian marriage was purely religious. Marriage was felt to be the symbol in man's life of the relationship which the One God established with His one people and the One Christ with His one Church.

From then on, a completely different mankind was in the making. This shows itself most clearly in the religious foundation of the family (the starting point of every form of human society and fellowship) and in the predominant tendency of all creation, which is in movement toward communism of love. The new men, called out and set apart by God, are deeply and firmly linked to the coming revolution and renewal of the whole moral and social order. It is a question of the strongest "yes" to the earth and mankind. From their Creator and His miraculous power, the believers expect the perfection of social and moral conditions among men. This was the most positive attitude imaginable: they waited for God's perfect love to become manifest for all men, comprehensively and universally, in answer to the need of their bodies as well as to the need of their souls.

HE CHRISTIANS KNEW that such a transvaluation of all values, such a turning upside down of all strata of society, can never be achieved by human power. Because of this knowledge and their boundless faith in the Almighty God, their insight reached down into immeasurably deeper levels than any human politico-revolutionary threat to the present power structure and judiciary order. Yet the very fact that theirs was not a rebellion based on human opposition and violent insurrection, which could have been easily crushed by the coercive power of the State, made these representatives of the impending judgment and the coming Kingdom appear all the more dangerous. It was they who called themselves "foreigners" and "strangers" in contemporary State and society, "citizens" of a quite different "political, suprapolitical order"! Indeed, it could be proved that the apocalyptic and prophetic books they read, as well as their own Revelation of John, were full of revolutionary opposition to the existing civic order. Was it not they, vassals of the coming Christ, Christians, who put themselves up against the Roman worshipers of the Emperor?

Yes, they felt they were "God's people," a "new people," the "first people," the "people of the future," the beginning, the central point, and the end of all human history! Nor did they hesitate to represent that the Church unity they experienced would be the dominant power in the Kingdom of the future! They even went so far as to assert that the councilors of their own communities would be capable of administering any large city of God, if such could exist in the present age of the world,

whereas contemporary government leaders had no right to
claim administrative superiority in view of their low moral
conduct, their bad character, and their poor performance.[53]

The sharp condemnation with which the Christians opposed
the dishonesty and impurity, the murderous violence, the mam-
monism and subservience in public life weighed much more
heavily against them than their acceptance of the existing law
and order counted in their favor. For they did recognize the
government as a transitory necessity, although they considered
it of but very relative moral value. However, the fact that
these revolutionaries of the Spirit knew that they were actually
the State's best helpers and allies in the cause of morality and
world peace[54] proves that theirs was quite a positive attitude
to the ethical importance of the State. They realized clearly
that, until the time of God's decisive intervention, they of
themselves were unable to change the structure of the present
order. They did not feel able to bring about any substantial
improvement for the masses, not even in the direction of social
reform. For this reason the Christians tolerated even slavery
and social oppression. For them these evils were but one expression of the status quo, only a partial aspect of the total crime
perpetrated by the State against freedom and equality. It was
typical of their way of protesting with their actual conduct
that they reacted by invariably giving full recognition to their
slave brothers. Frequently they bought or gave them their freedom; but they did not recognize any demand or legal claim
on the common purse to pay such ransom, as this would have
meant substituting a legal claim for the faith and hope and
the life of surrender and sacrifice to which any Christian
was committed.

However much they protested and proved their loyalty,
though, the Christians were misfits in society. The Jews with
their separatism and imageless worship of God, which made

them a "second race," were already an affront to society. The faith in God that the Christians had went a decisive step further. It was divested even of the seeming national character of the "Jewish God" and His Temple and sacrifices. For the pagans this explained the repulsively novel life the Christians led: it was god-less. Christians were looked upon as a downright monstrous "third race" and accused of intolerable atheism. This explains why at that time the Roman State fought against the Christians as "criminals," "desperate and forsaken people," "lawless men," "public enemies," "dregs of the nations," "monstrous phenomena."

In the eyes of the Christians, however, the religious idolatry that they found everywhere was the principal crime committed by humankind, the crux of the indictment against this age, the real cause of the judgment to come.[55] This struck at the very core of a concept which set up the State as absolute — the sole judge of its own interests, laws, and actions. The worship of Caesar as a god rested on the omnipotence of the Empire, on the identification of the State and its laws with culture, religion, and morality. The Christians abhorred and attacked this mixture of the religious and the patriotic. They abhorred any State religion that forced back God's rule; they loathed all religiosity influenced by the politics of the moment and fought against any permanent establishment and veneration of the existing power structure and any political system with a religious emphasis. These things had to be regarded as the inheritance of Babylon, the systematization of sin and demonism; they were nothing short of the Devil's State and the service of Satan.

Therefore it was inevitable that in return the State would accuse these people of high treason and of being the enemies of civilization. After all, they declared openly that "the emperors could only then have believed in Christ if they had not been emperors, or if Christians could have ever been emperors."[56] Belief in God's Kingdom stood in sharpest opposition to the deification of the Empire and the ensuing imperial cult.

And yet these same Christians subordinated the Emperor only to God. After God he is the first in this world. Precisely because he remains in their demonic ranks, he stands above all pagan gods. The Christians saw in the imperial government as in the entire existing order of mankind merely a passing, albeit necessary, historical phenomenon. Accordingly, the Creator's moral order is valid even now in the midst of the demonic rule of Satan's throne. Therefore even the existing government (representing that rule) is instituted by God. For Christians, it is a serious matter of conscience to honor and respect the moral task of the State and its ruler, for the State is ordained by God to be a bulwark against the most serious excesses of sin and demonism in these times. The State, custodian of public morals, must be highly respected. This conviction (which grew stronger in later Christianity) was never lacking, not even in the most radical circles during times of acute conflict. The condition of the world being as it is, even the most extreme among them were not anarchists in the sense that they would have wanted, or actually taken measures toward, the abolition of the State as it existed then or now. The early Christians knew therefore only one form of disobedience to government authority: passive resistance of utmost endurance, even unto death. There was no other attitude by which they could have demonstrated their certainty that the existing powers of the State can and will be abolished only by the new order of all things, hence by God alone. They themselves, however, took their stand firmly on the side of this new order coming from God.

Because they were revolutionaries of the Spirit, heralds of the last judgment and of the coming transformation, the Christians had to be ready for martyrdom at any moment.

Their life-witness meant the certainty of being sentenced to death by State and society. To them, therefore, a "martyr" was each "witness" ready to die for his faith, one who bore this testimony before kings and judges with the steadfastness of a soldier of God. He was a "martyr," that is a "confessor," even if, ready for anything, he did not have to die because of his witness. To give witness is the essence of martyrdom. The martyr upholds the factual, objective truth of his testimony as an eye-witness of the Lord and His resurrection. He sees Christ and becomes His prophetic Spirit-bearer. Through the Spirit, the blood-witness of the martyr-confessor is translated into the sphere of the decisive battle waged by Jesus, that battle in which He, champion and leader of the future, Himself died and by dying finally judged and routed the hostile powers of the present age. Put to death by the most devout people, the Jews, and the best State, that of the Romans, their Christ fettered and disarmed the demons and their thick darkness through His Cross. Since then, each new death of martyrdom is turned into a celebration of victory over these forces. Over and over again, the rout of the Satanic powers becomes a deadly serious reality in the dying with Christ.

Their beloved Jesus had foretold for Himself and for His disciples that the drinking of this cup would mean baptism in this blood-bath: again and again, the Church gathered around the martyrs as for a Lord's Supper in blood. Each time, the repulsive spectacle of execution was to them the solemn victory of Christ over Satan's rule, the certainty of faith in the Lord's resurrection, the meal of death celebrating His rising from the dead—that event which guaranteed the rule of the dying Victor for all times.

Today it is impossible to visualize how real the heroic soldiership of the Spirit actually was for the first Christians. From the beginning the military equipment given by the Spirit

was something infinitely more real in their lives than a mere
parable or metaphor. The two basic principles of army life—
the right to military pay and the injunction against economic
and political involvement—aptly characterized Jesus' commission to His apostles on their journeys; He stressed their right
as soldiers of Christ to receive maintenance for their service
(although they remained poor on principle) and enjoined
them to refrain from any business enterprise and from acquiring possessions. By virtue of the oath of allegiance or Rule of
Faith, by virtue of this oath of the sacrament, all Christians
were committed to the apostolic and prophetic soldiership of
the Spirit. Non-Christians were therefore called "civilians" or
*pagani* from which stems the word "pagan." Equipped with
the unblemished weapons of the Spirit, these militaries were
ready to die; hence every martyr-death was a solemn high-
festival for the fighting troop of the believers.

To gather around the martyrs was the tremendously powerful culmination of early Christian meetings, despite the presence of the pagan populace. But Jesus came also into every
peaceful meeting, however small, He who alone was both leader and fellow-fighter among His followers. Often in meetings
of this nature, the radiant Cross and the thronging mass of
people watching the execution of Jesus were all but visible.
The voices raised at the crucifixion of Jesus and the shouts of
His friends and enemies rang out from Golgotha.

What was seen and heard in such Spirit-filled gatherings
often led to unintelligible speech and to actions that were hard
to understand. Nevertheless, what dominated their meetings
was the fiery judgment of the last battle, which gave flaming
birth to light and warmth and brought the fresh air of the
future world; for here the Christ was truly present in person,
in the power of God's Word pregnant with the Spirit, and

in the powerful virtue of goodness, pureness, and strength.

In prayers, psalms and hymns, and in commentaries on the Bible made by the prophets and teachers during the meetings, the Word came into its own. The moral impact of Biblical truth exacted purity and truthfulness in actual life, practical love in actual work. There was nothing of the exaggeration and intoxication of one's own human emotions in the exultant enthusiasm which broke in freely from the Holy Spirit. On the contrary, this genuine, surging power of the Spirit revealed the authority of the Christ, which came down straight from the other world like a stroke of divine lightning. Sometimes, on hearing for the first time the proclamation from those who had been taught by the apostles, whole crowds would embrace the faith under this impact of God.[57]

The clearness of the divine Word, the actual fact of the accomplished work of salvation, was the sole content of such ecstatic and enthusiastic experiences. At times, the light of Biblical truth would flow from the Spirit-bearers like a visible force when the Word was proclaimed, or the book of the Law and the Prophets was read, and the ancient psalms and hymns of praise were sung. Tertullian tells the typical example of a prophetically gifted sister, whose visions were prompted by nothing but the readings of Scriptural passages, by the things described in song, psalm, and Biblical discourse. The Word which was read out became reality before her eyes and ears. She saw the Lord himself and the angelic hosts, the victorious battle of the Christ, and His return with the princely armies of Heaven.[58] Others filled with the Spirit saw with their own eyes how an angel prince drove demons out of a fasting wayfarer.[59]

Such demons were often seen as darkened light, smoke, snakes, and black shapes. These forms made plain the lying, slanderous, seductive character of evil darkness. Yet what really mattered here too was the religious and moral effect on the people. There is a story about a prostitute who listened for hours to the singing of psalms and apostolic hymns and was so deeply stirred that she broke down under the burden of her former life and started on the new way.[60] Another story tells how the aged John of Ephesus looked for a young renegade in the mountains. He threw his arms around the young bandit, who, lamenting bitterly, asked pardon. The apostle assured him with the power of his authority that the Healing Savior had given him complete forgiveness. John then fell on his knees before the young bandit and covered his right hand with kisses, the hand that had wielded the murderous weapon and was now washed clean of blood. He brought him back and restored him to the Church as a living example of repentance and regeneration, a trophy of Christ's power of resurrection.[61]

As this story of the apostle John shows, there can never be any reverence for the authority of the Holy Spirit without the unshakable, concrete reality of God's personal presence and clearly defined cause. What the Holy Spirit does is always identical with the Spirit of the Law and the Prophets, with the Spirit of Jesus and the apostles, with the Bible itself. The Spirit breaks into men's lives bringing the apostolic, prophetic freedom that leads to obedience to God-given authority. This authority guarantees the true fulfillment of freedom. There is only one determining will behind the mystery of the Spirit at work: God himself, the Creator, the Lawgiver, and the coming Ruler of humankind. The Spirit, since He reveals God, invariably engenders strictest moral responsibility. The inner voice, which speaks in every conscience awakened by the Spirit, is consistent with the intent and goal of God's way. Therefore, this voice knows when to be still in hushed reverence to hear God speak and "rightly and worthily" to praise Him.[62]

Whenever God reveals Himself, just because He brings boundless forgiveness and renewal, He brings on sharpest chastisement and purification. For instance, there was a woman whose hypocritical and impure life was unmasked by the Spirit working in Paul; she was thrown to the ground, paralyzed.[63] Again, the hands of a young man withered when he shared in the Meal, because he tried to conceal a murderous act from the all-seeing Spirit.[64] The Spirit-bearers were equipped with both the power to reveal the true state of a person and the authority to forgive; both gifts were inseparable; both revealed the truth. To be filled with the Spirit meant purity, truth, and love in daily life; hence, anyone filled with the Spirit was guided in every circumstance by that same true Spirit. Only then could the Spirit tell him what was in other people's hearts and which was the moment when Christ himself granted forgiveness of sin and strength for a new life.[65] Because forgiveness meant the taking away of sin by God himself, it showed itself as a power coming from God that broke and abolished the rule of sin.

We see, then, that the commission of the Spirit-bearers was to proclaim the Word, to expose evil, and to bring judgment into every situation; theirs was the authority to forgive and to impart the strength for healing and new life. Men of prophecy, they pronounced the Word God spoke.

LL THAT IS SAID ABOVE throws a clear light on the threefold gift of leadership that held sway over the whole Church during the early years. The Spirit-bearers, those who had the leadership and responsibility, were "first, apostles; second, prophets; third, teachers." God himself gave them to the Church in this trinity and in this order of their spiritual rank.[66] This divine appointment was first given to the primitive Church at Jerusalem. Like many other things, this too was of Jewish origin. Each of these three services could be found among the Jews; they had similar functions, although the Jews did not have that triune responsibility of leadership.

The unconditional respect the "teachers" were accorded among the Jews is well known. It went so far that, in case of captivity, one's teacher had to be ransomed before one's father; the teacher had to be relieved of his burden before the father. For the Christians as well, the teachers were among the honored leaders in the Spirit, only they were expressly assigned third place after the apostles and prophets. Yet they too were bearers of the Word of truth and of the Holy Spirit. They too had the power to raise up sons of the Spirit, to beget children of the Spirit as it were. Those who desired baptism were brought to them. Even in Origen's time, in some Churches the Spirit-filled teachers were still able to speak freely in the presence of the overseers and presbyters. It was the teachers' task to represent the truth to those outside through mission, and to give full instruction in the Bible and the Confession of Faith as their service within the Church. It was their service to make known the content and the strength of the new life in all its breadth and depth. Their instructions, given as coming from the Spirit of truth, were universal and binding; they carried a quite different weight from anything otherwise spoken in meetings.[67]

Therefore, Tertullian still considered the teachers as not counting among the administrative services of each Church community—overseers, elders, deacons—but rather among the leaders and heroes gifted with the Spirit who in his time were the martyrs and whom Tertullian regarded as witnesses of the prophetic Spirit. Teachers who attested to a mandate from the Spirit could be disowned by the Church only if their deeds did not match their words: for instance, if arrogant confidence in themselves robbed God of His honor. Otherwise, the teachers were subordinate only to the higher echelons of the Spirit's mandate, the prophets and apostles, because to these the Spirit entrusted the specific gift of insight and discernment. All presentations of teaching done under the Spirit's command could have no other character than that of the Spirit Himself and no other content than the Spirit's witness to the truth. The undisputed power and authority of the witnesses, who were shaken and moved and filled by the Spirit of God, could never allow the human instruments to become the deciding factor; only the Spirit of Christ, sole bearer of truth and strength, was allowed to prevail.

The absoluteness and directness of the Spirit at work reveals the Church, the Church that has reality only in God and in the Spirit, the Church that time after time breaks in anew, and that alone has final jurisdiction. In the presence of such spiritual oneness, such a bond of unity given by the Spirit, there was no question at that time of any human organization and conformity. That is why in those first years the terms were not sharply defined that were used for the local adminis-

tration services, such as "overseers," "presidents," and "elders,"
who were the leaders of their respective groups. That is why
the Church, just like the Holy Spirit, the Father, and the
Son, remained an object of faith for the first Christians. This
historical fact is of crucial significance.

Rudolf Sohm clearly recognized that the individual communities of the Christian brotherhood could only be understood
as the irradiance on earth from that ultimate reality which
has its life in God—the Church. Therefore, the gift and guidance of the freely moving Holy Spirit was the only valid, original Church order. As an object of faith, the divine, invisible
Church in its entirety and perfectness is expressed and becomes
operative in the individual believer and in every single worship
meeting. The Church must not be looked for where man is,
but where God is. She is the mistress and mother of the believers, the bride of the coming Messiah, the Eve of the heavenly
Adam, the Body of the Christ, which has reality in the Spirit.
The Lord is the Spirit. The Spirit is the Church. Thus, Christ
in the members becomes the Church. He becomes the Church
as the "coming Messiah."[68] This shaping of individual, human
communities of Christians is in the very image of the Church
that has being in God alone; this shaping is nothing less than
the action of God turned toward mankind. Here is the religious
and social manifestation of the Spirit at work now on this
earth.

From all this there resulted the gathering of men and women
into an order committed to a clearly defined way of living
whose members belonged together for life, an order quick
and alive in practical sharing and in the daily strengthening of
faith and deepening in the Spirit. It was the teachers' task
to advocate the practical consequences resulting from the
principle of such a brotherly order: to fit into the whole, to
accept the supreme, all-embracing cause, to seek the common

good for the whole community.[69] From this wide viewpoint the teachers had to see to it that all Christians met one another daily and gathered constantly.[70]

While maintaining these practical aims, the Spirit-filled teachers were commissioned to uphold the teaching of the apostles, to hand down the apostolic tradition unadulterated, as the sole plumb line for the lifeway in faith, as the Canon of Truth by which all things are measured. Belief in the Church was an integral part of the Apostolic Confession of Faith that grew out of the baptismal formula, according to which the believer was dipped into the death of Jesus in the name of the Father, the Son and the Holy Spirit. In early years, this oath of allegiance was passed on by word of mouth like a military watchword, so that it could not conceivably have been written down at that time. Harnack and other leading scholars proved that in its earliest form the confession was ninefold. In just the following simple words it confessed the belief in God, the Father, the Almighty; in Jesus the Christ (who is the coming Messiah), in the Son, our Lord; in the Holy Spirit, in His Church, and in His resurrection of all flesh (which is the transformation of matter for the new Kingdom).[71] Thus belief in God points vertically to Jesus as to the coming Prince in God's reign, and further to the Holy Spirit in whom God's person is at work now. Further, belief in the Father points to the Son and to the Church, who, working through God, is the mother of all believers. Finally, the belief in God's all-powerful might confesses Christ as our Lord and expresses the expectation of the Kingdom on earth under His rule in its most intense manifestation which is the resurrection of the flesh.

God alone matters here. For this very reason, to confess Him is to confess the lasting purpose of His creation, as it will be renewed by Him. The Word Incarnate will take God's creation in hand to make it new again. The Word went out from Jesus in the mission of the apostles, and, through the Spirit gathering the Church, the Word invades human conditions. God is the one God, and the coming Christ-Messiah is both the creating Logos and the historical Jesus. He is one and the same, He is now the Lord of the Church, He is the Healing Savior of all. "Accept Him! Draw near! Live as He lived, and do as He said!" Thus, teachers gifted with the Spirit led people to the Church of the one faith and witness, to Christ himself, and so to a new life governed by the divine citizenship which belongs to the future.

In the hands of these teachers the old Book, the Bible of the Jews, pointed again and again in that same direction. The Bible was and remained the permanent source of knowledge for all meetings, for all personal instruction, and for quiet, individual reading. Origen demanded that each Christian devote one to two hours daily to this study.[72] The powerful yet simple language of the Bible, particularly of the prophets and psalmists; the convincing account of the creation of the world; the prophetically inspired foreknowledge of the future; the ethical, divine power and spiritual clarity of the Mosaic law-givers—all these made a powerful impact on the first Christians. Tatian, Justin, and the author of the Proclamation of Peter spoke for many contemporary Christians when they described how they themselves were converted to the Christian faith through the Old Testament.[73]

From the beginning, the ancient Biblical prophecies of truth together with their fulfillment and their increased power in the Good News were the essence of the Spirit's mandate to teach. Everywhere, the "Lord's Sayings" and the events of Jesus' life (Papias owned an outstanding collection of such sayings[74]) were passed on from one to another. They were the very substance of the commission to teach. Called "Memoirs of the Apostles" already by Justin,[75] they were the original form of the Gospels as we know them. The memories of Jesus, called Gospels at an early date, were soon augmented by the apostolic letters, and so the permanent foundations for the New Testament were laid already by the first teachers of Christendom. Their mandate to teach was the charge to proclaim the Word and therefore was committed to the Spirit-given word of the first apostles and the first prophets. The word engendered by the apostles and prophets and spread by them to people everywhere was shaped, interpreted, and represented by the teachers.

That the teachers were placed after the prophets and apostles, particularly after the apostles, is clear from their very commission and also from the different intensity of their life-commitment. The apostles owned nothing and traveled constantly, while the prophets were only required to give up their possessions, and the teachers were not absolutely bound to renounce their property or to take to the road. And yet it was the itinerant life of the apostles which carried so much weight that early Christianity has rightly been called an itinerant religion, the way which traverses the whole world. Time after time, the example of the apostles was an incentive to the amazing mobility of the Christians as they traveled from place to place. This lively intercourse, together with the exchange of letters and of the writings they held in common, is the primary explanation for the fact that the same bond was kept between all the communities. Origen still emphasized that the apostles and prophets journeyed from town to town, from village to village, and took upon themselves the hardships of these travels, barely accepting even from believers the necessities of life.

In fact, the intensity of the early Christian struggle and mission task called for this encouragement through the example of the apostles. Fasting and lifelong celibacy were often the

results of a self-control that was born of hearts moved to live
up to the great intensity of purpose inherent in that task. The
example of the four prophetic daughters of Philip, who were
virgins, and later that of the Montanist prophetesses, likewise
virgins, illustrates the life of many apostles and prophets at
that time. But we must not confuse this soldier-like self-
discipline of the Christians, the sole purpose of which was the
eschatological task and fight, with the asceticism of later times,
which was valued for its own sake. Theirs was no striving for
redemption through ascetic, religious exercises. It was purely
and exclusively the concentration of all their powers on the prophetic proclamation of the coming Kingdom; it was the
tempering of all their energies for the arduous battle of the
spirits to which they were summoned; it was purely and
exclusively the focusing of all their energies on the one object,
the task on hand. The prophets wanted but one thing, that
God was heard, that God himself spoke and acted.

People who took this calling from God so seriously could
not remain hidden. Pagans like Lucian knew of prophets who,
in worship-meetings of the communities and even on their
travels from place to place with their friends, proclaimed their
Spirit-given word.[76] From his own experience, Celsus tells of
many prophets in his time who prophesied in holy places and
moved about in the cities and traveled on the highways. When
they were gripped in ecstasy, the Word of God and of Christ
spoke through them:

> I am God, I am God's Son, I am the Spirit of God. I
> have come because the destruction of the world is at hand.
> From this I will save you. Soon you shall see me returning
> again in heavenly power when the fire of judgment shall
> come upon city and land.[77]

A mighty spiritual flood at first, Christian prophecy ebbed
slowly away until its force was spent by the end of the second

century. Melito of Sardis still called himself a prophet. Among the Jews, prophecy had become a matter of the past only a little earlier, after the destruction of Jerusalem. Also until that time there had been among them an immense prophetic activity, preserved in the names of certain Jewish prophets and in the abundance of contemporaneous Jewish apocalypses and oracles, which however, because they served a literary purpose, lacked the power and authority of the prophets of old. Like the true Jewish prophets before them, the Christian prophets alone now claimed and upheld unconditional recognition of the authority of the Holy Spirit speaking through them as God's voice. What a mighty reality were God and the Holy Spirit for those first communities! An ancient fragment says of the prophetic Spirit common to both apostles and prophets that which Origen later says of the apostles alone:[78]

> The prophetic Spirit is what makes the firmly established prophetic order of life into a body. He endows the body of the flesh of Jesus Christ with a living soul.[79]

The Body of Christ as the living Church is indeed the all-determining, the God-given reality; this fact depends entirely on faith, and rests upon the ensoulment of this Body by the Spirit of the apostles and prophets.

And yet the principal task of the apostolic ambassadors was not entrusted to the prophets: at all times the standing and importance of apostolic calling far surpassed that of prophethood. What was said about the prophets was just as fundamentally true for the apostles. They too had the prophetic Spirit. For they too were prophets and teachers, often—perhaps always, after the very first apostles—being recognized from among the prophets and teachers and set apart for the apostolate. But God entrusted the apostles, in this same Spirit, with tasks which far exceeded prophetic utterance and instructive address. The ambassadorship of the apostolic messengers of the

Spirit carried more weight than the mission of prophecy, and much more weight than the charge of teaching all the people; it went beyond prophecy just because it alone had, above and beyond all the other inherent tasks, the power to lay the foundation for the Church. The apostle Thaddaeus said he would be silent in a small circle, because he knew he was sent to proclaim the word in public. Therefore he demanded that all the citizens of the town should assemble. "Then I will speak to them."[80]

Eusebius reports how those men, consumed with burning love and fulfilling the mission charge of Jesus, distributed their possessions among the poor and set out on an uninterrupted journey to speak of Christ to those who had never heard about Him. As soon as they had appointed shepherds in one place, they hurried on straightaway to other people in other lands.[81] The world-wide mission of the apostles included all men. They were charged, everywhere in all regions, to found and build up Church communities. Of all the inspired bearers of the Word the apostles were the molders and leaders throughout the earth. The work of these first ambassadors of the Messiah was felt to be so fundamental, so exclusively given by God, so much a part of the faith in the Spirit, that their work was even included in the Confession of Faith.[82] Only God himself, only Christ himself could call men to an apostolate of such consequence. That this was really a call from God was proved beyond doubt by tangible miracles wrought in the Spirit's authority, and by the visible building up of the Church everywhere through the first apostles. It is all the more astounding that *The Teaching of the Twelve Apostles* and the *Shepherd* of Hermas use the term "apostle" in a much broader sense than later generations, including ourselves, are used to.[83] But God did call out other, new apostles, even after He had sent out the Twelve and Paul. Tertullian and Origen confirmed this conviction of earlier Christendom and gave the name of apostles to the seventy disciples in the Gospels, among others.

That the God-given mandate of Christian apostleship towered high above everything else is brought into sharper focus by the fact that the word "apostle" originally applied to emissaries of non-Christian Judaism. The task of the Jewish apostles was limited to carrying letters from Jerusalem headquarters to the scattered Jews everywhere, to collecting contributions for headquarters, and, in the exercise of supervisory and disciplinary powers, to upholding the bond of all Jews with Jerusalem. In the same way, the primitive Church in Jerusalem as the Christian headquarters, once she had recognized Paul as an apostle, laid the well-known financial obligation on him as well as the decision of the "Apostolic Council." However, the power and authority of the Kingdom, which as God's reality stand behind the apostolic ambassadorship, have singularly greater tasks than these. Therefore, both the work carried out by the apostles and the power manifested by them had to be equally singular. It was not to be compared with the Jewish apostolate, which was purely organizational.

The work of the apostles was direct revelation of God's truth by the Spirit. Thus it became the foundation for the entire vision of faith given to the Church. It follows, therefore, that the apostles exercised the necessary supervision and discipline in the Church, which for that very reason spelled both unity and freedom for the Church communities. Because it was a mandate given by God, apostolic power could but manifest itself in miraculous deeds of the same nature as those wrought by Him who was the Bringer of the Kingdom: the lame walked, the blind saw, the deaf heard, the sick became well, the dead rose, all evil spirits were conquered and driven out. That the sick did not remain sick, that evil men became good, proved that Jesus was personally present in the apostles, through the immediacy of His Spirit working in them. Real healing from sin and feebleness took place, demonstrating that the apostolic news was God's medicine, God's restoration to health for His new life. The apostles healed without herbs, without drugs, without magic, through faith in God. In the apostolic laying on of hands, what made all the difference was the proclamation of His healing Christ. The fighting nature of the apostles' mandate often let illnesses reach a dangerous climax so that, when the demonic character underlying the illness had broken out in the most frightful way, the power of healing became all the more mightily revealed.

The apostles and prophets went out into the world to drive out demons. The first Christians knew of the existence of dark spiritual beings at work behind the demonism and the mortal sickness of the present era. Under the monarchic leadership of a high-ranking spiritual Prince, those beings work toward the destruction of humankind by means of sickness and spiritual corruption, through wrecking mind and soul, and breaking down morality. For they stand in hostile opposition to the Creator and Restorer of the world. The apostles challenged these powers to decisive battle. Because they were certain of victory, they could do this. Every demon was conquered and driven out through the name of Jesus Christ and the recounting of His life story.[84] To destroy the demons, the Son of God became man. By the authority of His Holy Spirit the demons were driven out.[85] The Son of God is come to destroy the works of the Devil. Therefore much more is at stake than the healing and betterment of individual people. The vital issue is the purification of the earth's whole atmosphere, the freeing of the entire social and political life, the victory over our present world-age in its totality. For indeed, our aeon is ruled by the princely power of the Evil One. He is the god of this world. He is the spirit controlling men. The pagan gods are demons. All public affairs and conditions are under their influence.

Only the Christian is already now ruling with royal prerogative over the mighty host of the raging enemy.[86] That the demonic powers acknowledge this rule reveals the supreme power of Christ.[87] For every believing Christian is capable of unmasking every demon. No demon can offer any resistance to his command or persist in any lie. The demons must surrender to the servants of God and Christ because they fear Christ in God and God in Christ. In fear, in anger, and in pain, they must abandon each place whenever by virtue of the Spirit's apostolic gifts of prophecy the proclamation of the Crucified comes into force:[88]

If you would only hear the demons and see what happens when they are driven out from possessed bodies, exorcised by us as though tortured by the whips of the Spirit and by tormenting words; when, under the impact of divine power, howling and groaning, they must feel the scourge and whip of God's might and must thereby confess the judgment to come! Come yourself and see how true it is what we say, and you will see how we are entreated by those whom you entreat and feared by those whom you fear and worship.[89]

NCE MORE, the militancy inherent in this unparalleled battle of the spirits broke out at the end of our period in the mighty revival movement which is generally called "Montanism" after one of its leaders. Originating in Phrygia, this movement affected most of the important regions of contemporary Christendom, principally Asia Minor, Gaul, and Africa. For a time, it dominated entire Churches, like that of Thyatira. Some overseers moved with their congregations into the country, where they lived together, caring for each others' economic needs, completely filled with the expectation that the Kingdom would now break in. Even Rome, attempting to preserve for the institutional Church the power and spirit of this movement, composed a letter of recognition but never sent it.

Here we are confronted with the crisis of early Christian eschatology, which had become a historical necessity. Montanism was the last mighty eruption of that intense expectation of the future, which eagerly awaited the intervention of God's future in history and, through it, that revolution which transforms all conditions and relationships. The genuine heroism of faith born of this conviction sought to establish itself once more in the Montanist prophets. Here, the God-given freedom alive in the bearers of the prophetic Spirit and their all-inclusive title to valid leadership strove once more toward victory. Through the New Prophecy, the representative Advocate promised in John's Gospel, who is the Holy Spirit of Jesus Christ, was to guide and direct the unity of the Church, the community of saints. Originally, therefore, this movement had no intention of severing itself from the body of Christendom. On the contrary, it was a typically internal, ecclesiastic movement and crisis, if one can apply the term "ecclesiastic" to the Church communities of that time.

Above all, the movement wanted the same, original Christian faith of the apostles that all Church communities tried to represent, and only that. Like the first apostles and prophets, the New Prophecy of Montanism wanted to defend the ancient Bible of the Law and the Prophets, the New Testament (which was in the process of being more sharply circumscribed), and the gradually expanded Rule of Faith, against all attacks and perversions. And only when their meaning seemed obscure, especially in the Pauline letters, did the New Prophecy attempt to throw new light on them through the clarification and illumination of the prophetic Spirit.

But at the last moment, from Rome, the Church[89a] declared herself in opposition to this renewal through the direct gift and working of the Spirit. At the same time, the Montanist movement itself degenerated into a sect, an increasingly formal organization of prophets, and thus became narrow, legalistic, and moralistic beyond measure. This reciprocal effect made the moment of separation a crucial turning point in the early history of Christianity.

For the purpose of this book, the reign of the great Emperor Marcus Aurelius (who died in the year 180) is considered the closing period of the early Christian time that followed directly after the primitive Church and the first apostles, so that this collection of sources covers one century. The basic change of direction which later led to the institutional Church ⟨*Kirche*⟩ revealed itself at this point in numerous acute symptoms, the most important of which we must describe here to mark the boundary of our period.

From now on large masses of people were involved, of whom the same demands could no longer be made as of the first little band of messengers filled with the Spirit. The question now arose how to preserve and promote Christianity in this world since the revolutionary renewal expected from God was so long in coming. From this state of affairs, the emerging institutional Church concluded that it was her binding task to carry forth into all circles and strata of mankind as much as possible of the revealed light even if, while so doing, the bright daylight of the Creator and of His coming day would have to be turned into the dusky dimness of mystic, cultic twilight. Conversely, the emerging sects sought to carry on the fight of the first Christians with clear sharpness, neither dimming nor darkening the light, even if, in the effort, the Light of the World would have to be hid under the bushel of human narrowness and small-group separatism.

At this turn of events, the curse hanging over the whole history of the organized Church erupted with elemental force: the curse of mutual loveless misrepresentation, which changed Christ's purpose to unite men in love through the Spirit into fanatical injustice bringing hate and division among men. The fact that the incipient institutional Church was unable to bear the spirit of incisive truth (which leads to the formation of a sect), while the incipient sect was unable to bear the spirit of diffusive love (which leads to the formation of a large ecclesiastic institution), marked the beginning of heresy-hunting, so characteristically "Christian," yet so completely un-Christian. The historical reasons for the Montanist mistrust of the growing worldliness in the institutional Church are evident. On the other hand, the censure and mistrust displayed by the institutional Church against the free-working Spirit have historical causes which are just as important.

By the end of the second century, there was every reason to look for protection from the influence of false prophetic spirits at all costs. From the religions of Hellenistic and Oriental civilizations, a mighty stream of pagan mysticism flooded into the Church communities, with philosophic and religious speculations and the spell of magic mystery rites. The institutional Church recognized in this wave of Gnosticism an hour of temptation and unprecedented peril. It could be compared only with the crisis caused by Jewish legalism which Paul had overcome. Nobody in the Church or in the Montanist movement wanted to be in any way associated with that Satan's brew. In the name of what was recognized, just in time, to be a false spirit of profound knowledge, the Church communities were all but destroyed and driven into the hands of demons. Often at the end of his life the aged Polycarp is said to have exclaimed, "Dear God, for what times hast Thou preserved me, that I should endure these things!"[90] He even went so far as to call a leader of the Gnostic movement the firstborn of Satan.[91] Under no circumstances would the Christians recognize anything "Christian" in this "Gnosis" or "mysterious knowledge," not even as another version of Christianity. The slightest contact with these counterfeiters was considered to be dangerous beyond measure. In Ephesus John fled from a building fearing it would fall on top of him, because one of those enemies of the truth was inside.[92] For all these reasons, in collecting the texts for this book we have as far as possible disregarded this Gnostic mixture of paganism and Christianity, although it is a fact that, even at that time and to a far greater extent later, the institutional Church incorporated numerous, effective pagan elements into her religious practices.

At the conclusion of the early Christian period, Christendom defended itself against this dangerous inroad mainly in two ways: by fixing the dogma and the literary form of the creeds and of the New Testament writings and by consolidating the power of the bishops. These steps clearly mark the end of the early period covered by our book. It was at this time that the creative work on the New Testament was provisionally brought to completion. Thereby, and at that point, the period of earliest Christian revelation by the Spirit was marked off; the creative, primitive time of Christendom, the time when God established new facts in history, was declared terminated. Between the years 140 and 200 the New Testament was given its primary form. From now on it was held as the sole authoritative gift of the Holy Spirit and was placed not only on the same level as the Old Testament but far above it. Side by side with this supreme result of Christianity's creative epoch, the Apostolic Creed became established, for now the gradually expanded Rule of Faith was set down in writing.

In these two documents, the message of early Christian revelation, the message given by the Spirit in that first period which had now irrevocably passed, was put on record for all times. Here the Spirit forged once more the keen weapons wielded by Him in the time of great battle, sharp weapons which were from now on to be turned primarily against deviations and false teachings, not least of all against those of the institutional Church itself. Was not even the Revelation of John included in this armory, side by side with the Gospels and the Acts of the Apostles and the apostolic and catholic Letters! And is not this the revolutionary Book of the Spirit, the eschatological Book tense with the expectation of the future! Indeed, this Book, with its antagonism to this age, goes all out to condemn the Roman Babylon of our present age! It is taken for granted that the reader of the sources collected here has access to all these writings included in the New Testament, and we hope that the study of the present volume will contribute toward a clearer understanding and appreciation of the New Testament as *the* Book of early Christian revelation.

The other protective measure against the dangers threatening at that time was the transformation of the Church into an ecclesiastic organization through the office of the bishops. In the first Christian communities—built with no thought of permanence and ready to break camp at any moment—the ever-present danger of disunity was and remained overcome owing to the free leadership in the Spirit given by the apostles, prophets, and teachers, and to the brotherly love in the Spirit ruling among all members of the Church. From now on, the uniformity of the Catholic world was ensured by the organization of the monarchical rule of the bishops, their synodal decrees, and finally by the ascendancy of the Pope. The episcopate declared itself the legitimate successor to the apostolate and prophetic Spirit; it restricted the Spirit to the office. But for this myth, the bishop's office could never have gained supremacy. The free-working Spirit and its object of faith, the Church of God as the Body of the Invisible One, were replaced by a different reality, the visible Church of the bishops. Already Irenaeus clearly defined this episcopal Church as that which she claims to be: the teaching of the apostles, the system of the Church, the succession of the bishops, and the perfect tradition of the Holy Scriptures. Already in his time no addition or curtailment of the Holy Scriptures was tolerated. Already he regarded every bishop as appointed by the apostles through the successive laying on of hands.[93]

Theodore of Mopsuestia described the gradual dying out of apostles and prophets and the ascendance of Church episcopacy as follows. After the death of the first apostles, the weakness of the second-generation apostles was patent in the breakdown of the apostolic power to work miracles. As a result, they voluntarily renounced their overall leadership and transferred part of their authority to Church overseers, who became provincial bishops.[94] In fact, the power of the provincial synods asserted itself for the first time in connection with the fight against Montanism, which again brings us to the end of our period.

Sohm saw in this an outrage committed by the organized Church against ultimate truth, namely that from now on, by virtue of the episcopal constitution, one individual human part, the overseer of an individual human community, became law for the whole. For those individual human parts served now to construct the envisaged whole like a tower, an organization, built by human hands. The first symptoms of the institution of the papacy, which was the very apex of this structure, were apparent already at our terminal date, after A.D. 180: in 190 the Roman Bishop Victor laid the foundation for that crowning ecclesiastical edifice by excluding from the fellowship of the Church all who refused to accept the Roman Easter practice. Around the year 200, Tertullian was still able to regard all apostolic sees as having equal status, whereas by 220 he felt compelled to attack the rising power of the papacy in the Bishop of Rome. Even Johannine Asia Minor, which had until then been the very hub of the Christian world, now receded before the leading influence of the see of Peter, while Jewish Christianity had become sectarian and from A.D. 135 on could no longer exert any kind of influence. Tertullian still considered all Christians priests and sacrificers, with equal title to the fellowship of peace, to the name of "brother," and to mutual hospitality. As he saw it, the authority to forgive sins still belonged entirely to the Spirit-bearers.[95] And it was pre-

cisely the authority to forgive sins that became the basis for
the ecclesiastical law of the bishops, a fact clearly recognizable
as late as A.D. 375.[96]

However external it seemed at first sight, the nascent
juridical power of the bishops gained a firm foothold in the
religious sentiment of Church life in the beginning. In regard
to the religious life, a previously undreamt-of proliferation
of Church ceremonials stands out at the close of our period;
in fact, an utterly different and new kind of piety took over
at this point.

Infant baptism, too, can be traced to the time immediately
following the period we have dealt with. It supplanted the baptismal bath of immersion, which hitherto had tremendous significance, with a totally different concept of the "sacrament"
of baptism and its mystery. Now baptism per se became a
value, signifying acceptance into God's Church and all her instruments of grace. Only now, with infant baptism, Christian
proper names came into use; before, the proper name "Christian" common to all was simply used alongside the old pagan
one.

As late as A.D. 170, Celsus noted that the Christians had no
altars.[97] But by A.D. 200, the table was often called "altar."
The Lord's Supper had already been separated from the
Lovemeal after the middle of the second century; originally
an offering of thankful hearts and tangible gifts by all believers,
it changed (again at the end of our century) into the oblation
of the Mass offered by the priest. Transubstantiation and
the re-enactment by the priest of the body and blood sacrifice
now took the place of Christ's presence and the descent of
the Spirit upon the gathered Church: the Spirit and the crucified Christ were now materialized in the substance of wafer
and wine as "Corpus Christi." In the third century, the shift
from the early celebration of the Meal to the Catholic Mass

was still in full progress.[98] The mystery of the Mass and the entire ritual with all its wondrous sacraments show more crassly than anything else how all the pagan religious currents flowed together in the institutional Church. As a result, the hybrid religion of the Church supplied for all manner of people the broadest religious satisfaction of their need for atonement and salvation.

The expectation of the future Kingdom that had depended entirely on God was now extinct, and the religiously motivated ego found rich nourishment in the otherworldly belief of the Church. With all the believer's religious self-gratification, the Deity threatened to vanish from under his hands as a result of the unbridgeable distance between this life and the life hereafter.

Together with Oriental mystery cults, it was Greek philosophy, especially Plato's, that exercised an increasingly dominant influence in this direction. Again in the years between 180 and 250, ecclesiastical Christianity became a great power in the field of learning and literature by extensively absorbing contemporary culture and philosophy. To the same degree that it found favor with the educated, it departed from the central message of the Kingdom of God. As late as the third century, men like Irenaeus, Hippolytus, and Tertullian tried in vain to hammer out the purest possible form of primary Christian truth; in vain, those believers who were disdainfully called "ignorant," "uneducated," and "simple-minded" continued to protest vigorously against the invasion of learning. But even these simple people gradually lost the strength for that kind of religious and moral exertion which in early times had sprung from the expectation of God's future Kingdom.

The Church contented herself with developing a quite tolerable middle-class morality for the masses, under which one could obtain—and this too since the third century—the desired, comforting forgiveness again and again by means of the Holy Sacrament of penance. The great success of the institutional Church achieved by her growing identification with the whole of contemporary society necessarily entailed that by and large one had Christianity without being Christian, that by and large one did not have Christianity although one was called Christian. In sum, by the end of the time-span covered in this book, the Church had "ceased to be the Virgin of Christ."[99] Consequently, there was now no longer the courage to call Christians saints ⟨holy ones⟩, and from now on one spoke only of a holy calling, holy sacraments, and holy scriptures.

The power underlying sanctification, the love to God and to the brothers alive in the early times, was now transformed into monastic asceticism and the Church piety of the masses. Christian ethics split into the dualistic way of simultaneously rejecting and accepting the world, for after all, the world followed its own laws and therefore was in any case unchangeable. The Church could not but accept the status quo, now unchangeable, and attempt to leaven it and make use of it. Some took revenge for this on the physical world of the senses, which in their eyes seemed more and more hostile to God, by embracing asceticism for its own sake. On the other hand, the reasonableness of compromise and the worldly wisdom of practical realism, which had now become necessary, very quickly produced the familiar conservative character of Church Christianity. Once more, the end of our period (again around A.D. 180) marks the turning point in the social and political stance of the Church. From now on, Christians exerted more and more power and influence in politics and public affairs; now they could no longer be criminals in the eyes of the State as the first Christians had been throughout.

Set forth in the baptismal instructions of *The Teaching of the Twelve Apostles,* the Sermon on the Mount stressed the unbridgeable gulf sharply dividing the two ways of death and of life; but now the Sermon on the Mount faded more and more into the background. The early Christian ideal of a communism of love was not completely abandoned, as John Chrysostom exemplified as late as A.D. 400; it was inconceivable to give it up, but it was still less conceivable for the Church to put it into practice. True, the theory of total love and surrender of all goods continued to be upheld; but it could not prevent the stance of Christians in regard to property from becoming indistinguishable in practice from that of non-Christians. Wealth and luxury spread. From the third century on, more and more high-ranking civil servants and army officers, traders in luxury goods, wealthy wholesalers, and big estate owners belonged to the Churches. Economic differences and class distinctions now were so little questioned that soon the episcopal Church herself owned slaves and became richer and richer, although nominally Church property still remained the property of the poor. While Tertullian and Origen, still influenced by the early years, represented that the profession of judge (which is to punish) and that of soldier (which is to kill) were out of the question, the sequence of events led later, in A.D. 314, to the punishment of deserters by excommunication, with no questions asked about their conscience.[100]

Nevertheless, the sacrifice of precious early Christian legacy was not altogether in vain. We find that the institutional Church achieved a partial softening of the rigid Roman concept of property and, still more important, public acceptance of the Christian concept of marriage. The eventual termination and re-molding of the Roman Empire can be traced back, not least of all, to the organized Church whose influence contributed both to the gradual disintegration and to the new growth. At the same time, it was within the Church that monasticism once again achieved that radical "anarchism" of faith responsible to God alone which had been alive in the beginning. Here, as in the first Church, private property was overcome by the communism of love. Here too, a new value was given to labor, similar to that which it had in the earliest time. Monasticism was simply a late phenomenon in which the heroism of early Christian faith grew one-sided and otherworldly. Thus the tremendous monastic movement was just one example of what was to become evident time and again throughout the history of the organized Church: her whole religious life in the Chrisian spirit can be nourished only from that powerful early time when the Spirit Himself became revealed in authority and in freedom.

By recasting Christianity; the institutional Church became a recognized world power with a dominant role in world history. But despite all the deviations from the early time of revelation, no Church or sect in Christendom has ever completely forgotten that love remains "the supreme sacrament of faith, the treasure of the Christian faith."[101] Bearing in mind the radicalism of all sects, the narrowness of all monastic exercises in devotion, and the vast responsibilities of the organized Churches, Irenaeus was right in saying, "It remains, as in the time now past, that the greatest is the free gift of brotherly love, which is more glorious than knowledge, more marvelous than prophecy, and more sublime than all other gifts of grace."[102]


With the present book we want to render the practical service of allowing the original testimonies of the transition period between earliest Christianity and the organized Church to speak to our times today. For in the fire of first love, in the abundance of God's manifestations, the rich, primitive force of the early Christian spirit speaks to us once again. Page by page it will become evident to the serious reader that all the moments of power and truth characteristic of New Testament Christianity can be sensed here as well as the beginnings and roots of those later developments that led to the organized Churches. All the texts belonging to this century of transition that are in this sense significant and authentic have been newly selected and translated for this book. In the annotations, references, and explanations at the end of our book, mention is made of the standard books and translations (often unequaled in their skill) which the editor compared and drew upon.

In this sense the editor owes a special debt of gratitude to Kösel's *Bibliothek der Kirchenväter,* and to the books of Harnack, Hennecke, and Preuschen, Mehlhorn, Rinn, and Jüngst, Klein, Zahn, Wetter, Troeltsch, and Achelis. The editor wishes to express his deepest gratitude to his father, Carl Franklin Arnold. How much he owes to his books, to his guidance in the whole domain of Church history, and to his comprehensive knowledge and his biblical and ecclesiastical orientation, and what the atmosphere of his parental home meant to him and opened up for him from the days of his early childhood—all this became increasingly clear to him as the years brought a growing sense of independence in his own life and work. That is why he dedicates this book to his parents.

For the editor a clearly defined way of life and faith results from the manifestation of God in earliest Christian times. In spite of rigidity in later centuries and the changes which affected Christianity then, this way continues to be a living force today, because it comes from the wellspring of living truth and can never become a mere imitation of outward traditions.

There is but one criterion for this way: the direct, spontaneous testimony which the Spirit Himself brings to all believers from God and from Christ. It is the witness of faith that speaks to us from apostolic and prophetic experience through the pages of this book. The original witness of the Church must lead us all, placed as we are today in very different camps, into the unity and purity of the clear light. The period of original revelation must be the point of departure for any dialogue between the many Churches, sects, movements, and trends of our own day.

The awakening and uniting of all who seriously want to be Christians, so much needed today, will be given at the Source and nowhere else.

Sannerz, 1925 and 1926.
Hesse, Germany

*Eberhard Arnold*

# SOURCES OF
# THE FIRST CENTURIES

# STATE, SOCIETY, and MARTYRS

L et no one have gods on his own, neither new ones nor
strange ones, but only those instituted by the State.

No one may hold meetings at night in the city.

Law from the Twelve Tables, 450 B.C. Cicero, *On the Laws*
II.19. (1)

O f those people who introduce new religions with unknown
customs or methods by which the minds of men could be
disturbed, those of the upper classes shall be deported, those
of the lower classes shall be put to death.

Legal decree according to the second-century pagan jurist
Julius Paulus. Five books of *Collected Sentences* V.21. (2)

W hen we assert that He who ordered this universe is the
One God, then, incomprehensibly, a law is put in force
against us.

Athenagoras, *A Plea Regarding Christians* 7, c. A.D. 177. (3)

We are charged with being irreligious people and, what is more, irreligious in respect to the emperors since we refuse to pay religious homage to their imperial majesties and to their genius and refuse to swear by them.

High treason is a crime of offense against the Roman religion. It is a crime of open irreligion, a raising of the hand to injure the deity. . . . Christians are considered to be enemies of the State, enemies of the public well-being. . . . In dealing with religious veneration of the second majesty, we Christians are accused of a second sacrilege because we do not celebrate the festivals of the Caesars along with you.

We wage a battle when we are challenged to face the tribunals of law. There, in peril of life, we give testimony for the truth. Police and informers bring up accusations against the Christians as sex criminals and murderers, blasphemers and traitors, enemies of public life, desecrators of temples, and criminals against the religion of Rome. Look, you do not deal with us in accordance with the formalities of criminal cases even though you consider the Christian guilty of every crime and an enemy of the gods, emperors, laws, morals, yes, of the whole of nature. "You do not," so they tell us, "worship the gods, nor do you make sacrifices to the emperors." Accordingly we are charged with sacrilege and high treason.

We are publicly accused of being atheists and criminals who are guilty of high treason.

Tertullian, *To the Heathen* (Nations) 1.17; *Apology* 24,27,35, 50,2,10; Justin, *Second Apology* 8. (4)

The Christians form among themselves secret societies that exist outside the system of laws, . . . an obscure and mysterious community founded on revolt and on the advantage that accrues from it.

Origen, *Against Celsus* VIII.17; III.14. (5)

They charge us on two points: that we do not sacrifice and that we do not believe in the same gods as the State.
Athenagoras 13. (6)

Tiberius suppressed foreign cults and Egyptian and Jewish religious rites and forced those who were enslaved by this kind of superstition to burn their religious vestments and all the paraphernalia of their cults. He dispersed Jewish youths to provinces with a more rugged climate, ostensibly to do military service. Others belonging to this people, or persons holding similar beliefs, he removed from the city on pain of slavery for life if they did not want to obey.
Suetonius (died A.D. 140) on Tiberius, who ruled A.D. 14-37, ch. 36. (7)

No humane endeavors, no princely generosity, no efforts to placate the gods were able to dispel the scandalous suspicion that the burning of the city was the result of an order. To silence this rumor, Nero pushed the Christians forward as the culprits and punished them with ingenious cruelty, as they were generally hated for their infamous deeds.

The one from whom this name originated, Christ, had been executed during the reign of Tiberius at the hands of the procurator, Pontius Pilate. For a time this pernicious superstition was suppressed, but it broke out again, not only in Judea where this evil thing began, but even in the city itself where everything atrocious and shameful from all quarters flows together and finds adherents.

To begin with, those who openly confessed were arrested, and then a vast multitude was convicted on the basis of their disclosures, not so much on the charge of arson as for their hatred of the human race. Their execution was made into a game: they were covered with the skins of wild animals and torn to pieces by dogs. They were hung on crosses. They were burned, wrapped in flammable material and set on fire as darkness fell, to illuminate the night. Nero had opened his gardens for this spectacle and put on circus games. He himself mingled with the crowd dressed as a charioteer or stood up high on a chariot. Although these people were guilty and deserved the severest penalty, all this gave rise to compassion for them, for it was felt that they were being victimized, not for the public good, but to satiate the cruelty of one man. (In the year 64) Tacitus, *Annals* XV.44.		(8)

When the Emperor [Nero] learned of the death of Festus, he sent Albanus as procurator to Judea. The King [Herod Agrippa II] took the office of high priest [in Jerusalem] away from Joseph and gave it to the son of Ananos, who was also called Ananos. The younger Ananos was an extremely violent and bold character. He belonged to the group of the Sadducees, who are more cruel in trials than the rest of the Jews.

Being this kind of man, Ananos thought that now was a favorable time for him since Festus had died and Albanus was still on his way. Therefore he convened the high council of judges and brought before them James, the brother of Jesus (called the "Messiah"), and several others. He accused them of transgressing the laws and had them stoned. Those citizens who were regarded as the most reasonable and law-abiding were vexed by this and sent secretly to the King to ask him to order Ananos not to do this kind of thing again, for he had not acted rightly in this case.
(In the year 62 or 63) Josephus, *Antiquities of the Jews* XX.9.1.		(9)

In the same year [A.D. 95] Domitian had executed, among many others, the Consul Flavius Clemens even though he

was a cousin of his, and his wife, Flavia Domitilla, was also related to Domitian. The accusation against both was that of atheism. On the basis of this accusation, many others who had adopted the customs of the Jews were also condemned. Some of them suffered death. Others were at least deprived of their property. Domitilla was merely banished to the island of Pandateria.
Dio Cassius, *Roman History* 67, ch. 14 (after A.D. 200). (10)

Gaius Pliny, Governor in Asia Minor, to the Emperor Trajan:

It is my custom, Sire, to report to you everything about which I am in doubt, for who could better guide my uncertainty or instruct my ignorance?

I have never been present at trials of Christians; therefore I do not know what or how much to punish or to investigate. I am also very unsure whether age should make any difference, or whether those who are of tender age should be treated just the same as the more robust; whether those who repent should be pardoned, or whether one who has once been a Christian shall gain nothing by having ceased to be one; finally, whether the name [of Christian] as such should be punished even if there is no crime, or whether only the crimes attributed to this name should be punished.

Meanwhile I have followed this procedure with those who were denounced to me as Christians: I asked them whether they were Christians. If they confessed I repeated the question a second and third time and, moreover, under threat of the death penalty. If they persisted I had them led away to their death, for I had no doubt that, whatever it was that they confessed, their stubbornness and inflexible obstinacy certainly deserved to be punished.

There were several others, Roman citizens, who showed the same madness, and I noted them to be sent to the city. As often happens during legal investigations, the crime became more widespread and there were some particular incidents. An anonymous accusation was presented denouncing a large number of persons by name. I felt that I should acquit those who denied that they were or had been Christians if they followed my example and called upon the gods; if they offered before your image incense and wine, which I had ordered to be brought for this purpose with the statues of the gods; and if they reviled Christ besides. It is said that those who really are Christians cannot be compelled to do any of these things in any circumstances. Others, whose names had been given by an informer, first said they were Christians but then soon denied it, saying in fact they had been but had ceased to be, some saying three years ago, others longer, and some as long as twenty years ago. All of these worshiped your image and the statues of the gods and cursed Christ.

They continued to maintain that the sum of their guilt or error lay in this, that it was their custom to meet on a fixed day before daylight and, alternating with one another, to sing a hymn to Christ as to a god. They also bound themselves mutually by an oath, not in order to commit any crime, but to promise not to commit theft, robbery, or adultery; not to break their word; and not to deny entrusted goods when claimed. After doing this, it was their custom to part from one another and then to meet again to share an ordinary and harmless meal. But even this they said they had ceased to do since my edict in which, in compliance with your injunction, I had forbidden closed societies.

I thought it all the more necessary, then, to find out finally what was true by putting to torture two girls who were called serving girls. But I found nothing but a depraved and enormous superstition. Consequently I adjourned the investigation and now turn to you for advice.

The matter seems to me worthy of consultation especially because of the large number of those imperiled. For many of all ages, of every rank, and of both sexes are already in danger, and many more will come into danger. The contagion of this superstition has spread not only in the cities but even to the villages and to the country districts. Yet I still feel it is possible to check it and set it right. Of this much I am sure, that people are beginning once more to frequent the beautiful temples which have been almost deserted, so that the long-neglected sacred rites are being restored and so that fodder for the animals to be sacrificed, for which there was until now scarcely any demand, is being bought and sold again. From this it is evident that a very great number of people can be brought back to better ways if they are given the opportunity to repent.

Trajan to Pliny:

Pliny Secundus, you have followed the correct procedure in examining those who were accused before you as Christians, for in general no hard and fast rule can be laid down. They should not be sought out. Those brought before you and proved guilty should be punished provided that anyone who denies that he is a Christian and actually proves this by worshiping our gods is pardoned on repentance, no matter how suspect his past may have been. Anonymous accusations, however, should not be admitted in any criminal case, for this would give a very bad precedent and would not be worthy of our age.
Correspondence of the Emperor Trajan with Pliny, *Letters* X.96-97, A.D. 112. (11)

I have received a letter addressed to me by your most esteemed predecessor, Serenius Granianus. It does not seem right to me now to let this matter pass by without examination, lest the people should be perturbed and the informers find opportunities for mean actions. If, therefore, the people of the province are able to base their petition against the Christians on clear grounds, so that they can be answerable even before a court of law, then let them use these legal channels only; let them not just resort to petitions and outcries. It is far more fitting that you should begin a detailed investigation if anyone brings up an accusation. Therefore if anyone acts as an accuser and shows proof that the people concerned are acting against the law in some way, then you should pass your sentence in accordance with the extent of the offense. But, by Hercules! if anyone should bring forward his accusation with slanderous intention, you should take such a shameful thing properly into account and see that it is punished.

Emperor Hadrian, (A.D. 117-138) to Minucius Fundanus, Proconsul of Asia, quoted in Justin, *First Apology* 68. (12)

The Church of God at Smyrna to the Church of God at Philomelium [in Phrygia, Asia Minor] and to all the communities of the holy all-embracing Church everywhere.

We write to you, brothers, concerning that which took place with those of us who have given witness unto death, in particular with the blessed Polycarp, who put an end to the persecution by sealing it, as it were, with his own witness.

Cut by scourges until the anatomy of the body was visible, even to the veins and arteries, they endured everything. Even the spectators pitied and bewailed them. The noble martyrs of Christ attained such towering strength of soul that not one of them uttered a cry or groan. They proved to all of us that in the hour of their torture they were free of the body, or rather that the Lord himself stood by them and talked with them.

In the same way they endured fearful torment when they

were condemned to the wild beasts. They were rolled over shells and were subjected to all kinds of other tortures, for the tyrant hoped to induce them to deny their faith by the prolonged torture, if that were possible.

The Infernal Tempter used many devices against them, but thanks be to the Lord he was powerless against them all. The noble Germanicus strengthened the weakness of others by his steadfastness. He wrestled gallantly with the wild beasts. When the proconsul tried to persuade him, saying that he had pity on his youth, he forcibly pulled the wild beast towards himself, wishing to be freed more quickly from this godless and unjust life. The whole mob, horrified at the heroism of the godloving and godfearing Christian sect, shouted, "Away with the atheists! Get moving! Look for Polycarp!"

Only one man, a certain Quintus from Phrygia, who had just recently come from there, turned coward when he saw the wild beasts. He was the one who had voluntarily given himself up to the court and had also persuaded some others to do the same. After earnest entreaty the proconsul persuaded him to take the oath and to sacrifice. Therefore, brothers, we do not find it praiseworthy if some of us voluntarily give ourselves up. The Gospel does not teach this. But Polycarp, in contrast, when he first heard of all this, acted admirably by showing no fear. . . . When they did not find him, they arrested two young slaves, one of whom became a traitor under torture.

Taking the young slave with them, the constables set out against him on a Friday around supper time with a squadron of mounted men and their usual arms. Late in the evening they came upon him and found him in an upper room of a small cottage. . . . They were amazed at his great age and his calm dignity. . . . He immediately ordered food and drink to be served them, as much as they wanted, and he asked them to give him an hour for undisturbed prayer. . . . And when the moment of departure came, they seated him on a donkey and in this way brought him into the city.

It was a great Sabbath. Herod, the chief of police, and Nicetes, his father, rode to meet him. They took him into their carriage and sitting next to him urged him by saying, "What is wrong with saying 'Lord!' and 'Caesar!' and sacrificing, and the rest of it, and thereby saving your life?"

At first he did not answer them, but when they did not leave him in peace he said, "I am not willing to do what you advise me.". . . When he entered the arena there was such a tremendous uproar that nobody could be understood.

When he was led forward, the proconsul asked him if he was Polycarp. This he affirmed. The proconsul wanted to persuade him to deny his faith, urging him, "Consider your great age," and all the other things they usually say in such cases. "Swear by the genius of Caesar; change your mind. Say, 'Away with the atheists.'" Polycarp, however, looked with a serious expression upon the whole mob assembled in the arena. He waved his hand over them, sighed deeply, looked up to heaven, and said, "Away with the atheists."

But the proconsul pressed him further, and said to him, "Swear and I will release you! Curse Christ!"

And Polycarp answered, "Eighty-six years have I served Him, and He has never done me any harm. How could I blaspheme my King and Savior?"

When the proconsul still pressed him saying, "Swear by the genius of Caesar," he replied, "If you desire the empty triumph of making me swear by the genius of Caesar according to your intention, and if you pretend that you do not know who I am, hear my frank confession: I am a Christian. If you are willing to learn what Christianity is, set a time at which you can hear me."

The proconsul replied, "Try to persuade the people."

Polycarp answered him, "You I consider worthy that I should give an explanation, for we have been taught to pay respect to governments and authorities appointed by God as long as it does us no harm. But as to that crowd, I do not consider them worthy of my defense."

Thereupon the proconsul declared, "I have wild beasts. I shall have you thrown before them if you do not change your mind."

"Let them come," he replied. "It is out of question for us to change from the better to the worse, but the opposite is worthy of honor: to turn round from evil to justice."

The proconsul continued, "If you belittle the beasts and do not change your mind, I shall have you thrown into the fire."

Polycarp answered him, "You threaten me with a fire that burns but for an hour and goes out after a short time, for you do not know the fire of the coming judgment and of eternal punishment for the godless. Why do you wait? Bring on whatever you will."

As Polycarp spoke these and similar words, he was full of courage and joy. His face shone with inward light. He was not in the least disconcerted by all these threats. The proconsul was astounded. Three times he sent his herald to announce in the midst of the arena, "Polycarp has confessed that he is a Christian!"

No sooner was this announced by the herald than the whole multitude, both pagans and Jews, the entire population of Smyrna, yelled with uncontrolled anger at the top of their voices, "He is the teacher of Asia! The father of the Christians! The destroyer of our gods! He has persuaded many not to sacrifice and not to worship." This they shouted, and they demanded of Philip, the high priest of public worship, that he let loose a lion upon Polycarp. He explained that he was not allowed to do this since the wild-beast combats had been closed. Then there arose a unanimous shout that Polycarp should be burned alive. In this way the vision had to be fulfilled in which he had seen his pillow burning while he was praying. To the faithful who were with him he had spoken the prophetic words, "I must be burned alive."

Now everything happened much faster than it can be told. The mob rushed to collect logs and brushwood from the workshops and the public baths; the Jews as usual were especially zealous in this work. When the woodpile was ready, Polycarp took off all his outer clothes, opened his belt, and tried to undo his shoes. This he had not usually done himself because each of the faithful was eager to be the first to touch his body. Already before his martyrdom he had been very much honored because of the goodness of his life.

The fuel for the pyre was very quickly piled around him. When they wanted to fasten him with nails, he refused. "Let me be. He who gives me the strength to endure the fire will also give me the strength to remain at the stake unflinching, without the security of your nails.". . . When he had spoken the Amen and finished his prayer, the executioners lit the fire.

In the end, when the godless mob saw that his body could not be consumed by the fire, they ordered the executioner to thrust a dagger into his breast. . . . When the Tempter, the Slanderer and Evil One, the Enemy of the race of the righteous, saw the whole greatness of his martyrdom and his blameless life from the beginning, . . . he prompted Nicetes, the father of Herod and the brother of Alce, to ask the proconsul not to give up the body, ". . . for fear," those were his words, "that they should abandon the Crucified and start worshiping this man." They said this through the instigation and urging of the Jews who also had been watching when we wanted to take him out of the fire. They do not know that we will never abandon Christ. He suffered for the salvation of all those who are being saved on the whole earth, the One without guilt for the guilty ones. We can never worship anyone else. We worship Him because He is the Son of God. To the martyrs we give the love we owe them as disciples and followers of the Lord. They have, after all, loved their King and Master with boundless love. How we wish that we may become their companions and fellow disciples! When the officer in charge saw the commotion caused by the Jews, he had the body put in the middle of the pyre and burned, according to their custom. So afterwards we were able to take up his bones, more valuable than jewels and more precious than gold, and to lay them to rest in our burying place. There we will come together as often as God will grant us, in jubilation and joy, as much as we are able. There we will celebrate the anniversary of his martyrdom and death like a birthday, in memory of those who have fought and won the fight before, and for the strengthening and preparation of those who still have to face it. Such is our report about the blessed Polycarp who, counting those from Philadelphia, was the twelfth to suffer martyrdom at Smyrna.

*The Martyrdom of the Holy Polycarp,* written on February 22, 156. (13)

When the proconsul was present in Pergamum [Asia Minor], Carpus and Papylus, joyful martyrs of Christ, were brought to him. The proconsul sat down and asked, "What is your name?"

The one who was questioned answered, "My first and chosen name is Christian. But if you are asking for my name in the world, then I call myself Carpus."

The proconsul declared, "The decrees of the emperors are known to you, that you must worship the all-controlling gods.

Therefore I advise both of you to come forward and sacrifice."

Carpus replied, "I am a Christian. I honor Christ, the Son of God, who has come in the latter times to save us and has delivered us from the madness of the Devil. I will not sacrifice to such idols. Do what you please. It is impossible for me to offer sacrifices to these delusive phantoms, these demons, for they who sacrifice to them become like them."

The proconsul flared up, "Both of you, sacrifice to the gods and listen to reason!"

Carpus said joyfully, "Away with the gods who have created neither Heaven nor earth."

The proconsul said, "You must sacrifice; the Caesar has commanded it."

Carpus answered, "The living do not sacrifice to the dead."

The proconsul asked, "Do you believe that the gods are dead?"

Carpus replied, "If you would like to know, they were never even men, nor did they ever live that they could die. Believe me, you are caught up in a grave delusion."

The proconsul replied, "I have let you talk too much nonsense and thus have misled you to blaspheme the gods and the majesty. You shall not continue in this way. You will sacrifice or else—! What do you say?"

Carpus said, "I cannot sacrifice. I have never yet sacrificed to idols."

At once the proconsul ordered him to be hung up and had his skin flayed with tools of torture, but he cried out again and again, "I am a Christian! I am a Christian! I am a Christian!" After this torture had gone on for a long time he lost his strength and could not speak any more.

The proconsul therefore turned his attention from Carpus to Papylus and asked him, "Are you a councillor?"

He answered, "I am a citizen."

The proconsul asked, "Of what city?"

Papylus answered, "Thyatira."

The proconsul asked, "Do you have any children?"

Papylus replied, "Oh yes, many of them, through God."

One of the surrounding crowd shouted, "He means he has children by his Christian faith."

The proconsul shouted at him, "Why do you lie, saying that you have children?"

Papylus answered, "Will you understand that I am not lying but saying the truth? In every district and city I have children in God."

The proconsul said, "You will sacrifice or else—! What do you say?"

Papylus answered, "I have served God since my youth. I have never sacrificed to idols. I am a Christian. You cannot learn anything else from me. There is nothing I can say which is greater or more wonderful than this." Then he also was hung up and his body was flayed with three pairs of iron instruments of torture. He did not utter a sound, but as a courageous fighter he endured the rage of the Tempter.

When the proconsul saw their outstanding steadfastness, he ordered them to be burned alive. They descended into the amphitheater with brisk steps, that they might be freed from this world as quickly as possible. Papylus was the first to be nailed to the stake. When the flames leaped up he prayed quietly and gave up his soul. Carpus was nailed on after him. He was full of joy. . . . When he had spoken and the fire was burning, he prayed, "Praise be to Thee O Lord, Jesus Christ, Son of God, that Thou didst deem me, a sinner, also worthy of this part in Thee!" After these words he gave up his soul.

Agathonica was present when these things happened. She saw the glory of the Lord which Carpus had seen and described. In this she recognized a call from Heaven and raised her voice straightaway. "This Meal has been prepared for me. I must partake in it. I must receive the Meal of glory."

The people cried out, "Have pity on your son."

Agathonica joyfully answered, "He has God who can care for him, for He is the provider for all. But I, why do I stand here?" She threw off her clothes and jubilantly allowed herself to be nailed to the stake.

Those standing by burst into tears and cried, "A cruel sentence! What unjust orders!"

But she, standing erect and caught by the fire, cried out three times, "Lord, Lord, Lord, help me, for I flee unto Thee." Then she gave up her soul and was perfected with the saints. About the year 165. Acts in Eusebius IV. 15–48.        (14)

Rusticus, the City Prefect, said to Justin before the judgment seat, "First of all trust the gods and obey the Emperor."

Justin answered, "Obedience to the words of our Savior Jesus Christ does not call for blame or condemnation."

City Prefect Rusticus asked, "Which branch of knowledge do you study?"

Justin answered, "I endeavored to acquaint myself with all systems. In the end I surrendered to the true teachings of the Christians. These teachings do not please those who are caught up in false beliefs."

City Prefect Rusticus answered, "And you enjoy the teachings of these people, you utterly wretched man?"

Justin replied, "The worship of the God of the Christians consists in our belief in the one God ... who has made and brought forth the whole creation, visible and invisible; and in the Lord Jesus Christ whom the prophets foretold in this way: He would appear to the human race as the Herald of salvation and the Proclaimer of precious truth. Being only a man, I feel too insignificant to say anything appropriate about His boundless divinity. I do however acknowledge a prophetic power. He whom I have called here the Son of God has been proclaimed beforehand. I know that through inspiration from God the prophets foretold His future coming to men."

City Prefect Rusticus asked, "Where do you assemble?"

Justin answered, "Where each one wants to and is able to. You probably believe that we all come together in one and the same place. This is not so, for the God of the Christians is not limited to any one place. He fills Heaven and earth. He is honored and glorified by the faithful everywhere."

City Prefect Rusticus said, "Answer, where do you assemble, or in what place do you gather your followers?"

Justin answered, "I live up on the hill, close to the baths of Timothy; during all this time (and I am now living in Rome for the second time) I have not known any other meeting place. I communicated the teachings of truth to anyone who wished to see me there."

Rusticus asked, "You still insist that you are a Christian?"

Justin answered, "I am a Christian."

The City Prefect turned to Chariton. "Now you tell me, are you also a Christian?"

Chariton answered, "I am a Christian by the will of God."

The City Prefect now asked the woman Charito, "What do you say, Charito?"

Charito answered, "I am a Christian by the gift of God."

Rusticus turned to Euelpistus. "Tell me, what are you?"

Euelpistus, a slave of the Emperor, answered, "I, too, am a Christian; through Christ I have been freed, and by the gift of Christ I share the same hope."

The City Prefect asked Hierax, "And you are a Christian too?"

Hierax answered, "Yes, I am a Christian, for my homage

and worship belong to the same God."

Rusticus, the City Prefect, asked, "Did Justin make you Christians too?"

Hierax replied, "I was a Christian, and I will be a Christian."

Paeon, who was not among the accused and was standing by, said, "I, too, am a Christian."

City Prefect Rusticus asked, "Who taught you?"

Paeon said, "From our parents we accepted this wonderful Confession."

Euelpistus said, "I heard the words of Justin with joy. But I also learned to be a Christian from my parents."

Rusticus, the City Prefect, asked, "Where are your parents?"

Euelpistus said, "In Cappadocia [Asia Minor]."

Rusticus also asked Hierax, "Who are your parents?"

He answered, "Christ is our true Father, and our faith in Him is our Mother. My earthly parents died. I was taken away from Iconium in Phrygia [Asia Minor], and from there I came here."

The City Prefect, Rusticus, turned to Liberian. "What do you say now? Are you a Christian too? Are you also godless?"

Liberian answered, "I, too, am a Christian, for I worship and give homage to the only true God."

The City Prefect now turned once more to Justin. "Listen, you who are called a learned man. You think that you possess true insight; if you should be scourged and beheaded, do you believe you will ascend into Heaven?"

Justin answered, "I believe that if I endure these things I shall have what He promises. For I know that the divine gift will stay with all who live this way until the end of the world."

City Prefect Rusticus said, "Do you suppose, then, that you will ascend into Heaven and receive some reward there?"

Justin said, "I do not suppose it; I know it. I am certain of it."

The City Prefect, Rusticus, said, "We have to come now finally to the matter in hand. It is getting urgent. Come here and with one accord offer a sacrifice to the gods."

Justin answered, "No right-thinking person slanders communion with God by going to godlessness."

Rusticus, the City Prefect, said, "Unless you obey, you will be mercilessly punished."

Justin answered, "It is our wish to be martyred for the sake of our Lord Jesus Christ and so be saved. This will be our salvation and our confidence at the much more fearful judgment seat of our Lord and Savior, who will demand that the whole world come before His forum."

So also said the other martyrs, "Do what you will, for we are Christians and do not sacrifice to idols."

Then Rusticus, the City Prefect, pronounced sentence: "These people, who have refused to sacrifice to the gods and do not obey the command of the Emperor, shall be scourged and taken away to be beheaded according to the laws."
Martyrdom of Justin, Chariton, etc., in Rome, about 163 or 167. (15)

The servants of Christ who live as aliens at *Vienna* and *Lugdunum* [Vienne and Lyons] in Gaul, to the brothers in Asia Minor and Phrygia. . . . The Adversary has fallen upon us with all his might. He has given us a foretaste of the ignominy of his future when it breaks in.

One of our brothers was called Vettius Epagathus. He was filled with abundant love towards God and his neighbor. He never hesitated to do a service to his neighbor. He carried a great zeal for God in his heart. He burned with the fervor of the Spirit. He also was received into the select circle of the martyrs as a defender and advocate of the Christians, he who carried within him the defending Advocate, the Spirit of

Zechariah. He was and is a true disciple of Christ in the full sense of the word. He followed the Lamb wherever He went.

In the presence of all the people, the Governor had given the order that all of us with our households should be investigated. Prompted by Satan, fearful of the tortures which they saw God's people suffer, and under pressure from the soldiers who talked them directly into it, pagan slaves in our service brought forth lies against us. These lies were the usual accusations of cannibalism, unnatural sex unions, and similar ghastly things which we should never speak or think about or even believe that they have ever happened among human beings. When this became known among the pagans, they all flew into a truly bestial rage against us.

Through the slave girl, Blandina, Christ revealed that what men regard as mean, insignificant, and unattractive is accounted worthy of great glory in the sight of God because of the fact that love towards Him proves itself with power and does not vaunt itself for the sake of making an impression. Her comfort, her relief, her refreshment, her pain-killing remedy for everything she suffered was the cry, "I am a Christian, and nothing evil happens among us."

Also Sanctus, a serving brother, steadfastly endured tortures beyond all measure and all human strength—all the tortures that human beings are able to inflict. Those lawless men hoped that, through the persistence and cruelty of their tortures, they could force him to say something that would be harmful to the Christians. But he resisted with unshakable firmness. He did not even say what his name was, or his race or native city, or whether he was a slave or free. To every question he gave only one answer, in Latin, "I am a Christian." This was his glory; it was his answer to all and everything instead of giving his name, native city, and family. No other sound did the pagans hear from his lips. The Governor and his torturers became very bitter on account of this. When they could think of nothing else they pressed red-hot metal plates against the most sensitive parts of his body. These burned until they grew cold, but still he stood firm in his confession.

Biblis was one of those who had denied Christ. She was the only one to come to her senses actually during the agony of torture, awaking out of a deep sleep as it were. The tortures of the present age reminded her of the punishments of eternity, and she flatly contradicted the slanderers.

Even the blessed Pothinus, the overseer of the Church at *Lugdunum,* who had reached the great age of more than ninety years, was dragged before the tribunal. He was physically so feeble that he was scarcely able to breathe, but he was strong with inward joy and full of longing for the crown of martyrdom. His body was tired to death because of his great age and his physical ailments, but his soul was kept in him so powerfully that Christ was to triumph through him. He was led before the tribunal by soldiers accompanied by the city authorities. A great multitude yelled and shouted in a wild uproar. It happened in just the same way as when Christ was condemned. He gave a good witness. When the Governor asked him, "Who is the god of the Christians?" he answered, "If you were worthy you would know." Thereupon he was ill-treated in the most merciless way. Those closest to him pounded him and kicked him viciously from all sides, not respecting his old age in the slightest. Those further away hurled at him whatever came into their hands. Scarcely breathing any more Pothinus was thrown into prison, and after two days he gave up his soul.

Maturus, Sanctus, Blandina, and Attalus were taken to the wild beasts in the amphitheater, to give the pagan crowd which was gathered there a public spectacle of inhumanity. They ran the gauntlet of whips. They were already used to this.

They let themselves be dragged around and mauled by the wild beasts. Everything the raving, yelling mob wanted, now from this side, now from that, they endured. They sat upon the iron chair which roasted their bodies so that the fumes rose up. Yet they heard nothing from Sanctus beyond the confession of faith he had repeated over and over again from the beginning. When they were still found alive in spite of the terrible and prolonged torture, they were finally killed. Blandina was hung on a post, delivered up to the wild beasts for food. Hung up like this in the shape of the Cross, she could be seen from afar, and through her ardent prayers she aroused increased zeal in those who were fighting, for during this fight they saw with their own eyes, right in and through the person of their sister, the One who was crucified for them. In this way it was shown to all who believe in Him that everyone who suffers for the glory of Christ is always in fellowship with the living God. As none of the wild beasts had yet touched Blandina, she was taken down from the post and thrown into prison once more, to be kept ready for a new fight.

Most of those who had denied their faith were received back into the bosom of the Church. The fire of their lives was rekindled and burned brightly. They learned to confess and stood before the tribunal again, full of life and vigor, once more to be plagued by the Governor. In the meantime the command of the Emperor had arrived: those who denied their faith should be set free; the others should be executed.

The great festival had just begun. Large numbers of people had flocked together from many faraway places. Before the eyes of the crowd the Governor had all the blessed ones conducted to the tribunal in a ceremonial procession. Again he started to examine them. All those who clearly possessed Roman citizenship were beheaded. The rest were sent to the wild beasts. Christ was glorified magnificently by those who had formerly denied Him. The pagans could not grasp it. They gave witness. Attalus sat in the iron chair. His body burned. The fumes rose up. On being asked, "What is God's name?" he answered, "God does not have a name as a man has."

The glorified Blandina had already learned to know the scourging, the wild beasts, and the red-hot griddle. Finally they tied her in a fishing net and threw her to a bull. For a long time the animal tossed her about, and so she was killed. She did not feel anymore what was happening to her because she lived only in the hope and expectation of the things that were prepared for her through her communion with Christ. Even the pagans had to admit that none of their women had ever suffered so many tortures for so long. Yet not even this was enough to satisfy their rage and cruelty towards the holy ones.

The bodies of those that had perished in prison they threw to the dogs, watching carefully night and day that none of us could be buried. The remains of those who had been torn to pieces by the wild beasts and those charred by the fire they put on public view just as they were. The heads and trunks of the others, carefully guarded by soldiers, they also left unburied for many days. Some of them were raging and gnashing their teeth, seeking to take even more vengeance on them. Others laughed and jeered at them and exalted their own idols, to whom they attributed the punishment of the martyrs.

The more reasonable ones, those of whom one could believe that they knew pity to a certain extent, slandered them, crying, "Where is your god? How were they helped by the faith which they loved more than their own lives?" For six days the bodies of the martyrs, mocked in every possible way, were exposed to the elements. Finally they were burned to ashes by these lawless men and swept into the Rhône, which flows nearby.

No trace of them was to remain on earth. This they did thinking that they could defeat God and deprive them of their
restoration. They said that they should not be allowed to
have any hope of resurrection, for it was through their faith
in this that they introduced a strange and new religion. "Now
let us see whether they will rise again, whether their god can
help them, and whether he can deliver them out of our hands."
*Letter from Vienne and Lyons* (Southern France) to Phrygia:
Eusebius V.1 ff. In the year 177.                            (16)

O n the sixteenth day before the Calends of August [July
17, 180], in the consulship of Praesens and Claudianus
(Praesens being consul for the second time), Speratus, Nartzalus, Cittinus, Donata, Secunda, and Vestia were brought into
the senate house of Carthage.

The Proconsul Saturninus said, "You can win the leniency
of our Lord the Emperor if you return to reason."

Speratus answered, "We have never done wrong. We have
not taken part in any crime at all. We have never cursed. Even
if we were ill-treated, we only gave thanks. Therefore we honor
our Emperor."

The Proconsul Saturninus said, "We too are religious people,
and our religion is simple. We swear by the genius of our Lord
the Emperor and offer sacrifices for his well-being. You must
do that too."

Speratus answered, "If you lend me a quiet ear I will tell
you the secret of simplicity."

Saturninus said, "As soon as you begin to say evil things
about our rites, I will not lend my ear to you. Swear by the
genius of our Lord the Caesar!"

Speratus answered, "I do not recognize any empire of this
present age. I serve that God whom no man has seen, or can

ever see with these eyes. I have not stolen. On the contrary, when I buy anything I pay my taxes, for I know only one Lord, the King of kings, the Ruler of all nations."

The Proconsul Saturninus said to the others, "Give up this persuasion."

Speratus replied, "It is an evil persuasion to commit murder and bear false witness."

The Proconsul Saturninus said, "Give up this madness."

Cittinus spoke up now, "There is no one whom we fear except the Lord our God who is in Heaven."

Donata said, "Honor Caesar as Caesar, but fear God."

Vestia said, "I am a Christian."

Secunda said, "What I am, I want to remain."

The Proconsul Saturninus asked Speratus, "Do you remain a Christian?"

Speratus replied, "I am a Christian," and they all agreed with him.

The Proconsul Saturninus said, "Do you want some time to consider?"

Speratus replied, "In such a just cause there is nothing to consider."

The Proconsul Saturninus said, "What do you have in your satchel?"

Speratus said, "The letters and writings of Paul, a just man."

The Proconsul Saturninus said, "You shall have thirty days' grace to consider the matter."

Speratus said again, "I am a Christian," and all agreed with him.

The Proconsul Saturninus read the sentence from his tablet: "Speratus, Nartzalus, Cittinus, Donata, Vestia, and Secunda, and the rest who confessed that they want to live according to the Christian custom shall be executed by the sword, since they remained obstinate, although the opportunity was offered them to return to the Roman tradition."

Speratus said, "We give thanks to God."

Nartzalus said, "Today we are martyrs in Heaven, thanks be to God."

The Proconsul Saturninus ordered it to be proclaimed by the herald: "I have commanded that Speratus, Nartzalus, Cittinus, Veturius, Felix, Aquilinus, Laetantius, Januaria, Generosa, Vestia, Donata, and Secunda be led forth to execution."

They all said, "Thanks be to God," and were immediately executed with the sword.

*Acts of Martyrs,* official court minutes from Carthage, about July 17, 180.                                                        (17)

Romans, the things that have recently taken place in your city under Urbicus and that are likewise being done against all reason by the authorities, compel me to address the following words to you.

Whenever anyone is admonished by father or neighbor, child or friend, brother or husband, or wife, for any shortcoming he seeks to put these to death. He does this because he is stubborn and intemperate and because he is hard to move to the good. In turn, the evil demons try to kill us because they hate us and because they find suitable judges to act as their tools and servants. It is just as if the authorities were possessed by them. That you may understand the reason for all that took place under Urbicus, I will now tell what occurred. There was a certain woman who lived with a dissolute husband. She herself had formerly lived licentiously. After having learned the teachings of Christ she changed and then tried to persuade her husband to live a purer life too. . . . She forced herself to stay with him, for her friends had persuaded her to continue the marriage in the hope that her husband might change his ways at some future time. However when he traveled to Egypt and news reached her that his conduct was worse than ever, she separated herself from him in order not to participate in his vices and impieties by remaining married to him and sharing his table and bed. She gave him a bill of divorce according to Roman custom. Her noble husband should have been delighted that she, after her former reckless behavior with servants and employees and her indulgence in drink and every vice, had now given up all this and even wanted to dissuade him from these things. Instead he brought a charge against her. Since she had separated herself from him against his will, he charged her with being a Christian. She submitted a written petition to you, O Emperor, that she might be granted permission to put her household affairs in order first, and afterwards she would defend herself against the charge. You gave her your permission, so that her former husband could not legally prosecute her for the time being. The husband now turned against Ptolemaeus and had him summoned by Urbicus because he had instructed this woman in the Christian teachings. This is what happened. The former husband persuaded his friend, the centurion who had arrested Ptolemaeus, to summon Ptolemaeus and ask him only this one question: whether he was a Christian. Now when Ptolemaeus, who loved the truth and detested lying and deceit, confessed that he was a Christian, the centurion had him put in chains and tortured for a long time in prison. Finally the prisoner was brought before Urbicus, but here again, the same as before, only the one question was asked: was he a Christian? And again he confessed to Christ's teachings, conscious of the good things he owed to Christian instruction. Now when Urbicus

ordered Ptolemaeus to be led away to execution, a certain
Lucius, who was a Christian too, in the face of this unreason-
able sentence asked the City Prefect, "For what reason did you
order this man to be taken away? He is neither an adulterer
nor a fornicator nor a murderer nor a thief nor a robber, nor
has he broken any other law. He has only confessed to the
Christian name. Your judgment, Urbicus, will bring honor
neither to the Emperor Pius, nor to the Emperor's son, the
philosopher [later the Emperor Marcus Aurelius], nor to the
sacred Senate."

The only answer the City Prefect made to Lucius was, "You
too seem to me to be such a one." When Lucius answered yes,
he ordered him also to be led away to death. Lucius said he
could only be grateful because now he would be freed from
such evil rulers and would be allowed to go to the Father and
King of Heaven. Then a third who also came forward was
condemned to the same punishment.

Justin, *Second Apology* 1,2, in A.D. 150.　　　　　　　(18)

We too were the same as you. We were blind and callous,
sharing your ideas in supposing that the Christians
worshiped monsters, devoured children, and joined in lascivious
feasts. At that time we undertook the legal defense and protection of individual cases of sacrilege or incest or even par-
ricide, but we regarded them [the Christians] as not entitled
even to a hearing. Yes, sometimes the struggle with our own
pity made us torture those who confessed with all the more
savage cruelty.

Minucius Felix, *Octavius* 28.2,3 (about 160).　　　　　(19)

You [the Jews] chose special men and sent them from
Jerusalem throughout the world to proclaim that with

Christianity a godless sect had arisen and to bring those accusations against us which now are raised by all those who do not know us.

Justin, *Dialogue with Trypho the Jew* 17.1. (20)

Y ou also accuse Him [Jesus] of having taught the same godless, wicked, and criminal teachings which you bring up in condemnation of all those who everywhere confess Christ to be their Teacher and the Son of God. Moreover, not even now, after your city has been conquered and your country laid waste, do you repent, but dare to curse Jesus and all who believe in Him.

Justin, *Dialogue with Trypho the Jew* 108.2.3. (21)

M y friends, is there any matter in which you blame us other than this, that we do not live according to the Law, and that we do not circumcise the flesh as your forefathers did or keep the Sabbaths as you do? Or are our life and morals also slandered among you? I must ask you this: do you also hold the opinion about us that we actually eat men and that, after a carousal, we extinguish the lights and engage in promiscuous intercourse? Or do you simply condemn us because we follow the one or the other teaching but do not follow that belief which you hold to be the true one?"

Trypho replied, "This is what amazes us. But concerning the things of which the masses speak, they are not worth believing, for they go right against human nature. Moreover, I know that your teachings, written down in the so-called Gospel, are so wonderful and so great that in my opinion no man can keep them; for I have read them with interest. But this is what we cannot grasp at all: that you want to fear God and that you believe yourselves favored above the people around you, yet

you do not withdraw from them in any way or separate yourselves from the pagans, you observe neither the festivals nor the Sabbaths, you do not circumcise, and you set your hopes on a man who was crucified and believe you will receive good things from God in spite of the fact that you do not obey His commandments."
Justin, *Dialogue with Trypho the Jew* 10.1.2. (22)

In every country there is a throng of females, hermaphrodites, and perverts ready for wicked acts, and you [the Roman State] accept rent, taxes, and tribute from them instead of eradicating them from your Empire. What is done in public by you and recognized by the State, you hold against us as if we practiced it in darkness after overturning the light.
Justin, *First Apology* 27. (23)

Our accusers impute godless feasts and indiscriminate intercourse to us. They do this on the one hand to convince themselves that there are good reasons for hating us; on the other hand, they do it in the hope of drawing us away from our way of life by intimidation, or they do it to influence the authorities against us and to incite them to treat us harshly and implacably because of the enormity of the accusations.
Athenagoras, *A Plea Regarding Christians* 31. (24)

Because we do not make any distinctions in rank and outward appearance, or wealth and education, or age and sex, they devise an accusation against us that we practice cannabalism and sexual perversions.
Tatian, *Address to the Greeks*. (25)

They form a rabble of profane conspiracy. Their alliance consists in meetings at night with solemn rituals and inhuman revelries. They replace holy rites with inexpiable crimes. They despise temples as if they were tombs. They disparage the gods and ridicule our sacred rites. They look down on our priests although they are pitiable themselves. They despise titles of honor and the purple robe of high government office though hardly able themselves to cover their nakedness.

Just like a rank growth of weeds, the abominable haunts where this impious confederacy meet are multiplying all over the world, due to the daily increase of immorality. Root and branch, it should at all costs be exterminated and accursed. They recognize each other by secret signs and symbols. They love one another before being acquainted, so to speak. Everywhere they practice a kind ·of religious cult of lust, calling one another "brother" and "sister" indiscriminately. Thus, under the cover of these hallowed names, ordinary fornication becomes incest.

They consecrate and worship the head of a donkey, the meanest of all animals. They even reverence the genitals of their president and priest, adoring in this the creative power of their father. This suspicion may be false, but at any rate it fits the character of their secret nocturnal rites. To venerate an executed criminal and the gallows, the wooden cross on which he was executed, is to erect altars which befit lost and depraved wretches. The blood of the infant—oh, how abominable— they lap up greedily, they distribute its limbs with passionate eagerness.

Their feastings are notorious. Even Cornelius Fronto, the teacher of Emperor Marcus Aurelius [about 175], testifies to this. . . . After a surfeit of feasting, when the blood is heated and drinking has inflamed impure passions, a dog which has been tied to the lampstand upsets and extinguishes the tale-telling light. Darkness covers their shamelessness, and lustful embraces are indiscriminately exchanged. All single acts cor-

respond to the will of all. . . . Otherwise why do they have no altars, no temples, no images? Why do they not speak in public? Why do they never meet in the open? Is it not simply because what they worship and conceal is criminal and shameful?
Minucius Felix, *Octavius* 8.4; 9.1-6; 10.2.               (26)

They say I am incestuous, . . . I murder babies, . . . I am a malefactor against the gods, against the emperors. . . . Yet they do not give me a hearing.
Tertullian, *Apology* 4.                                    (27)

The Emperors Severus and Antoninus made a rescript: "From now on no one who accidentally damages a statue of our Emperor by throwing a stone shall be proclaimed guilty of high treason unless premeditated intention can be proved."
Quoted by the jurist Marcian shortly after A.D. 200.        (28)

Celsus says, "The Christians boast that they blaspheme and strike the images of the gods."
Origen, *Against Celsus*.                                   (29)

When a Christian passes through temples, he will spit down upon the smoking altars and blow them out.
   As to rooting out the strange gods in every way, it has been commanded, "You shall utterly destroy all places where the pagans sacrifice to their gods. You shall overturn their pillars and dash them in pieces. You shall cut down their groves. You shall burn their graven images. You shall destroy their names."
Tertullian, *On Idolatry* 11; *Scorpiace* 2.               (30)

Was one of us ever accused on any other ground [than that of bearing the name "Christian"]? The Christian never has to suffer for any other affairs except those of his sect, which during all this long time no one has ever proved guilty of incest or any cruel act. It is for our singular innocence, our great honesty, our justice, purity, and love of truth, yes, it is for the living God that we are burned to death. Thus you inflict a punishment on us which usually you do not inflict on actual temple robbers or enemies of the State or on the great number guilty of high treason.
Tertullian, *To Scapula* 4.                                              (31)

It becomes evident that the entire crime with which they charge us does not consist in any wicked acts, but in the bearing of a name. The issue is not the name of a crime, but the crime of bearing a name. Again and again it is the Name that must be punished by the sword, the gallows, the cross, or the wild beasts.
Tertullian, *To the Heathen* 1.3.                                        (32)

I am concerned to demonstrate from those things which are considered honorable among you that our morals are pure, but yours are mad in many respects.... How is it that you are not ashamed to slander the good name of our women—you who have such a large number of vile and useless poetesses, wanton women, and worthless men?... Who can endure it any longer that even fratricide is honored among you?... Be ashamed, you who are known to be disciples of women yourselves, that you scoff at the women who join us as well as at the Church who stands by them!
Tatian, *Address to the Greeks,* from chapters 33 and 34.
                                                                        (33)

If only somebody would climb up on to a high platform and cry out at the top of his voice, "Be ashamed, oh, be ashamed, you who accuse innocent people of the very crimes you yourselves openly commit, you who attach to those who do not have the slightest part in them the things of which you and your gods are guilty! Change your lives, and come to your senses!"

Justin, *Second Apology* 12. (34)

 **CHRISTIAN
SELF-PORTRAITS**

Christianity is not a matter of persuasive words. It is a matter of true greatness as long as it is hated by the world. Ignatius, *Letter to the Romans* 3.3. About A.D. 110.     (1)

The Lord will send thee a scepter of power out from Jerusalem. This is a prophecy of the mighty Logos which His apostles, going out from Jerusalem, proclaimed everywhere. Him we worship and teach everywhere although death is decreed for all those who teach or even profess the name of Christ.
Justin, *First Apology* 45.     (2)

Our Jesus, without yet appearing in radiant splendor, has sent a rod of power to Jerusalem. This is the Word that summons, the Word of transformation by the Spirit. This Word went out to all nations over which the demons ruled, as David testifies, "The gods of the nations are demons." And so it happened that many, powerfully gripped by His Word, abandoned the demons whom they had served. Now through Jesus they have come to believe in the Almighty God.
Justin, *Dialogue with Trypho* 83.4.     (3)

The prophecy, "O ye princes, lift up your gates, and be ye lifted up, O ye eternal gates!" was spoken only of this our Christ. As Isaiah, David, and all the Scriptures testified, He appeared without splendor or honor. He is the Lord of all the powers because it was the will of the Father to give them all to Him. He arose from the dead and ascended into Heaven as the Psalm and the other Scriptures had revealed. You can recognize Him more easily as the Lord of all the powers especially today if you will but look at the things that are happening before your eyes. For every demon is exorcised, conquered, and subdued in the very name of this Son of God, the Firstborn of all creation, who became man through a virgin, who suffered and was crucified by your people under Pontius Pilate, who died and rose from the dead and ascended into Heaven.

Justin, *Dialogue with Trypho* 85.1-2.                    (4)

Demons are outsiders from divine religion. We ourselves used to worship them. We constantly plead with God through Jesus Christ to be liberated from them in order that through Him we may turn to God and be without reproach. For we do call Him Savior and Redeemer! The demons shudder at His mighty name. Even in our days they surrender to Him when they are subdued in the name of Jesus Christ, who was crucified under Pontius Pilate, Governor of Judea. From what happens today it is clear to all that His Father gave Him so great a power that even the demons surrender to His name and to the saving power of His suffering.

Justin, *Dialogue with Trypho* 30.3.                    (5)

Among us you can find uneducated people, artisans, and dear old mothers who would not be able to put into words the usefulness of their teaching, but by their deeds they demonstrate the usefulness of their principles. They do not repeat words learned by heart, but they show good deeds: when hit they do not hit back, when robbed they do not go to court, they give to those who ask, and they love their fellowmen as themselves.

Athenagoras, *A Plea Regarding Christians* 11. (6)

We, more than all other men, are your helpers and allies for peace.

Justin, *First Apology* 12. (7)

If everyone were to act the same as you [Christians], the national government would soon be left utterly deserted and without any help, and affairs on earth would soon pass into the hands of the most savage and wretched barbarians."

Celsus next exhorts us to help the Emperor and be his fellow soldiers. To this we reply, "You cannot demand military service of Christians any more than you can of priests." We do not go forth as soldiers with the Emperor even if he demands this, but we do fight for him by forming our own army, an army of faith through our prayers to God.

Origen, *Against Celsus*, Celsus against the Christians, VIII. 68,73. (8)

We ourselves were well conversant with war, murder, and everything evil, but all of us throughout the whole wide earth have traded in our weapons of war. We have exchanged our swords for ploughshares, our spears for farm tools. Now we cultivate the fear of God, justice, kindness to men, faith, and the expectation of the future given to us by the Father himself through the Crucified One. . . . We do not give up our confession though we be executed by the sword, though we be crucified, thrown to wild beasts, put in chains, and exposed to fire and every other kind of torture. Everyone knows this. On the contrary, the more we are persecuted and mar-

tyred, the more do others in ever-increasing numbers become
believers and God-fearing men through the name of Jesus.
Justin, *Dialogue with Trypho* 110.3,4.                    (9)

I do not wish to be a ruler. I do not strive for wealth. I
refuse offices connected with military command. Fornication
I detest. No insatiable hunger for gold drives me to go to sea.
I do not fight for a victor's laurels. I am free from the mad
thirst for fame. I despise death. I stand above every illness.
No grief consumes my soul.
Tatian, *Address to the Greeks* 11.2.                    (10)

We must then offer no resistance. He never wanted us to
imitate the wicked. Rather, He challenged us to lead
everyone away from shamefulness and pleasure in evil by patience and kindness. We can in fact show that many who were
once among you have been transformed in this way. They gave
up their violent and domineering ways. Either they were conquered by the sight of their neighbors' patient life, or they were
convinced by noticing the extraordinary kindness and patience
of some defrauded traveling companions, or they were overcome by encountering and testing this attitude in people with
whom they had business dealings. Anyone who is not found
living in accordance with His teachings should not be regarded
as a Christian even if he confesses to Christ's teaching with
his lips. For He said that only those shall be saved who do
not just talk, but who also do the corresponding works.
Justin, *First Apology* 16.                    (11)

Even to this day, spiritual gifts of prophecy are to be found
among us. You [the Jews] should realize from this that
these gifts that once were alive among your people have now
been transferred to us. And just as there were false prophets

among you alongside your holy prophets, so there are many false teachers in our midst now. Our Lord himself in His day warned us against such men.

Therefore we will not let ourselves be taken by surprise in any way, for we are aware that He knew in advance all that would happen to us after His resurrection from the dead and His ascension into Heaven. He told us that we would be killed and hated for the sake of His name and that many false prophets and false Christs would come in His name and seduce many, and this has actually happened. Many in their craftiness have spread godless, blasphemous, and sinful teachings in His name. Whatever the Devil, that impure spirit, has put into their minds they have taught and continue to teach to this day. We do our utmost to change these people's minds as well as yours and to dissuade them from error.

Justin, *Dialogue with Trypho* 82.1–3. (12)

They teach blasphemies, some in one way and some in another, against the Creator of the universe and the crowned Messiah, whose coming was prophesied by Him, blasphemies against the God of Abraham, Isaac, and Jacob. With none of them have we fellowship, for we know that in their impiousness and godlessness, in their sinfulness and slanderousness, they confess Jesus in name only without really worshiping Him. They style themselves Christians as those pagans do who write God's name on the work of their hands and then indulge in wicked and godless rites. . . .

As I said before, we know not only from these events [the appearance of false teachers] that Jesus knew the future in advance, but we know it also from many other happenings He predicted to those who believed and confessed that He is the Christ. He even prophesied all that we would suffer when we are put to death by our own relatives. Consequently, it is obvious that nothing in His words and actions can be rejected.

We pray that you may believe in Him and that you may be saved when He comes again and appears in shining glory.

Justin, *Dialogue with Trypho* 35.5-8.                    (13)

We, on the other hand, have been taught — and we believe it firmly — that God accepts in mercy only those who live in accordance with the good that dwells in God, namely, self-control, justice, love of our fellowmen, and whatever else is characteristic of God, of Him to whom no name can be allotted by which to call Him.

Justin, *First Apology* 10.                    (14)

When we are together we remind one another of these things, and help all who suffer want as best we can, and keep together in harmony. We praise the Creator of the universe through His Son Jesus Christ and through the Holy Spirit for everything we receive.

Justin, *First Apology* 67.                    (15)

We who ourselves used to have pleasure in impure things now cling to chastity alone. We who dabbled in the arts of magic now consecrate ourselves to the good and unbegotten God. We who formerly treasured money and possessions more than anything else now hand over everything we have to a treasury for all and share it with everyone who needs it. We who formerly hated and murdered one another and did not even share our hearth with those of a different tribe because of their customs, now, after Christ's appearance, live together and share the same table. Now we pray for our enemies and try to win those who hate us unjustly so that they too may live in accordance with Christ's wonderful teachings, that they too may enter into the expectation, that they too may receive the

same good things that we will receive from God, the Ruler of the universe.
Justin, *First Apology* 14. (16)

M any men and women who were Christ's disciples from their youth remain chaste even though they live to the age of sixty or seventy. I believe I am able to prove that there are such people in every class of men—not to mention the countless throng of those who, after leading a licentious life, have repented and accepted these teachings. Christ did not call the righteous and abstemious to a change of heart but the godless, the dissolute, and the unjust.
Justin, *First Apology* 15. (17)

T hose who lived in innocence, following God's command, were called "children" in the earliest times as Papias tells in the first book of his *Sayings of the Lord Explained.*
Clement of Alexandria in *The Tutor;* Maximus Confessor, *Comments on Dionysius the Areopagite's Ecclesiastical Hierarchy* 2. (18)

E ither we marry for the sole purpose of bringing up children, or else we renounce marriage altogether and remain continent.
   Recently one of our people handed a petition to Felix, the Prefect of Alexandria, requesting him to allow his surgeon to remove his sex glands, for the physician there stated they were not allowed to do this without the prefect's permission. When Felix refused to sign such a permission under any circumstances, this young man remained single and was satisfied with that, a conscious attitude of mind which he and his fellow believers shared.
Justin, *First Apology* 29. (19)

Must it not be entirely wrong to accept as good one part of what God has created for men's use, but to reject another part as useless and superfluous?
*Letter to Diognetus* 4.                                    (20)

Women who wear gold ornaments are evidently afraid that without their ornaments or stripped of their jewelry they might be taken for slaves. True nobility, however, is found in the beauty and substance of the soul. It does not recognize the slave by the price he fetches at a sale but by his unfree spirit. For us, what corresponds to freedom is not a mere semblance, but a being free because God, who even accepted us to be His children, is our educator. Therefore we must attain the highest degree of freedom in the way we bear ourselves at rest or in motion, in the way we walk and dress: in a word, in every part of life.
Clement of Alexandria, *The Tutor* III.11.59.            (21)

That we for the most part must be considered poor is no disgrace to us but an honor. A life of luxury weakens the spirit. Frugality makes it strong. And yet, how can anyone be considered poor who does not feel any want, who does not covet what belongs to others, who is rich in God's eyes? Much more should he be considered poor who always craves for more while he already has much.

Let me tell you what I think. No man can be as poor as he was at birth. The birds live without any inheritance, and cattle find their fodder each day. Yet these creatures are on the earth for our sake. We possess all of them if we do not covet them. Just as a man traveling on the road is the better off the lighter his bundle, so too, he who makes himself light by poverty, who does not need to pant under the burden of wealth, is happiest on his journey through life. If we regarded wealth as useful

we would ask God for it. He surely could give us a share of it, for everything belongs to Him, but we would rather despise wealth than have it in our hands.
Minucius Felix, *Octavius* 36.3-7.                    (22)


Happiness does not consist in ruling over one's neighbors or in longing to have more than one's weaker fellowmen. Nor does it consist in being rich and in oppressing those lowlier than oneself. No one can imitate God by doing such things. They are alien to His sublimity. On the contrary, anyone who takes his neighbor's burden upon himself, who tries to help the weaker one in points where he has an advantage, who gives what he has received from God to those who need it, takes God's place, as it were, in the eyes of those who receive. He is an imitator of God. In this way, though living on earth, you will know with awe that there is a God who reigns in Heaven, and you will begin to proclaim the mysteries of God. Then you will learn to love and admire those who are punished by death because they refuse to deny God. In this way you will despise the deception and error of the world.
*Letter to Diognetus* 10.                              (23)


It is the Christians, O Emperor, who have sought and found the truth. We have realized it from their writings; they are closer to the truth and to a right understanding than all the other peoples, for they acknowledge God. They believe in Him, the Creator and Builder of the Universe, in whom all things are and from whom everything comes. They worship no other God. They have His commandments imprinted on their hearts. They observe them because they live in the hope and expectation of the coming age of the world. They do not commit adultery. They do not live in fornication. They speak no untruth. They do not keep for themselves the goods entrusted to them. They do not covet what belongs to others. They honor father and mother. They show love to their neighbors. They pronounce judgments which are just. They do not worship idols in human form. They do not do to another what they would not wish to have done to themselves. They do not eat the food sacrificed to idols, for they are pure. They speak gently to those who oppress them, and in this way they make them their friends. It has become their passion to do good to their enemies. Their women, O Emperor, are pure like virgins. Their daughters are chaste, kind, and gentle. Their men refrain from all unlawful intimate relationships. They keep free from all impurity, for they live in the expectation of the recompense to come in the other world. Any male or female slaves or dependents whom individuals among them may have, they persuade to become Christians because of the love they feel towards them. If they do become Christians, they are brothers to them without discrimination.

They worship no alien gods. They live in the awareness of their smallness. Kindliness is their nature. There is no falsehood among them. They love one another. They do not neglect widows. Orphans they rescue from those who are cruel to them. Every one of them who has anything gives ungrudgingly to the one who has nothing. If they see a traveling stranger they bring him under their roof. They rejoice over him as over a real brother, for they do not call one another brothers after the flesh, but they know they are brothers in the Spirit and in God. If one of them sees that one of their poor must leave this world, he provides for his burial as well as he can. And if they hear that one of them is imprisoned or oppressed by their opponents for the sake of their Christ's name, all of them take care of all his needs. If possible they set him free. If anyone among them is poor or comes into want while they themselves have nothing to spare, they fast two or three days for him. In this way they can supply any poor man with the food he needs.

They are ready to give up their lives for Christ, for they observe the words of their Christ with much care. Their life is one of consecration and justice, as the Lord their God commanded them. Every morning, yes, every hour, they give praise and honor to their God for all the good things He gives to them. They thank Him for their food and drink. If any one of them who is righteous passes from this world, they rejoice and give thanks to God. They escort his body as though he were simply moving from one place to another. When a baby is born to one of them, they honor God, and if it should happen that the little child dies, they honor God even more, for it has passed through the world without sin. But if they have to experience that one of them dies in godlessness or sin, they weep bitterly over him. They sigh for him because he must go to meet his punishment. This, O Emperor, is the rule of life of the Christians, and this their manner of life.

As men who know God, they ask of Him the things that are proper for God to give and right for them to receive. Thus they run the course of their lives. They acknowledge the good deeds of God towards them. And see, because of them, good flows on in the world! Truly it is they who have sought and have found the truth, and from what we have understood here we must conclude that they alone are close to the knowledge of truth. Yet they do not cry out in the ears of the masses the good deeds they do. Rather, they take care that no one should notice them. They hide their giving like someone who conceals a treasure he has found. They strive after righteousness because they live in the expectation of seeing their Christ in His radiance and receiving from Him the fulfilment of the promises He made to them.

Take their writings and read in them, and you will see that I have not invented anything here and that I have not spoken as their partisan. Rather, through reading their writings I came to these firm convictions, also regarding the future things to which they bear witness. It is for this reason that I felt urged to declare the truth to those who are ready for the truth and ready to seek the world of the future.

Aristides, *Apology* 15,16. About A.D. 137. (24)

It is good to be lowly in heart, to hate designs that are
        evil,
And, above all, to love one's neighbor as oneself,
To love God with all one's soul and to serve Him.
For this we shall be called "brothers," who stem from the
        holy race
Of the Messiah in Heaven. In our meetings for worship
We remember the joy; we tread the paths of godliness
        and truth.
Never may we approach the inner shrines of the temples,
Or make offerings to idols, or honor them with vows
And the delightful fragrance of flowers and the gleam of
        torches,
Or adorn [them] with splendid gifts and oblations,
Nor may we light the altar with flames and the perfume
        of incense,
Nor when sacrificing a bull may we send with the libation
The blood of a sacrificed sheep, as a ransom for earthly
        punishment,
Nor may we pollute the purity of the ether with the oily
        smoke
Of flesh-consuming pyres and abominable smells.
But let us be glad with a holy mind and understanding,
With joyful hearts, with abundant gifts of love,
And mild and generous hands. With gracious psalms and
        songs

Worthy of our God, we are urged and impelled
To sing to Thee, the everlasting, ever-faithful God:
The Father of all, the all-knowing God.
*Sibylline Oracles* Book VIII.480-500. (25)


When people are challenged to participate in other mysteries, the proclamation is issued to "anyone who has pure hands and something wise to say!" or to "anyone who is free of all guilt, whose soul is not conscious of any evil, and who has lived a noble and just life!" Such is the propaganda of those who promise deliverance from sin.

Hear now what sort of people these [Christians] invite: "Everyone who is a sinner, who is foolish, who is simple"— in a word, everyone who is an unhappy wretch—"such a one the Kingdom of God will receive." You should realize that a sinner is an unjust man, a thief, burglar, poisoner, a desecrator of temples, and a grave-robber! If one wanted to call together a band of robbers, these would be just the ones to invite.

The Christians make this offer, "Let no well-educated man, no wise man, no great man come to us—such we consider bad. But if anyone is uneducated, foolish, and ignorant, let him take courage and come!" By maintaining that such people are of themselves worthy of their God, they prove that they desire and are able to win only the simple, the lowly, the foolish, the slaves, old women, and little children.

They say, "God has been sent to sinners." What does that mean? Is He not sent to those who are free from sin? What does evildoing consist in then? In not having sinned, perhaps? If someone speaks out a sin and humbles himself, conscious of his wickedness, God will accept him!
Celsus against the Christians, in Origen, *Against Celsus* III.44, 59-62. (26)

The new ones to be accepted are questioned by the teachers about the reason for their decision before they hear the Word. Those who bring them shall say whether they are ready for it and what their situation is. . . . Whoever has a demon needs purification before he takes part in the instruction. The professions and trades of those who are going to be accepted into the community must be examined. The nature and type of each must be established. A pander, one who keeps a brothel, shall give it up or be rejected. A sculptor or an artist must be warned not to make idolatrous pictures; he shall give it up or be rejected. If anyone is an actor or impersonator in the theater, he shall give it up or be rejected. A charioteer, an athlete, a gladiator, a trainer of gladiators, or one who fights wild beasts or hunts them or holds public office at the circus games shall give it up or be rejected. A pagan priest or guardian of idols shall give it up or be rejected. A military constable must be forbidden to kill. If he is commanded to kill in the course of his duty, he must not take this upon himself, neither may he swear; if he is not willing to follow these instructions, he must be rejected. A proconsul or a civic magistrate who wears the purple and governs by the sword, shall give it up or be rejected.

Anyone taking part in baptismal instruction, or anyone already baptized who wants to become a soldier shall be sent away, for he has despised God. A prostitute, a sodomite, one who has mutilated himself or who does unmentionable things shall be rejected because he is defiled. A magician shall not come up for examination either. An enchanter, an astrologer, a diviner, a soothsayer, a seducer of the people, one who practices magic with pieces of clothing, one who speaks in demonic riddles, one who makes amulets: all these shall desist or be rejected. The slave who is a concubine and who has reared her children and has no relationship except with her master may become a hearer. If it is otherwise she must be rejected. Whoever has a concubine shall leave her or marry her legally. If he refuses he must be rejected. Should we have missed anything here, practical life will teach you, for we all have the Spirit of God.

Hippolytus, Church Order in *The Apostolic Tradition* 16. About A.D. 218. (27)

Christians cannot be distinguished from the rest of mankind by country, speech, or customs. They do not live in cities of their own; they do not speak a special language; they do not follow a peculiar manner of life. Their teaching was not invented by the ingenuity or speculation of men, nor do they advocate mere book learning, as other groups do. They live in Greek cities and they live in non-Greek cities according to the lot of each one. They conform to the customs of their country in dress, food, and the general mode of life, and yet they show a remarkable, an admittedly extraordinary structure of their own life together. They live in their own countries, but only as guests and aliens. They take part in everything as citizens and endure everything as aliens. Every foreign country is their homeland, and every homeland is a foreign country to them. They marry like everyone else. They beget children, but they do not expose them after they are born. They have a common table, but no common bed. They are in the flesh, but they do not live according to the flesh. They live on earth, but their citizenship is in Heaven. They obey the established laws, but through their way of life they surpass these laws. They love all men and are persecuted by all. Nobody knows them, and yet they are condemned. They are put to death, and just through this they are brought to life. They are as poor as beggars, and yet they make many rich. They lack everything, and yet they have everything in abundance. They are dishonored, and yet have their glory in this very dishonor. They are insulted, and just in this they are vindicated. They are abused, and yet they bless. They are assaulted, and yet it is they who show respect. Doing good, they are sentenced like evildoers. When punished with death, they rejoice in the certainty of being awakened to life. Jews attack them as men of another race, and Greeks persecute them, yet those who hate them cannot give any reason to justify their hostility.

In a word: what the soul is in the body, the Christians are in the world. As the soul is present in all the members of the body, so Christians are present in all the cities of the world. As the soul lives in the body, yet does not have its origin in the body, so the Christians live in the world yet are not of the world. Invisible, the soul is enclosed by the visible body: in the same way the Christians are known to be in the world, but their religion remains invisible. Even though the flesh suffers no wrong from the soul, it hates the soul and fights against it because it is hindered by the soul from following its lusts; so too the world, though suffering no wrong from the Christians, hates them because they oppose its lusts. The soul loves the flesh, but the flesh hates the soul; as the soul loves the members of the body, so the Christians love those who hate them. The soul is enclosed in the body, yet it holds the body together; the Christians are kept prisoners in the world, as it were, yet they are the very ones who hold the world together. Immortal, the soul lives in a mortal house; so too the Christians live in a corruptible existence as strangers and look forward to incorruptible life in Heaven. When the body is poorly provided with food and drink, the soul gains strength. In the same way the number of Christians increases day by day when they are punished with death. Such is the important task God has entrusted to the Christians and they must not shirk it.

*Letter to Diognetus* 5,6 (end of second century).          (28)

We are a united body. We are bound together by a common religious conviction, by one and the same divine discipline and by the bond of common hope. We form a permanent society and come together for communal gatherings as if forming an army around God and besieging Him with our prayers. This is the kind of force in which God rejoices. We pray also for the Emperor and for all those who hold responsible offices and positions of authority. We pray for the postponement of the end. We gather to bring to mind the contents of the Holy Scriptures as often as the world situation gives us a warning or a reminder. In every case we nourish faith with holy words, quicken expectation, and strengthen trust. We reinforce discipline by inculcating our precepts. In these meetings of our society there is also encouragement, admonition, and divine correction, for holding judgment is a matter which carries great weight among us, as it should be among men who are sure of God's presence. Thus when someone has sinned so much that he is excluded from the fellowship of prayer, from the entire sacred intercourse of the community, it is a deeply moving prelude of the judgment to come.

The most proved men preside, the "elders" as we call them. They have attained this honor only through their good name, never through the use of money, for nothing that is of God can be bought for money. Even though we have a kind of cash box, the money does not come from admission fees, as when one buys membership or position in a society. That would be like "buying religion." Rather, every man contributes something once a month, or whenever he wishes to, and only if he wishes to, and if he can; for no one is forced, but everyone gives his share freewillingly. These contributions might be called the deposit funds of fellowship with God as they are not spent on banquets or drinking parties or on gluttony. Rather they are used to feed and to bury the poor; for boys and girls without means and without parents to help them; . . . for shipwrecked sailors; and for those doing forced labor in the mines, or banished on islands, or in prison, provided they suffer for the sake of God's fellowship. That makes them beneficiaries by virtue of their confession of faith. But even such acts of great love set a stain on us in the eyes of some people. "Look," they say, "how they love each other" (for they hate each other). "See, how ready they are to die for one another" (for they would sooner kill each other). Furthermore, they get excited because we are called by the name of "brothers." I think the only reason for this is that every word of blood relationship used to express heartfelt affection is hypocrisy with them. But we are brothers even to you by the law of nature, our common mother, although you are not true men as long as you are bad brothers! How much more does it express the truth to call and look upon those as brothers who have recognized their one Father, God, and who have come, startled and amazed, from the same womb of ignorance to the one light of truth. But maybe we are not considered quite legitimate because our brotherliness is not loudly declaimed in a tragedy, or because we are brothers with regard to our family possessions too, at which point your brotherliness ceases to exist as a rule.

We who are inwardly bound together in spirit and in soul can have no hesitation in surrendering our property. We hold everything in common except our wives. At this point we dissolve our community, and this is precisely the one point in which the rest of men practice community. Oh, this example of ancient Greek wisdom and Roman dignity! Procurers both, the philosopher and the government official!

How can anyone be surprised if such a great love as ours comes to expression in our communal meals! But you slander even our modest meals as wasteful after you have discredited them as criminal. Investigations are made only into the

Christian banquets. Legally they are not allowed because they are regarded as unlawful meetings. According to the law such banquets are to be condemned as soon as anyone files a complaint on the basis of the paragraphs of the law enacted against secret societies. But have we ever met to hurt anyone? In our meetings we are the same as when we are scattered; jointly we are the same as individually. This we are without damaging or hurting anyone. When upright and good people gather, when believing and pure men join together, that should not be called a secret society, but a senate. On the contrary, those gatherings should be called secret societies which conspire to hate good and honest men, which call out for blood of innocent people. To justify their hate they use as a pretext their mad and groundless belief that the Christians are the principal cause of every public disaster and every misfortune of the people. If the Tiber rises over the city walls, or the other way around, if the Nile does not flood the fields, if the weather is not favorable, if there is an earthquake, or if there is a plague, then the cry is immediately raised, "The Christians to the lions!" Tertullian, *Apology* 39,40, in the year 198. (29)

W e know that the followers of the Stoic school were also hated and killed because, at least in their ethical teaching, they showed a love of order by virtue of the seed of the Logos implanted in all mankind. It is similar with some of the poets. As examples I could give Heraclitus (whom I like to mention) and Musonius of our own time and others, for the demons, as we already pointed out, were always eager to make those hated who in some way tried to live according to the Logos and to avoid evil. No wonder then that the demons try to make those much more hated who live according to the vision and knowledge of the whole Logos, which is the Christ, instead of only a little part of the Logos, scattered like a seed among men. It had to be like that after the demons had been unmasked by Him. And the demons will always carry on like this until they are confined to everlasting fire and suffer just punishment and torment. Even now they are overcome by men in the name of Jesus Christ.

Justin, *Second Apology* 8. After A.D. 150.                    (30)

Clearly, our faith is more sublime than any human doctrine, for the very reason that Christ, who appeared for our sakes, is the whole Logos, the Body as well as the Word and the Soul. . . . Socrates, the most forceful of them all, was in his time accused of the same crimes as we are. They claimed that he introduced new gods and spurned the gods recognized by the State. . . . "It is not easy to find the Father and Creator of all things, and when one has found Him, it is indeed not without danger to proclaim Him before all men." Yet our Christ did all this in His own power. No one believed so much in Socrates that he was willing to die for his teachings, and yet Socrates knew of Christ to some extent. . . . After all, He was and is the Logos who dwells in every man, who foretold things to come, first through the prophets, and then in person when He took on our human nature and brought us this teaching! But not only philosophers and scholars believed in Christ; no, it was much more simple laborers and quite ordinary people who even scorned honor, fear, and death. Thus He is revealed as the power of the ineffable Father, in complete contrast to mere instruments of human reason.

Justin, *Second Apology* 10.                    (31)

I must admit it is the object of all my prayers and earnest endeavors to be found a Christian. Not that the teachings of Plato are alien to those of Christ, but what I mean is that

they are not equivalent in all things; neither are those of the others, the Stoics, the poets, and historians. Each of those men spoke admirably in as far as he was endowed with the seed of the divine Logos disseminated everywhere and saw what is related to its nature. They contradicted each other in important issues however, showing a lack of far-sighted knowledge and clear, infallible understanding. Everything which was said by them rightly belongs to us Christians. For next to God we worship the Logos, who came from this same unbegotten and ineffable God, and we love Him because He became man for our sakes and even took part in our suffering that He might heal us. All these writers could see only a demonlike glimpse of the truth through the indwelling, innate seed of the Logos, for the seed of something, and its imitation, given according to one's receptivity, are always quite different from the thing itself.
Justin, *Second Apology* 13. (32)

You have learned enough now, I believe, to see that the Christians are right in keeping aloof from the common error and lack of judgment, and therefore also from the meddlesomeness and boastfulness of the Jews. But you cannot expect to learn from any man the mysterious nature of their own worship of God.
*Letter to Diognetus* 4. (33)

Every generation of men is under a curse, as is shown in the Law of Moses. The Father of the whole universe willed that His Christ, out of love to men of every generation, should take upon Himself the curse that is on all men. He fully realized that He would raise Him up again after His death by execution.
Justin, *Dialogue with Trypho* 95.1,2. (34)

The words of the Law, "Cursed is anyone who hangeth on a tree," strengthen our hope, which clings to the crucified Christ. . . . You can see with your own eyes what is actually happening now, for in your synagogues you Jews curse all those who have become believers through Jesus Christ, and the pagans put your curse into effect by executing anyone who simply confesses that he is a Christian. For all of them we have this answer, "You are our brothers. Recognize God's truth." Even if the pagans, as well as you, instead of following us, do all in their power to make us deny the name of Christ, we nevertheless prefer to die. We suffer because we are convinced that through Christ God will give us all the good things that He promised us.
Justin, *Dialogue with Trypho* 96.1–2.                              (35)

The first elders were very distressed unless they had to suffer physically in some way all the time. They preferred to speak the truth rather than to write it down.
Clement of Alexandria about the oral Tradition of the Elders in early Christian times. *Selections* from the Prophets 11.27.
(36)

Neither would we be put to death, nor would unjust men and demons have any power over us, were it not for the fact that every man who is born must die, without exception. We are glad, therefore, when we are allowed to pay off this common debt.
Justin, *Second Apology* 11.                                        (37)

And now I want to turn to the man who asserts or believes that we are initiated by the murder and the blood of a little child. Can you think it possible that such a tender, tiny body should be gashed with mortal wounds, that any man alive would slaughter a little baby hardly come into being, to spill, drain, and drink its innocent blood? Nobody can believe such a thing unless he is capable of doing it himself. But I do see people among you at times expose newly born children to wild beasts and birds and at other times put them to death by strangling or by other horrible means. Some women destroy the unborn child in their womb by taking drugs, thus committing infanticide before they are delivered.

For us it is not permissible even to see or to hear of murder. Yes, we shrink so much from human blood that we do not even use the blood of animals in the food we eat.

Moreover, the rabble of demons has concocted the grandiose fable of incestuous banquets against us to throw the mud of ugly shame upon the good name of our chastity. They tried, through the horror of these outrageous opinions about us, to turn people away from seeking the knowledge of the truth. Even Fronto, whom you cite, did not produce any evidence based on affirmed testimony but simply gave vent to rhetorical abuse. The banquets that we organize are as chaste as they are sober. We do not like sumptuous eating, nor do we prolong our meals with drinking bouts. We know how to temper our gaiety with seriousness.

Minucius Felix, *Octavius* 30.1,2,6; 31.1,5. (38)

We are so far from practising promiscuous intercourse that we are not even allowed a lustful glance. What could justify any doubt as to the purity of the life led by those who are not allowed to use their eyes for any other purpose than that for which God created them, namely to look in the light, for whom even a lustful glance is called adultery! For them the coming judgment applies even to thoughts!

We are not accountable to human laws, which a wicked man may evade. Right from the beginning I tried to convince you of the divine origin of our teaching. We have quite a different law. We have a task which has led us to see that the full measure of justice is to be found in rightly loving ourselves and our neighbors. With this in mind we look upon some, according to age, as sons and daughters; some we treat as brothers and sisters; and those who are older we honor as fathers and mothers. It is of the utmost importance to us that their bodies remain undefiled and uncorrupted: they belong, after all, to those we consider our brothers and sisters or some other relation! The Logos speaks to us once more, "If anyone kisses a second time, because he enjoyed it . . . !" adding, "Thus one must give the kiss and exchange greetings with great care, for if it should be defiled by any wrong thought it would rob us of eternal life."

Therefore, because we are expecting eternal life, our contempt of the world extends even to the pleasures experienced only in the world of the imagination. Thus each of us has only one wife, whom he has married according to our own laws and, what is more, for the purpose of begetting children. The farmer, after entrusting the seed to mother earth, waits for the harvest without sowing more seed. In the same way our desire reaches its goal in the procreation of children. Nevertheless you can find many fellow-believers, both men and women, who grow old without ever marrying, in the hope of a closer inner communion with God. If, then, to persevere in the state of virginity brings both sexes nearer to God, and if a mere thought or lustful desire drives us away from Him, how much more shall we despise the deeds the very thought of which we forbid ourselves? Our life does not consist in making up beautiful phrases but in performing beautiful deeds and in working toward them. Every man shall remain as he is born or marry only once, for a second marriage is only camouflaged adultery. . . . He who severs himself from his first wife, even after her death, is an adulterer in disguise. He oversteps the ordinance of God who in the beginning created only one man and only one woman.

But why should I speak about things which are mysteries? In spite of such sublime principles we hear the most serious accusations against us, proving the saying, "The harlot reproves the chaste." The very people who organize a regular white-slave traffic; who avoiding the law offer young people every type of vile debauchery; who do not even abstain from males but perform shocking acts, males with males; who defile in every way just the most graceful and beautiful bodies; who drag the glorious handiwork of God's creation in the dust— for beauty is not on the earth of itself but because it is sent by the hand and grace of God—these very people dare to lay at our door all the infamous things they are conscious of in themselves and even attribute them to their "ideal" gods, evidently because they consider them noble deeds, worthy of their gods!

Adulterers and corrupters of boys want to defame us who live in virginity or in strictly monogamic marriages! They, who actually live like fish of prey, gulp down everyone who comes their way, the stronger hunting down the weaker. Oh, what an outrage against human flesh when the laws, enacted by you and your ancestors with just consideration, are violated, when people are put under such pressure that the very governors appointed by you cannot cope with the lawsuits, when over and above this the people who have to suffer these things are not even allowed to hit back when struck and are expected to use only kind words when reviled! To be just alone is not enough because to be just means to repay like for like, but we have been commanded to go far beyond this, to be kind and patient.

How could anyone in his right mind accuse us of murder when we hold to such principles, for you have to kill someone if you want to eat human flesh!

Just as they lie in the first charge, so do they also in the second. If anyone were to ask them whether they have actually seen what they assert, not one of them would be brazen enough to say 'yes.' And yet we have slaves too, some more, some fewer. Nothing can remain hidden from them, but not one of them has ever invented such fables about us. We cannot bear to see a man put to death, even justly! How then can anyone accuse us of murder and cannibalism?. . . How can we possibly kill anyone when we cannot even look on lest we are polluted with the guilt of murder and sacrilege! How can we possibly kill anyone, we who call those women murderers who take drugs to induce an abortion, we who say they will have to give an account before God one day! We are convinced that with God nothing goes unexamined, and that the body, after serving the irrational urges and lusts of the soul, will have its share in punishment. We have, therefore, every reason to detest even the slightest sin.

Athenagoras, *A Plea Regarding Christians* 32-35.        (39)

Consider, then, whether those who have received such teaching can possibly practice promiscuous and unlawful intercourse, or, most godless of all, eat human flesh! We are forbidden so much as to look at gladiator fights lest we become privy to and participants in murder! We also consider it immoral to watch other shows because our eyes and ears shall not be defiled with sympathy for acts of murder as they are celebrated there in song. As for speaking about cannibalism: there the children of Thyestes and Tereus are devoured. As for speaking about adultery: with them it is the theme of their tragedies, not just as a misdeed of men, but even more so of gods, celebrated as a heroic act in elegant language during their contests!

May the very thought of doing such things be far from the Christians! They exercise wise self-control. They practice continence, observe monogamy, guard chastity, and wipe out injustice, destroying sin with its root. With them justice is lived out, laws are kept, and faith is witnessed to by deeds. They confess God. They consider truth supreme. Grace protects them. Peace shields them. The holy Word leads them. Wisdom teaches them. Life is decisive. God is their King.

Theophilus of Antioch, *To Autolycus* Book III.15. (40)

We are accused of being "Christians," [*chresteu* = excellent] but it is not right to hate what is excellent. And again, when one of the accused denies his faith and simply says he is not one, you acquit him as though you knew of no charge to bring against him. But if anyone confesses that he is one, you punish him because of his confession. It would be your duty rather to investigate the conduct of both the confessor and the renegade so that the deeds of each one establish his guilt or his innocence.

Justin, *First Apology* 4. (41)

Our persecutors are actually not primarily interested in our property when they prosecute us, nor in our good name as citizens when they publicly heap insults on us, nor in any of the less important values when they plunge us into ruin. All these things we hold in contempt, no matter how important and worthwhile they may seem to the masses. We have been taught not to hit back at people who harass us, not to go to court against those who expel us and rob us. Rather are we enjoined to offer the other side of the face for more blows when they ignominiously smite us on the one side. When they take away our coat, we are to give them our overcoat as well.

No, it is clearly our body and our life that our persecutors plot against when there are no more goods they can take away from us. This is the only explanation for the many accusations they spread about us. If anyone can convict us of unjust acts, whether small or big, we are the last to beg off punishment; we would in fact demand the most severe and relentless punishment if this were to happen. . . . While others accused of transgressions are not punished before they are convicted, in our case the judges do not inquire whether the defendant has committed any wrong but are provoked about the name as if that were in itself a crime.

Athenagoras, *A Plea Regarding Christians* 1.2. (42)

What a beautiful sight it is for God when a Christian wrestles with pain; when he takes up the fight against threats, capital punishment, and torture; when smiling he mocks at the clatter of the tools of death and the horror of the executioner; when he defends and upholds his liberty in the face of kings and princes, obeying God alone to whom he belongs; when triumphantly and victoriously he challenges the very one who has passed sentence on him! For he is victor who has reached the goal of his aspirations.

Is there any soldier who would not face danger more boldly under the eyes of his general? Only he who proves himself receives the prize, and yet the general cannot give what is not his: he cannot prolong life. He can do nothing but give military honors.

But the fighter for God does not feel forsaken in his pain nor will he be destroyed by death. Thus it may seem as if the Christian were miserable, but that he can never be, in reality. You yourselves extol unfortunate men such as Mucius Scaevola to the skies. He would have perished among his enemies if he had not sacrificed his right hand. But how many from among us have sacrificed not only their right hand but much more than that: they suffered the scorching and burning of their whole body without uttering one single cry of pain! And they had it in their power to obtain their release. However, why do I compare men with Mucius or Aquilius or with Regulus? Among us, boys and frail women laugh to scorn torture and the gallows cross, the wild beasts and all the other horrors of execution! In their pain they show an endurance that comes from Heaven.

Minucius Felix, *Octavius* 37.1-5. (43)

The poor wretches have got it into their heads that they are altogether immortal.

Lucian, died 180 (writer of comedies), in *Peregrinus* 13.

(44)

How they are thrown to the wild beasts to make them deny the Lord! How unconquerable they are! Do you not see that the more of them are executed, the more do the others grow in number? That is clearly not the work of men. That is the power of God. That is proof of His presence.

*Letter to Diognetus* 7. (45)

# CONFESSION of FAITH and SCRIPTURES

I believe in One God,
The Father Almighty,
And in His only begotten Son
Jesus Christ, our Lord,
And in the Holy Spirit,
Giver of new life,
And in the resurrection of the flesh,
And in one only, apostolic, holy Church
everywhere,
Which is His Church.

Earliest Coptic baptismal symbol, still shorter in several other Egyptian texts. (1)

We confess our faith:
In the Father, the Ruler of the whole world,
And in Jesus Christ, our Savior,
And in the Holy Spirit, the representative Advocate,
And in the holy Church,
And in the forgiveness of sins.

About 150-180 in the *Epistle of the Apostles* 3-5. (2)

After entering the baptismal water, we confess the Christian faith in the words of His law and declare with our own mouths that we have renounced the Devil, his pomp, and his angels.

The unity of the Church is proved by the mutuality of the greetings of peace, by the use of the name "brother," and by mutual hospitality: the granting of these privileges depends on no other condition than the matching tradition of the same oath of allegiance in all.

There is one Rule of Faith: this is the belief [testified to in the following]. There is one and absolutely only one God and no other than the Creator of the universe, who, through His own Word sent down before all other things, brought into being everything out of nothing. This Word is called His Son, perceived in different ways under the Name of God by the patriarchs, heard at all times in the Prophets, brought down at last into the virgin Mary by the Spirit and in the power of God, His Father, became flesh in her womb, and was born of her as Jesus Christ. Thereafter He proclaimed the new law and the promise of the Kingdom of the Heavens and wrought great acts of power; nailed to the Cross, He rose again the third day; having ascended into the Heavens, He sits at the right hand of the Father and has sent the Holy Spirit as His representative power to move those that believe; and He shall come again in glory to receive the saints into the fulfillment of eternal life and the heavenly promises, and to judge the sinners with incessant fire, after the raising of both from the dead has been brought about by the restoration of the flesh. This norm was established by Christ and is in no way questioned among us.

We believe as we have always done—and even more now since we have been better instructed by the representative Advocate, who truly leads men into all truth—we believe that there is only one true God, namely in that administration of His Household which we call Economy, that there is only one Son of the one and only God, who is His own Word, who proceeded from Him, through whom everything was made and without whom nothing was made, who was sent down by the Father into the virgin and was born of her, man and God, son of a human being and Son of God, who is called Jesus Christ, the same who suffered, who died and was buried in accordance with the Scriptures, and was raised by the Father, and was received to sit at the right hand of the Father, and shall come again to judge the living and the dead. He is the same who in accordance with His promise sent down the Holy Spirit from the Father, the representative Advocate who sanctifies the faith of those who believe in the Father, in the Son, and in the Holy Spirit. This norm has been current since the beginning of the Good News.

The Rule of Faith is definitely only one; it alone is immovable and unchangeable. It is the following: to believe in the one and only God, who has power over all things, the Creator of the world, and in His Son Jesus Christ, born of the virgin Mary, crucified under Pontius Pilate, raised again from the dead on the third day, received into the Heavens, now sitting at the right hand of the Father, and who shall come again to judge the living and the dead through the resurrection of the flesh.

Tertullian, *On Shows* 4; *The Prescription of Heretics* 20,13; *Against Praxeas* 2; *Concerning the Veiling of Virgins* 1.   (3)

He who holds immovable in his heart the plumb line of the truth, which he took hold of through baptism, is able to see through all deceptions of false teachers.

A spiritually minded disciple has the constant help of faith in the one God, of firm conviction about Christ, and of true recognition of the Holy Spirit. This teaching of the apostles is the age-old fellowship of the Church throughout the whole world.

The Church spreads out over the whole world to the uttermost ends of the earth. From the apostles and their disciples she received the faith: in the one God, the Almighty Father, Creator of Heaven and earth, the sea, and all that is in them; in the one Christ [Messiah] Jesus, the Son of God, who for our salvation took on flesh; and in the Holy Spirit who through the prophets proclaimed God's plan of salvation and the twofold coming of the Lord, His birth from a virgin, His suffering, His resurrection from the dead, the bodily ascension into Heaven of our beloved Lord, the Christ [Messiah] Jesus, and His future coming from the Heavens in the glory of the Father "to make all things new" and to raise up anew all flesh of the whole human race in order to execute judgment justly on all.

Irenaeus, *Against Heresies* I.9.4; IV.33; I.10.1.          (4)

I believe in God, the Almighty (Father),
And in the Messiah Jesus, His only begotten Son,
Who is Ruler over us,
Who was born of the Holy Spirit and of Mary, the
          virgin,
Who was crucified under Pontius Pilate and was
          buried,
And on the third day rose from the dead,
Who ascended into the realms of Heaven
And sits at the right hand of the Father,
From where He will come to judge the living and
          the dead,
And in the Spirit, who is Holy,
One holy Church,

Forgiveness of sins,
And the resurrection of the flesh.

Amen.

The Roman Baptismal Confession, used in the whole East in
the Roman version, in this form since A.D. 125-135. Sources
in the annotation.                                          (5)

O you happy and glorious ones in the Lord, you who keep
your Confession of the perfect apostolic faith in your
hearts and until now knew nothing of any written creeds! You
did not need the letter because you overflowed with the Spirit.
Nor did you desire to use your hands for writing because for
your salvation you confessed with your mouths what you believed in your hearts. There was no need for you as bishops to
read what you knew by heart because you were reborn and
newly baptized.
Hilary of Poitiers to the bishops of Gaul, Germany, and Britain
in the year 360.                                            (6)

We who worship the Creator of this world are not atheists.
What sensible man will not admit this?
Moreover, we want to make it known that we recognize
Jesus Christ, who is our Teacher in these things, who was born
for this purpose and was crucified under Pontius Pilate, Procurator of Judea at the time of the Emperor Tiberius, as the
true Son of God. To Him therefore we give the second place,
and with good reason we honor the prophetic Spirit in the
third place.
Justin, *First Apology* 13.                                 (7)

I have shown sufficiently that we are not atheists, for ours is
the one God, uncreated and eternal, invisible, immutable,

incomprehensible, inconceivable, to be grasped only by the mind and by reason, surrounded by light and beauty, by Spirit and power to an ineffable degree: He by whose Word the universe was created, was set in order, and is ruled.

However, we also acknowledge a Son of God. Let no one think it ridiculous that God should have a Son! For our thoughts about God the Father and the Son are very different from the myths of the poets who represent that the gods are in no way better than men. The Son of God is the Word [Logos] of the Father. He is thought that shapes, and power that creates; for according to His pattern and through Him is everything made, the Father and the Son being one. Since through the unity and power of the Spirit the Son is in the Father and the Father in the Son, the Son of God is the thought [mind] and the Word [Logos] of the Father.

If, however, in your superior intelligence you should wonder what is meant by the expression "Son," I will give you a brief explanation. He is First-begotten to the Father, but not as if He were created. From the beginning God, who is eternal mind, had the Word in Himself, because He is never without the Word. Rather, the Son came forth to be formative thought and creative power for all things material. With this the prophetic Spirit also agrees, saying, "The Lord created me in the beginning of his ways for his works."

Further, we teach that the Holy Spirit, who shows Himself at work in the Prophets, is also an effluence of God, flowing from Him and returning to Him like a ray of the sun. How can a man know his way about if he hears people decried as atheists who confess one God, the Father, and one God, the Son, and one Holy Spirit, and who prove that these have power in their oneness and yet are different in their order?

Athenagoras, *A Plea Regarding Christians* 10.          (8)

From ancient times wicked demons in human form defiled women, corrupted boys, and showed men such terrifying sights that whoever did not have the insight to discern what was happening became confused. Obsessed by fear, they failed to recognize them as evil demons. They called them "gods" and gave to each the name which each demon had given to himself.

Socrates tried by true reason and exact inquiry to bring these things to light and to draw man away from these demons. That is why the demons, working through men who delighted in evil, knew how to bring about his execution as an atheist and sacrilegious person. They accused him of having introduced new gods. And now they try to do the very same thing to us. For it happened not only among the Greeks that these things were brought to light, (through Socrates) but also among the barbarians. It happened through the same Logos who took form and became man and was called Jesus Christ. Him we follow, and we deny that the spirits who have done those things are true deities but assert that they are wicked and infamous demons, in no way even capable of such actions as men are who strive for goodness and merit.
Justin, *First Apology* 5. (9)

Crosses also we do not worship, nor do we desire to worship them. But you, who consecrate gods of wood, very possibly worship wooden crosses as being parts of your gods.
Minucius Felix, *Octavius* 29.6. (10)

So, then, we are called atheists. We confess that we are atheists as far as such false gods are concerned but not with respect to the true God, the Father of justice, self-control, and of all other good qualities, the God who is free from all taint of evil. No. We worship and adore Him and the Son who came

from Him and taught us these things, the host of other good
angels who follow Him and are very much like Him, and the
prophetic Spirit. To these we give honor in reason and in truth.
Justin, *First Apology* 6.                                    (11)

We think of God the Creator of all things as being far
above all that is corruptible.
Justin, *First Apology* 20.                                   (12)

Is it right, I ask, to charge us with atheism, we who clearly
distinguish God from matter and prove that matter is something quite different from God and that there is a tremendous
distance between them? We show that the divine Being is uncreated and eternal, to be grasped only by mind and spirit.
Matter on the other hand is created and corruptible.
Athenagoras, *A Plea Regarding Christians* 4.               (13)

The sacrifice most pleasing to Him is that we try to recognize who stretched out and vaulted the heavens and set the
earth as the center, who gathered the water into seas and
separated light from darkness, who adorned the ether with
stars and made the earth bring forth all manner of seed, who
called the animals into being and created man. If we follow
God as the Molder who holds all things together and watches
over all things with that same wisdom and skill with which He
governs the universe, and if we lift up holy hands to Him, what
need does He have then of ritual sacrifices?

Beautiful indeed is the world, glorious in its magnitude, in
the arrangement of the stars, both in the zodiac and around
the constellation of the Great Dipper and in its form as a
sphere. Yet the world for these reasons does not deserve to be
worshiped; rather does its sublime Artificer. . . . God himself

is everything: Unapproachable Light! Perfect Beauty! Spirit! Power! Word!

If the world were a well-tuned instrument played in rhythm, I would not worship the instrument but Him who made it and tuned it, who strikes the notes and sings the song that fits the melody. God is the Perfect Good and eternally does only good. Athenagoras, *A Plea Regarding Christians* 13,16.     (14)

The presbyter, a disciple of the apostles, expressed himself in the same way concerning the two Covenants, showing that both came from one and the same God and that there is no other God except Him who created and formed us. The argument of those who maintain that this world surrounding us was made by an angel or by any other kind of power, or by another god, has no basis at all, for once a man is driven away from the Creator of all things and concedes that the world in which we live was made by another or through another, he has to fall into many absurd and contradictory notions; he will not be able to render an account either of the probability of these or of their truth.
"Traditions of the Elders" in Irenaeus, *Against Heresies* IV. 32.1.     (15)

There will never be another God, nor has there ever been another God from eternity, except the One, who created and ordered this universe. Furthermore, we believe that our God is none other than yours. According to our faith He is one and the same God as He who with a strong hand and an outstretched arm led your fathers out of Egypt. We have placed our trust in no other God (for there is no other) but only in Him whom you also have trusted, the God of Abraham, Isaac, and Jacob.

The Law proclaimed on Horeb is of course obsolete and belongs to you alone, whereas ours is for all men everywhere and at all times. Now whenever a law is laid down in opposition to another law, it supersedes the former one. In the same way, a later compact annuls the former one. Christ has been given to us as the eternal and final Law. We can rely on the Covenant, after which there will be no further law, no precept, no command.

Justin, *Dialogue with Trypho the Jew* 11.1,2. (16)

Do you think we conceal the object of our worship because we have no temples and altars? What image of God can I invent since in reality man himself is God's image? What temple shall I build Him when the whole world, the work of His hands, cannot contain Him? And I, a man who lives comparatively spaciously, should I shut up the greatness of such majesty in a single small cell? Should we not rather make a sanctuary for Him in our souls? Should we not consecrate a holy place to Him in our inmost hearts? Shall I sacrifice little and big animals to Him? After all, He created them for my use, and so I could only return to Him His own gift.

Certainly, we cannot show or see the God we worship. He is God for us just because we can know Him but cannot see Him. In His works, in all the movements of the universe, we perceive His power always, whether in thunder, lightning, and approaching storm, or in the clear sky.

And you believe that this God knows nothing of the doings and dealings of men? You believe that from His throne in Heaven He cannot visit all men or know individual men? Man, in this you are mistaken and deceived. How can God be far away! The whole Heaven and the whole earth and all things beyond the confines of the world are filled with God. Everywhere He is very close to us, yes, much more than that, He is in us. Look at the sun again! Fixed in the sky, its light is still poured out over all the earth. It is equally present everywhere and penetrates everything. Its splendor is nowhere dimmed. How much more is God present, He who is the Creator of all things and sees all things, from whom nothing can remain hidden! He is present in darkness, present even in our thoughts, which are a darkness of another kind as it were. All our deeds are done under His eyes. I would almost say: we live with Him. Minucius Felix, *Octavius* 32.1,2,4,7-9. (17)

It is He who has manifested Himself. He revealed Himself through faith. To faith alone is it given to see God. God, the Ruler and Creator of the Universe, He who made all things and arranged them in proper order, was man's friend and full of kindness and patience. This He always was, is, and always will be: kind and good, slow to anger, and true. He alone is good. When He had conceived the great and ineffable thought, He communicated it only to His Son. Now, as long as He kept and guarded His wise counsel within Himself as a secret, it could appear as if He were not concerned and did not care about us. But He disclosed what He had in mind from the beginning through His beloved Son. Through Him He revealed it. Thus He granted us all things at once, to share in His blessings, to perceive, and to understand. Which of us could have expected all this?
*Letter to Diognetus* 8.5-9. (18)

The Father of the Universe is unbegotten. Therefore He cannot have any name attached to Him, for whenever someone receives a name, the giver of the name is the older one. The words Father, God, Creator, Lord, and Ruler are not names but only descriptions of attributes derived from His good deeds and His works. However His Son, who alone is called His Son in the proper sense, being the Logos who was in the Father before all creation, was begotten when He created and set in order all things through the Son in the beginning. He is called the Christ because He was anointed, and because God set all things in order through Him.

Christ is a name that also contains an incomprehensible concept, just as the term "God" is no real name but the concept of an inexplicable Being, inborn in human nature. However, "Jesus" points to the name and concept of a man and a redeemer, for, as we have said already, He became man. He was born in accordance with the will of God the Father for the sake of believing men and for the downfall of all demons, as you can see even now in that which takes place before your own eyes. After all, many of our people (the Christians namely) have healed a great number of possessed persons who did not receive healing from any other exorcist, sorcerer, or herb doctor. They did this throughout the whole world, and even in your own capital city, by driving out the demons in the name of Jesus Christ, who was crucified under Pontius Pilate.

Justin, *Second Apology* 6.                                              (19)

Chosen King of the world to come, He took up battle against the one who received the rulership for the present time, as it was ordained beforehand. What grieved Him most sorely was this, that He was attacked in ignorance by the very people for whom He waged the fight as for His own children. And yet He loved those who hated Him, mourned over those who did not believe in Him, blessed those who abused Him, and prayed for His enemies. He not only acted like a father Himself, but He also taught His disciples to do the same in their attitude [toward others], to act toward them as toward their own brothers. In this way He was a Father, in this way a Prophet. Hence follows the expectation that in this way also He shall be King over His children and that a time of eternal peace shall break in by virtue of His fatherly love toward His children and of the indwelling reverence of the children toward their Father.

Clementine *Homilies* III.19. (20)

The Christians trace their lineage from Jesus Christ. He is called the Son of God Most High. Concerning Him the testimony is given that He descended from Heaven as God and took and put on flesh from a Hebrew virgin, and that in this way the Son of God dwelt in a daughter of man. This is taught in the Good News which, so they testify, has been spread abroad in recent times. You too will be able to grasp its significance when you read it. This Jesus, then, is descended from the people of the Hebrews. He had twelve disciples through whom His wonderful work of salvation was to be accomplished. He Himself was pierced by the Jews, and it is testified that He lived again after three days and was lifted up into Heaven. After that, these same twelve disciples went out into the known parts of the world and proclaimed His majesty with loving-kindness and serious intent. For this reason those who believe in this proclamation today are called Christians, a name by which they have become well known.

Aristides, *Apology* 2.6-8. (21)

Christ alone is begotten as the real Son of God because He is His Logos, His Firstborn, and His Power. Become man according to His counsel, He gave us these teachings for the transformation and leading upward of mankind.

Justin, *First Apology* 23. (22)

The Christian teaching is more sublime than any other because in Christ the divine Logos became man.

Whoever does not know Christ does not know the will of God. Whoever despises and hates Christ obviously despises and hates Him who sent Him. And if a man does not believe in Christ, he does not believe in the words of the prophets, in which His Joyful News was proclaimed to all men.

If you knew the words of the prophets, you would not be able to deny that Jesus is God, Son of the one unbegotten and ineffable God.

Justin, *Dialogue with Trypho the Jew* 26.10.       (23)

He is eternal, although He came to be born of the virgin Mary and became man. It is with Him that the Father begins to renew Heaven and earth. Through Him shall He bring about the New Creation. It is He who shall shine as the eternal Light in Jerusalem.

Justin, *Dialogue with Trypho the Jew* 113.4,5.       (24)

From the fortieth and fiftieth year the span of life begins to decline toward older age, and our Lord taught at this age as the Gospel and all the elders testify. They were together in Asia with John, the Lord's disciple, [and say] that John handed this information down to them, for he stayed with them until the times of Trajan. Some of them, moreover, saw not only John but other apostles as well and heard the same account from them, and they bear witness to this report.

"Traditions of the Elders" in Irenaeus, *Against Heresies* II. 22.5.       (25)

You can see that the crucified Christ possesses the hidden power of God: every demon, in fact every single power and authority on earth, trembles before Him.

The Word revealed that the nations shall believe in Him. You can see it with your own eyes, for we who are men of all nationalities have become God-fearing and righteous through our faith in Christ, and we wait for His future coming.

Justin, *Dialogue with Trypho the Jew* 49.8; 52.4.     (26)

Through miracles, too, you can be led to an understanding of Jesus. In miracles we recognized Christ, the Son of God, who was crucified, who rose from the dead, who ascended into Heaven, and who shall come once more to judge all men who ever lived, even as far back as Adam.

Justin, *Dialogue with Trypho the Jew* 132.1.     (27)

If such miracles are shown to have accompanied the power of His suffering and still now accompany it, how great will be the miracles when He appears again in glory! As Daniel revealed, He shall appear on the clouds as the Son of Man, accompanied by angels.

Justin, *Dialogue with Trypho the Jew* 31.1.     (28)

But if Jesus at His first coming which took place in lowliness, without honor or glory, revealed so much light and power that now every nation knows Him—so much that the old positions of international corruption are abandoned in a general retreat, so much that even the demons submit to His Name and all the powers and kingdoms have greater fear of His Name than of the whole world of the dead—shall He not then, at His future appearance, which will take place in radiant glory, destroy completely all His enemies and all those who in their sins have turned their backs on Him! How He will then reward His own with all the things they expected and lead them to peace!

Christ, my Lord, the "Mighty and Powerful One," shall come and demand what is His own from all.
Justin, *Dialogue with Trypho the Jew* 121.3; 125.5.     (29)

Oh, foolish people! They do not understand what has been proved again and again, that two manifestations of His arrival are prophesied: in the one He suffers, is robbed of glory and honor, and is crucified as was prophesied; in the other He will appear in glory from Heaven. This will come about when the man of great apostasy, who utters improper things against the Most High, will be bold enough to commit sinful acts on earth against us Christians—against us, who have learned the true worship of God from the Law and from the Word which went out from Jerusalem by way of the apostles of Jesus and who have taken refuge in the God of Jacob and the God of Israel.
Justin, *Dialogue with Trypho the Jew* 110.2.     (30)

Whatever else is mentioned in prophecy shall be fulfilled at His second appearance. When those are mentioned who are oppressed and cast out, that is, cast out from the world, this means: As far as you and all other men have it in your power, every Christian is cast out not only from his property but even from the world itself. You dispute his very right to live.
Justin, *Dialogue with Trypho the Jew* 110.5.     (31)

I already pointed out that Moses, too, showed in a symbol two appearances of our Christ. The same truth was figuratively foretold and announced by the actions of Moses and Jesus [that is, Joshua]. The one remained on the hill until evening with his arms stretched out and supported, representing the type (foreshadowing) of the Cross; the other, whose byname was Jesus, took charge of the battle and led Israel to victory. Now in the case of both these holy men and prophets of God, we can perceive that neither of them alone was worthy of bearing both mysteries together, the type of the Cross and the mystery of the Name, for One alone is, was, and shall be capable of this, before whose Name every power shudders in fear of being destroyed by Him in the future. Justin, *Dialogue with Trypho the Jew* 111.1,2. (32)

Since all things which have happened were predicted before they occurred, we should trust that similar prophecies, which are not yet fulfilled, will quite certainly happen. The prophecies already fulfilled came true even though they were not understood. In the same way the other prophecies will also quite certainly come true, even though they are not understood and not believed. The prophets foretold a twofold coming of Christ: the one, belonging already to history, was the coming of a dishonored and suffering man; the other shall take place when, as the prophets announced, He shall appear from Heaven in glory with His angelic throng. Then will He raise up the bodies of all men who ever lived and clothe the bodies of the worthy with incorruption, but the bodies of the unrighteous, eternally subject to pain, He will cast into eternal fire together with the evil spirits.
Justin, *First Apology* 52. (33)

The blessing [Gen. 27:27-29] undoubtedly refers to the times of the Kingdom, when the just shall rise from the dead and reign, when also creation, made new and set free, shall produce an abundance of all kinds of food from the dew of heaven and the fertility of the earth [Gen. 27]. So this

is what the elders who had seen John, the Lord's disciple, remembered hearing from him concerning the things the Lord had taught about those times.
Irenaeus, *Against Heresies* V.33.3 (cf. Eusebius III.39.1).
(34)


The first elders bear witness that when Christ comes again, when He rules over all, there will in truth be unity, harmony, and peace among the different kinds of animals, which by nature are opposed and hostile to each other.
Irenaeus, *Demonstration of the Apostolic Proclamation* 61.
(35)


Papias maintained that after the resurrection of the dead there will be a period of a thousand years when Christ's Kingdom will be established on this earth in physical form.
He is said to have maintained the Jewish teaching [Mishna] of a millennium.
Papias in Eusebius *chronic. a. Abr.* III.39.11; ⟨Jerome, *On Illustrious Men* 18⟩.
(36)


You are very zealous to be on sure ground when you refer to the Scriptures. But tell me, do you really maintain that our city of Jerusalem shall be built up again, and do you really expect that your people will gather there joyfully with Christ, together with the patriarchs, the prophets, and the men of our nation, and those who became proselytes before your Christ came?"

"Trypho, I am not so mean as to say one thing and think another. I have already pointed out to you that many more share this conviction with me. We are quite certain that the future will be like this. . . .

"I am not on the side of men or human teachings, but of God and His truth. If you have ever met any who call themselves Christians but do not share this conviction and even make bold to blaspheme the God of Abraham, the God of Isaac, and the God of Jacob, and moreover assert that there is no resurrection from the dead, saying that after death their souls will be taken up to Heaven instead, do not take such persons for Christians. . . . But I, and every other Christian who has the right beliefs in all things, know that there is a resurrection of the flesh, followed by a thousand years in the rebuilt, beautified, and enlarged city of Jerusalem, as the prophets Ezekiel, Isaiah, and the others announced."

Justin, *Dialogue with Trypho the Jew* 80.1,2,4,5. (37)

Isaiah spoke a clear word about this period of a thousand years:

There shall be a new heaven and a new earth. Former things shall not be remembered or come into mind. But gladness and joy shall be found on earth, and it is I who create it all. Behold, I make Jerusalem a joy and my people a gladness. I will rejoice over Jerusalem and be glad in my people. No more shall there be heard the voice of weeping or the cry of lamentation. No more shall anyone die before his time, only a few days old, nor shall the old man pass away without completing his time, for the youth shall live to a hundred years. And if he is a sinner he will die only at the age of a hundred and then be accursed.

They shall build houses and inhabit them; they shall plant vineyards and themselves eat the fruit of them. No more shall others inhabit what they build, nor shall others eat what they plant. For as the days of the tree of life shall be the days of my people. The fruits of their labor shall endure. My chosen ones shall not labor in vain. They shall not bring forth children for destruction, for they shall be a righteous generation blessed by the Lord. Their offspring shall stay with them. For before they call I will hear them; while they are still speaking, I will say, "What is it?" In those times the wolf and the lamb shall feed together, the lion shall eat hay like the ox, and the serpent shall eat dust like bread. There shall be no harm or destruction done on my holy mountain, says the Lord. "Now," I explained, "if these words say, 'Like the days of the tree shall be the days of my people; the fruits of their work shall endure,' according to our belief they mysteriously point to the period of one thousand years. When Adam was told that he would die on the day he ate of the tree, Adam as we know had not completed a thousand years. We also are firmly convinced that the words 'a day of the Lord is like a thousand years' apply to our teaching. Moreover, a certain man called John, who was amongst us and belonged to the apostles of Christ, prophesied in a revelation that those who believe in our Christ shall dwell in Jerusalem for a thousand years, and that afterwards there will be, for all men without exception, universal and so-called eternal resurrection and universal, so-called eternal judgment. Our Lord himself said the same with the words, 'They shall neither marry nor be given in marriage, but they shall be equal to the angels. Children of God through the resurrection shall they be.' "

Justin, *Dialogue with Trypho the Jew* 81.                    (38)

The linkage of all conditions and activities must relate to some unified goal. The origin and nature of man, his living, doing, and suffering, the whole course of his earthly existence, and the end befitting his nature—all these must become one, must find harmony, unity, and complete accord throughout his being.

Late Athenagoras, *On the Resurrection of the Dead* 15. (39)

The intention of the Creator in creating man was to make an intelligent being who should look upon the works of God and serve his Creator.

Since this destiny of man will never come to an end, the human being will never come to an end either. Body and soul together make up the human being, for the soul without the body is not man.

Athenagoras, *On the Resurrection of the Dead* 12–15.    (40)

The salvation of the soul would be the final goal of only a part of the human being, not of the whole. In order that the final goal can be realized, the body must be united with the soul, which is possible only through resurrection.

Athenagoras, *On the Resurrection of the Dead* 24–25.    (41)

Therefore the resurrection of bodies which are without souls or even entirely disintegrated must most certainly take place. The same people must reappear in the twofold nature of their being.

Late Athenagoras, *On the Resurrection of the Dead* 25. (42)

The first elders tell us that some men who have been found worthy of dwelling in Heaven shall go there, others shall enjoy the delights of Paradise, while others again shall find the glory of the City, for in every place the Healing Savior will be seen in different measure according to the worthiness of each one who beholds Him. The first elders say that the different dwelling places shall be determined according to whether men bring forth fruit a hundredfold, or sixtyfold, or thirtyfold; the first shall be taken up into Heaven, the second shall live in Paradise, and the third shall inhabit the City.

All things are God's. To each one He gives the appropriate
dwelling. His Word says, to each one will the Father give according to how worthy each one is or will be. That is the
table at which those who are invited to the Wedding shall
recline in their different places to share in the Meal. The first
elders, the disciples of the apostles, say that this is the arrangement and distribution of those who are being saved. Through
these steps they go forward, that is, through the Spirit to the
Son, and through the Son they ascend to the Father. Finally,
however, the Son delivers up His work to the Father, as the
Apostle also said.

Therefore the first elders, who were the disciples of the
apostles, say that those who are being translated from the earth
will be taken to Paradise, for Paradise has been prepared for
the righteous and for those gifted with the Spirit. The apostle
Paul was carried there too, where he heard unspeakable words,
unspeakable for us in our present life. There those who were
translated shall remain until the end of the world, and this
shall be the beginning of their immortality.

Since it was through a tree that we lost the Logos in Paradise, it was through a tree again that the Logos was made
manifest to all when He showed in Himself the length, the
height, the depth, and the breadth and, as one of the oldest
Christians said, He gathered together the two peoples to one
God by stretching out both His hands.
"Traditions of the Elders" in Irenaeus, *Against Heresies* V.
36.1,2; 5.1; 17.4.                                           (43)

What we cannot know of ourselves, we have learned
through the prophets. They firmly believed that the
spirit, the heavenly armor of our mortality, shall gain immortality together with the soul. Thus, far in advance of their time,
they spoke out things that other souls had not yet recognized.

Everyone can recognize this in detail if he does not in puffed-up conceit reject the most holy revelations, which have been written down in the course of time. Through them everyone who has an open ear is made a friend of God.
Tatian, *Address to the Greeks* 20.6; 12.6. (44)

M oses was the first prophet. He said in these very words, "A ruler shall never be lacking in Judah nor a leader from his thigh until He comes for whom it is reserved. And He shall be the expectation of the nations." The words "He shall be the expectation of the nations" were meant to be a testimony that people of every nation would expect His return, as you can see with your own eyes and be convinced by the fact.
Justin, *First Apology* 32. (45)

A s I heard from one of the first elders, who in turn heard it from those who had still seen the apostles and had been their pupils, the only punishment which came into question for the ancients who sinned unknowingly was the punishment due to them according to the Scriptures.

So it was with David. He pleased God when, unjustly persecuted by Saul and having to flee from him, he did not take revenge on his enemy; when he sang psalms about the advent of the Messiah; when he taught wisdom to the nations and did everything according to the counsel of the Spirit. But when lust overcame him and he took Bathsheba, the wife of Uriah, the Scripture said about him, "The thing which David did was wicked in the eyes of the Lord." And the prophet Nathan was sent to him to show him his sin. Thus he had to pass sentence upon himself and condemn himself so that he could obtain mercy and forgiveness from Christ.

It was similar with Solomon. He pleased God as long as he continued to judge rightly and to speak wisdom; as long as he

built the true type foreshadowing the Temple and proclaimed
the glory of God; as long as he announced the peace to come
upon the nations and pictured the Kingdom of the Messiah
beforehand; and as long as he spoke his three thousand parables
about the expected arrival of the Messiah. But when he took
wives from all the heathen nations and allowed them to set
up idols, the Scripture condemned him very strongly in order
that no man might glorify himself in the sight of God. That
is what this elder said.

Therefore the Lord descended into the kingdom of the Underworld to speak there also, proclaiming His advent, for now
there was forgiveness of sin for those who had believed in Him.
All those believed in Him who had put their hope in Him,
all those who had proclaimed His advent beforehand and had
served His plan: the righteous men, the prophets, and the patriarchs, whose sins He forgave in a befitting way as He forgave
ours. Nor should we lay these sins to their charge unless we
want to despise the grace of God. Just as these men did not
charge us with our lack of self-restraint, which we were guilty
of before the Messiah was revealed to us, so neither is it for us
to blame those who sinned before the Messiah came. "For all
men fall short of the glory of God." They are not made
righteous of themselves but only through the coming of the
Lord, if they earnestly seek His light. Their deeds were recorded for our discipline, that we should recognize two things:
first of all, that we and they have one and the same God,
whom sins do not please even when committed by eminent
people; and secondly, that we should refrain from evil. Thus
this elder tells us that we must not be arrogant; neither
should we condemn the ancients. Rather, now that we have
recognized the Messiah, we should take care not to do anything
that does not please God. Otherwise we would have no for-

giveness of sins anymore and would be excluded from His Kingdom. . . . Then as now, the punishment of God's justice remains the same: then it was foreshadowing, temporal, and less severe; now it is real, eternal, and final.

Hence the elders declare those men very foolish who, from the experiences of those who disobeyed God in ancient times, want to conclude that there is a second God. In contrast, the first elders pointed out to these men what God in His compassionate love has done for the salvation of those who received Him when He appeared.

"Traditions of the Elders" in Irenaeus, *Against Heresies* IV. 27,28. (46)

The men of God, vessels of the Holy Spirit and prophets, were inspired and instructed by God himself. They were God-taught, holy, and just men. Therefore they were considered worthy of the reward of becoming God's instruments and receiving the wisdom flowing out from Him. In this wisdom they spoke prophetically about the creation of the world and all other matters. Thus they spoke out prophetic revelations about pestilences, famines, and wars. And this was not done by just one or two; no, a great number arose among the Hebrews, according to the times and circumstances, and among the Greeks too there was the Sibyl. All their sayings stand in perfect harmony with each other: what they spoke about the time that had gone before them, their utterances about what happened in their own time, and their words about the things being fulfilled now in our own time. Therefore we are convinced that future events will come about in the same way as past events did, which have already occurred in accordance with their words.

Theophilus of Antioch, *To Autolycus* II.9. (47)

God has foreknowledge of what all men will do, and it is His principle to reward or punish every man in the future according to the merits of his actions. Therefore He foretells through the prophetic Spirit what will come to them from Him according to the merit of their actions. In this way He leads the human race to reflection and consideration at all times, showing men that He cares for them and provides for them. At the instigation of evil spirits, the death penalty was decreed on all those who read the books of Hystaspes, or the Sibyl, or the prophets. Thus, fear was to prevent people into whose hands these books might fall from acquiring knowledge of good things from them; fear was to keep them in servitude to the demons. However, they were not able to achieve this permanently, for we occupied ourselves with these writings fearlessly. As you see, we even offer them to you for examination because we are convinced that they will find everyone's approval.

There were individual men among the Jews who came forward as prophets of God. Through them the prophetic Spirit predicted the things of the future before they actually happened. Successive kings reigning over the Jews got possession of these prophecies written down by the prophets themselves in their own Hebrew language exactly as they were spoken, and preserved them carefully. [Seventy] men were asked to translate them into Greek. This was done, and the books remained with the Egyptians to the present day. They are also in the hands of all the Jews wherever they may be. However, though they read these books, they do not understand their meaning.

Justin, *First Apology* 44,31.                              (48)

Now, in the Books of the Prophets we find predicted that Jesus our Christ would come into the world born of a

virgin and that, reaching manhood, He would heal every disease and ailment and raise the dead; that He would be hated,
misunderstood, and crucified, would die, rise again, and ascend
into Heaven; that He would be in fact and in name the Son of
God; that messengers would be sent by Him to all peoples with
this message; and that people from the pagan nations would
believe in Him. This was prophesied partly five thousand
years before He appeared, partly three thousand, partly two
thousand, one thousand, and partly eight hundred years before
He appeared, for as one generation after another arose, new
prophets arose time and again.
Justin, *First Apology* 31.　　　　　　　　　　　　　　　(49)

Sometimes the Holy Spirit performed clearly recognizable
acts which foreshadowed the future. At other times He
spoke in unmistakable words about future events as if indeed
they were happening now or had already happened. The
reader must understand this manner of speaking in order to
be able to follow rightly the words of the prophets.
Justin, *Dialogue with Trypho the Jew* 114.1.　　　　　(50)

If then we were to be satisfied with reasonings, our justification could seem to lie in human words, but the statements
of the prophets confirm our arguments. You, with your intel-
lectual curiosity and great learning, will have heard of the
sayings of men like Moses, Isaiah, Jeremiah, and the other
prophets. Lifted in ecstasy above their own ways of thinking
by the impulse of the Holy Spirit, they prophesied the things
they were prompted to say. The Spirit used them in this way
just as a flute player blows the flute. Let us hear, then, what
they say.
Athenagoras, *A Plea Regarding Christians* 9.　　　　　(51)

Howdever, when you find the words of the prophets put into the mouth of a person, you must not consider them as spoken by Spirit-filled persons, but by the divine Word [Logos as Spirit] moving in them. Sometimes He proclaims the future events in the manner of a prediction, sometimes He speaks in the person of God the Lord and the Father of all things, sometimes in the person of Christ, and at other times from the mouth of the peoples themselves, replying to the Lord or to His Father.

Justin, *First Apology* 36.                                                        (52)

To give you an illustration of this, the following words were spoken in the name of the Father through the prophet Isaiah, "What kind of house will you build for me? says the Lord. Heaven is my throne and the earth is my footstool." And again elsewhere:

> My soul hates your new moons and sabbaths; I cannot endure the great day of fasting and idleness any longer; nor when you appear before me will I listen to you. Your hands are full of blood. And when you bring me wheat flour and incense it is an abomination to me. Fat of lambs and blood of oxen I desire not. For who has demanded this from your hands? But loose every bond of injustice, tear apart the knots of forced contracts, shelter the homeless and clothe the naked, break bread with the hungry!

You can understand from this what truths were pronounced by the prophets in the name of God.

Justin, *First Apology* 37.                                                        (53)

When the prophetic Spirit speaks in the person of Christ, this is what He says: "I stretched out my hands to a disobedient and contradicting people, to those who walk in ways that are not good." And again:

I offered my back to scourges and my cheeks to blows.
I did not turn my face away from the shame of spittings;
the Lord was my helper, and therefore I did not waver.
I held out my face like a hard stone, and I knew that I
would not be put to shame, because he who justifies me
is at hand.

And again He says, "They cast lots for my clothing and pierced my feet and hands." "But I lay down and slept and have risen again because the Lord has taken charge of me."

And again He says, "They made mouths at me, shook their heads and said, 'Let him deliver himself.' " That all this happened to Christ at the hands of the Jews you can find out, for as He was being crucified they curled their lips, shook their heads and said, "Let him who raised the dead now save himself!"

Justin, *First Apology* 38. (54)

When, however, the prophetic Spirit speaks as Proclaimer of the Future, He says:

The law shall go out from Zion and the Word of the Lord from Jerusalem, and he shall judge among the nations and rebuke many people. They shall turn their swords into ploughshares and their spears into sickles; nation shall not lift up sword against nation any longer, and they shall study war no more.

You can be convinced that this has really happened now, for twelve men, illiterate and unskilled in speaking, went out from Jerusalem into the world. Through the power of God they revealed to the whole of mankind that they were sent by Christ to proclaim the Word of God to everyone. Now we who once murdered one another not only refrain from all

hatred of our enemies, but more than that, in order to avoid
lying or deceiving our examining judges, we meet death
cheerfully for confessing to Christ.

Justin, *First Apology* 39.                                        (55)

Just now I quoted the Scriptures again in the Septuagint
translation, for when I quoted from them earlier according
to your version, I was only trying to find out your point of
view.

Justin, *Dialogue with Trypho the Jew* 137.3.        (56)

What was unbelievable, what men deemed impossible,
was foretold by God through the prophetic Spirit as
taking place in the future. Therefore, when it actually happens,
it should not be doubted but believed  because it was foretold.

Justin, *First Apology* 33.                                        (57)

Since I base my proofs and arguments on the Scriptures and
on actual events, do not delay or hesitate to believe me,
for these words are not thought up by me, nor are they embel-
lished by human skill. On the contrary, they are sometimes
words from the Psalms of David, sometimes joyful news from
Isaiah, sometimes words of proclamation from Zechariah, or
words from the Writings of Moses. You will recognize them,
Trypho. They can be found in your Scriptures—no, not really
in yours, but rather in ours, for we obey them, whereas you, in
spite of reading them, do not grasp their meaning. Indeed,
many considered the teachings of the Law to be foolish
and unworthy of God, for they were not given the grace to
understand that God has called your people to a rightabout
turn, to a change of spirit, because of their sin and spiritual disease. However, what the prophets said after the death of Moses

stands eternally. The Psalms, too, have prophecies which are
eternally valid.
Justin, *Dialogue with Trypho the Jew* 28.2; 29.2; 30.1,2.
(58)


We who have been led to God through this crucified
Christ, we are the true Israel of the Spirit, the real descendants of Judah, Jacob, Isaac, and Abraham, who though
uncircumcised was approved and blessed by God because of
his faith and was called to be the father of many nations.
Justin, *Dialogue with Trypho the Jew* 11.5.          (59)


If I tried to base my proof on human teachings or human
arguments, you would not need to take any notice of me.
Yet when I constantly bring up so many relevant passages of
Scripture and try to make them understandable to you, you
show your hardness of heart in not being able to understand
God's thoughts and His will.
Justin, *Dialogue with Trypho the Jew* 68.1.          (60)


The clear insight I drew from the Scriptures and my
trust in them have only been confirmed by the deceitful
mimickings that the so-called Devil has circulated among
the Greeks, and by all that he did likewise through Egyptian
sorcerers and false prophets at the time of Elijah.
Justin, *Dialogue with Trypho the Jew* 69.1.          (61)


It is said that seers and prophets lived at the time of the
great writers, who wrote down the truths they learned from
them. How much more are we able to comprehend the truth,
we who are taught by the holy prophets, by those who had
received God's Holy Spirit within them! For this reason the

sayings of all the prophets foretelling the destiny of the whole world are in complete mutual accord.

From this elucidation one can see how our Holy Scriptures prove more ancient and true than those of the Greeks and Egyptians or of any other historians.

When past times are reviewed together with all that has been said above, the great antiquity of the Prophetic Writings and the truly divine nature of our faith can be recognized. These truths are not new, and our teachings are neither mythical nor false.

Theophilus of Antioch, *To Autolycus* III.17,26,29.     (62)

That, and that alone, is true which we testify as the teachings of Christ and of the prophets who preceded Him, and it is older than any writer who ever lived. It is not because we say the same things as they do, however, that we want our teaching to be accepted, but because we speak the truth.

Justin, *First Apology* 23.     (63)

Moses was the oldest prophet. He lived before any of the Greek writers. Through him the prophetic Spirit proclaimed how, and from what, God in the beginning formed the world. "In the beginning God created heaven and earth."

Justin, *First Apology* 59.     (64)

It is the prophets and those who openly throughout the whole world came to worship God through the name of the Crucified One who led us to this faith.

Listen therefore to these words from the Scriptures! They need no explanation, but only an open ear.

To understand God's Scriptures I needed the grace He gave me.

But you are mistaken if you think you can drive me into a corner because of a quotation, and if you want me to find a contradiction in the Scriptures. I would never venture to think or to admit such a thing. Even if a passage which seems to contradict another were laid before me, I still remain firmly convinced that no passage contradicts another. In such a case I would rather say that I cannot understand the words and shall do my utmost to get those who imagine contradictions in the Scriptures to share my conviction.
Justin, *Dialogue with Trypho the Jew* 53.6; 55.3; 58.1; 65.2.
(65)

Do you suppose that we would ever have been able to grasp the truths set forth in the Scriptures if the grace of understanding had not been given to us by the will of Him who wanted to reveal them?
Justin, *Dialogue with Trypho the Jew* 119.1.          (66)

God's milk mixes ill with plaster.
Papias or "Traditions of the Elders" in Irenaeus, *Against Heresies* III.17.4.          (67)

It is not true that our teaching is the same as that of the others. The others in fact only echo ours. You can hear and learn the truth among us from simple, uneducated people who do not even know the letters of the alphabet, people who are unpolished in speech but wise in discernment. Some of them are crippled and blind. You can see from this that the Word does not spring from human knowledge but is pronounced by the power of God.
Justin, *First Apology* 60.          (68)

Once, making up my mind to seek absolute peace and avoid all human distractions, I went to a place near the sea. As I approached the spot where I wanted to be alone, an old man of prepossessing appearance and gentle and earnest demeanor followed me at a short distance.

He asked me, "Does our mind possess such and so great a power that it reaches God? Will the human mind ever be capable of seeing God without the aid of the Holy Spirit?"

"What teacher," I asked the old man in turn, "shall one turn to, and what system of philosophy can be of use if the truth is not to be found even in the systems of Plato and Pythagoras?"

"A long time ago," he answered me, "long before all these so-called philosophers, there lived men who were happy, just, and loved God, who spoke in the Spirit of God, foretelling the future and all the events which are now actually taking place. We call these men prophets. It is they alone who have seen the truth and proclaimed it to men without fearing or flattering them or thirsting for personal glory. Filled with the Holy Spirit, they expressed only that which they heard and saw.

"Their Writings are still extant. Whoever concerns himself with them and believes them can profit by them greatly. They are concerned with the origin and end of things, and with anything at all which is a necessary part of a philosopher's basic knowledge. For those men at that time there was no need to turn to human proofs to verify their teachings. On the contrary, they dispensed with all arguments of reason. Just those men, nevertheless, are trustworthy witnesses to the truth, for the history of the past and of the present compels us to agree with their words. Also the miracles they wrought make them trustworthy. In all these things they glorified God, the Father and Creator of the World, and proclaimed Christ as His Son, who was to come from Him.

"Pray that above all the gates of light may be opened to you! For no one can perceive and understand unless God and His Christ grant him the grace of comprehension."

My spirit was immediately set on fire, and a love for the prophets and for those who are friends of Christ took possession of me.

Justin, *Dialogue with Trypho the Jew* 3.1; 4.1; 7.1-3; 8.1.
(69)

After Christ not a single prophet appeared among you Jews. Your prophets owe what they did and said, which is known also to us from the Scriptures, only to God's powers. One of them had received one, another another! Solomon received the spirit of wisdom, Daniel of discernment and counsel, Moses of strength and devoutness, Elijah of fear, and Isaiah of knowledge. Likewise, one or two gifts were received by Jeremiah, the twelve prophets, David, and all the other prophets who appeared among you.

As soon as He came, the gifts of the Spirit were suspended, that is, they ceased. After His coming, they had to cease among you according to the Plan of Salvation, which is being realized in history among those who belong to Him. The powers of the Spirit came to rest in Him so that they would become gifts again in accordance with the prophecies. He grants them to each believer whom He deems worthy through the graciousness of that mighty Spirit.

The Logos spoke this: "He went up on high, took captivity captive, and gave gifts to the sons of men." Another prophecy says, "After this I will pour out my Spirit over all flesh, over my servants and handmaids, and they shall prophesy."

Justin, *Dialogue with Trypho the Jew* 87.3,4,6.        (70)

Among us you can see both men and women who have received gifts of grace from God's Spirit.
Justin, *Dialogue with Trypho the Jew* 88.1.                    (71)

I will prove to you that we have not believed vain and empty myths or teachings that cannot be verified; on the contrary, we have believed men who were filled with the divine Spirit, overflowing with grace and power.
Justin, *Dialogue with Trypho the Jew* 9.1.                    (72)

Unlike the great multitude, I did not take pleasure in those who talk much  but in those who teach the truth; not in those who stamp alien commandments on the memory  but in those who keep the traditions given to the believers by the Lord and derived from truth itself. If by chance, though, someone came my way who had been a pupil and follower of the first elders, I inquired into the teachings of these elders: what Andrew or Peter said or what Philip or Thomas or James or John or Matthew or any other disciple of the Lord said, and further what Aristion and the elder presbyter John say, the disciples of the Lord; for I assumed that the wisdom to be gleaned from books would not be so profitable to me as the living Word, a Voice which is abiding because it is living.
Papias, quoted in Eusebius III.39.3-4.                    (73)

Because the Prophets and the Gospels were bearers of the one and only Spirit of God, they both spoke out through the Holy Spirit with equal emphasis for that justice which the Law demands.
Theophilus of Antioch, *To Autolycus* III.12.                    (74)

I flee to the Gospel for refuge as to the flesh of Jesus, and to the apostles as to the body of the elders of the Church.

Let us love the prophets too, for they foretold about the Gospel and hoped in Him and waited for Him. By faith in Him were they saved into the unity of Jesus Christ, holy men worthy of our love and admiration, witnessed to by Jesus Christ and included in His Father's Gospel of our common hope.
Ignatius, *Letter to the Philadelphians* 5.                    (75)

I have heard certain people say, "What I cannot find in the ancient records, I do not believe in the Gospel." And when I said to them, "It is written!" they answered me, "That is just the question." But my records are Jesus Christ. The unassailable records are His Cross, His death, His resurrection, and the faith bestowed through Him; by these I want to be justified through your prayers.

The priests, too, were good, but better is the High Priest to whom alone is entrusted the Holy of Holies, to whom alone are entrusted the hidden things of God. He is the Door to the Father through which alone enter Abraham and Isaac and Jacob and the prophets, and the apostles and the Church. All this comes together in the unity of God. One thing, however, makes the Gospel stand out above all: the advent of the Healing Savior, our Lord Jesus Christ, His suffering, and His resurrection. Certainly, the beloved prophets pointed to Him in their prophecies, but the Gospel is the consummation of incorruption. All these together are good if you have faith through love.
Ignatius, *Letter to the Philadelphians* 8–9.                    (76)

In the Memoirs, which in my opinion were compiled by the apostles of Jesus and their followers, it is written that as He prayed His perspiration poured down like drops of blood.

Moreover, it is written for us in the Memoirs of the Apostles that Jesus is the Son of God.

He was the Only Begotten of the Father of all; He proceeded from Him in a special way as Logos and Power, later to become man through a virgin, as we know from the Memoirs of the Apostles.
Justin, *Dialogue with Trypho the Jew* 103.8; 100.4; 105.1.
(77)

The Memoirs of the Apostles or the Writings of the Prophets are read among us as long as time permits.
Justin, *First Apology* 67.
(78)

The apostles in their Memoirs, which are called Gospels, handed down as they were commanded: "Jesus took bread, gave thanks, and said, 'Do this in remembrance of me.'"
Justin, *First Apology* 66.
(79)

This is what the elder said: "Mark, Peter's interpreter, wrote down from memory everything that was said or done by Christ, though not in proper order. For he had not heard the Lord nor had he been one of His followers, but, as I said, later became a follower of Peter, who adapted his teaching to the practical needs of the Churches. Mark had only one purpose in mind: not to omit anything he had heard or to make any false statements. Matthew compiled the Lord's Sayings in the Aramaic language, and everyone translated them as well as he could."
Papias also quotes from the First Letter of John and likewise from the First Letter of Peter.
Here begins the account of the Gospel according to John; John's Gospel was made known and given to the communities by John during his lifetime, as Papias of Hierapolis, a beloved disciple of John, related in his interpretations, that is, in his five books.

I do not need to dwell on the inspiration of John's Book of Revelation since from the earlier times the blessed Papias, Irenaeus, Methodius, and Hippolytus bear witness to its genuineness.

Papias, sources in annotations. (80)

The third Gospel Book we accept is that according to Luke. Luke was a physician. He wrote his book after Christ's ascension and after Paul had taken him as his companion on the way. He wrote in his own name and to the best of his knowledge though certainly he himself did not see the Lord in the flesh. Therefore he began his story, as far as he was able to ascertain it, with the birth of John [the Baptist].

The author of the fourth Gospel is John. When his fellow apostles and bishops urged him to write it down, he said, "Fast with me from now on for three days, and let us share with one another whatever is revealed to each one of us." The same night it was revealed to Andrew, one of the apostles, that John should write everything down in his own name and that all the others should check it.

Though the beginnings of the individual Gospel Books may differ, nothing in them deviates from the faith of the believers. Everything is stated by the one leading Spirit in all of them concerning the birth, His suffering, His resurrection, His life with His disciples, and His twofold coming, the first time despised in lowliness, which has already happened, and the second time glorious in kingly power, which is yet to come. No wonder John is so emphatic in his Letters when he describes specific things and says about himself, "What we have seen with our eyes and heard with our ears, and what our hands have felt, these things we are writing to you." Thus he declares himself not only an eyewitness who himself saw and heard all the Lord's miracles, but also the one who wrote them down in order.

The Acts of all the apostles, however, are compiled in only one Book. Luke collected them for the excellent Theophilus because these different events took place in his own presence. These are all he wants to report, as is clearly borne out by his omission of the martyrdom of Peter and by the fact that he does not report anything about the journey of Paul from the City [Rome] to Spain.

To all those who want to know, the Letters of Paul themselves make it clear who wrote them, and from what place and for what reasons they were written. First of all he writes to the Corinthians, forbidding all dissension, to which they were inclined; next, to the Galatians, forbidding circumcision; to the Romans however he writes more fully, introducing them to the order of the Scriptures and showing them that Christ is the crux of everything. It is not necessary for us to dwell on individual Letters because he, the blessed apostle Paul, following the order of his predecessor John, writes only to seven Churches by name, and in this sequence: first to the Corinthians, second to the Ephesians, third to the Philippians, fourth to the Colossians, fifth to the Galatians, sixth to the Thessalonians, seventh to the Romans. Although he writes to the Corinthians and Thessalonians a second time to admonish them, yet it is clearly evident that there is only *one* Church spread over the whole earth, for though John writes to only seven Churches in his Revelation, nevertheless he always addresses all. The Letter to Philemon, though, and the one to Titus and the two to Timothy were written out of love and personal affection and yet are held in great honor in the whole Church everywhere. They are held sacred for the carrying out of Church discipline in the Church. There is also in circulation a Letter to the Laodiceans and another to the Alexandrians, forged in Paul's name for the dissenting group of Marcion, as well as several others that cannot be accepted by the whole Church every-where, for it will not do to mix gall with honey.

Certainly, the Letter of Jude and two bearing the name of John are accepted by the whole Church and also the *Wisdom of Solomon* written by his friends in his honor.

We also accept a Revelation by John and one by Peter, al-though some of us do not want the latter to be read aloud in the Church. The *Shepherd* was written very recently in our times by Hermas of Rome when his brother Pius was occupying the chair of the Church of Rome. Therefore it is proper that it be read. Yet, to the end of time, it cannot be read aloud to the people in the Church either with the prophets, whose number is complete, or with the apostles.

*Muratorian Canon,* Rome, c. A.D. 180. (81)

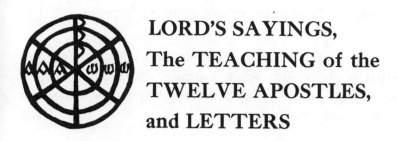

# LORD'S SAYINGS,
# The TEACHING of the
# TWELVE APOSTLES,
# and LETTERS

He who is near me is near the fire. But whoever is far from me is far from the Kingdom.
Origen, *Homily XX.3 on Jeremiah;* Didymus, *Commentary on Psalm 88:8.* (1)

Where there is one alone, I say: I am with him. Lift up the stone, and there you will find me; split the wood, and I am there.
Oxyrhynchus Papyrus I, 1897, discovery of Grenfell and Hunt. ⟨See also *Gospel according to Thomas* 77.⟩ (2)

I am the door of life. He who enters through me enters into life.
Clementine *Homilies* III.52 quoting Jewish Christian Gospel of the Ebionites. (3)

Be saved, you and your soul!
Clement of Alexandria, *Excerpts from Theodotus* 2.2. (4)

T hy Holy Spirit come upon us and cleanse us!

Minuscule MS 700; Gregory of Nyssa, Maximus; Ropes No.
56; quoting the Lord's Prayer according to Marcion.        (5)


U nless you make what is right left, and what is left right,
what is above into what is below, and what is behind
into what is in front, you will not learn to know the Kingdom.

*Acts of Peter* 38; *Acts of Philip* 34.                    (6)


I f you lean on my breast but do not do the will of my
Father in Heaven, I will push you from my breast.

Jewish Gospel in the Zion Gospel Edition; *Second Letter of
Clement* 4.5.                                              (7)


W hy do you say Lord, Lord to me, and yet not do what
I say?

Clementine *Homilies* VIII.7.4; *Recognitions* IV.5; quoting
Jewish Christian Gospel of the Ebionites; Syriac *Didascalia*
XXVI ⟨see also Connolly, p. 256⟩.                          (8)


Y ou go wrong because you do not know the truth of the
Scriptures. Therefore you do not know the power of
God. . . . Why do you not know that the Scriptures are based
on good reason?

Clem. *Hom.* III.50; II.51; XVIII.20; quoting Gospel of the
Ebionites.                                                (9)


Y ou hear with your one ear, but the other you have closed.

Oxyr. Papyr. I, 1897.                                     (10)

He who has grieved the spirit of his brother is guilty of a most serious offense.

And you should never be joyful unless you look at your brother in love.

Jerome, commentaries *On Ezekiel* 18.7; *On Ephesians* 5.3-4; quoting the Nazaraean Gospel of the Hebrews and the Gospel of the Ebionites. (11)

Woe to those who live in wealth and luxury and give nothing to the poor! They shall have to render an account, for they ought to love their neighbors as themselves. They did not have compassion for them when they were destitute.

Clem. *Recog.* II.29. (12)

How can you say, I have fulfilled the Law and Prophets, since it is written in the Law: Thou shalt love thy neighbor as thyself? Look, many of your brothers, sons of Abraham, are covered with filth and dying of hunger while your house is filled with many goods and not a thing goes out of it to them.

Origen, *Comm. XV.14 on Matthew* (Latin) quoting the Gospel of the Hebrews. (13)

Woe to those who have and like hypocrites take more, or who can help themselves and yet receive. For everyone who receives something shall render an account to God the Lord on the Day of Judgment why he received. . . . He who simply gives to everybody gives well and is blameless. He who accepts when destitute . . . accepts well and shall be exalted by God in eternal life.

*Didascalia* XVII ⟨see also Connolly, pp. 154 f.⟩; cf. *Apostolic Constitutions* IV.3. (14)

I took my stand in the midst of the world and appeared to them in the flesh, and I found them all glutted, and not one among them did I find thirsting, and my soul labors for the sons of men because they are blind in their hearts.
Oxyr. Papyr. I, 1897. ⟨See also *Gospel according to Thomas* 28.⟩            (15)

The seeker shall not rest until he has found, and he who has found shall marvel. He who has marveled shall rule like a king, and he who rules shall find rest.
Clem. Alex., *Misc.* V.14.96; cf. II.9.45; Oxyr. Papyr. 654, 1904; from the Gospel of the Hebrews.     (16)

A city that is built on the top of a high mountain and is fortified can neither fall nor be hidden.
Oxyr. Papyr. I, 1897. ⟨See also *Gospel according to Thomas* 32.⟩            (17)

Ask for what is great, and what is small will be given to you as well.
Clem. Alex., *Misc.* I.24.158; Origen, *On Prayer* 2.2; 14.1.              (18)

Seek to grow from smallness, and from the higher place move down to the lowest!
Codex Bezae (D) and others, after Mt. 20:28. See Ropes No. 153.           (19)

The weak shall be saved through the strong.
*Apostolic Church Order* 26 (Ethiopic text).     (20)

Everything that does not lie open before your eyes and is hidden from you shall be revealed to you, for there is

nothing hidden that shall not be revealed and nothing buried that shall not be raised up.
Oxyr. Papyr. 654, 1904. ⟨See also *Gospel according to Thomas* 5, 6.⟩ (21)

How can they who seize us say that the Kingdom remains in Heaven? The very birds of heaven shall convince them, and every beast under the earth or upon the earth and the fishes of the sea, they all shall convince you. And the Kingdom—Heaven—is within you. Whoever knows himself shall find; but when you know yourselves you will know that you are sons of the Father, the Perfect One. You shall know yourselves.
Oxyr. Papyr. 654, 1904; from the Gospel of the Hebrews. (22)

He saw a man working on the Sabbath, and He said to him: Man, if you know what you do, you are blessed, but if you do not know, you are cursed and a transgressor of the Law.
Codex Bezae (D) after Luke 6:4. (23)

My mystery for me and for the sons of my house!
Clem. Alex., *Misc.* V.10.63; Clem. *Hom.* XIX.20; quoting Gospel of the Ebionites. Cf. Symmachus at Isaiah 24:16. (24)

Become trusty money changers who reject the false coins and accept only the good ones.
Clem. *Hom.* II.51; III.50; XVIII.20; *Didascalia* IX ⟨see also Connolly, p.101⟩; *Apostolic Constitutions* II.36; Clem. Alex., *Misc.* I.28.177. (25)

I choose for myself the right men; the right men are those whom my Father in Heaven has given me.
Eusebius, *On the Theophany* 4.12, on Mt. 10:34-36 (Syriac).
(26)

If you do not abstain from the world, you will not find the Kingdom of God.
Oxyr. Papyr. I, 1897; Clem. Alex., *Misc.* III.15.99.     (27)

Jesus says, "Take no thought ... from morning until evening and from evening until morning either for the food you shall eat or for the clothes you shall wear. If you own one garment, what more do you need? Who would add to your stature? He Himself will give you your clothes." His disciples say to Him, "When will you be revealed to us, and when shall we see you?" He says, "When you shall be undressed and shall not be put to shame."
Oxyr. Papyr. 655, 1904. ⟨See also *Gospel according to Thomas* 36-37.⟩     (28)

This world is only a bridge. Cross over it, but do not build your house on it!
On an archway in northern India. "The Secret of the Presence."     (29)

This age of lawlessness and unbelief stands under the dominion of Satan, who, through the influence of impure spirits, hinders men from grasping the genuine power of God. Therefore reveal your justice and righteousness now!" Thus they asked Christ.

Christ answered them: "For Satan's power the measure of the years is fulfilled. But new horrors are drawing near. They will also come upon those for whom I was delivered to

death because they have sinned. They should turn back to truth and sin no more in order to inherit the glory of righteousness, which is in Heaven because it belongs to the cause of the Spirit and to incorruption."
Freer Gospel Manuscript, H.A. Sanders, 1908; Jerome, *Dialogue Against Pelagius* 2.15; cf. *Acts of John* 41.          (30)

The days shall come when vines will grow, each with ten thousand runners, and on each runner ten thousand branches, and on each branch ten thousand shoots, and on every shoot ten thousand sprouts, and on every sprout ten thousand bunches, each bunch with ten thousand grapes, and every grape pressed will yield twenty-five quarts of wine. Should one of the saints lay hold of a bunch, another bunch will cry out, "I am better, take me. Glorify the Lord through me!" Accordingly, a grain of wheat will produce ten thousand ears, every ear will have ten thousand grains and every grain will yield five double pounds of pure, clear wheat flour. And with all other fruits, seeds, and plants it will be the same. And all animals will feed only on what the earth offers them. They will become peaceful and live in mutual harmony, subject to men in all obedience. They who enter there [in the Kingdom of God] shall see these things.
Papias quoted by Irenaeus, *Against Heresies* V.33.3,4.     (31)

Behold, I make the first things last and the last things first.
*Didascalia* XXVI ⟨see also Connolly, pp. 234, 235⟩; *Letter of Barnabas* 6.13.          (32)

That man is counted rich in God who has recognized that the old things of the past are new and that the new things are old.
Clem. *Hom.* VIII.7; cf. *Recog.* IV.5.          (33)

If you keep my word, you shall know the eternal Kingdom beforehand.

Justin, *Dialogue with Trypho the Jew* 116.2.          (34)

I give you a great inheritance such as the whole world does not have.

Macarius of Egypt, *Homily* 12.17.          (35)

I will judge you in those things in which I encounter you.

Justin, *Dialogue with Trypho the Jew* 47.6.          (36)

God will come to those who have faith in me, to those who hunger and thirst, and to those who test their souls in this life; and He will judge the sons of lawlessness.

*Apocalypse of Peter* 14, Akhmim Fragment.          (37)

There is a confusion that leads to death and there is a confusion that leads to life.

Jerome, *Commentary on Ezekiel* 16.52.          (38)

There is something greater than raising the dead and feeding the multitudes: Blessed are they who have believed with their whole heart.

Gospel fragment in Coptic *Acts of Paul*.          (39)

My disciples are bathed in living waters pouring down from above.

Oxyr. Papyr. 840, 1907.          (40)

If the neighbor of one of the chosen sins, the chosen one sins. For if he had kept himself as the Word demands, his

neighbor would have been so ashamed on seeing the other
one's life that he would not have sinned.

The Traditions of Matthias in Clem. Alex., *Misc.* VII.13.82.

(41)

T he Son of Man is come today and has found the lost.

Clem. Alex., *Misc.* IV.6.35.                              (42)

W hoever seeks me shall find me in children, for there
will I be made manifest.

Hippolytus, *Philosophumena* V.7.20 quoting Jewish Christian
Gospel of the Naassenes.                                    (43)

H ow many go around the well, and nobody draws from
it? Why do you not risk anything when going this way?
It is not manifest to you that with me there is courage and a
sword.

Celsus in Origen, *Against Celsus* VIII.15, from a lost Christian
writing, *Heavenly Dialogue*.                              (44)

S eek and find, and realize that the truth does not lie openly
on the surface.

Clem. *Hom.* III.52.                                        (45)

Y ou are whitewashed tombs, full of dead men's bones inside,
for the living man is not in you.

Hippolytus, *Philosophumena* V.3.                          (46)

T he Word that was freely given must not be sold.

Clem. *Hom.* III.71.3.                                      (47)

Blessed is the man whom his Lord shall appoint to the service of his fellow laborers.
Clem. *Hom.* III.64.1. (48)

Do not grieve the Holy Spirit that is in you, and do not quench the light that shines in you.
Pseudo-Cyprian, *Against Dice-Throwers* 3. (49)

My Mother, the Holy Spirit, seized me.
Sources: Origen, Jerome. See annotation. (50)

I myself am here, the One who speaks, the One who speaks in the prophets.
Pseudo-Cyprian, *On the Unbelief of the Jews* 4; Epiphanius, *Panarion* 23.5; 41.3; 66.42. (51)

Give me now Thy power, O Father, that with me they may endure the world. Amen. I have received the diadem [scepter] of the Kingdom. In their lowliness they were despised, for they were not recognized. Through Thee, Father, I am become King. Thou wilt subject all things to me.

I reveal my full glory to you and show you all your power and the secret of your apostleship.

A Gospel fragment from the Strasbourg Coptic Papyrus, 1900. (52)

I chose you twelve to be disciples, esteeming you worthy of me, sending you into the world to proclaim the Joyful News to men throughout the earth so that they know there is *one* God. Reveal the future events through faith in me so that those who hear and believe shall be rescued.
Clem. Alex., *Misc.* VI.6.48; Proclamation of Peter 4 ⟨see also E. Hennecke, *New Testament Apocrypha*, vol. 2, p. 101⟩. (53)

The Lord's teaching by the twelve apostles to the heathen: There are two ways: the one is that of life and the other is that of death. There is a great difference between the two ways. The way of life is this: first, you shall love the God who made you; second, you shall love your neighbor as yourself. Everything that you do not wish to be done to you, do not do to another!

Now the teaching of these words is this: Bless those who curse you, and pray for your enemies. Fast for those who persecute you, for what grace would it be if you love those who love you? Do not even the heathen peoples do that? But love those who hate you, and you will have no enemy. Abstain from the cravings of the flesh and of the body. If someone strikes you on the right cheek, turn the other to him also, and you will be perfect. If someone presses you to go with him one mile, get ready for two. If anyone takes away your coat, give him your jacket as well. If any man seizes what is yours, do not demand it back, for you cannot anyway. Give to everyone who asks of you and never demand a return, for it is the Father's will that all should share the gifts we have received.

Blessed is he who gives according to the commandment, for he is not guilty. Woe to him who receives. Certainly, if any man is in need and receives help, he is not guilty, but he who is not in need will have to render account why he received and for what purpose. He will be put in prison, his action will be thoroughly examined, and he will not be released until he has handed over the last penny. However, for this case it has also been said: let the gift from your heart sweat in your hands until you find the one to whom to give.

The second commandment of the teaching is this: You shall not kill. You shall not commit adultery. You shall not corrupt boys. You shall not practice sexual promiscuity. You shall not steal. You shall not practice magic. You shall not mix poison. You shall not procure an abortion or kill the newborn child. You shall not covet the share that falls to your neighbor. You shall not commit perjury. You shall not bear false witness. You shall not speak evil about others. You shall not be resentful. You shall not be double-minded or double-tongued, for to be double-tongued is a deadly snare. Let your speech be neither dishonest nor empty, but let it be full of significance through action. You shall not be rapacious and always want to have more, or be deceitful, or malicious, or imagine yourself to be great. You shall not plot evil schemes against your neighbor. You shall not hate any man. You shall admonish people, you shall pray for people, and you shall love men more than your own life.

My child, flee from all evil and from everything resembling it. Do not get angry, for anger leads to murder. Do not get into passionate tempers or be quarrelsome or boil with rage, for all these things breed murder. My child, do not be lustful, for lust leads to promiscuity. Do not use foul language or cast lewd eyes, for all these things lead to adulterous acts. My child, do not foretell the future from natural signs, for this leads to idolatry. Do not use magic formulas, or astrology, or purification charms; you should not even wish to watch such things, for they all breed idolatry. My child, do not be a liar, for lying leads to stealing. Do not love money, and do not fall a prey to vain ambition, for all these things lead to theft. My child, do not grumble, for this leads to blasphemy; do not be self-willed or evil-minded, for all these things breed blasphemy. Be gentle-minded, for those of a gentle mind shall possess the earth. Be patient and have a loving heart. Be guileless. Be quiet and good, trembling in all things at the words you have heard. You shall not exalt yourself or allow your heart to be bold and presumptuous. Your heart shall not cling to the high and mighty, but turn to the good and humble folk. Accept as good whatever happens to you or affects you, knowing that nothing happens without God.

My child, night and day remember him who speaks God's Word to you. Honor him as the Lord, for the Lord himself is in the place where the Lordship of the Lord is proclaimed. Seek daily the presence of the people dedicated to God so that you are refreshed with their words. Do not be divisive, but reconcile quarrelers. Be just in your judgments, and do not show partiality in reproving transgressions. Do not be in doubt whether or not this should be done.

Do not be one who stretches out his hands to receive but closes them when it comes to giving. If you have earned something by the work of your hands, pass it on as a ransom for your sins. Do not hesitate to give, and do not grumble when giving, for you will know who is the glorious Giver of your reward. Do not turn away from those who are in need, but share all things in common with your brother. Do not claim anything as your own, for if you have fellowship in the immortal, how much more in perishable things!

Do not withdraw your hand from your son or your daughter, but from their youth teach them the fear of God. Do not give orders in anger or bitterness to your man or woman slaves who hope in the same God lest they lose the fear of God who is Ruler over you both, for He does not come with His call showing partiality; instead He comes to those whom He has prepared by His Spirit. And you slaves, be subject to your masters as to God's image, in shame and fear. Hate all shamming and everything that is not pleasing to the Lord. Never depart from the commandments of the Lord. Guard what you have received. Add nothing to it and take nothing away. Confess your trespasses in the Church and do not go to prayer with a guilty conscience. This is the way of life.

But the way of death consists in this: First of all, and above all, it is accursed and full of evil: murders, adulteries, covetous passions, promiscuous sex acts, thefts, idolatries, witchcrafts, magic poisonings, robberies, false testimonies, hypocrisies, doubleness of heart, deception, arrogance, malice, conceit, greed, filthy talk, jealousy, impudence, haughtiness, and boastfulness. It is the way of those who persecute the good and hate the truth, who love lying and do not know the reward of righteousness, who do not cleave to the good and to just judgment, who never tire of following evil instead of good, from whom gentleness and patience are remote, who love vanity and are out for reward, who have no heart for the poor and do not stand up for the oppressed, who do not know Him who made them, who kill their children and destroy God's creatures, who turn their backs on the poor and oppress the afflicted, who are advocates of the rich and judge the workers unjustly. They are sinners in all things! Save yourselves, children, from all these!

Be careful that nobody leads you astray from the way of this teaching lest with his teachings he leads you away from God, for if you can carry the whole yoke of the Lord you will be perfect; but if you cannot, do what you can. In matters of eating take upon yourself what you can, but keep away completely from meat offered to idols, for it represents the worship of dead gods.

Now concerning baptism, baptize in this way: after you have said all these things, baptize in running water, in the name of the Father and of the Son and of the Holy Spirit. If you have no running water close by, however, dip in other water. If you cannot do it in cold water, do it in warm water. If you have neither close by, pour water on the head three times, in the name of the Father and of the Son and of the Holy Spirit. Before baptism the baptizer and the one who is to be baptized shall fast, and a few others as well if they can. Challenge the one who is to be baptized to fast one or two days. Your fasts shall not take place with those of the hypocrites, for they fast on the second and the fifth day after the Sabbath. Fast instead on the fourth day and on the day before the Sabbath. And do not pray as the hypocrites do but as the Lord commanded in His Gospel. Pray thus:

Our Father, Thou who art in the Heavens,
Thy Name be honored;
Thy Kingdom come,
Thy will be done
As in Heaven so on earth;
Give us this day our daily bread,
And forgive us our debts
As we also forgive our debtors,
And do not lead us into temptation,
But deliver us from the evil one.

For to Thee belong the power and the glory into the ages. Pray thus three times a day.

Concerning the Meal of Thanksgiving, give thanks in this way, first with the cup:

We give thanks to Thee, our Father, for the holy vine of David, Thy servant. This vine Thou didst make known to us through Jesus, Thy child. Glory be to Thee into the ages!

Then with the broken bread:

We give thanks to Thee, our Father, for the life and knowledge which Thou hast made known to us through Jesus, Thy child. Glory be to Thee into the ages! Just as this broken bread was scattered over the hills and became one when it had been brought together, so shall Thy Church be brought together from the ends of the earth into Thy Kingdom. For to Thee belong the glory and the power through Jesus Christ into the ages. Do not allow anybody to eat and drink of your Meal of Thanksgiving except those who have been baptized in the name of the Lord, for concerning this, too, the Lord said, "Do not give that which is holy to dogs." After you are satisfied give thanks in this way:

We give thanks to Thee, Holy Father, for Thy Holy Name, for which Thou hast made a dwelling in our hearts, and for the knowledge, faith, and immortality which Thou hast made known to us through Jesus, Thy child. To Thee be glory into the ages! Thou, all-powerful Ruler, hast established the universe for Thy name's sake, and Thou hast given men food and drink to enjoy, that they may give thanks to Thee. But to us Thou hast given the food of the Holy Spirit and the drink of the Holy Spirit and eternal life through Thy child. Above all, we give Thee thanks because Thou art Power. To Thee belongs the glory into the ages! Remember, O Lord, Thy Church, to deliver her from all evil and to make her perfect in Thy love. Gather her, the consecrated Church, from the four winds into Thy Kingdom which Thou hast prepared for her. For Thine is the power and the glory into the ages.

May grace come, and may the world pass away!

May the help of the God of David triumph!

If anyone is holy, let him come; if anyone is not, let him change from the root up!

Our Lord comes!

So it is.

Trust the prophets to give thanks as much as they wish.

Should anyone come and teach you all these things said above, receive him. However, if he himself is a false teacher and teaches a different teaching leading to dissolution, do not listen to him; but if his teaching increases justice and knowledge of the Lord, receive him as the Lord.

Regarding apostles and prophets, act in accordance with the directions of the Gospel. Every apostle visiting you shall be received as the Lord. He should stay only one day and if it is necessary a second day also. If he stays for three days, he is a false prophet. When the apostle leaves he shall not accept anything except bread for the time until he reaches his next night's lodging. But if he asks for money he is a false prophet.

As to any prophet who speaks in the Spirit, this holds good: Do not inquire or censure! For every sin shall be forgiven, but this sin shall not be forgiven. However, not every man who speaks in the Spirit is a prophet, but only if he has the manner of the Lord. Thus the false and the true prophet shall be known by their manner of life. No prophet speaking in the Spirit who orders the table spread will eat from it unless he is a false prophet. Further, every prophet who teaches the truth is a false prophet if he does not do what he teaches. However, every tested, true prophet who does something related to the universal mystery of the Church, yet does not teach others to do so great a thing as he himself does, shall not be judged among you. His judgment rests with God, for the prophets of old also acted in the same way. But if anyone says in the Spirit, "Give me money" or anything else, do not listen to him. However, if he asks you to give something to others in need, nobody shall judge him.

Anyone who comes in the name of the Lord shall be received. You will then test him and you will know him, for you will have the understanding to decide between right and left. If the one coming to you is only a traveler, help him as much as you can, but he shall stay with you only for two days, if necessary three. If someone wants to settle among you, let him work in his trade for a living. In case he has no trade or craft, use your discretion and see to it that no idle Christian lives in your midst. But if he will not act accordingly, he wants to make a business proposition of his Christianity. Beware of such men.

Every true prophet who wishes to settle among you is worthy of his food. Likewise, a true teacher is just as worthy of his food as a laborer. Therefore always take the firstfruits of the produce of winepress and threshing floor, of cattle and sheep, and give these firstfruits to the prophets, for they are your highest priests. If however you have no prophet, give them to the poor. When you bake something take the firstfruits and give them according to these directions. Likewise, when you open a fresh jar of wine or oil, take the firstfruits and give them to the prophets. Also of money and clothing and of any other valuables, take the firstfruits as you think right, and give them according to these directions.

On the Lord's own day come together, break bread and give thanks, but first confess your transgressions so that your offering may be pure. No one, however, who has a quarrel with his friend shall join you until they are reconciled so that your offering is not defiled. For this is what was said by the Lord: "In every place and at all times you shall offer me a pure sacrifice, for I am a great King, says the Lord, and my name is wonderful among the nations."

Elect for yourselves overseers and servants worthy of the Lord, men of gentle disposition who are free of the love of money, honest and tried, for they are those who, in serving you, render you the service of the prophets and teachers. Therefore do not ignore them, for they are the men honored among you along with the prophets and teachers. Admonish one another, not in anger but peaceably, as you see it in the Gospel. Moreover, if anyone has wronged another, let no one speak with him, and do not let him hear a word from you until he repents. Your prayers and the gifts you give from your heart and all that you do shall be as you find it in the Gospel of our Lord.

Watch over your life! Do not let your lamps go out, and do not loosen the belt around your loins; be ready, for you do not know the hour when our Lord is coming. Come together often and seek that which concerns your souls since the whole time of your faith will be of no use to you unless you are made perfect at the last hour. For in the last days great numbers of false prophets and corruptors will appear. The sheep will turn into wolves, and love will turn into hate. As lawlessness increases, men will hate, persecute, and betray one another. And then the World-deceiver will appear in the likeness of the Son of God. He will do signs and wonders; the earth will be given into his hands; and he will commit abominable deeds such as have never been done since eternity. Then the race of men will come into the fire of testing, and many will be thrown down by this impact and will perish. But those who remain steadfast in their faith will only just in time be snatched away from the World-deceiver, the Cursed One. Then the signs of the truth will appear: first the sign of the out-stretched hands in the sky; then the sign of the sound of the trumpet; and third the resurrection of the dead, yet not of all, but as it was said, "The Lord will come, and all the holy ones with Him." Then the world will see the Lord coming on the clouds of the sky.
*Didache*. (54)

The Church of God that lives as an alien in Rome to the Church of God that lives as an alien in Corinth—to those who are called and made holy by the will of God through our Lord Jesus Christ: may grace and peace from the Almighty God come to you abundantly through Jesus Christ.

Because calamities and misfortunes broke in upon us suddenly and in quick succession, we have been rather tardy, it seems to us, in concerning ourselves with the disputes that have arisen among you, dearly beloved. The vile and godless rebellion, so utterly inappropriate and foreign to the chosen of God, provoked a few rash and bold people to such a high degree of folly that your honorable and widely renowned name, cherished by all men, has been defamed.

For who among your guests did not experience your glorious and steadfast faith? . . . make honorable mention of the splendid character of your hospitality? call your perfect and secure knowledge a happy thing? You did everything without considering rank or station in life; you lived in accordance with God's commandments; you were obedient to your overseers and paid your elders the respect due to them; and your younger people you urged to a modest and reverent attitude. You practiced obedience rather than demanding it, you were more joyful in giving than in receiving; you were content with and mindful of what Christ gave you for your way through life; you carefully locked up His words in your hearts; and His sufferings were before your eyes. Thus a deep and radiant peace had been given to all of you and an insatiable longing to do good awakened in you. The Holy Spirit was poured out abundantly upon you all. Day and night you labored on behalf of the entire brotherhood. You were sincere and guileless and bore no grudge against one another.

Fame and abundance were bestowed upon you in full measure, and then it happened as it is written: "The beloved ate and drank, . . . and then he kicked out." From this sprang jealousy and envy, strife and dissension, persecution and disorder, war and captivity. Thus those who were not honored rose up against the honored, those who were not esteemed against the esteemed, the unwise against the wise, the young against the elders. As a result, justice and peace are far removed. . . . Everyone follows the cravings of his evil heart; he is filled with that unjust and godless jealousy through which indeed death came into the world.

We are writing this, beloved, not only for your admonition but also as a challenge to ourselves, for we are in the same arena and the same struggle faces us. . . . Let us fix our eyes on the blood of Christ and recognize how precious it is to His Father. Poured out for the sake of our salvation, it brought the gift of complete change to the whole world. Let us survey all generations of men. Let us recognize that from generation to generation the Lord has given to those who are willing to turn to Him an opportunity to change their lives. Noah called to repentance; those who heeded him were saved. Jonah prophesied destruction to the Ninevites; they turned away from their sins. By their supplications they moved God's heart and were spared by Him although they were not of God's people. The servants of God's grace called men to a complete change of heart and mind through the Holy Spirit. Yes, He himself, the Ruler of the Universe, spoke of this change of heart with an oath, "As truly as I live, says the Lord, I do not desire that the sinner dies but that he turns around."

Christ belongs to those who want to be small, not to those who exalt themselves above His flock. The Scepter of God's majesty, the Lord Jesus Christ himself, came in lowliness, just as the Holy Spirit proclaimed Him in saying:

He is like a small child, like a weak root in poor soil. He has no comeliness or glory. We saw him. He had neither comeliness nor beauty. His form was despised. It was uglier than the form of men usually is. . . . He was despised; he was disregarded. He bears our sins. For our sakes he is afflicted. We regarded him as one afflicted and bruised and martyred. But it is for our sins that he was wounded, it is for our iniquities that he was bruised. He was under punishment that we might have peace. By his stripes we were healed. He did not open his mouth while he was abused. Like a sheep he was led to slaughter, and as a lamb is dumb under the hand of his shearer, he did not open his mouth.... Because of the sins of my people did he come to his death.... He took upon himself the sins of many, and he was delivered up because of their sins.

And again Christ himself says:

But I am a worm and not a man, mocked by men and despised by the people. All who saw me scorned me, they muttered with their lips and shook their heads, "He hoped in the Lord, let him deliver him; let him rescue him, for he has delight in him."

You see, beloved ones, what example is given to us, for if the Lord was so small, what should we do then, who by Him have been led under the yoke of His grace? Let us also imitate those who were clad only in goatskins and sheepskins and who proclaimed the coming of the Messiah.

Let this text of the Scriptures never apply to us where it says:

Wretched are those who doubt, who are divided in their souls and say, "We heard these things already in the days of our fathers. But see, we have become old, and none of all these things has happened." Oh, you foolish people! Compare yourselves to a tree. Think of a vine: first it sheds its leaves; then a fresh shoot grows, then a leaf, then a flower; after this the unripe fruit develops; and finally there is the ripe bunch of grapes.

You see, the fruit of the tree has ripened in a very short time.

Truly God's will shall be accomplished quickly and suddenly. The Scripture also bears witness to this when it says, "He will come quickly. He will not delay. Suddenly the Lord will come to his temple—he, the Holy One for whom you are waiting!"

Let us consider, beloved, how the Lord continually proclaims to us the future resurrection, of which He made the Lord Jesus Christ the firstfruits when He raised Him from the dead. Let us contemplate the resurrection that recurs in a regular fashion. Day and night show us the resurrection: night goes to rest, day breaks in; day departs, night comes on. Let us consider the crops. How and in what manner does sowing take place? The farmer goes out and casts all the seeds on the soil: they are dry and bare; they fall on the soil; they decay. After they have decayed, the Lord's sublime providence raises them up, and from each single seed many grow and bear fruit.

Let us consider the strange sign which is seen in the Orient in the region of Arabia. There is a bird called the phoenix there. It is the only one of its kind, and it lives five hundred years. When its end draws near and it must die, it builds itself a coffin of frankincense, myrrh, and other fine herbs. When its time of life is fulfilled, it settles down in the coffin and dies. As its flesh decays, a worm is engendered that feeds on the putrid juices of the dead animal and grows wings. Then, when it has grown strong, it takes up the coffin containing the bones of the former bird and carries it from Arabia to Egypt, to the city called the City of the Sun. In broad daylight, before everybody's eyes, it alights upon the altar of the god of the sun, puts down its burden there, and flies back home again. Then the priests look up their calendar records and discover that its return comes after a lapse of five hundred years. Shall we then consider it something great and marvelous that the Creator of the Universe will raise up those who have served Him in holiness and in the trust of a good faith since He uses even a bird to show us His mighty promise?

No one was ever honored and made great through himself or his own efforts or through the good works he has done, but only through His will. Therefore we too, who have been called through His will in Jesus Christ, will never become righteous of ourselves or through our own wisdom, understanding, and devotion, or through the actions we have done in purity of heart, but through that faith by which the Almighty God has made all men good from the very beginning. To Him be glory forever and ever. Amen.

Let us therefore endeavor to belong to those who wait for Him so that we may share in the promised gifts. Yet how will this come about, dearly beloved? If our heart is turned toward God in steadfast faith, if we strive toward what gives joy to Him and is dear to Him, if we carry out what is in harmony with His unassailable will and follow in the way of truth, throwing off from ourselves all injustice and evil, covetousness, quarrelsomeness, malice and falseness, all slander and calumny, all hatred of God, all pride and arrogance, all empty boasting and thirst for fame. All who do such things are hateful to God and not only those who do such things but also those who approve of them.

This is the way, dearly beloved, in which we found our salvation, Jesus Christ, the High Priest of our sacrifice, the guardian and helper of our weakness. Through Him we look into the heights of Heaven. Through Him we recognize God's unblemished and exalted countenance, as in a mirror. Through Him the eyes of our hearts were opened. Through Him our unwise and darkened mind springs up into the light. Through Him the Lord allowed us to taste immortal knowledge.

Particular duties are prescribed for the high priest; a particular place is assigned to the priests; and again, particular tasks are laid upon the Levites. The laymen are bound by the rules that apply to them. Each one of us brothers shall please God in his own station and keep a good conscience. Let each one of us with all dignity keep to the boundary assigned to his service without overstepping the limits. The sacrifice is made in the court of the altar only, in front of the sanctuary, and, what is more, by the high priest and his helpers. Further, those who act in opposition to the ordinance of His will suffer death as the fate they deserve. Look, brothers: the greater the knowledge that has been entrusted to us, the greater the danger we have to face.

The Joyful News was proclaimed by the Lord to the apostles for our sake. Jesus Christ was sent from God. Hence, Christ came from God, and the apostles came from Christ. Both these things happened in proper order in accordance with God's will. Thus the apostles received their commission, filled with certainty through the resurrection of our Lord Jesus Christ and strengthened in God's Word; thus they went forth full of the joy of the Holy Spirit, proclaiming the joyful news that the Kingdom of God is at hand. They spoke in villages and cities, and they appointed the firstfruits of their labor to be the bishops and deacons of the future believers, after testing them through the Spirit. Blessed are the elders who completed their course and came to a fruitful and perfect end. They need not fear any more that someone will dislodge them from the place given to them.

We see, however, that elders who were leading a good life were removed by you from the service they fulfilled blamelessly and honorably. Why are there quarrels, anger, dissension, divisions, and war in your midst? Do we not have *one* God and *one* Christ and *one* Spirit of grace poured out upon us—*one* calling in Christ? Why do we rend and tear to pieces the members of Christ? Why do we separate ourselves from our own body and push our folly to such an extreme as to forget that we are members one of another? Remember the words of the Lord Jesus!

Your division has brought confusion to many, it has discouraged many, and it has brought many to have doubts. It has plunged us all into anguish.

Who can describe the bond of the love of God? Who can put into words the majesty of its beauty? The height to which love leads is ineffable. Love unites us with God. . . . Love knows nothing of division, love causes no quarrel, love does everything in harmony. All the chosen ones of God are made perfect in love. Without love there is nothing that pleases God. In love the Lord accepted us. Because of the love He felt for us, our Lord Jesus Christ by the will of God gave His blood for us, gave His flesh for our flesh and His soul for our souls.

We know of many among our number who have given themselves up freewillingly to imprisonment so that they might bring freedom to others. Many have sold themselves into slavery to feed others with the money they received.

Therefore, you who started this contention submit to the elders, accept discipline in repentance, and bend the knees of your heart. Learn obedience, and rid yourselves of the boastful and arrogant impudence of your tongues! It is better for you to be found small in Christ's flock yet chosen, than to be exceedingly important yet excluded from the hope He gives.

*First Letter of Clement to the Corinthians* (about the year 94).
(55)

Ignatius, also called Theophorus, . . . wishes the Church at Ephesus in Asia all joy in Jesus Christ.

As imitators of God, you have been given new life by the

blood of God to complete the task that corresponds to your character. You hastened to see me when you heard that for the sake of our common name and expectation I was led away in chains from Syria and that I hope through your prayer to obtain the favor of fighting with the wild beasts in Rome so that I may attain to discipleship.

It is fitting, therefore, that in every way you glorify Jesus Christ who has glorified you. Be firmly joined together in unanimous obedience, obeying the overseer and the body of elders, and be made holy in all things. Your deserving body of elders, worthy of God, is attuned to the overseer as the strings are to a lyre! Therefore the song of Jesus Christ resounds in your unity and in your harmonious love. Yes, one and all of you should become one choir so that in perfect harmony, taking your keynote from God in unity, you may with one voice sing praises to the Father through Jesus Christ so that He may hear you and recognize you by your good deeds as members of His Son.

Certain people with wicked thoughts at the back of their minds are in the habit of flaunting the Name while they practice other things unworthy of God. These you must shun like wild beasts. Mad dogs they are, biting treacherously. You must be on your guard against them, for they are hard to cure. There is only one Physician: He who in flesh and in Spirit alike, begotten and unbegotten, is God come into the flesh, He who in death is true life, who sprang from Mary and from God, who first suffered and then did not suffer pain any more, Jesus Christ our Lord!

You are stones for the Father's temple, prepared for the house-building of God the Father. You are raised high up by the hoist of Jesus Christ, which is the Cross, while the Holy Spirit is your rope. Your faith is your windlass. Love is the path that leads up to God. You are all traveling companions,

God-bearers, temple-bearers, Christ-bearers, bearers of holy things, in everything adorned with the words of Jesus Christ.

Let us be eager to become imitators of the Lord. Who could have suffered more than He? Who could have been so robbed, who so despised?

The last times are here. Let us feel shame at last! Let us fear God's patience lest it become judgment upon us! Either let us fear the future wrath or let us love the grace that is given now, one or the other. Let us be found only in Christ Jesus so that we live the true life!

Be eager, then, in coming together as often as possible for God's Meal of Thanksgiving and for His praises, for if you meet frequently, Satan's powers are broken; what threatens you from him is dashed to pieces on the unity of your faith. There is nothing better than the peace by which all warfare waged by heavenly and earthly powers is abolished.

Of all these things none is hidden from you if you are single-hearted and if you direct your faith and love toward Jesus Christ. These are the beginning and the end of life: the beginning is faith, the end is love. The two bound together in unity are God. Everything else that belongs to goodness follows from these. No one who professes faith sins, and anyone who possesses love does not hate. The tree is known by its fruit. Those who profess to belong to Christ will be recognized by their actions. However, what matters now is not a mere professing of faith. Now the crucial thing is whether a man is found in the power of faith to the end. He who truly possesses the Word of Jesus can even hear His silence speak. In this way shall he be perfect: he will act in accordance with his words and will be known even by his silence.

Our God, Jesus the Christ, was conceived by Mary of the seed of David and yet of the Holy Spirit according to God's plan of salvation. He was born and baptized so that through

His suffering He would purify the water. From that time on every evil spell was exposed, all bonds of evil vanished, and ignorance was removed. The ancient kingdom was shattered. God revealed Himself in human form to bring the newness of eternal life! Now began that which had been prepared by God. From now on everything came into motion, for now the destruction of death was taken in hand.

Ignatius, *Letter to the Ephesians,* before the year 120.  (56)

The most wonderful thing is unity with Jesus and with the Father. In Him we shall partake in God if we firmly resist and flee all the arrogant attacks of the Prince of this World.

Unity of prayer, unity of supplication, unity of mind, unity of expectancy in love and in blameless joy: this is Jesus Christ and there is nothing greater than He. Flock together, all of you, as to one temple of God, as to one altar, to one Jesus Christ, who proceeded from the one Father, who is in the One and returned to the One.

Therefore, breathed upon by His grace, they were persecuted in order fully to convince the disobedient that there is one God, who revealed Himself through Jesus Christ His Son, Christ who is God's Word which came forth from His silence and who in every way was a joy to Him who sent Him.

Ignatius, *Letter to the Magnesians,* before the year 120. (57)

Take up kindness and renew yourselves in faith, that is, the flesh of the Lord, and in the love, that is, the blood of Jesus Christ. Let no one among you hold anything against his neighbor. Be deaf toward anyone who tells you tales that do not lead to Jesus Christ, who was of David's lineage, Mary's son; who was really born; who ate and drank; who was really persecuted under Pontius Pilate; and was really crucified and died while the powers of Heaven, earth, and the Underworld looked on; who also really rose from the dead because His Father awakened Him. In His likeness the Father will also awaken us, who believe in Him, through Christ Jesus, without whom we have no true life.

Ignatius, *Letter to the Trallians,* before the year 120. (58)

Ignatius, also called Theophorus, . . . salutes the Church that presides in the district of the Romans. Grant me nothing more than to be a sacrifice to God while there is still an altar ready. Having become one choir in love, you should sing praises to the Father in Christ Jesus that God has made the overseer and supervisor of Syria worthy of being deported from the rising to the setting of the sun. It is wonderful to set thus away from the world toward God in order that I may have my rising in Him!

I beseech you, do not show me any misplaced kindness! Let me become fodder for the wild beasts! Passing through them, I shall reach God. I am God's grain. Ground by the teeth of wild beasts, I shall become the pure bread of Christ. I would rather that you coax the wild beasts to become my tomb and leave no trace of my body lest I should become a burden to anyone after my death. In this way I shall truly become a disciple of Jesus when the world sees nothing of my body anymore. Plead with Christ for me that by these instruments I may become a public sacrifice to God.

Now I am just beginning to be a disciple. Nothing visible or invisible shall prevent me from reaching the presence of Jesus Christ. Come fire, cross, and packs of wild beasts; come cutting to pieces, tearing to bits, dispersion of bones, mangling of limbs, crushing of my whole body; come all the evil tortures of the Devil upon me—if only I attain the presence of Jesus Christ!

All the wide bounds of the world and the kingdoms of this age will profit me nothing. Better to die for the sake of Jesus Christ than to be king over the utmost ends of the earth. Him I seek who died for us. Him I want who rose for our sake. The day of my birth pangs is upon me. Allow me to imitate the suffering of my God! If anyone bears Him within himself, he will understand what is my desire. He will have compassion with me, for he knows what urges me on.

My love has been crucified. That fire which burns for earthly things is not in me. There is, however, living water speaking in me and saying within me, "Go up there, go to the Father!" Perishable food does not tempt me anymore, nor the allurements of this life. I desire the bread of God, which is the flesh of Jesus Christ, who is of the seed of David. For drink I want His blood. This is an imperishable Lovemeal. Ignatius, *Letter to the Romans,* before the year 120.     (59)

My brothers, my love for you is boundless. I am strengthening you with loud shouts of joy. Of course it is not I who am strengthening you but Jesus Christ, because I am still fearful in my chains as one who is not yet fully prepared. Your prayers though will prepare me on my way toward God so that I may win the lot which through mercy has fallen to me. It was the Spirit who proclaimed and said: "Do nothing without the overseer. Keep your flesh as God's temple. Love unity. Flee from all division. Become and act like Jesus, the Christ, who is the image of the Father in Heaven."
Ignatius, *Letter to the Philadelphians,* before the year 120.
     (60)

Ignatius, also called Theophorus, sends the Church at Smyrna in Asia joyful greetings!

I praise Jesus Christ, the God who has filled you with such

wisdom. I did indeed see you armed with immovable faith as though nailed to the Cross of the Lord Jesus Christ in flesh and in spirit and firmly joined together in love through the blood of Christ. You are fully convinced by faith in our Lord that He is truly of the lineage of David according to the flesh and that He is the Son of God according to the will and power of God, truly born of a virgin and baptized by John so that all righteousness might be fulfilled by Him, truly nailed for us on the Cross in the flesh under Pontius Pilate and Herod (we are the fruit of this, His most blessed suffering) so that through His resurrection He might set up a banner of victory throughout all ages for His saints and believers, whether among Jews or Gentiles, in the one Body of His Church. He suffered all this for our sake that we might be saved. He truly suffered just as He also truly raised Himself from the dead.

Why have I given myself up to death, fire, the sword, and the wild beasts? To be near the sword is to be near God. To be in the midst of wild beasts is to be in the midst of God, only it must be done in the name of Jesus Christ. To suffer with Him I endure everything, for He who became the perfect Man is powerful in me. Let no man deceive himself. Judgment will come even over the heavenly powers, even over the splendor of the angels, and over the earthly and the invisible principalities unless they believe in the blood of Christ. Let him grasp it who can.

Learn to know those who teach errors about the grace of Jesus Christ which has come to us; recognize how they are opposed to the mind of God. Such teachers do not care for love and the Lovemeal; they have no concern for widows or orphans, for anyone in need, for those in prison or released from prison, for the hungry or the thirsty. They keep away from the Lord's Supper and from prayer, for they do not confess that the Lord's Supper is the flesh of our Savior Jesus

Christ, which flesh suffered for our sins and was raised up by our Father in His goodness. Because they speak against the gift of God, they are dying of their disputes. It would be better for them to hold the Lovemeal so that they too might rise from the dead. It is proper to shun such people and not to speak about them either privately or together. Rather should we hold to the prophets and above all to the Gospel in which the Passion is revealed to us and the resurrection is accomplished.

Flee from divisions as the beginning of all evil! Follow the overseer, all of you, as Jesus Christ follows the Father, and follow the council of elders as you would follow the apostles. Honor the brothers who serve as you honor God's command. In Church matters let no one do anything without the overseer. ... Where the overseer is present, there the Church should be also, just as wherever Jesus Christ is, there is the universal Church.

Ignatius, *Letter to the Smyrnaeans,* before the year 120.  (61)

Ignatius also called Theophorus, sends heartiest greetings to Polycarp, overseer of the Church of the Smyrnaeans, or rather to one who has God the Father and the Lord Jesus Christ for his overseer.

If you love the good disciples it does not bring you any credit; rather restore the corrupted ones by kindness. Not every wound is healed with the same plaster. Relieve fits of fever with poultices.

Men who seem trustworthy but teach errors must not intimidate you. Stand firm, like the anvil under the blows of the hammer. A good wrestler wins the fight even though he suffers blows. Above all, we ought to endure everything for God's sake so that He may also endure us. Be more zealous than you are now. Learn to understand the times. Expect

Him to come who is above time, the timeless One, the invisible One who became visible for our sake, the untouched One, the One beyond suffering who came to suffer for us, who in every way endured for our sake.

Toil together, fight, run, suffer, rest, and rise up together as God's stewards, companions of His table, and His servants! Please Him who is your warlord, Him from whom you will also receive your soldier's pay. Let none of you desert the flag! Let your baptism remain your armor, faith your helmet, love your spear, patience your weapon.

Ignatius, *Letter to Polycarp*, before the year 120.          (62)

Polycarp and the elders with him to the Church of God that lives as an alien in Philippi:

Believe in Him who raised our Lord Jesus Christ from the dead and gave Him glory and a throne at His right hand. Everything that is in Heaven and on earth is made subject to Him. Everything that has breath serves Him who is coming, a Judge of the living and the dead, whose blood God will require of those who disobey Him. He who raised Him from the dead will raise us also if we do His will and live in His words; if we love what He loved; if we keep clear of all injustice, avarice, greed for money, slander, and lying; if we do not return evil for evil, bad word for bad word, blow for blow, or curse for curse; but at all times bear in mind what our Lord said.

Brothers, I do not write these things to you about justice on my own initiative but because you asked me to do so. Neither I nor anyone else like me is able to follow in the wise footsteps of the blessed and glorious Paul, who lived among you. He stood face to face with the generation of his time and took a clear and firm stand for the word of truth. When absent he wrote letters to you that will enable you, if you consider them carefully, to be established in the faith given to you, which is the mother of us all. Love to God and Christ and to our neighbor goes before her, and hope follows her. He who lives in these things has fulfilled the commandment of righteousness, for he who has love is far from any sin.

The love of money is the beginning of all evil. We know that we brought nothing into the world and that we can take nothing out of it. If we live in this present age in a way that is pleasing to Him, we shall partake in the age to come according to His promise to raise us from the dead. If we conduct our life in accordance with His nature, we shall also rule with Him if only we have faith.

Let us therefore hold unceasingly to our expectation, to the guarantee of our future righteousness. This is Jesus Christ, who carried our sins on His own body up to the Tree, who committed no sin. No guile could be found in His words, but He suffered everything for our sake so that we should live in Him. Therefore let us become imitators of His patience, and if we must suffer for the sake of His name, then let us glorify Him. In this He gave us an example in His own person, and in this we believed.

Polycarp, *Letter to the Philippians*. Attested to by Irenacus, *Against Heresies* III.3.4; Eusebius, III.36.13-15.       (63)

When I see the great and extensive demands made on you by God, I feel an extraordinary and overwhelming joy at your blessed and glorious life in the Spirit. The grace of the gift of the Spirit has been deeply implanted in you. Our Ruler has made the past and the present known to us through the prophets. He also gave us a foretaste of the things of the future. Thus, when we see how these things become a reality one after another just as He said, we ought through this to come to a richer and deeper sense of the fear of God. Not as a teacher but as one from your midst, I want to point out a few things that could be an encouragement to you in the present situation.

The days are evil now, and he who makes them so still has power. Therefore we should inquire into the demands of the Lord and watch over ourselves at the same time. He says to us:

> Behold, this is the fast which I have chosen, says the Lord (not the fast of a man who chastises his soul but quite different): Undo every unjust fetter. Untie the knots of forced contracts! Set free the oppressed! Tear up every unjust bond! Break your bread with the hungry! When you see someone naked, give him clothes. Bring the homeless into your house! And if you see a humble man you shall not despise him. You shall not turn your eyes from those who belong to your own flesh and blood. Then your light shall break forth at dawn.... Then justice will go before you. Then God's righteousness will encompass you. Then you will cry out and God will hear you, and while you are still speaking he will say, "Behold, I am here!" This he will do if you have given up binding with fetters, raising your hand, and speaking unfriendly words; if from your heart you give your bread to the hungry and show compassion to those who are oppressed.

Let us flee completely all the works of lawlessness lest the works of lawlessness take hold of us! Let us hate the error of the present age so that we may find love in the age to come! Let us not give our souls freedom as if we were allowed to go on the same way with the sinners and the wicked lest we become like them! The final stumbling block recorded in the words of Enoch is at hand. Our Ruler has cut short the times and the days so that His beloved One may hasten His coming and enter into His inheritance. The Old Covenant was shattered so that the Covenant of the beloved Jesus might be sealed into our hearts. This takes place through the expectation that belongs to faith in Him.

Let us be watchful during these last days! Our whole life-long faith will be of no profit to us unless we resist now, in this godless moment of history and in the cataclysm to come, as becomes children of God. To make sure then that the Black Spirit cannot creep in, let us flee from every kind of vanity, let us hate utterly the deeds of the way of vice! Do not withdraw into self-satisfied solitude as though your right-eousness were already assured, but gather together instead, and participate in seeking out what serves the common good. The Scripture says, "Woe to those that are wise in their own estimation and clever in their own conceit!"

Let us become men of the Spirit! Let us become a perfect temple for God! As far as it lies in our power, let us surrender to the fear of God. Let us fight to keep His words so that we feel joy in His commandments. The Lord will judge the world without respect of persons. Everyone will receive accor-ding to his actions: if he is good his justice shall go before him; if he is evil the wages of evildoing will await him. On no account let us give ourselves over to rest! Let us who were called never fall asleep over our sins! Let the Prince of Evil never gain power over us and force us away from the Lord's Kingdom! Take this to heart, my brothers: you see that Israel, after the many signs and miracles that were performed in her midst, has nevertheless been abandoned. Let us be watchful then lest the word which is written, "Many are called, but few are chosen," be one day applied to us!

The reason then that the Lord took it upon Himself to give His flesh over to destruction was that we might become pure through the forgiveness of sin. This takes place through His blood of atonement. Therefore we ought to give most fervent thanks to the Lord for making known to us the past, for giving us light about the present, and for not leaving us without discernment of the future. But the Scripture says, "Not unjustly are nets spread out for birds." This means that a man shall justly perish if he has knowledge of the way of justice and yet remains on the way of darkness.

Further, my brothers, the Lord took it upon Himself to suffer for our souls, He, the Lord of the whole world, to whom God spoke immediately after the foundation of the world. "Let us make men after our image and in our likeness!"

Hear then how He came to take it upon Himself to suffer at the hands of men. The prophets, thanks to the gift of grace they received from the Lord himself, prophesied concerning Him. He had to be revealed in the flesh in order to abolish death and to manifest the resurrection from the dead. He also took this suffering upon Himself to fulfill the promise given to the fathers and to prepare a new people for Himself. During His life on earth He wanted to demonstrate that He himself will bring about the resurrection, and that He himself will then exercise judgment.

Furthermore, He proclaimed the truth. He taught Israel and performed so many great miracles and signs because He loved them to the utmost. He chose His own apostles, those who were to proclaim His Joyful News, from among those who had been the very worst of sinners. By this He proved that He did not come to call the righteous but the sinners. After He had made this choice, He revealed Himself as God's Son. If He had not appeared in the flesh, men could never have survived the sight of Him. They even have to shut their eyes when looking at the sun, which is nothing but the work of His hands and will perish one day.

Furthermore, the Son of God came in the flesh to fulfill the measure of sin of those who had already persecuted His prophets to death. He took suffering upon Himself also for this reason. Even before His flesh was wounded, God said that it was caused by them: "When they have struck down their shepherd, the sheep of the flock will perish." But, as is known, it was by His own choice that He suffered in this way.

Thus speaks the Lord God: "Enter into the good land which the Lord swore to Abraham, Isaac, and Jacob, and take possession of it, a land flowing with milk and honey." Learn now what knowledge [*gnosis*] has to say about this. "Hope," it says, "in Jesus, who shall reveal Himself to you in the flesh in the time to come. For 'land' as something capable of suffering stands for 'man' since Adam was formed out of the earth." But what then does it mean, "into the good land"? The prophet means the Lord in a symbolic way; but only he will grasp it who is wise and understanding and loves his Lord.

Now, by renewing us through the forgiveness of sins, He made us to be of a different stamp, just as though He were giving us the souls of children and creating us again. . . . Now the Lord says, "Behold, I make the last things like the first." . . . We have experienced a new creation in ourselves as He announced through another prophet. Therefore we are those whom He has led into the good land. Just as a child is kept alive with honey first and then with milk, so we also are filled with the strength of life, first by faith in the promise and then by the Word, and in this way we attain life in full possession of the land.

He also foretold: "They shall increase and multiply and rule over the fish." But who is presently able to rule over quadrupeds or fish or the birds in the sky? We ought to realize that such rulership depends on the authority to assert lordship by a mere word of command. Though this is not the case now, yet He did tell us when it would happen, namely, when we ourselves have been made perfectly ready to become the heirs of the Lord's Covenant. Thus the Son of God, who is the Lord and who will have the judgment over the living and the dead in the future, suffered in order that His wounds should secure life for us. Let us believe, then, that the Son of God could not suffer except for our sake.

Observe what instructions He gave us in order to show what He would have to suffer at their hands: "Take a pair of fine goats, alike to each other." The one, He says, shall be the object of curses—note how Jesus appears symbolized in this!—and you shall spit upon it, all of you, goad it, put scarlet wool around its head and chase it out into the desert! . . . Take note what is meant by this, that one of the goats is destined for the altar, the other is to be cursed, and the accursed one is to be crowned with a wreath. It relates to this, that on that day to come they shall see Him clothed with the scarlet robe around His body and they will cry, "Is not this the One whom we once scorned, spat at, goaded, and finally crucified? Truly this was the man who said at that time that He is the Son of God."

Therefore the two goats must be alike, shapely and well matched, so that when they see Him [Jesus] coming again, they will be terrified at the similarity.

What do you think is symbolized by the command given to Israel that men whose sins are consummated should offer a heifer, kill it, and burn it? that young boys should then collect the ashes, put them into containers, and put scarlet wool and hyssop around a piece of wood — here again we see a foreshadowing of the Cross and the scarlet!—and with this the boys should sprinkle the people one by one that they may be cleansed from their sins?

Take note with what plainness He speaks to us here! The slaughtered animal is Jesus; the sinful men who offer it signify those who offered Him to be slaughtered. The young boys who did the sprinkling are those who brought us the Joyful News of the forgiveness of sins and the cleansing of the heart, to whom He gave authority to proclaim the Joyful News. Their number is twelve, pointing to the twelve tribes of Israel. Why are there three sprinkling boys, though? This points to Abraham, Isaac, and Jacob because they are great in God's sight. And why is there wool on the piece of wood? Because the royal reign of Jesus rests on the Wood and because whoever hopes in Him will live forever.

Blessed are those who, setting their hope on the Cross, went down into the water. . . . Again in another writing it says, "And there was a river meandering to the right, and graceful trees arose from it, and whoever eats of them will live forever." This indicates that we go down into the water full of sin and dirt, but then we come up from it laden with fruit, bearing reverence in our heart and hope in Jesus in our spirit. And whoever eats from them will live forever. With this He wants to say: whoever hears this proclamation and believes shall live forever.

The Spirit spoke into the heart of Moses telling him to make the symbol of a cross and thus foreshadow Him who was to suffer. Then Moses piled shield upon shield in the thick of the battle, and when he had reached a point high above them all, he stood up there and stretched out his arms.

And the Spirit spoke through another prophet, "All day long I stretched out my arms to a disobedient people that resists my way of justice."

For this Jesus was sent, that through His appearance He would free from darkness our hearts which are already wasted unto death and given up to the error of godlessness, and through His Word He would establish the Covenant in us.

When His Son comes, when He puts an end to the age of the Unjust One, when He judges the godless and transforms the sun, the moon, and stars—then He will rest with honor on the seventh day.

We ourselves must have been made just and must have received the promise. There must be no godlessness anymore, and all things must have become new through the Lord. Only then shall we be able to keep the Sabbath Day holy. First we ourselves must have been made holy.

"I cannot endure your new moons and sabbaths." Take heed what He means by this! It is not the present Sabbaths which I find acceptable but only the one I have ordained, on which I will put all things to rest and then make the eighth day begin. This means a different world. This is why we celebrate the first day of the week so joyfully, the same day also on which Jesus rose from the dead and, after He had manifested Himself, ascended into Heaven.

Let us become clear whether there is a Temple of God! Yes, there is. It is where God himself promises to build and prepare one. . . . Before we came to believe in God, our innermost heart was exposed to corruption. It was frail, just as a temple built with hands truly is, for it was full of idolatry. It was a dwelling-place of demons because we did what was offensive to God. Yet it shall be built upon the Name of the Lord. Take heed of the word that "the Temple of the Lord shall be built in glory!"

By receiving forgiveness of sins, by setting our hope on His name, we became new men, we were created all over again. Now God really dwells in us, in our innermost being. How? The word of His faith, the invitation to His promise, the wisdom of His ordinances, the commandments of His teaching—they all dwell in us. By speaking through us prophetically Himself, by dwelling in us Himself, by opening the door of the temple, which is our mouth, He gives us who were under the lordship of death a change of heart and leads us into His imperishable Temple. Let him who wants to be saved look not to the man who speaks but to Him who dwells in him and speaks through him.... Be simple in heart and rich in the Spirit!

Love your neighbor more than your own soul. Share everything with your neighbor and call nothing your own. As the apple of your eye, love everyone who proclaims the Word of the Lord to you. Night and day, remember the day of judgment, and daily seek the presence of the holy ones. Summon all your energy, yes, venture your life, to remain pure.

I urge those of you who are better off, if you will accept my well-meant advice, you have among you those to whom you can do good: do not fail to do so! The day is at hand when everything will perish together with the Evil One. The Lord is at hand, and His reward.

I urge you again and again: Be good lawmakers to each other, remain your own faithful counselors, keep away from all hypocrisy.

*Letter of Barnabas* in the Codex Sinaiticus, about A.D. 120.

(64)

# MEETINGS
## and
# WORSHIP

Wherever there are two together, they are never men without God.
Lord's saying according to a sheet of papyrus from an ancient collection of sayings. Oxyr. Papyr. I, 1897, Grenfell and Hunt.

(1)

Still daily some become disciples of His Christ and forsake the way of error. Enlightened by the name of this Christ, they receive gifts according to their merits. One receives the spirit of understanding, the other of counsel, this one the spirit of fortitude, that one of healing, the one the spirit of prophecy, the other of teaching, and yet another the spirit of the fear of God.
Justin, *Dialogue with Trypho the Jew* 39.2.

(2)

In whom have all the nations believed but in Christ who is already come? In whom have they believed—the Parthians, Medes, Elamites, and those who inhabit Mesopotamia, Armenia, Phrygia, Cappadocia; those who live in Pontus, Asia, and Pamphylia, in Egypt, in Africa beyond Cyrene; those born here and those who came here from Rome; also the Jews in Jerusalem and other national groups, as now the various tribes of the Gaetulians and of the wide regions of the Moors, and the Spaniards to their remotest boundaries; the different nations of Gaul; the haunts of the Britons, inaccessible to the Romans; the lands of the Sarmatians, Dacians, Germans, Scythians; and many remote nations, provinces, and islands, which are unknown to us and which we cannot enumerate?

We are but of yesterday, yet we have filled all that is yours: cities and islands, forts and towns, assemblies and even military camps, tribes, councils, the Palace, the Senate, the Forum. We left you only the temples.

Tertullian, *Against the Jews* VII; *Apology* 37.          (3)

When our Lord sent us to the ignorant nations to baptize them for the forgiveness of sins, He commanded us to teach them first.

*Homilies* XVII.7; cf. IX.23; *Recognitions* II.33; IV.32. From the Ebionite "Gospel of the Twelve" in the Homilies and Recognitions ascribed to Clement.          (4)

All those who are convinced that what we say and teach is the truth have the faith and pledge themselves that they will have the strength to live accordingly. (Anyone who accepts baptism must feel the power in him to overcome himself.) All those who confess this are led to prayer. Fasting, they ask God's forgiveness for their past sins. We also pray and fast with them. Then we lead them to a place where there is water. They are born again. They experience rebirth in the same way as we ourselves experienced it. In the name of God, the Father and Lord of all things, and in the name of our Healer and Savior Jesus Christ and of the Holy Spirit, they now take a bath in the water.

Christ said, "Unless you are born again you will not be able to enter into the Kingdom of Heaven." Now it is clear to everybody that it is impossible for those who have once been born to reenter their mothers' wombs. It was said through the prophet Isaiah in what way those who have sinned and repent shall be freed from their sins. These are his words:

Wash yourselves, make yourselves clean. Banish the wickednesses from your hearts. Learn to do good. Defend the orphans and plead for the rights of the widow. Come now and let us reason together, says the Lord: Though your sins be as scarlet, I will make them as white as wool; and though they be red as crimson, I will make them as white as snow. But if you will not hear me, the sword shall devour you. For the mouth of the Lord has spoken.

The apostles gave us the following reason for this: When we were first born we were begotten of nature's compulsion without our knowledge, from moist seed, through the intercourse of our parents, and grew up in bad customs and wicked principles. In order that we do not remain children of necessity and ignorance but become children by free choice and insight and gain forgiveness of our former sins, there is pronounced in the water, over the one who longs for the new birth and who has repented of his misdeeds, the name of God, the Father of all, and the Lord. He who leads to the bath the one to be baptized uses these words only, for nobody is able to give a name to the ineffable God. Should anyone want to assert that there is one, he is smitten with hopeless insanity. This bath is called illumination by us, for those who experience these things happening to them become enlightened in their minds and spirits. Furthermore, the washing of the one who is enlightened is also done in the name of

Jesus Christ, who was crucified under Pontius Pilate, and in the name of the Holy Spirit, who foretold everything concerning Jesus through the prophets.
Justin, *First Apology* 61. (5)

Indeed, Isaiah did not command you to bathe yourselves so that you would be able to wash away murder and other sins in this way. All the waters of the ocean would not be enough to cleanse you. Rather, the bath of salvation which he meant from the beginning is, as one might expect, that taken by those who repent, who no longer cleanse themselves through the blood of goats and sheep or through the ashes of a heifer or through the offering of wheat flour, but quite differently: on the way of faith, through the blood of Christ and through His death. That Christ suffered death for this purpose was said by Isaiah himself.
Justin, *Dialogue with Trypho the Jew* 13.1. (6)

We have become believers, then, through the bath which brings repentance and knowledge of God, which was given, according to Isaiah's word, to heal the sins of the peoples of God. We tell you that this bath foretold by him is the one which alone has the power to purify men provided they repent. This is the water of life. The wells you have dug for yourselves have caved in and are useless. . . . Wash your souls clean of anger, greed, envy, and hate, and you will see that the whole body will be pure.
Justin, *Dialogue with Trypho the Jew* 14.1. (7)

The nature of our Meal and its purpose are explained by its very name. It is called *Agape,* as the Greeks call love in its purest sense. However much it may cost, it is always a gain to be extravagant in the name of fellowship with what is God's, since the food brought is used for the benefit of all who are in need. To respect the lowly is all-important with God.

If then the motive for our Meal is honorable, consider the discipline ruling during the Meal in that light. That which is rooted in religious commitment does not tolerate vileness and licentiousness. The participants do not go to the table unless they have first tasted of prayer to God. As much is eaten as is necessary to satisfy the hungry; as much is drunk as is good for those who live a disciplined life. When satisfying themselves they are aware that even during the night they should worship God. They converse as those who are aware that God is listening.

After the hands are washed and the lights are lit, all are asked to stand forth and to praise God as well as each is able, be it from the Holy Scriptures or from his own heart. From this it will be recognized "how he drank." In like manner the Meal is closed with a prayer. After this we part from one another, not to gang together to brawl or to roam about in bands, or to go in secret byways of licentiousness, but always pursuing the same self-control and purity as befits those who have taken in a truth rather than a meal. This is the way Christians meet.

Tertullian, *Apology* 39. (8)

God has announced in advance that He has joy in all the sacrifices offered in the name of Jesus that are made in accordance with the precepts of Jesus Christ, that is, in the Meal of Thanksgiving of the bread and the cup, which is celebrated by Christians in all places throughout the earth.

Justin, *Dialogue with Trypho the Jew* 117.1. (9)

I too assert that prayers and thanksgivings, offered by men who live up to them, are the only perfect sacrifices pleasing to God. In accordance with their tradition, the Christians know only these sacrifices. They offer them when they celebrate the Meal of Remembrance by eating and drinking. In this way they commemorate the suffering which the Son of God endured for their sake.

Justin, *Dialogue with Trypho the Jew* 117.3.               (10)

We assert that God has no need of bloody sacrifices, libations, and incense. We honor Him by prayer and by words of thanksgiving and by praising His Name whenever we consume anything. We have realized that the only homage truly worthy of Him is not to consume by fire the things He created for our nourishment  but rather to consecrate them to our use and to the use of those who need them  and to thank Him for these things by sending up homage to Him with words of prayer and with hymns. We give thanks to God for our own creation, for everything which gives life and health, for the bounties of nature, and for the changes of the seasons. We send up supplications to Him that we may rise in incorruption through faith in Him.

Justin, *First Apology* 13.                                (11)

After he has been immersed, we lead the one who has become a believer and united with us to the place where the brothers, as we call ourselves, are assembled. There, all together, we pray fervently for ourselves, for the one who has been "enlightened," and for all others everywhere in the world. We pray that after we have recognized the truth we may be made worthy through our actions to prove ourselves good stewards and keepers of that which has been entrusted to us so that we may attain eternal salvation. At the end of the prayer we greet one another with a kiss.

Then bread and a cup containing water mixed with wine are brought to the overseer of the brothers. He takes both and gives praise and glory to the Father of the Universe through the name of the Son and of the Holy Spirit. He offers copious thanks that by Him we have been deemed worthy to receive these gifts. At the end of the prayer and the thanksgiving all the people assembled give their assent, saying, "Amen." The word "Amen" in Hebrew means "So be it!" When the overseer has given thanks and all the people have assented, those we call table stewards [deacons] give each one present some of the bread and wine with water that was accepted with thanksgiving and take some of it to the homes of those who are absent.

This meal we call Thanksgiving [Eucharist]. No one is allowed to take part in it except he who believes that the things we teach are true, who has received the bath for the forgiveness of sins and for the new birth, and who lives according to the teachings handed down by Christ. For we do not partake of this meal as if it were ordinary food or ordinary drink. Rather, through the Logos of God, our Healing Savior Jesus Christ became flesh and accepted flesh and blood for the sake of our salvation. Hence, as we have been taught, the food taken with thanksgiving in the words of prayer He handed down to us is the flesh and blood of that Christ who became flesh. Our flesh and blood are strengthened by this eating and drinking for our transformation.

The apostles in their own memoirs, which are called Gospels, handed down as they were commanded:

> Jesus took the bread, gave thanks, and said, "Do this in remembrance of me. This is my body." In the same way he took the cup, gave thanks, and said, "This is my blood." And he gave it to them alone.

It was the invention of evil demons that something similar could be done in the mystery-cult of Mithras in aping mimicry, namely, by giving bread and a cup of water to the initiates with the corresponding words in their secret initiation rites. You know this quite well, or you can easily find out.

We constantly remind each other of these things. Those among us who are well-to-do support all those who are in need! We always hold together. For everything we receive, we praise the Creator of the Universe through His Son Jesus Christ and through the Holy Spirit.

On the day named after the sun, we hold a meeting in one place for all who live in the cities or the country nearby. The Memoirs of the Apostles or the Writings of the Prophets are read as long as time permits. When the reader has finished, the overseer gives a talk urging and inviting us to imitate all these good examples. Then we all stand up together and send up our prayers. As said before, bread is brought and wine and water after we have finished our prayer. The overseer likewise sends up prayers and thanksgivings with all his might. The people give their consent by saying, "Amen." Now the distribution takes place, and each one receives what has been accepted with thanksgiving. Those who are absent receive their share through the table stewards [deacons].

Those who are well-off and freewillingly wish to do so contribute as much as each one wants to. What is collected is deposited with the overseer. He uses it for the care of orphans and widows, for those who are suffering want arising from illness or any other cause, for prisoners, and for travelers staying with us for a short time. Briefly, he provides for all who are in need in the town.

We all choose Sunday for our communal gathering because it is the first day, on which God created the universe by transforming darkness and primal matter, and because Jesus Christ,

our Healing Savior, rose from the dead on the same day. For
they crucified Him on the day before the day of Saturn; on
the day after the day of Saturn, that is on the Sunday, He
appeared to His apostles and disciples and taught them
these things which we have put before you also for your
consideration.

Justin Martyr, *First Apology* 65-67, about A.D. 138.    (12)

Let one who has been chosen by all the people be ordained
as overseer. When he has been nominated and has pleased
all, the whole people, with the elders and the overseers present,
shall assemble on the Lord's Day. With the agreement of all,
they shall lay their hands upon him. The elders shall stand
by in silence. All shall pray silently in their hearts that the
Holy Spirit may descend upon him  while, at the request of
all, one of the overseers present lays his hand on the one who
has been chosen to be overseer and prays:

> Pour forth now that power which comes from Thee, the
> Spirit of leadership! Thou gavest it to Thy holy apostles
> through Thy beloved servant Jesus Christ. They estab-
> lished the Church in every place that became Thy
> sanctuary that Thy Name be praised and thanked un-
> ceasingly!

All shall offer the kiss of peace to the one who has been
ordained. The serving brothers [deacons] shall bring to him
the offered gifts, on which he shall lay his hands with all the
elders. The thanksgiving follows now, beginning with an
antiphon with the Church.

When an elder is ordained, the overseer shall lay his hand
upon his head. The elders also shall touch him and pray in the
same way as it was said above concerning the overseer:

> God, Father of my Lord Jesus Christ, look upon this
> Thy slave, and impart to him the Spirit of grace and

counsel, ... as Thou didst command Moses to choose
elders, whom Thou didst fill with Thy Spirit, which Thou
gavest to Thy servant.

When a serving brother is ordained he receives the laying
on of hands by the overseer. On a confessor who has been
imprisoned, hands shall not be laid for the service of deacon
or that of elder, for he already has this honor by virtue of his
confession. A widow shall not be ordained but chosen. ... The
appointment shall be by the Word; the widow's task is that
of prayer, which is the task common to all. A reader shall be
appointed by the overseer giving him the Book. Hands shall not
be laid upon a consecrated virgin, for it is her decision alone
that makes her a virginal person. If anyone says, "I have received a gift of healing or knowledge or tongues by revelation,"
hands shall not be laid upon him. He will have to prove it.

Hippolytus, *The Apostolic Tradition,* chapters 2, 4, 8–15
⟨see also B. S. Easton, pp. 33–35, 37–41⟩.　　　　　　(13)

P rayer used with the laying on of hands and anointing:
　　Come, Thou holy Name of Christ
　　Which is high above every name;
　　Come, Thou power of the Most High and perfect mercy;
　　Come, Thou highest gift. ...
　　Come, messenger of the five members:
　　Understanding, thought, insight, consideration,
　　　　　　　　judgment.
　　Impart Thyself to these young people!
　　Come, holy power of the Spirit.
　　Purify their reins and heart,
　　And seal them in the name of the Father
　　And of the Son and of the Holy Spirit.

*Acts of Thomas* II.27.　　　　　　　　　　　　　(14)

For the expulsion of demons: O nature that did not turn to higher things! O fountain of the soul that persists in defilement. Seat of corruption, full of darkness! O death dancing among those that are yours! O tree without fruit, full of smoldering fire! O tree that bears nothing but coal for fruit! O forest of trees full of poisonous shoots! Consort of unbelief, you have disclosed who you are! With your children you are convicted. The means to honor greater things you do not know, for you do not possess it. Your end is like your root and your nature. Detach yourself from those who are waiting for the Lord! Depart from their thoughts and from their minds! Depart from their souls and their bodies! Detach yourself from their actions, their life, their behavior; depart from their activities, their occupations, their plans! Depart from their resurrection to God, from their fastings, from their prayers, from their holy baptism, from their Meal of Thanksgiving, from their daily food and drink, from their clothing, from their love, from their rest, from their continence, and from their justice. From all these, most wicked Satan, hated by God, shall Jesus Christ our God banish you, He who has the power over those who are like you and bear your stamp.

We glorify Thy Name that has turned us away from error and from pitiless lust. We testify to Thy goodness abundantly revealed to us by Thee. We praise Thy good Name, O Lord! Thou didst expose the spirits convicted by Thee! We thank Thee, O Lord Jesus Christ, that we believe in Thine immutable grace. We thank Thee, whose longing is for human nature that is saved. We thank Thee for giving us this unwavering faith that Thou alone art God, now and forever.

To Thee I call who art God alone: the One who is exceedingly great, the unutterable One, the incomprehensible One; to whom all powers of government are subject; before whom every authority bows, and before whom all that is

high falls down and remains silent; at whose voice the demons take fright; and beholding whom all creation surrenders in silent adoration.
*Acts of John* 84, 85, 79.                                        (15)

Salvation shows itself. The apostles are given Light. The Lord's Passover draws near. Burning candles are brought together and arranged fittingly. The Spirit of the Word [Logos] who teaches the saints rejoices. Through Him the Father is glorified. To Him be the glory for ever and ever! Amen.
*Letter to Diognetus* 12.                                         (16)

Through whom will the last Enemy be destroyed?
      Through Christ.  Amen.
Through whom is the sting of death destroyed?
      Through the Only Begotten.  Amen.
To whom belongs the rulership?
      It belongs to the Son.  Amen.
Through whom has everything come into being?
      Through the Firstborn.  Amen.

A Gospel fragment from the Strasbourg Coptic Papyrus, 1900.
                                                            (17)

Thou art our Savior.
      Thou art our Helper.
Thou . . . our Refuge.
Thou art our Support.
Do not forsake us,
But deliver us from every peril.
Save us and our entreaties,
For Thine is the power, O Holy Ruler,
Whose name is Lord,

Who dwells in the Heavens
And looks down upon what is low.
Honor be to Him for evermore.
Amen.
All things sanctify Thee everywhere.
With all those who sanctify Thy Name,
Accept us, who sanctify Thee too,
As we call to Thee:
Holy, holy, holy is the Lord of Sabaoth!
Heaven and earth are full of Thy glory!
Fill us also with Thy glory.
Deign to send down Thy Holy Spirit
On these gifts of Thy creation, ...
And make the bread to be the body
Of our Lord and Savior Jesus Christ,
And the cup to be the blood
Of the New Covenant!

We proclaim Thy death
And we confess Thy resurrection.
Grant us to share in Thy gift
To bring the power of the Holy Spirit,
To confirm and increase faith,
To give hope for future eternal life
Through our Lord Jesus Christ,
Through whom we glorify Thee, O Father,
With the Holy Spirit, for ever and ever.

Liturgical Papyrus from Dêr-Balyzeh. (18)

The Lord be with you!
And with thy spirit.
Lift up your hearts!
We lift them up to the Lord.

Let us give thanks to the Lord!
This is fitting and right.

We thank Thee, O God, through Thy beloved servant Jesus
Christ. Thou didst send Him to us in these last days, a
Healing Savior and Redeemer and the messenger of Thy
will. Thou didst make all things through Him, the Logos
proceeding from Thee. In Him Thou art rejoicing. From
Heaven Thou didst send Him into the virgin's womb. Dwelling within her, He became flesh, was manifested as Thy Son,
born of the Holy Spirit and of the virgin. He fulfilled Thy
will and prepared a Holy People for Thee. He spread out
His hands when He suffered so that He might set free from
suffering those who trusted in Thee. He was delivered to suffer
freewillingly so that He might put an end to death, break
the bonds of the Devil, tread the Underworld underfoot, give
light to the righteous, set up a boundary, and proclaim
resurrection!

He took bread, thanking Thee, and He said, "Take, eat,
this is my body which will be broken for you!" Likewise, He
also took the cup with the words, "This is my blood, which
will be shed for you. As often as you do this, you do it in
remembrance of me." Remembering therefore His death and
His resurrection, we offer this bread and this cup to Thee,
giving thanks to Thee that in this Thou hast counted us
worthy to stand before Thee and to serve Thee as priests.

We ask Thee to send Thy Holy Spirit as a gift to Thy Holy
Church. Make us one through this! Grant to all who partake
in Thy holy things that they may be filled with the Holy
Spirit so that their faith may be strengthened in the truth
and we may praise and glorify Thee through Thy servant
Jesus Christ through whom be glory and power to Thee

with the Holy Spirit in the Holy Church both now and throughout the ages for ever and ever.

Hippolytus, *The Apostolic Tradition* 4 ⟨see also Easton, pp. 35–36⟩. (19)

O Jesus, hidden mystery that has been revealed to us, Thou art He who has disclosed to us the rich treasury of mysteries. Thou hast said to me words which have set me on fire and which I can speak of to no others.

Jesus! Man! Slain, dead, buried! Jesus! God! Out of God, and Redeemer! Thou who givest life to the dead and health to the sick! O Jesus, Thou who art needy like one of the poor and dost redeem like one who has no need! Thou who dost catch fish for breakfast and dinner and who dost satisfy all with a little bread, Jesus, who dost rest from the toil of the journey like a man and walk upon the waves like a God.

O Jesus Most High! Voice of the rising sun, mighty in perfect compassion! Healing Savior of all, right hand of the Light. Mighty hand, which overthrows the Evil One by revealing his nature and by gathering all of his kind into one place. Thou, Only Begotten, who dost manifest Thyself in the most various forms. Thou, who art the Only Begotten of many brothers! God from God Most High, and man despised until now!

O Jesus Christ, who dost not forget us in those things for which we call upon Thee; who art become the source of all life for the whole of mankind; Thou who for our sake wast judged and imprisoned, whereas by Thee are all those who are captive made free; Thou who hast been called a deceiver, whereas by Thee have all those who belong to Thee been delivered from deception: I beseech Thee for these who stand here and believe in Thee, for they long to receive Thy gifts. Joyfully they set their hope in Thy help. They take refuge in Thy majesty. Their ears are open to hear from us the words which are spoken to them. May Thy peace come and dwell in them! Renew them by purifying them from their former deeds so that they strip off the old man with his deeds and put on the new man, who is now proclaimed to them by me.

O Jesus, who hast made us worthy to take part in the Thanksgiving Meal of Thy holy body and blood, see, we make bold to approach Thy Meal of Thanksgiving and to call upon Thy Holy Name: Come, and have community with us!
*Acts of Thomas* V.47-49.                                    (20)

W e will entreat the Creator of the universe with constant prayer and supplication that He may keep intact the counted number of His elect in the whole world through His beloved servant Jesus Christ. Through Him He called us from darkness to light, from ignorance to the knowledge of His glorious Name.

O Lord, Thou hast called us to hope on Thy Name,
Thou, the Origin of all creation!
Thou didst open the eyes of our hearts
To know Thee,
Who alone art the Highest on High.
Thou art the Holy One who dwells among the holy,
Who humbles the pride of the lofty,
Who brings to naught the designs of the nations,
Who raises the lowly and humbles the lofty,
Who makes rich and makes poor,
Who kills, saves, and makes alive!
Thou, the only benefactor of spirits
And the God of all flesh,
Who looks into the chasms

And sees the works of man,
Helper of those in danger,
Savior of those in despair,
Creator and Overseer of every spirit,
Thou who dost multiply the nations on earth
And choosest from them those who love Thee
Through Jesus Christ, Thy beloved servant,
Through whom Thou hast taught us,
Made us holy, and honored us:
We beseech Thee, O Ruler,
Be Thou our helper and defender.
Save those who are in distress among us!
Have mercy on those who are disheartened!
Raise up those who have fallen,
Show Thyself to those who entreat Thee,
And heal those who are sick!
Turn back those who stray from Thy people,
Feed the hungry,
Free our captives,
Strengthen the weak,
Encourage those who lose heart!
All nations shall know
That Thou alone art God
And Jesus Christ is Thy servant
And we are Thy people and the sheep of Thy pasture.
Thou hast made manifest
The everlasting order of the universe
Through the working of powerful forces.
Thou, Lord, hast created the earth,
Thou who art faithful in all generations.
Thou art righteous in Thy judgments,
Marvelous in Thy strength and majesty.
Thou art wise in creating

And full of wisdom in maintaining what is created;
Thou art gracious in what can be seen
And faithful to those who trust in Thee.
Merciful and compassionate One,
Forgive us our lawlessness and unrighteousness,
Our trespasses and our failings.
Reckon not all the sins of Thy servants and handmaids,
But cleanse us with the cleansing of Thy truth!
And guide our steps
That we may live and act
In holiness and righteousness of heart
And do those things which are good and bring joy
To Thee and to our rulers.
Yes, O Ruler, let Thy face shine upon us
And bring us salvation and peace
That we may be sheltered by Thy mighty hand
And saved from all sin by Thine uplifted arm.
Deliver us from those who hate us without cause.
Grant harmony and peace to us
And to all the inhabitants of the earth,
Just as Thou didst grant it to our fathers
When they called upon Thee reverently in faith and in
        truth.
Grant it to us so that we shall be obedient
To Thine almighty and glorious Name.
Grant this also to those
Who rule and govern us on earth.

   Thou, O Ruler, hast given them the power of government through Thy majesty and unutterable might so that we, acknowledging the honor and dignity given to them by Thee, may be subject to them without opposing Thy will in anything. Grant to them, O Lord, health, peace, concord, and firmness so that they may administer without offense the Government which Thou hast given them! For Thou, O Heavenly Ruler, King of the Ages, hast given to the children of men glory and dignity and authority over the things which are on earth. Do Thou, O Lord, direct their counsels according to that which is good and pleasing in Thy sight so that they may with reverence exercise the authority Thou hast granted them, peacefully and benevolently, without violence, and thus obtain Thy mercy.

To Thee who alone hast power to do these and many more good things to us, to Thee we give praise through the High Priest and protector of our souls, Jesus Christ, through whom be glory and majesty to Thee now and from generation to generation and into all the ages forever. Amen.

*First Letter of Clement* 59-61. (21)

My Lord and my God!
Companion of Thy servants!
Guide and leader of those who believe in Thee!
Refuge and repose of the oppressed!
Hope of the poor and deliverer of the captives!
Physician of the souls laid low in sickness!
Healing Savior of every creature!
Thou who dost give new life to the world
And strength to the souls.
Thou who dost know future events
And dost accomplish them through us!
Thou, O Lord, who dost reveal hidden mysteries
And disclose secret words!
Thou, O Lord, art the planter of the good tree!
By Thy hands are all good works brought forth.
Thou art Lord,
Thou art He who is in all,
Who penetrates all,

Who dwells in all Thy works
And is manifest in all their workings:
O Jesus Christ, Son of Mercy!
Perfect Healing Savior,
Christ, Son of the Living God,
Undaunted Power, who has overthrown the Enemy!
Voice which is heard by spiritual princes,
Which calls into action all their mighty ones!
Ambassador sent from on High,
Who descended even into the Underworld,
Who opened its doors and led out
Those who had long been shut up in the chamber of
        darkness
And showed them the way that leads up to the heights:
I call to Thee, Lord Jesus!

*Acts of Thomas* I.10.                               (22)

Glory to Thee,
  O merciful and surrendered One!
Glory to Thee,
O wise Word!
Glory to Thy mercy,
Which is poured out upon us!
Glory to Thy compassionate love,
Which is spread out over us!
Glory to Thy majesty,
Which for our sake came down low!
Glory to Thy most exalted rulership,
Which for our sake humbled itself!
Glory to Thy power,
Which for our sake became weak!
Glory to Thy divinity,
Which for our sake appeared in the likeness of men!

Glory to Thy manhood,
Which for our sake died to make us live!
Glory to Thy resurrection from the dead,
Which brings resurrection and peace to our souls!
Glory and honor to Thy ascent into Heaven,
Through which Thou hast opened for us
The way up to the heights!
Thou didst promise us that we shall sit at Thy right hand
And with Thee judge the twelve tribes of Israel.
Thou art the Heavenly Word of the Father,
Thou art the hidden light of clarity.
Thou art He who shows the way of truth,
Who drives away darkness
And blots out error!

*Acts of Thomas* VIII.80.                                    (23)


Who is like Thee, O God,
    Who dost withhold from none
Thy tender love and Thy glowing zeal?
Who is like Thee in tenderness of heart,
Thou who hast delivered Thy creatures from evil?
Life, that has conquered death!
Peace, that has ended toil!
Glory to the Only Begotten of the Father!
Glory to the Compassionate One,
Who was sent out of compassion!
To Thee be glory,
Who lovest compassion!
To Thee be glory,
Name of the Messiah!
To Thee be glory,
O power that dwellest in Christ!

*Acts of Thomas* X.122, 132.                                (24)

Hope of the weak and confidence of the poor!
Refuge and lodging of the weary!
Voice that came forth from on high!
Comforter who dwells in our midst!
Shelter and haven of those
Who journey through dark countries!
Physician who heals without payment!
Thou who among men was crucified for many!
Thou who with mighty power descended into the
        Underworld,
The sight of whom the princes of death could not endure!
Thou who with great glory ascended!
Thou dost gather all those who take refuge in Thee;
Thou dost prepare the way.
In Thy footsteps followed all whom Thou hast redeemed.
Thou hast led them to Thy flock
And united them with Thy sheep,
O Son of mercies!
Thou who art the Son art sent out of love to men
From the perfect Fatherland above,
Lord of undefiled possessions,
Who serves Thy servants so that they may live!
Thou hast filled creation with Thy riches,
O poor One who was in need
And hungered for forty days,
Thou hast satisfied the thirsty with Thy good things:

Be Thou with these people,
Gather them into Thy sheepfold
And unite them with Thy number!
Be Thou their guide in the land of error!
Be Thou their physician in the land of sickness!
Be Thou their rest in the land of the weary!

Make them holy in an impure land!
Be Thou the physician of their bodies and souls,
Make them Thy holy temple,
And let Thy Holy Spirit dwell in them!
*Acts of Thomas* XIII.156.                                    (25)

G lory to God in the highest Heaven,
    And peace on earth to the men
With whom He is well pleased.
We praise Thee, we exalt Thee,
We glorify Thee, we worship Thee
Through Thy great High Priest,
Thou, the true God,
The only One who is uncreated,
The only One who is inaccessible.
We praise Thee for the sake of Thy great glory!
O Lord, heavenly King,
O God, Father Almighty, Lord, God,
Father of Christ the immaculate Lamb,
Who takes the sins of the world upon Himself:
Accept my entreaty,
Thou who sittest upon the throne
Above the cherubim.
For Thou alone art holy,
Thou alone art Lord,
God and Father of Jesus Christ,
The God of all creation,
And our King.
To Thee be glory,
Honor, and worship through Him.
Praise is Thy due,
Honor is Thy due,
Glory is Thy due,

O God and Father,
Through the Son
In the Holy Spirit
For ever and ever.   Amen.
Hymn in the *Apostolic Constitutions* VII.47,48.          (26)

Friendly Light of the holy splendor
    Of Thine eternal Father above,
In the blessed heights of Heaven:
O Jesus Christ!
At the setting of the sun
When we see the evening light,
We praise the Father and the Son
And God's Holy Spirit.
Worthy art Thou that we praise Thee
At all times with reverence,
O Son of God, Giver of life!
Creation therefore pays Thee homage.

Hymn, handed down as very old, in Basil and in other manuscripts.                                                (27)

Nature trembled and said with astonishment:
    What new mystery is this?
The Judge is judged and remains silent;
The invisible One is seen and does not hide Himself;
The incomprehensible One is comprehended and does
        not resist;
The unmeasurable One is measured and does not struggle;
The One beyond suffering suffers and does not avenge
        Himself;
The immortal One dies and does not refuse death.
What new mystery is this?
Melito of Sardis, Fragment 13.                          (28)

The primal element of all things, the first principle of
being and life, is the Spirit.

The second, poured forth from the first son of the Spirit,
is chaos.

The third, that received being and form from both, is the
soul.

And it is like the timid deer
Which is hunted on earth
By Death, who incessantly
Tests his power upon it.
Today it is in the Kingdom of Light,
Tomorrow it is thrown into misery,
Plunged deep into pain and tears.
Straying and lost in the maze
It seeks for the exit in vain.
But Jesus said, "O Father, look
Upon this tormented being,
How it roams the earth in sorrow,
Far away from Thy breath.
It seeks to flee the bitter chaos
Yet does not know the way of escape.
Send me down, O Father, to save it.
With the seals in hand I will descend,
Striding through the aeons,
Opening all the mysteries,
Revealing all the forms of gods.
The secret of the holy way—
I call it knowledge—I will bring."

Hippolytus, *Philosophumena* V.10. (29)

As the breath of the wind sweeps through the harp
And the chords sing,
So the breath of the Lord's Spirit

Sweeps through my members,
And I sing in His love.

For He destroys what is false
And all that is hostile.
Thus it has been from the beginning
And shall be to the end:
Nothing shall stand against Him,
And nothing shall resist Him.

The Lord has multiplied His knowledge
And is eager that we know
What His grace has given us.
Thus we give praise to His Name,
And our spirits sing praises
To His Holy Spirit.

A little stream sprang up
And became a river mighty and broad.
It swept away everything and broke it up
And tore down the temple.
No bulwarks or structures could check it,
Nor dams built by the art of man.

It streamed over the face of the whole earth
And filled everything;
All the thirsty on earth drank therefrom,
And their thirst was quenched and slaked,
For the drink was the gift of the Most High.

Blessed therefore are the servants of that drink,
To whom His water was entrusted,
For they freshened the dry lips
And quickened the flagging will.

The souls that were near departing,
They snatched away from death,
And they set up straight the members that had fallen.
They gave strength to their weakness
And light to their eyes,
For they all knew one another in the Lord
And were redeemed by the eternal water
Of immortality.
Hallelujah!

Ode of Solomon 6.                                    (30)

As the passion of anger toward a child,
So is the passion of joy toward the beloved,
Reaping her fruit unhindered.
My joy is the Lord,
My passion is toward Him.
This path of mine is beautiful,
For the Lord is my helper.

In full measure
He revealed Himself to me
In His simplicity,
For His kindness made His greatness small.
He became like me
That I might grasp Him.
He appeared like me in form
That I might put Him on.
I had no fear when I saw Him
Because He had mercy on me.
He became like my own nature
That I might comprehend Him.
His form was the same as mine
That I might not turn back from Him.

The Father of knowledge
Is the Logos of knowledge.
He who created wisdom
Is wiser than His servants.
And He who created me knew before I was
What I should do when I came into being.
Therefore He had mercy on me with rich compassion,
And He granted me to ask of Him
And to receive from His nature.

For He it is that is incorruptible,
The fullness of the ages and the Father thereof.
He gave and revealed Himself
To them that are His
That they might know Him who made them
And not suppose that they came of themselves.

He blazed a way for knowledge,
He widened and extended it and brought it to perfection.
He put the signs of His light upon it
And His footsteps, from beginning to end.

By Him it was prepared,
And it shone forth in the Son
To penetrate creation for its redemption,
To make the Most High known among His saints,
To proclaim the good tidings of the coming of the Lord
To the singers of psalms
That they might go forth to meet Him and play to Him
With joy, on harps of many voices.

They shall come before Him and see with their own eyes,
And they shall be seen before His countenance.

They shall praise the Lord for His love
Because He is near and allows them to see Him.

Hate shall be rooted out from the earth,
It shall be locked away together with envy,
For ignorance is now destroyed,
The knowledge of the Lord is come.

Therefore singers shall sing the grace of the Most High
And shall bring their songs before Him.
Their hearts shall be bright as the day
And their voices as beautiful as the Lord!
Nothing that lives shall be without knowledge or dumb,
For He gave a mouth to His creation,
A voice and mouth to open before Him
And to praise Him.

Confess His might,
Proclaim His grace!
Hallelujah!

Ode of Solomon 7. (31)


Open your ears,
And I will speak to you.
Give me your souls
That I may also give my soul to you:
The Word of the Lord and His decrees,
The holy plan that He has formed
Concerning His Anointed,
For it is upon the will of the Lord
That your redemption is built.
His thought is life everlasting,
And your perfection shall not pass away.

Become rich in God the Father,
And receive the thoughts of the Most High!
Be brave, and let His grace redeem you!
For I announce peace to you  His saints,
And all who hear it shall not fall in war,
And again, those who understand it shall not be lost,
And those who accept it shall not be ashamed.

An everlasting crown is truth—
Blessed are they who set it on their heads!
And it is a precious jewel.
Wars were even waged to win this crown.
Righteousness won it and gave it to you.
So put on the crown in firm alliance with the Lord!
All those who conquered shall be written in His Book,
For your own victory is your scribe
That chooses you beforehand
And wills that you shall be redeemed.
Hallelujah!

Ode of Solomon 9.                                    (32)

My heart was circumcised and its flower appeared.
Grace sprang up in it
And brought forth fruit for the Lord.
For the Most High cut me by His Holy Spirit
And opened my reins toward Him.
He filled me in His love
And His circumcision became my salvation.

I hastened on the way of His peace,
On the way of truth.
From beginning to end
I received His knowledge.

I was firmly established on the rock of truth
Where He himself set me up.

Speaking waters drew close to my lips
Abundantly from the fount of the Lord.

I drank, and became drunk
With the waters of immortality.
Yet my drunkenness was not one of ignorance,
For I left vanity behind.

I turned to the Most High, my God,
And became rich with His gift.
I left folly lying on the earth,
I stripped it off and threw it from me.
The Lord renewed me with His raiment
And created me by His light.

From above He refreshed me with immortality
So I became like a land
That blossoms and rejoices in its fruit.
Like the sun upon the face of the earth,
The Lord gave light to mine eyes,
And my face received the dew;
My breath delighted in the precious odors of the Lord.

He led me into His Paradise,
Where the pleasure of the Lord abounds.
I threw myself before the Lord
For the sake of His glory, and I said:
"Blessed are they that are planted in Thy land,
That have a place in Thy Paradise,
That grow like the growth of Thy trees
And have stepped from darkness into light!

"Behold, all Thy workers are fair
And do good works.
From unkindness they turn to Thy graciousness.

"They cast off the bitterness of the trees
When they were planted in Thy land.
Thus everything became a warning sign from Thee,
An everlasting memorial for Thy faithful servants.
For there is much room in Thy Paradise,
And there is nothing that is useless therein,
But everything is filled with Thy fruits!"

Glory to Thee, O God, eternal delight of Paradise!
Hallelujah!

Ode of Solomon 11.                                          (33)


The womb of the virgin received;
She conceived in her womb and gave birth,
And the virgin became a mother in great longing.
She travailed and bore a Son without pain,
For it would not have been seemly otherwise.
And she did not call for a midwife,
For He took away her pains.
She brought Him forth as a man, willingly.
She gave birth in revelation,
She gained in great power,
She loved in redemption,
She guarded in kindness
And revealed in glory.
Hallelujah!

Ode of Solomon 19.                                          (34)

He who leads me down from on high
And leads me up from the regions below,
Who captures the things that are between
And makes them subject to me,
Who scatters my foes and adversaries
And gives me power to loose fetters,
Who by my hands slew the dragon with seven heads
And set me upon His root
That I might destroy the dragon's seed:
Thou hast been with me and helped me,
Thy Name was about me in every place.
Thy right hand destroyed the venom of the blasphemer,
Thy hand leveled the path for Thy believers.
Thou didst choose them from out of the graves
And separate them from the corpses.
Thou didst take the dry bones
And clothe them with bodies.
Thou didst give power of life to the motionless,
And immortality became Thy way and Thy countenance.

Thou didst lead Thine age to corruption,
Thus to dissolve creation and to renew it
And to make Thy Rock the foundation of the universe.
Thy Kingdom hast Thou built upon it
And it became the dwelling-place of Thy saints!
Hallelujah!

Ode of Solomon 22.                                          (35)

Joy is of the saints:
Who shall put it on
But they alone?
Grace is of the elect:

Who shall receive it
But they who have trusted in it from the very beginning?
Love is of the elect:
Who shall put it on
But they who possessed it from the very beginning?
Walk in the knowledge of the Lord,
And you shall know the rich grace of the Lord
To His joy and to the perfection of His knowledge!

His plan of salvation was like an epistle:
His will came down from on high
And was sent like an arrow
Which is shot mightily from the bow.
And many hands fell upon the letter
To seize it and take it and read it.
But it escaped from their fingers,
And they were frightened of it
And of the seal upon it.
Because they had no strength to break the seal,
For the power upon the seal was greater than they.
But those who had seen it followed the epistle
To discover where it would come to rest
And who would read it
And who would hear it.

But a wheel caught it,
And the letter stayed on the wheel.
From then on there was with it
The sign of the Kingdom and of Government.
And everything that shook the wheel
Was mowed down and cut off by it.
And it gathered up all that was good for a weir,
It dammed up the streams and passed through them.

It uprooted many forests
And blazed a broad trail.

Thus the Lordship went down to the feet,
For to the feet the wheel had rolled,
And that which had come upon it
Was a letter of testament.
And when all the lands had gathered,
The Ruler was revealed
And was seen in His domain,
The true Son of the Father Most High.
He inherited all and took possession of all.
But the designs of the many were thwarted.
All the unfaithful rushed forward and fled,
And the persecutors were obliterated and wiped out.

But the letter was a great tablet
Written all over by the finger of God.
And upon it stood the Name of the Father
And of the Son and of the Holy Spirit,
To rule for ever and ever.
Hallelujah!
Ode of Solomon 23. (36)

The Lord is my hope.
In Him I shall not be confounded.
According to His honor He made me
And gave me according to His goodness.
According to His love He lifted me up
And exalted me according to His great glory.

He brought me out of the depths of Hell
And snatched me from the jaws of death.

He threw my foes to the ground
And justified me in His grace,
For I believed in the Lord's Anointed.
Therefore He appeared to me as the Lord
And showed me His sign.
He led me into His light
And gave me the scepter of His power
To subdue the designs of the nations
And bring down the power of the mighty,
To wage war by His Word,
And to win victory by His power.

The Lord threw down my enemy by His Word;
He became like chaff swept away by the wind.
I gave honor to the Most High,
For He exalted His Servant
And the Son of His handmaid.
Hallelujah!

Ode of Solomon 29.                                    (37)

We will praise the Lord, we all His children,
    And proclaim the truth of His faith.
By Him His sons are known,
Therefore we sing in His love.

We rejoice in the Lord through His grace
And receive life through His Christ.
For He caused a great day to shine upon us,
A wonderful day, because He gave us of His glory.
Therefore we will all join together in the name of the Lord
And praise Him in His goodness.
Our faces shall shine in His light,
And our hearts shall meditate in His love.

By day and by night let us exult
In jubilation about the Lord.
The Savior is come, who quickens our souls
And does not reject them.
The Man who humbled Himself
And was exalted for the sake of His righteousness,
The Son of the Most High,
He is come in the perfection of His Father.
And light has arisen from the Logos,
Light that was in Him from the beginning.

The Christ is One in truth
And was known before the foundation of the world
That He might quicken the souls forever
To establish the truth of His Name.

A new song of those who love Him,
Hallelujah!

Ode of Solomon 41.                                              (38)

I stretched out my hands and came to the Lord,
For the stretching out of hands is His sign,
And my stretching out is the outstretched Wood
That is set up for the righteous on His way.

I became of no use to those who knew me,
For I am hidden from those that do not take hold of me,
But I am come to those who love me.
Dead are all my persecutors,
But those seek me who believe that I live.
For I rose from the dead and am with them,
And I speak through their mouths.

I cast out those that persecute them,
And on them I threw the yoke of my love.

Like the arm of the bridegroom on the bride,
So my yoke lies on them who love me.
And like the canopy over the bed in the house of the
        bridegroom,
So is my love over those who believe in me.

I was not rejected though it seemed that I was.
I was not lost though they were troubled for me.
Hell saw me and became powerless.
Death spewed me out and many with me.
Gall and bitterness I have been to him,
And I went down with him to the utmost depths.
His head and his feet became limp,
He could not bear to see my face.
I created a Church of the living among his dead,
And I spoke to them with living lips.
Because my Word shall not be in vain,
Those who had died ran toward me  crying,
And said, "Have mercy upon us, O Son of God,
And do with us according to Thy grace!
Bring us out of the bonds of darkness,
Open the door to us by which we come out to Thee!
For we see that our death does not touch Thee.
Let us also be redeemed, together with Thee,
For Thou art our Redeemer!"

And I heard their voice,
I took their faith to my heart,
And I set my Name upon their heads,

For they are free men and they are mine.
Hallelujah!

Ode of Solomon 42.                                              (39)

G lory to Thee, Father.
Glory to Thee, Word.
Glory to Thee, Grace.
Glory to Thee, Spirit.
Glory to Thee, Holy One,
Glory to Thy glory.
We praise Thee, Father.
We thank Thee, O Light
In whom there is no darkness.


And that for which we give thanks is announced by Him:
I will be saved, and I will save.
I will be loosed, and I will loose.
I will be wounded, and I will wound.
I will be born, and I will give birth.
I will eat, and I will be eaten.
I will hear, and I will be heard.
I will be thought, being wholly thought.
I will be washed, and I will wash.
Grace leads the dance, I will make music,
You shall all dance in a ring.
I will lament, you shall all beat your breasts.
I will flee, and I will stay.
I will adorn, and I will be adorned.
I will be united, and I will unite.
I have no house, and I have houses.
I have no home, and I have homes.
I have no temple, and I have temples.

A lamp I am to thee that dost behold me.
A mirror I am to thee that dost perceive me.
A door I am to thee that dost knock at me.
A way I am to thee, a traveler.
Join thee now unto my dancing!
Dance Hymn. *Acts of John* 94, 95.                          (40)

O bridle of racing young horses,
   Wing of soaring birds,
Safe rudder of sailing boats,
Shepherd of the royal lambs!
Unite Thy simple children
That they may sing Thee praises
In holiness and clearness,
With consecrated lips,
O Christ, Thou leader of youth,
King of Thy holy people.
Almighty Word of the Father Most High,
Invincible stronghold of wisdom,
Eternal helper in anguish and fear,
O Jesus, immortal One,
Savior of mortal men,
Thou art the ploughing shepherd,
The steering helmsman Thou art,
Thou art the heavenly pinion
Of Thy surrendered people.
And from the sea of evil
Dost Thou pull out and save,
O fisher of men. Thou dost lift
Pure fish from hostile seas
To a life of sweetness and joy.
O holy shepherd, lead us,

Sheep gathered by Thy Spirit,
O prince of undefiled youth!
The footsteps of Christ
Show us the way to Heaven.
O Word, eternally welling,
O aeon which never ends,
Eternal light undying,
O fount of mercy and love,
O source of all that is good!
Holy life Thou art
For those who worship God!
O Jesus, Christ, our Lord!
Thou art the heavenly milk
Flowing from the beloved breast
Of wisdom, the blessed bride.
Little children are we, receiving food
From the breast of the Spirit
With pure and childlike mouths:
With the Spirit's breath are we filled.
We sing Thee simple praises.
Hymns from upright hearts
As thanks, O Christ our King,
We owe to Thee who saved us
And brought us into life.
With undivided hearts
We follow the mighty Son,
A company of peace,
Who are begotten of Christ.
O holy, chosen band,
In unity sing praises
To God, the King of Peace!

Hymn by Clement of Alexandria, at the end of *The Tutor*.

(41)

O Lord, all-powerful God, Thou who art the Father of Thy beloved and exalted Servant, Jesus Christ! Through Him we have received the knowledge of Thee. Thou, who art the God of angels and powers and of all creation and of the whole race of the righteous who live in Thy presence: I praise Thee because Thou hast made me worthy of this day and this hour to be received among the number of the martyrs, so that I share in the cup of Thy Christ for the resurrection of soul and body to eternal life in the incorruption of the Holy Spirit. May I be accepted among their ranks today in Thy sight as a rich sacrifice giving Thee joy, as a sacrifice which Thou hast prepared and revealed beforehand and hast now fulfilled! Thou art the true God in whom there is no falsehood! For everything, therefore, I praise Thee. I praise Thee, I glorify Thee, through the eternal and heavenly High Priest, Jesus Christ, Thy beloved Servant. Through Him honor is due to Thee and to Him and to the Holy Spirit, both now and in all the ages to come.    Amen.

Polycarp's Last Prayer, from *The Martyrdom of Polycarp*, A.D. 155.                                                                (42)

# PROCLAMATION
# and
# PROPHECY

He sent the Logos to appear to the world. He was slighted by His people, proclaimed by the apostles, and accepted and believed in by the Gentiles. This is He who was from the beginning. He appeared as the new and was found to be old. He is always born anew in the hearts of the saints. He is the Eternal One, who is declared to be "the Son today." Through Him the Church is made rich. Through Him the grace which unfolds in the saints is multiplied. This grace grants understanding. It unravels mysteries. It announces the appointed times. It rejoices in the believers. Grace imparts itself to the seekers. It gives itself to those who do not break the vows of faith or transgress the boundaries set by the fathers.

Then the fear of the law is glorified, the gift of prophecy is recognized, the faith of the Gospels is firmly established, and the tradition of the apostles is preserved. The grace of the Church exults. If you do not offend this grace, you will know what the Logos speaks through the mouth of those whom He chooses and when He chooses.

*Letter to Diognetus* 11. (1)

Hear now what was prophesied about the messengers of His truth and the heralds of His appearance; the King and prophet was inspired by the prophetic Spirit to speak thus:

> One day shouts the message to the other, and one night makes it known to the next; there is no speech or call whose voice is not perceived. Their voice goes forth throughout the earth and their words to the ends of the world. He has pitched his tent in the sun, which comes forth like a bridegroom leaving his chamber, like a giant running his course with joy.

And again in another prophecy the prophetic Spirit, testifying through the same David, said that after being crucified Christ would reign as King, for he said, "Let joy rule among the nations. The Lord reigns from the Tree!"
Justin, *First Apology* 40, 41.                              (2)


They will come from east and west and sit at table with Abraham, Isaac, and Jacob in the Kingdom of Heaven. But those who were born to the Kingdom will be driven into the darkness outside." This, I confirm, is what I proclaim; for I have but one concern, to speak the truth. I have no fear of anyone even if you were to tear me to pieces this very minute.
Justin, *Dialogue with Trypho the Jew* 120.6.               (3)


When the blessed Evangelist John, the apostle, had lived in Ephesus into his extreme old age and could hardly be carried to the meetings of the Church by the disciples anymore, and when in speaking he could no longer put together many words, he would not say anything else in the different meetings but this: "Little children, love one another!" When at last the disciples and brothers present got tired of hearing

the same thing again and again, they said, "Master, why do you keep saying the same thing?" John replied with a saying worthy of him: "Because it is the Lord's command, and it is enough if it is really done."
Jerome, *Commentary on Galatians* 6:10. A.D. 387-388.   (4)

When a man loves God with all his heart and with all his strength, his mind is filled with the fear of God. He will fear no other god; but he will, since God desires it, fear the messenger who is loved by the Lord and by God himself. Whoever loves his neighbor as himself will wish for him all the good things he claims for himself, and nobody wishes evil for himself. He who loves his neighbor will ask and do for him the same things he would for himself. A man's neighbor is whoever feels and thinks as he does: *that is man.* The Word tells us so! Whoever loves God the Lord with his whole heart and with all his strength and his neighbor as himself, whose religion is fully committed to this twofold service—service to God and service to men—such a man could truly be good.
Justin, *Dialogue with Trypho the Jew* 93.2,3.        (5)

The prophet Isaiah tells us that we should not, as some think, love only our own people: "Say to those that hate and curse you, 'You are our brothers!'" And the Gospel says, "Love your enemies!"
Theophilus of Antioch, *To Autolycus* III.14.        (6)

Jesus commanded us to love even our enemies. This was already announced through Isaiah in several passages, which also tell of the mystery of our new birth, a new birth belonging to all people who expect Christ's coming in Jerusalem and who strive to please Him through deeds. He was crucified so that

He might come again in glory according to the Scriptures. And the tree of life which was planted in Paradise was a mysterious sign pointing to Him and so was the history of all the just.

Justin, *Dialogue with Trypho the Jew* 85.7; 86.1.　　　(7)

Now there remains nothing for us to do but to seek what we once had but have lost: to join the soul to the Holy Spirit and thereby to achieve union with Him according to God's will.

Tatian, *Address to the Greeks* 15.1.　　　(8)

Our hearts have been so thoroughly circumcised from sin that we even rejoice when going to death for the sake of the Name of that glorious Rock from which living water gushes forth into the hearts of those who love the Father of the Universe through Him, quenching the thirst of those who desire to drink the water of life.

Justin, *Dialogue with Trypho the Jew* 114.4.　　　(9)

Die to the world by renouncing the madness of its stir and bustle. Live for God by throwing off the old man in you, through recognition of His nature. We were not born to die. We die because of our own guilt. Our freedom of will has ruined us. We who were free became slaves. We were sold because of our sin. God created nothing evil. It is we who brought forth wickedness. Those who brought it about can also do away with it again.

Tatian, *Address to the Greeks* 11.5-6.　　　(10)

We were saved as though from a fire. We were liberated from our former sins, from the torment, out of the conflagration prepared for us by Satan and all his servants.

And again it is Jesus alone, the Son of God, who snatches us from their hands. He has promised that, if we keep His commandments, He will dress us in the garments laid out for us and prepare for us an eternal Kingdom.
Justin, *Dialogue with Trypho the Jew* 116.2.          (11)

We ourselves, both men and angels, shall be the cause of our condemnation if we sin and do not repent while there is time. For the sake of your salvation take this hard struggle upon yourselves and immediately put the Messiah of the Almighty God in the place of your teachers!

All who desire can share in the divine mercy. They only need to repent. The Logos foretells that they shall be happy when He says, "Blessed is the man whom the Lord does not charge with sin," which means that anyone who repents of his sins receives from God full remission of his sins.

Therefore I challenge you: I can wish nothing greater for you, gentlemen, than the recognition that every man can obtain happiness on the way shown. May you come to share fully in our confession: Jesus is the Messiah of God!
Justin, *Dialogue with Trypho the Jew* 141.1; 142.2; 141.2; 142.3.          (12)

This much we know, that before any creatures were made He proceeded from the Father in the Father's power and in accordance with His will; He is the One whom the prophets call Wisdom, Day, Sunrise, Sword, Stone, Branch, Jacob, and Israel, sometimes one, sometimes another; and we also know something else, that He became man through the virgin in order that the sin caused by the Serpent would be abolished in the same way in which it had begun.

From the virgin Mary, Jesus was born, Jesus to whom a great many passages in the Scriptures refer as we have shown.

Through Him God destroys the Serpent and those angels and men who have become like the Serpent. Through Him God frees from death those who repent of their sins and believe in Him.

Justin, *Dialogue with Trypho the Jew* 100.4,5. (13)

When the cup of our wickedness was filled, when it had become quite clear that as its reward we were to expect punishment and death, and when the time had come which God had appointed to reveal from then on His goodness and His power, then—oh, overflowing kindness and love of God!—then He did not hate us or reject us; He did not hold our evil deeds against us. Instead, He was generous and forbearing. In His compassion He took our sins upon Himself. He gave His own Son as a ransom for us: the Holy for the unholy, the Innocent for the sinners, the Righteous for the unjust, the Incorruptible for the corruptible, and the Immortal for the mortal. What else could have covered our sins except His righteousness?

In whom else could we, criminals and godless men that we are, be justified except in the Son of God alone? What wonderful exchange, what inscrutable design, what unexpected act of goodness: the injustice of the many was to be covered by the *One* who is righteous, and the righteousness of the One was to justify the many sinners! In former times He proved to us the powerlessness of our nature to gain life; now He showed that the Redeemer has the power to save what is powerless. In both ways He wanted to lead us to have faith in His goodness, to learn to know Him as our Nourisher, as our Father, Teacher, Counselor, and Physician, as Spirit, Light, Honor, Glory, Power, and Life so that we no longer need to care anxiously for food and clothing.

*Letter to Diognetus* 9. (14)

He grew up like any other man. He lived in a fitting way and granted each stage of development its due. He used all kinds of food. He was thirty years old, more or less, when John appeared, who heralded His advent and went before Him on the way of baptism.

When Jesus came to the Jordan where John was baptizing and stepped down into the water, fire blazed up in the Jordan; and when He came out of the water, the Holy Spirit lighted on Him like a dove, as the apostles of this our Christ have written. We know that He did not go to the river because He needed either the baptism or the Spirit coming down upon Him in the shape of a dove. Nor did He want to be born and to die on the Cross because He needed to do this for His own sake. On the contrary, He was concerned only with the human race, which from the time of Adam had fallen prey to death and to the deceit of the Serpent, every man having burdened himself with guilt and sin.

Then Jesus came to the Jordan. He was known as the son of Joseph the carpenter and was without comeliness as the Scriptures foretold. He was also regarded as a carpenter; for when He was among men He made the things a carpenter makes, plows and yokes, in order to teach the symbols of justice and of an active working life.

Justin, *Dialogue with Trypho the Jew* 88.2-4,8.          (15)

His sayings were brief and to the point, for He was no Sophist, but His Word was the Power of God.

Justin, *First Apology* 14.                          (16)

He has the power to drive away every importunate, evil angel and to stop him from taking possession of our souls. . . . Therefore God teaches us through His Son to fight to the utmost for justice and, when we come toward the close of life, to pray that our souls may not fall into the hands of any of these evil powers.

Jesus knew what the words of the Psalm revealed: His Father would grant all His requests and would raise Him from the dead. He urged all who fear God to praise Him, for through the mystery of the crucified Jesus, God has compassion for all the believers of every race. He stood in the midst of His brothers the apostles and convinced them that He had warned them beforehand of the suffering He would have to endure and told them that this had been predicted by the prophets. Thus, after He had risen from the dead, the apostles were gripped with remorse that they had abandoned Him when He was crucified. He praised God while He was with them, as the Memoirs of the Apostles also testify. Justin, *Dialogue with Trypho the Jew* 105.3,5; 106.1.　　　(17)

We had lost it. By means of the Tree it was made newly manifest to all, showing in itself the height, the length, the breadth, and the depth as one of the witnesses who went before us said:

> Through the extension of His hands He gathered together the two peoples to the one God. There are two hands because there are two peoples scattered to the ends of the earth. And there is one Head in the middle as there is but one God who is above all and through all and in us all.

Irenaeus, *Against Heresies* V.17.4.　　　　　　　(18)

Hail, O Cross! I have come to thee whom I know to be mine; I have come to thee because thou longest for me. I know thy mystery for the sake of which thou art set up. Thou art fastened to the world to make firm what is unstable. In one direction thou reachest up into heaven to witness to the

Spirit above. In the other direction thou art spread out to the right and to the left that thou mayest put to flight the dreadful Hostile Power and draw the world into one. In a third direction thou art planted in the earth in order to join all that is on the earth and under the earth to the things that are in Heaven.

O Cross, tool of salvation of the Most High! O Cross, banner of Christ's victory over all enemies! O Cross, planted upon the earth and bearing fruit in Heaven! O Name of the Cross, that containest the universe!

Well done, O Cross, that hast bound the whole circumference of the world! Well done, O shape full of clarity, that hast given shape to thine own unshapely outward appearance! Hail to the invisible chastisement with which thou strikest at the very nature of the many gods and drivest out from this mankind him who invented them! Well done, O Cross, that hast cast off the ruler, brought home the robber, and called the apostle to repentance, and hast not thought it beneath thy dignity to accept us.

But how long am I speaking instead of letting myself be embraced by the Cross in order that in the Cross I may be awakened to Life! Through the Cross I go into the death common to all, and depart from life.

*Acts of Andrew* (Andrew's Death).                    (19)

This Cross of light is sometimes called Logos by me for your sakes; sometimes it is called Reason, sometimes Jesus, sometimes Christ, sometimes Door, sometimes Way, sometimes Bread, sometimes Seed, sometimes Resurrection, sometimes Son, sometimes Father, sometimes Spirit, sometimes Life, sometimes Truth, sometimes Faith, sometimes Grace.

Know me, then, as the repose of the Word, the piercing of

the Word, the blood of the Word, as the wounding of the
Word, as the hanging up of the Word, as the suffering of the
Word, as the nailing on of the Word, as the death of the Word!
*Acts of John* 98,101.                                    (20)

T he crucifixion is, as the Prophet predicted, the greatest
mystery of His power and rulership. This can be shown,
too, by the things you can perceive. Consider all the things in
this world and whether they could be used without this shape
or held together without it.

The sea cannot be plowed unless this sign of victory, here
holding the sail, remains unbroken. The land is not plowed .
without it. Diggers and artisans do no work without tools
having this shape. And man's form differs from that of the
irrational animals precisely in this, that he can stand erect
with his arms spread out. The symbols you are in the habit of
using display the force of this sign: I mean the standards and
trophies you use in all your processions by which after all you
brandish, though unconsciously, the insignia of His power and
dominion.

Justin, *First Apology* 55.                                (21)

T he symbol of the scarlet cloth, too, showed the mystery
of Christ's blood. The spies sent out by Jesus [Joshua],
son of Nun, had given it to Rahab the harlot in Jericho,
instructing her to tie it outside her window. Through this
same window she lowered them to escape from their enemies.
This symbol points to the blood of Christ by which people from
every nation who were once servants of fornication and wrongdoing are freed, provided they have received forgiveness of
sin and do not sin anymore.

We should grasp such passages of the Scriptures according
to their symbolic meaning. Or shall we understand them

in the foolish way your teachers do? Must we not see in the cross with the bronze serpent the same symbolic reference to Jesus, the Crucified? Did not your people owe their victory to the fact that Moses stretched out his arms and that the name Jesus [Joshua] was given to the son of Nun?

If we see things in this light, we shall no longer be troubled by this story concerning the Lawgiver. He did not turn away from God, as you might think, urging the people to place their hope in the very Beast which caused sin and disobedience in the beginning. Rather, what the blessed prophet did and said at that time contains a wealth of wisdom and deep mystery.
Justin, *Dialogue with Trypho the Jew* 111.4; 112.2-3.   (22)

By this sign God has declared a mystery. By this He proclaims that He destroys the power of the Serpent which first caused Adam to sin; that He saves from the bites of the serpents, from the works of sin (that is, from idolatry and other wrongdoing); and that He frees all who believe in Jesus. For He wanted to go into death through the same sign, the Cross.
Justin, *Dialogue with Trypho the Jew* 94.2.   (23)

The type or sign set up against the serpents, from whose bites Israel was suffering, was erected for the finding of salvation, the salvation of those who believe that at that time it was announced to the Serpent that it would die through Him who voluntarily went to His death. This sign concerns the belief in the salvation of all who, poisoned by the Serpent's bite, flee to Him who sent His Son into the world to be crucified. Not that the prophetic Spirit taught us through Moses to submit in faith to a serpent. On the contrary, He told us that the Serpent was cursed by God from the beginning; and through Isaiah He indicated that the Serpent would be slain as the

Enemy by the great sword, that means by Christ.

Since the Word is truth, it is God's will that you should not always remain foolish and self-seeking. It is His will that you may be saved by becoming one with Christ. Him God loves. To Him God bears witness. I have proved this by giving evidence from the Holy Words of the prophets.

Justin, *Dialogue with Trypho the Jew* 91.4; 92.5.        (24)

E lisha threw a stick into the Jordan to recover the iron axe head used by sons of the prophets to cut down trees. This was for building a house in which they were to read and study the Law and the commandments of God. Through the very heavy sins we committed we too went down to the bottom and were redeemed by our Christ through His death on the Cross and through the cleansing by water. In this way we were made a house of prayer and worship.

Justin, *Dialogue with Trypho the Jew* 86.6.        (25)

G od reveals that the day will come when the demons, who already dread God's name now, will be annihilated through the crucified Jesus, to whose entire life those symbols pointed beforehand; that because of His working, all the powers and kingdoms will look at Him with dread; and that the believers in Christ among men everywhere will be recognized as God-fearing men and bearers of peace.

Justin, *Dialogue with Trypho the Jew* 131.5.        (26)

I f it had not been ordained for Christ to suffer and if the prophets had not foretold that He would be brought to death by the sins of the people, that He would be reviled, scourged, counted among the sinners, and led as a lamb to the slaughter, one would indeed be justified in feeling astonished. Seeing, however, that these things so clearly mark Him

out and reveal Him to all the world, we had to surrender to Him in firm belief. Anyone who knows the words of the prophets and who hears that Jesus was crucified will have to confess that He, and no other, is the Messiah.
Justin, *Dialogue with Trypho the Jew* 89.3.                    (27)

His heart trembled and His bones quaked. His heart melted like wax in His breast. We must recognize, then, that the Son in reality endured these great pains for our sake according to the Father's will, and we cannot maintain that, since He was the Son of God, He did not feel what was done to Him and inflicted upon Him.
Justin, *Dialogue with Trypho the Jew* 103.8.                    (28)

Christ, the Firstborn of all Creation, became the beginning of a second race. This race He brought forth anew by water and faith and wood (the mystery of the Cross) just as Noah and his household were saved by wood when they rode over the waters. *By water, faith, and wood* those who prepare themselves in good time and awake to repentance for their sins shall escape the impending judgment of God.

We know that of the two peoples who were blessed (the descendants of Shem and Japheth) the Semites conquered the habitations of Canaan first, and that afterwards, in accordance with the prophecies, the Japhethites seized what the Semites had conquered, the one people (the Canaanites) being given into servitude under the other two. Christ, however, has come in the power of the Almighty Father to call men to friendship, blessing, change of heart, and life together as brothers in that time to come when all the holy ones shall live in the land whose possession He promised them, as has been shown before. Hence men of every nation, whether slaves or free men, realize now that they shall live with Christ in that land and inherit

everlasting, imperishable good if they believe in Him and recognize the truth taught by Him and His prophets.
Justin, *Dialogue with Trypho the Jew* 138.2; 139.4-5.    (29)

He called Abraham and commanded him to go out from the country where he was living. With this call He has roused us all, and now we have left the state and the evil ways we shared with its inhabitants. We shall inherit the Holy Land together with Abraham, and we shall take possession of our inheritance for all eternity, for having believed like Abraham, we are his children. Just as Abraham believed the Word of God, and this was counted to him as righteousness, in the same way do we believe the Word of God, which, after being spoken to us first through the prophets, was proclaimed to us again through the apostles of Christ. Therefore we have renounced all the things the world offers, even unto death.
Justin, *Dialogue with Trypho the Jew* 119.5-6.          (30)

Believe me, according to the teaching of Isaiah and the other prophets, at the second coming of Jesus no libations or sacrifices of blood will be offered on the altar  but true praises in the Spirit and thanksgivings!
Justin, *Dialogue with Trypho the Jew* 118.2.          (31)

Brothers! We must think of Jesus Christ as we do of God, as the Judge of the living and the dead. We must not think little of our Salvation.

For how many proofs of His bountiful love do we thank Him! He gave us light. Like a father He has called us sons. He has saved us when we were lost. The air surrounding us made us weak; our eyes were full of darkness. And then we learned to see. We cast off the dark cloud which had enveloped us. That happened through His will, for He had mercy on us.

He sorrowed for us. He saved us since He saw great error and ruin in us. He saw that we had no hope of salvation unless it came through Him. He called us when we were not there. He willed us to come into being out of nothing.

Those who are lost must be saved. It is a great and wonderful thing to support, not what is standing, but what is collapsing. Thus it was the Messiah's will to save what was lost, and He saved many when He came and called us who were already lost. What then can we offer Him in return as our thanks and recompense? Only this, that we confess Him through whom we were saved! But how do we confess Him? By doing what He says and not ignoring His commandments so that we honor Him not only with our lips but rather with all our heart and soul.

So then, brothers, let us confess Him with our actions by loving one another, by not committing adultery, not speaking evil of each other, and not being envious, and by being self-controlled, compassionate, and kind! We ought to suffer together the things which are hard to bear. It is our obligation not to love money. We want to confess Him with such actions and not do the opposite.

Be aware, brothers, that the stay of our fleshly nature in this world-age has little significance. It is of short duration. But Christ's promise is great and wonderful. It brings the peace of the future Kingdom and of eternal life. What then should we do to gain these things? We must lead a holy and upright life, regarding things of the present age as alien. We must not covet them, for in desiring to possess them we fall from the right path.

The world to come and this world-age face one another as enemies. This age spreads abroad adultery and corruption, avarice and deceit, while the world-age to come renounces all these things. We cannot be friends of both. We must give up the present age and keep to the age to come. Therefore, as long as we are in this world-age, let us repent with our whole heart for the wicked things we have done in the flesh so that we may be saved by the Lord while there is still time to turn around.

In what state were you saved, in what state did you learn to see? It happened in this life of the flesh. Therefore it is the flesh which we must guard as God's temple, for just as you were called in the flesh, you will reach the goal in the flesh. If Christ the Lord, who saved us and who at first was pure Spirit, became flesh and called us when He was in that state, we also shall receive our reward in this very flesh.

Let us therefore love one another so that we may all enter the Kingdom of God. Let us expect the Kingdom of God from hour to hour in love and justice! Indeed we do not know the day when God will appear. When someone asked the Lord when His Kingdom would come, He only said, "When that which is now two shall become *one,* the outside like the inside, and the male with the female shall be neither male nor female!"

Now, "two shall become one" means the time when we tell one another the truth, the time in which two bodies are one soul without deception. That "the outside" shall be "like the inside" shows us this: the inside means the soul, the outside means the body. Just as your body is clearly visible, so your soul shall be manifest in the good deeds you carry out with your body. "The male together with the female shall be neither male nor female" means that a brother when seeing a sister does not think of the woman in her, just as on the other hand the sister does not think of him as a man. He says therefore: When you act like this and are like this, my Father's Kingdom will come.

When the heathen hear the words of God from our lips, they marvel at them as something beautiful and great. However, when they find out that our deeds are unworthy of the words we speak, they turn from this to blasphemy. They say it is a myth and a delusion. If we do the will of God our Father, we shall belong to the first Church, the one of the Spirit, who was created before the sun and the moon. But if we do not do the Lord's will, we shall be like those of whom the Scripture says, "My house is become a den of thieves." Let us choose, then, to be a part of the Church of life so that we shall be saved.

I believe that you are not unaware that the living Church is the Body of Christ, for the Scripture says that God made man male and female—the male is Christ, the female is the Church. To this belong the Books of the Prophets and the Apostles, and so the Church is not merely of today but existed from the beginning, for she was present in the Spirit just as our Jesus was. But He was revealed in the last days to save us.

The Church, being present in the Spirit, was made manifest in the flesh of Christ. She shows us through Him that each one among us who guards her and does not corrupt her in the flesh shall receive her in the Holy Spirit, for this flesh is the counterpart of the Spirit. No one, therefore, who destroys the counterpart can receive the original. This is what it means then: Brothers, guard the flesh so that you may receive the Spirit! If we say that the flesh is the Church and that the Spirit is Christ, then he who dishonors the flesh dishonors the Church. Whoever acts like this will not be able to receive the Spirit who is the Christ. If we renounce the pleasures of the flesh and master our soul by not yielding to its evil lusts, we shall gain the mercy of Jesus.

Realize that the Day of Judgment is at hand like a blazing furnace. Heaven upon heaven shall dissolve. The whole earth shall be like lead melting in the fire, and then the secret and the open deeds of men shall appear as they are. For the Lord says, "I am coming to gather all nations, tribes, and tongues." This refers to the day of His appearing when He will come and redeem us, each according to his works. Even the unbelievers shall see His glory and might. They will be dismayed when they see the rulership of the world in the hands of Jesus. Let us have faith, then, brothers and sisters! We are standing the test of the Living God and training ourselves in the present life so that we shall be crowned by the life to come.

*Second Letter of Clement,* one of the oldest Church sermons, about A.D. 150. (32)

THE SHEPHERD OF HERMAS: People who think out evil in their hearts bring death and captivity upon themselves, especially those who seize upon this present world for themselves and boast of their wealth and do not turn their will toward the good things that are to come. The Lord is near to those who turn to Him, as is written in the Book of Eldad and Medad, who prophesied to the people in the desert. Because the Church was created before all other things, she is old. It was for her sake that the world was formed.

The stones that are white and round and do not fit into the building are the people who have faith but at the same time possess the riches of this world. When the suffering of persecution comes upon them, they deny their Lord because of their wealth and their business affairs. Once their wealth which entices their souls is cut off from them on all sides, they will be useful to God. Just as a round stone cannot be squared and made useful for the building unless it is hewn and thus loses one part of itself after another, so also the

wealthy in this world-age cannot be used by the Lord unless
their wealth is cut off from them on all sides. Learn this first
from your own life's experience: when you were rich you were
useless, but now you are useful, now you can be accepted into
life. Be useful to God, all of you! For you yourself will also
be taken from these very stones.

Do you not see that the tower is still being built? Only when
the construction of the tower is finished will the end come.
But it will be built up quickly. Let this reminder and this
renewal of your spirits be sufficient for you and for the saints.

Listen to me now: Stand together in peace! Look after one
another! Be concerned each for the other! Do not use for
yourselves alone what God has created, but share it with the
poor! By eating too much, some are bringing sickness upon
their bodies and ruining them, while the bodies of others
who have nothing to eat are ruined by lack of food. Their
bodies are wasting away. High living is harmful to you who
are well off and do not share with the poor. Think of the
coming judgment! You who are privileged, seek out those who
are going hungry, while the tower is still incomplete. Once
the tower is finished you will wish to do good, but you will
not have an opportunity anymore. You who enjoy your wealth,
take care that the poor do not groan lest their groaning go
up to the Lord and you be shut outside the door of the tower
with all your riches.

Why did the figure appear to you in the first vision as an
old woman sitting in a chair? Because you had become old
in spirit and were already dying and had no strength anymore.
Your soft living and your doubts had brought you to this point.
You became enervated by the affairs of daily life and fell into
lethargy just like old men who, once they have given up all
hope of regaining strength, expect nothing but to fall asleep.

But all who have repented will be quite new again. They

will be firmly founded once they have repented with all their hearts. As I prayed at home and sat on my bed, a man of splendid appearance came in. He was dressed like a shepherd. He wore a white goatskin about his shoulders and had a satchel on his back and a staff in his hand. The following is what the shepherd, who is the angel of repentance, commanded me to write down.

First Command: Above all, believe that God is One, He who created all things, who set them in order, and who brought all things from non-existence into existence; He contains all things who alone is uncontainable. Therefore put your trust in Him and fear Him, and in fearing Him exercise self-control.

Second Command: Do good, and with a simple heart share the fruits of your labor which God gives to you with all those who are poor, not wondering to whom you should give and to whom you should not give. Give to all, for God wishes that you give to all from His gifts to you.

Third Command: Love truth. Let your mouth speak nothing but the truth, for the Lord is truthful in every word. In Him there is no falsehood. Liars wound the Lord. They become thieves who steal from the Lord because they do not return to Him the gift in the same way as they received it, for they received a Spirit from Him that does not lie.

Never in my life have I spoken a true word, but I have always talked deceitfully with everybody, and I even twisted my lies in such a way that to everyone they appeared to be true.

Fourth Command: I command that he who has sinned must sin no more. For his former sins there is One who can give healing because He is the One who has all things in His power. I am in charge of repentance, and to all who repent I give discernment. To repent is great discernment.

Fifth Command: If you are patient, the Holy Spirit who

lives in you will remain pure. Then the shadow of a hostile, evil spirit will not darken Him, but, dwelling in a wide, open room, He will rejoice and be glad. . . . But when a spirit of anger tries to push itself in as well, the Holy Spirit, who is so tender, straightaway feels constricted. The Lord dwells in patience, but the Devil dwells in anger. When such spirits dwell in one and the same vessel with the Holy Spirit, that vessel can never contain them all. It overflows as it were. For the tender Spirit is not accustomed to live together with an evil spirit or with harshness. He departs from such a man and seeks to dwell in a place where gentleness, patience, and quiet are at home.

Sixth Command: The angel of righteousness is tender and chaste, gentle and calm. When he stirs in your heart, he straightaway speaks with you about justice, purity, holiness, and self-control and about all just deeds and every glorious virtue. Whenever these impulses stir your heart, know that the angel of righteousness is with you. When anger flares up in you, however, or when a mood of bitterness overcomes you, know that the angel of wickedness is in you. And further-more, when the urge for much bustle and for the stimuli pro-vided by many kinds of food and drink arises in your heart, when intoxication and plenty of amusements, when desire for women, passion for money, and the power of arrogance and ostentation, or when anything like them or akin to them arises in your heart, know then that the angel of wickedness is in you.

Seventh Command: If you fear the Lord you will master the Devil, for he does not have any power. One who has no power need not be feared. He who has glorious power must be feared. Therefore fear the Lord and you will live for Him.

Eighth Command: Adultery and sexual promiscuity, much drinking, wicked sumptuousness, much eating, opulence, boast-fulness, pride and arrogance, lying, slander and hypocrisy, vindictiveness and abusive language—all these actions are the wickedest of all in the life of men. From all these actions the servant of God must abstain.

Listen now to the actions that are good, for which you must fight and which you must not lack: most of all faith, fear of the Lord, love, unity, words of justice, truthfulness, and patience. There is nothing in men's lives which is better than these.

Now hear what follows from these things: rendering service to widows, visiting orphans and the poor, giving them active help, delivering God's servants from every distress, being hospitable, ... resisting no one, being calm, becoming poorer than all other men, honoring the aged, practicing justice, observing brotherly love, putting up with abuse, being patient, not bearing any grudges, giving comfort, not letting those who are gravely tempted despair of their faith but helping them to turn around and encouraging them to be joyful and trusting, reproving sinners, not oppressing debtors and needy people, and doing whatever other actions are like these.

Ninth Command: Tear doubt out of your heart! Never allow doubt to hinder you from praying to God by perchance thinking to yourself, "How can I ask anything from the Lord, how can I receive anything from Him since I have sinned so much against Him?" Never think like this! Instead, turn to the Lord with your whole heart. Pray to Him without wavering and you will come to know His great mercy. He will never desert you. He will fulfill your heart's request because God is not like men, who harbor grudges. No, He does not remember evil, and He has compassion for what He has made.

Tenth Command: Man, you have no insight if you do not grasp that sadness is the most wicked of all the spirits and very terrible for the servants of God. Sadness ruins a man more than all the other spirits combined. It drives the Holy Spirit from him. Certainly, on the other hand, it also saves.

Whenever a doubting man starts out to do something and he fails in it because of his doubt, sadness enters into the man. It grieves the Holy Spirit and pushes Him out. These two things then grieve the Spirit: doubt because he did not succeed in his undertaking and the angry temper on the other hand grieves the Spirit because he did evil. God's Spirit, which was given into this flesh of yours, cannot endure either sadness or confinement. A gloomy man always does evil. The prayer of a dejected man never has the strength to ascend to God's altar. So cleanse yourself of all this wicked gloom, and you will live for God.

Eleventh Command: Whoever consults a false prophet on any matter is an idolater. Such a man is completely lacking in truth; he is foolish. No Spirit given by God waits to be consulted. Having the power of Divinity, it speaks all things of itself because it is from above, from the power of the Divine Spirit. But the spirit that waits to be consulted and speaks upon man's request is earthly and shallow. It has no power. And unless it is asked it has nothing to say.

Therefore test the true and the false prophet. By his life test the man who has the Divine Spirit. In the first place, the man who has the Spirit from above is filled with gentleness, patience, and calm. He knows himself to be small and abstains from all wickedness and from the vain desires of this world-age. He makes himself poorer than all other men. He makes no reply whatever to anyone who consults him. He does not speak in secret. Nor does the Holy Spirit ever speak when man wants to speak, but only then does He speak when God wants Him to speak.

The man who only imagines that he has the Spirit exalts himself. He wants to have the place of honor, and he straightaway becomes impudent, shameless, and talkative, given to excessive eating and drinking, and well versed in all kinds of trickery. He accepts payment for his prophesying, and if he does not get it he does not prophesy. It is impossible for a prophet of God to act like this. For your part, then, trust the Spirit who comes from God and has power, but do not believe the earthly, empty spirit at all, for it has no power because it comes from the Devil. Listen now to the parable I am going to tell you. Take a stone and throw it up to heaven; see whether you can hit the firmament with it! Or again, take a water-squirt and squirt water up to heaven; see whether you can make a hole in the firmament with it.

Just as this is impossible, so are the earthly spirits impotent and weak. In the same way, the Divine Spirit who comes down from above is mighty. Therefore trust this Spirit, but keep away from the other one!

Twelfth Command: Hear then by which acts evil desire destroys the servants of God! What stands out more than anything is the desire for someone else's wife or husband, for extravagant wealth, excessive eating and drinking, and for all other foolish luxuries. All excess is foolish and futile for the servants of God. When evil desire finds you armed with the fear of God and determined to resist, it will flee far away from you and you will never see it again, for it fears your weapons.

Cannot man master these commands—man who is master over *all* creatures and has been given dominion over *all* things? Yes, that man who has the Lord in his heart is able to master all things and all these commands. Those, however, who have the Lord merely on their lips while their hearts are hardened and who are far from the Lord find these commands hard and impossible to fulfill.

So you who are empty and fickle in faith, let the Lord enter into your hearts! Then you will know that nothing is easier than these commands, nothing sweeter, nothing kindlier! Turn around, you who live under the commands of the Devil. Though the Devil can wrestle with God's servants, he cannot throw them. If you resist him, he will be beaten back and will flee from you in disgrace. Empty jars sour quickly, and so their contents no longer taste good. All who are filled with faith stoutly resist the Devil, and he goes away from them because he can find no place to break in. Then he goes to the people who are empty. There he finds room. He forces his way in to them and does in them as he pleases. And they become his slaves.

But I, the angel of repentance, say to you, be not afraid of the Devil! I was sent to be with you who repent with all your hearts. I was sent to strengthen you in your faith. Believe in God, you who because of your sins have despaired of your life, adding new sins to the old and weighing down your lives! Believe in God. Believe that the Lord will heal you of your former sins if you turn toward Him wholeheartedly and do good in the remaining days of your lives, serving Him rightly in accordance with His will. Believe that strength will be given you to overcome the works of the Devil.

Hear the parables which the shepherd, who is the angel of repentance, told me:

First Parable: You know that you who are God's servants are living in a foreign country, for your own City-state is far away from this city-state. Knowing, then, which one is to be your own City-state, he continued, why do you acquire fields, costly furnishings, buildings, and frail dwellings here? Anyone who acquires these things for himself in this city cannot expect to find the way home to his own City.

Foolish, double-minded, wretched man: Do you not realize that all these things here do not belong to you, that they are under a power alien to your nature? The ruler of this city-state here will say, "I do not want you to live in my city! No! Get out of this city, for you do not observe my laws!" Now you own fields, buildings, and many other possessions, and you are driven out by the overlord! What are you going to do now with your fields, your houses, and all the other things you have amassed? Quite rightly the ruler will tell you, "Either observe my laws or get out of my country!"

What are you going to do now? In your own City you have a clearly defined law. Will you, for the sake of your fields and the rest of your possessions, altogether renounce your own laws and actually live in accordance with the laws of this city-state? Take care lest it prove fatal to you to repudiate your own laws, for if you wish to come home to your own City, you will not be received there because you have denied the laws of your own City-state. You will be expelled. You should realize, then, that you live in a foreign country. Acquire no more here than what is absolutely necessary, the bare necessities of life. Be ready at any time so that, whenever the ruler of this city wishes to expel you because you disobey his laws, you can leave his city and move to your own City to live there in accordance with your own laws, in great joy, without having to suffer torture! Instead of fields, buy for yourselves people in distress in accordance with your means. It is far, far better to buy this kind of field, property, or building, which is quite different and which you can find again in your own City when you come home. This "extravagance" is beautiful and holy; it brings no grief and no fear; it brings nothing but joy. Do not practice the extravagance of the pagans, for it is damaging to you who are the servants of God. . . .

Third Parable: The present world epoch is wintertime for the righteous. Just as in winter all the trees are alike and, once they have shed their leaves, it is not easy to tell which trees are dead and which are still alive; in the same way in this world-age, it will not be easy to tell the righteous from the evildoers. They all look alike. Those budding trees are the righteous, who shall live in the future world-age. The future age will be summertime for the righteous; but certainly for the evildoers it will be winter. Just as in summer the fruits of each individual tree appear, and one can tell to which species it belongs, in the same way the fruits of the righteous will appear. They will all be visible when they blossom and ripen in the world to come. . . .

Fifth Parable: My servant carried out the command I gave him to fence the vineyard and did a great deal more to my vineyard besides: he dug it up and weeded it. In the same way on the day when you are fasting, take nothing but bread and water, and calculate according to the value of what you otherwise would have eaten the amount of the sum you would have spent on it each day. Give it to a widow, an orphan, or a poor person. Never let the thought arise in your heart that this flesh of yours is perishable and that you could abuse and defile it on that account! If you defile your flesh, you also defile the Holy Spirit; and if you defile the Spirit, you will not attain life. For the two belong together, and the one cannot be defiled without defiling the other. Keep them both pure, then, and you will live for God! . . .

Eighth Parable: He showed me a great willow that overshadowed valleys and mountains. All who are called by the name of the Lord gathered under the shelter of this willow. A radiant angel of the Lord, of tremendous height, stood beside the willow. With a great sickle he cut branches from it and gave them to the people who stood in the shade of the willow. He gave them little sticks from the branches.

This great tree that casts its shade over valleys and mountains and over the whole earth is the Law of God, which is given to the whole world. Indeed, this Law is the Son of God, who is proclaimed to the ends of the earth. The people standing in the shade are those who came to believe in Him through hearing the proclamation. The tall and radiant angel is Michael, who has authority over this people and who guides them, for it is he who put the Law into the hearts of the believers, and now he tests those to whom he gave it, to see whether they have kept it well.

Now you see many sticks that are useless. The people whose sticks were found withered and worm-eaten are the apostates and traitors to the Church who heaped shame upon the Lord by their sins. They were ashamed of the Name that was called down upon them, which is the Name of the Lord. These people are utterly lost to God. You will see that not one of them has repented although they heard the words you spoke to them as I commanded you to do. From such men life has departed. All those who do not repent have lost their lives. Those among them who did repent became good and were given their places within the outer walls; some even were allowed to go up into the tower. You see, then, that repentance holds life for the sinner. Unwillingness to repent spells death.

Those who gave up their sticks green but full of cracks are the people who were always faithful and good but jealously vied with each other for first places, honors, and privileges. However, they quickly repented and were given their dwellings in the tower. But if anyone should turn to such dissension again, he will be removed from the tower. He will lose his life. Life is given to all people who keep the Lord's commandments. His commandments say nothing about "first" places, honors, or privileges; instead, they speak of patience and of man's readiness to be small.

The people who returned their sticks half green and half withered are those who are absorbed in their own business affairs and consequently do not hold to the saints. That is why they are half alive and half dead. Many of them did repent when they heard my commands, and all who have repented are given a place in the tower. Only a few of them fell away completely; there is no repentance in them. Go and tell all men to repent so that they can live for God, for the Lord has sent me to them in His compassion and in His will to give repentance to all.

Ninth Parable: I want to show you all the things the Holy Spirit showed you, who spoke to you in the form of the Church; for that Spirit is the Son of God. He showed me in the middle of the plain a great white rock rising from the plain, higher than the mountains, square like a cube, and of such immense size that it could contain the whole world. The rock was ancient. A gateway was cut into it. The gateway seemed to me to be new. The gateway beamed more brightly than the sun. I marveled at the brilliance of the gateway. Around the gateway stood twelve maidens. I saw that six men had arrived, tall and splendidly built and of like appearance. They called many more men to come, and they came, tall, handsome, strong men.

And the first six men ordered them to build a tower upon the rock above the gateway: "You are not to deliver any stones directly for the building. Put them down by the tower. The maidens are to carry them through the gateway and hand them over for the building. Unless they are carried through the gateway by the hands of these virgins, they cannot change their colors as is necessary. The tower cannot be completed until its Master comes and inspects this building, for the tower is being built according to his will."

After a little while I saw a great body of men approaching. In their midst was a man of such tremendous stature that he rose above the tower. The six men who had been in charge of the building walked at his right and at his left, and all who had worked on the building were with him, and many other splendid figures were surrounding him. The virgins who guarded the tower ran up to him and kissed him and began to walk at his side around the tower. He inspected the building thoroughly, so thoroughly that he touched each individual stone. He held a rod in his hand with which he struck each of the stones that was built into the tower.

When the wonderful man who was the Master of the whole tower had completed this task, he called the shepherd to him and handed over to him all the stones lying beside the tower which had been thrown out from the building, and he said, "Clean all these stones carefully and use them in the construction of the tower as far as they will fit in with the others. Those that will not fit throw away, far away from the tower!"

Now when the shepherd saw that the tower was splendidly built, he rejoiced greatly. So beautifully was the tower built that when I saw it I was filled with a longing to dwell in it. There was not a single joint in it. It looked as though it had been chiseled out of the rock. There it stood, as if of one single stone.

Now I was alone with the maidens. They were joyful and friendly to me, especially the four most glorious among them.

The maidens said to me, "The shepherd is not coming here anymore today. You were entrusted to us, and you may not leave us!"

"Where am I to stay then?" I asked.

"You shall sleep with us," they said, "as a brother and not as a husband, for you are our brother and from now on we want to live with you, for we love you very much!"

But I hesitated to stay with them. The one who evidently was leader among them began to kiss and embrace me. When the others saw her embracing me, they too began to kiss me and lead me around the tower and rejoice with me. Some were pacing in a circle, others were swinging in dance, and again others were singing. Silently I walked with them around the tower, and I rejoiced with them. But when it became late, I wanted to go home. However, they did not let me go, and held me back. So I stayed with them that night and slept beside the tower. The virgins spread their linen tunics on the ground and made me lie down in their midst. They did nothing at all but pray. I prayed unceasingly with them and not less than they. The virgins were glad to see me praying like that. I stayed there with them until the morning, till the second hour.

The rock and the gateway are the Son of God. The rock is old, the gateway is new! The Son of God came into being before the whole creation; therefore He was His Father's counselor at the creation. Yet because He was made manifest in the last days at the end of time, therefore the gateway is newly broken in so that those who are saved may enter through it into God's Kingdom. No man can enter the Kingdom of God except through the name of His Son, beloved by Him. All the glorious angels surround the Lord like a wall. The gateway is the Son of God; He is the only entrance to the Lord. No one shall enter into Him except through His Son. Also the glorious man [the Master of the tower] is the Son of God, and the other six are the radiant angels surrounding Him on His right and on His left. The tower that is being built is the Church.

The virgins here are holy spirits. If you receive the Name only and are not clothed by them, it will be of no use to you, for these virgins are powers of the Son of God. If you bear the Name but do not bear the power, you will bear the Name in vain. The stones that were rejected are those who bore the Name but did not put on the clothes of the virgins. Their very names are their clothes. Even the Son himself bears the names of these virgins! All the stones are clothed with the power of these virgins. That is why you see that the tower has become *one* stone with the rock. In the same way, too, those who have come to believe in the Lord through His Son and are clothed with these spirits will become *one* spirit and *one* body. Of *one* color will be their garments.

Hear now about the stones that were thrown out. All of them had received the Name of God's Son and the power of these virgins. . . . Some time later they were seduced by the beautiful women in black garments with bare shoulders and flowing hair, whom you saw. Consequently, they were cast out from the house of God and turned over to these women. This, he concluded, is the meaning of the stones that were thrown out. Certainly, they may return to the tower if they throw off the works of these women and accept once more the power of the virgins and live in accordance with their deeds. That is why there is a pause in the building, so that they can repent and be newly fitted into the building of the tower. But if they do not repent, others will get in, and they will be rejected forever.

For all these things I gave thanks to the Lord. He has mercy on all who are called by His Name. He sent the angel of repentance to us who had sinned against Him. He renewed our spirits. He gave us new life after we had wrought our own ruin once more and had no more hope of life whatever. The Name of the Lord is great and incomprehensible, and it supports the whole world. He Himself has become the foundation which supports those who wholeheartedly bear His Name.

Now hear the names of the stronger virgins first, those who stood at the corners of the tower. The first is Faith, the second Chastity, the third Strength, and the fourth Patience. The other virgins who stood between them bear the names Simplicity, Innocence, Purity, Cheerfulness, Truth, Understanding,

Unity, and Love. Whoever bears these names and the Name of the Son of God is able to enter God's Kingdom.

Hear also the names of the other women clothed in black. Of these, again, four are the most powerful. The first is Unbelief, the second Licentiousness, the third Disobedience, the fourth Deceit. The others that follow them are Sadness, Wickedness, Immodesty, Ill-temper, Untruth, Folly, Slander, and Hatred.

The first stones, those fitted into the building out of the deep, the ten stones of the foundations, signify the first generation of believers. The next twenty-five stones are the second generation of just men. The thirty-five stones after that are God's prophets and His servants. The following forty are the apostles and teachers of the proclamation of God's Son.

They had to rise up through the water to be made alive. The water is the seal. They go down into the water dead. Living they come up again. The Son of God will rejoice among them and be glad when He receives His people washed clean. Where there were many springs and all the Lord's creatures drank from these springs, there are the believers who were apostles and teachers and who proclaimed the Lord's Word throughout the whole world in holiness and purity and did not suppress a tittle on account of their own evil inclinations. They always lived in righteousness and truth. It was they who received the Holy Spirit. Such men will go in to the angels.

Where the trees are full of fruit, where they were adorned all over with fruit, there are the believers who suffered for the Name of the Son of God, suffered willingly and with their whole hearts, and laid down their lives. All those who did not deny but willingly took suffering upon themselves when questioned before the authorities have special glory before God.

From the white mountain are the believers who are like innocent children in whose hearts no sin has entered and who have not experienced what evil is. They always remained in childhood innocence. Such people will dwell steadfastly in God's Kingdom. All "children" are glorious in the sight of God and are foremost with Him. You will be the first of all to live for God. Let yourselves be healed while the tower is still being built! The Lord dwells in peace-loving men, for He loves peace. Do not trample on His mercy! Honor Him rather because He is so patient with you in your sins. He is not like you. Therefore find that repentance which will save you.

Be manly in your calling. Proclaim to every man the mighty things of God. You will find grace in this calling. Further, I tell you that every man must be rescued from his distress. Whoever is hungry and suffers want, lacking even the barest necessities of life, endures great anguish and need. Whoever is harassed by such need endures the same anguish and torture as a man who is in prison. Many even take their own lives because of such unbearable suffering. Whoever knows of such a man's misery and does not come to his rescue commits a grave sin; he is guilty of that man's blood. Unless you hurry to do what is good, the tower will be completed and you will be shut out.

Prophecies from the *Shepherd* of Hermas. In the years 140 and 150. (33)

The prophetic Spirit is the corporate body of the prophetic order. He is the fleshly body of Jesus Christ as that which endows it with a living soul.

Grenfell and Hunt, *Oxyrhynchus Papyri* Part I, No. 5, pp. 8-9. (34)

The Cross shall go before me when I come in my glory. Seven times brighter than the sun will I shine when I come in my glory with all my holy ones, with my angels. Then my Father shall set a crown upon my head, and I will judge the living and the dead and recompense every man according to his deeds.

Do you not understand that the fig tree is the house of Israel? Truly, I tell you, when its branches have sprouted at the end of the world, false Christs shall arise. They will arouse expectation and say, "I am the Christ who once came into the world." But this liar is not the Christ. When they reject him, he will murder with the sword. Then shall the branches of the fig tree, which is the house of Israel, shoot forth. There shall be many martyrs by his hand. Enoch and Elijah shall be sent to teach them that this is the Seducer who must come into the world to deceive with signs and wonders.

Through the suffering of the Son who is without sin, the creature that fell prey to destruction was made holy. As for you, you are chosen according to the promises I have given you. Spread my Good News of peace throughout the world! Truly, men shall rejoice. My words are the wellspring of expectant hope and of life. All of a sudden the world shall be filled with joy.

*Revelation of Peter* 1,2. (35)

Plead for few days so that the time will be shortened. The Kingdom is already prepared for you. Watch! I call Heaven and earth to witness: I have caused evil to perish and I have created the good, as truly as I live, says the Lord. Good mother, enfold thy sons in thine arms; give them joy like a dove feeding her young; give strength to their feet, for I have chosen thee, says the Lord. The nations will rage, yet they shall not prevail against thee, says the Lord. My hands shall protect thee so that thy sons will not see the Underworld! Rejoice, O mother, with thy sons, for I shall deliver thee, says the Lord.

Remember thy sleeping sons, for I will make them arise from the hidden graves in the earth and I will be merciful to them, for I am merciful, says the Lord, the Almighty. Clasp thy children in thine arms until I come and proclaim mercy unto them, for my wells are brimming over and my grace shall never cease.

Wait for your Shepherd! He will grant you eternal peace, for He is near who shall come at the end of the world! Prepare yourselves to receive the reward of the Kingdom, for the everlasting light shall shine upon you for ever and ever! Flee the darkness of this world; accept the happiness of your glory. I bear witness to my Healing Savior openly. Receive the gift of the Lord; rejoice and give thanks to Him who has called you to His Kingdom coming from the Heavens.

Arise! Stand and behold at the Lord's banquet the number of those who are sealed. All who have turned away from the darkness of the world have received shining raiment from the Lord. Zion, receive thy chosen band and enfold those who are clad in white, who have fulfilled the Law of the Lord. The number of thy sons, for whom thou didst long, is complete; pray earnestly for the rulership of the Lord to come so that thy people, who were called from the beginning, may be made holy! I, Ezra, saw upon Mount Zion a great company, which I could not count, and they all praised the Lord with singing. And in their midst stood a youth of noble stature towering above them all. He set a crown on the head of each one of them, and He grew even more in stature. And wonder held me spellbound.

Then I asked the angel, "Lord, who are these?"

He answered and said to me, "These are they who have laid aside their mortal clothing and put on immortal raiment and have confessed the Name of the Lord. Now they are being crowned and are given palms."

And I said to the angel, "Who is the youth who puts the crowns on their heads and gives them palms into their hands?"

He answered and said to me, "He is the Son of God, whom they confessed in the world." And I began to praise them because they had stood up valiantly for the Name of the Lord. Fifth Book of Ezra 2.13-47.                                                    (36)

Hear the Word, O my people! Prepare yourselves for the fight. In suffering, conduct yourselves like aliens on this earth. Whoever sells, let him do so as one who is fleeing! Whoever buys, let him do so as one about to lose everything! Whoever trades, let him trade as one who will make no more profit! Whoever builds, as one who will never inhabit! Whoever sows, as one who will not reap! Whoever prunes vines, as one who will not gather the vintage! Those who marry, let them do so as though they will not beget any children! And those who do not marry, as if they were widowed! Hence those who work, work in vain. Strangers will gather their fruit, they will rob them of their riches, destroy their houses, and lead their sons into captivity. Therefore those who marry should know that their children will come into captivity and famine.
Sixth Book of Ezra 16.41-47.                                                (37)

Behold, out of the land of Syria I begin to call a new Jerusalem. I will subdue Zion and it shall be taken captive. And the barren one who is childless shall be rich in children, and she shall be called the daughter of my Father, but to me she shall be my bride. For so it has pleased Him who sent me.
*Epistle of the Apostles* 33 ⟨see also James, *The Apocryphal New Testament,* pp. 496-497⟩.                                          (38)

O rolling waves! O fortress earth! Over you shall rise the
Sun that never sets! And all shall obey Him, who comes
once more to earth! Thus they knew His mighty power!

*Sibylline Oracles,* Book III.93–96.                              (39)

The mills of God grind late, but grind the finest flour.
Then will fire lay waste all things and grind to dust
The leafy-crowned peaks of mountains and all flesh.
The beginning of evil for all is love of money
And lack of true understanding.
Desire for treacherous gold and silver shall rule,
For nothing is greater than these in mortal eyes.
Not the light of the sun, nor heaven nor sea nor broad-
        backed earth
Whence all things spring, nor God the Giver, the Begetter
        of all,
Nor constancy nor faith have they preferred to these two
        things.
O source of godlessness, forerunner of disorder,
Lord of and means to all wars, hateful plague of peace,
Setting parents against children, and children against
        parents!
Even marriage itself, without the gold, will nowhere be
        valued,
Nowhere at all; and the earth shall have her boundaries
And every sea its watchers,
Partitioned off with deceit among those who have money.
They will exploit the poor as if they wanted for ever and
        ever
To keep the earth that feeds the masses of people,
Procuring land for themselves and yet more land,
Boasting and putting down the poor.
And if the vast earth did not have its place

Far from the starry heavens, men would not share the
    light;
It could be bought for gold and would belong to the rich.
For poor folk God would have to prepare another
        existence.
To thee, O stiff-necked Rome, shall come one day from
        above
The fitting blow from Heaven! Then shall first thy neck
        bow down!
Thou shalt be razed to the ground and wholly consumed
        by fire,
Laid low and stretched out on the ground.
The whole of thy riches shall perish.
Then thy ruins shall be the abode of wolves and of foxes,
And thou shalt be deserted as if thou hadst never been.
*Sibylline Oracles,* Book VIII. 14–42.                    (10)

R ejoice, O holy daughter of Zion that hast suffered
        greatly!
Thy King himself shall come, riding on a colt.
Filled with loving-kindness, He shall take away
Our yoke of slavery, so hard to bear,
That presses on our neck,
And He shall break the godless ordinances and the
        oppressive bonds.
Know Him for thy God, Him, who is God's Son.
Praise Him, hold Him firmly in thy heart.
Love Him with all thy soul and bear His name.
Deny thy former gods, and wash thyself with His own
        blood!
Thy songs will not propitiate Him, nor will thy prayers.
He heeds no short-lived sacrifices, for He himself is
        immortal.

Know then who He is,
When understanding mouths sing forth His praises!
And then shalt thou see thy Creator.
*Sibylline Oracles,* Book VIII.324-336.                    (41)


The representative, administrative Spirit speaks out what
Christ has foreordained. He bears witness above all to
Christ himself. The representative, administrating Spirit is
the restorer. The representative, administrating Spirit bears
witness to an abundance of truths. Without deviating from the
clarity and perfection revealed in Christ himself, He shall
seal and attest all things in accordance with our belief in
Christ and in the whole design of God the Creator.
Tertullian, *On Monogamy* 2,4.                    (42)


In the meantime the Son of God poured forth the gift He
received from the Father: the Holy Spirit, third Name of
the Divinity, the third degree of Majesty, the Proclaimer of
the one Rulership, the Administrator of the various branches
of the household, and—if one accepts the words of His New
Prophecy—the Leader into all truth that is in the Father,
in the Son, and in the Holy Spirit, according to the Christian
oath of allegiance.
Tertullian, *Against Praxeas* 30.                    (43)


God poured out over all flesh the gift He had foreordained,
His Spirit, to oppose the mighty spirits of unbelief and
perversity. In this way He breathed new life into diseased
faith. In this way He freed the Ancient Documents from all
obscurity and ambiguity by the bright light of the Word and
of understanding. It became necessary that the Holy Spirit
should no longer withhold the superabundance of His utterances so that no new seed might be provided for expositions

by false teachers, however subtle and cunning. Accordingly the Holy Spirit now really has overcome all the old ambiguities of obscure parables by proclaiming openly and clearly the entire mystery through the New Prophecy flowing in copious streams from the representative Advocate. If you draw from His springs, you will never thirst for any other teaching; no feverish craving after questions will ever consume you again.
Tertullian, *On the Resurrection of the Flesh* 63.          (44)

After the Apostle had written, Montanus came, so they say, and had that of the representative Administrator which is perfect, the giving nature of the Holy Spirit.
Didymus, *On the Trinity* III.41.2.          (45)

Justice, in its rudimentary beginning, had a natural fear of God. Then, through the Law and the Prophets it progressed to its infancy; through the Gospels it grew into the fervor of youth; and now it is brought to maturity by the representative Spirit. Grace is at work and keeps going forward to the end. After Christ, only the representative Spirit may be called and revered as Master. He alone leads the way because He alone succeeds Christ. Those who have received Him set truth above custom.
Tertullian, *On Veiling Virgins* 1.          (46)

The first gifts of grace are not like the last.
Epiphanius, *Panarion* 48.8.          (47)

We are now better instructed by the Spirit, the representative Administrator, who brings in the whole truth. We believe in the one and only God within that order we call Household Plan. In it the one God has also a Son, His own

Word, who proceeded from Him; and finally He sends the Holy Spirit, the representative Administrator, proceeding from the Father. According to the words of the New Prophecy, the unity of God is made manifest in the distinction between the Father, the Son, and the Holy Spirit through the distribution which differentiates and unifies, through the administration of the household which indicates the number.
Tertullian, *Against Praxeas* 2,13,30.                    (48)

The period of weakness in the flesh had to run its course until the coming of the representative Spirit. The Lord deferred until His coming what was unbearable before. But now no one has the excuse that a demand is too hard to be borne, for He who gives us the power to carry it out is no longer lacking.
Tertullian, *On Monogamy* 14.                    (49)

The Spirit is the representative Administrator whom, according to John's Gospel, the Lord promised to send. He leads into perfect truth. Once more He reveals the Covenant and the Promise—yes, He comes with even more glorious promises.
Epiphanius, *Panarion* 48.13; 48.10; Eusebius V.16.19.   (50)

The Lord challenges us to suffer persecutions and to confess Him. He wants those who belong to Him to be brave and fearless. He Himself shows how weakness of the flesh is overcome by courage of the Spirit. This is the testimony of the apostles and in particular of the representative, administrating Spirit. A Christian is fearless.

Yet do not even shepherds flee and forsake their flocks? If so, they are justly marked by the representative, administrating Spirit for what they are. The way is narrow. Few are chosen.

Therefore the representative, administrating Spirit has come to call to martyrdom and to give strength.
Tertullian, *On Flight in Persecution* 9, cf. 10,11.  (51)

If anyone recognizes the Spirit, he will listen to Him, how He brands the runaways.
Tertullian, *On Flight in Persecution* 11.  (52)

The divine banner and the human banner do not go to-gether, nor the standard of Christ and the standard of the Devil. Only without the sword can the Christian wage war: the Lord has abolished the sword.
Tertullian, *On Idolatry* 19; *On the Chaplet* 11-12.  (53)

If you ask counsel of the Spirit as to what is greater than the word that perfect love casts out fear, He will give you an answer. Nearly all sayings of the Spirit spur on to martyrdom and never to flight.
Tertullian, *On Flight in Persecution* 9.  (54)

Divine revelation is not dependent on human nature and reflection. Being God's work, it is given to those who respond to Him in purity of life and in holiness.
Pseudo-Justin, *Exhortation to the Greeks* 8.  (55)

Only a holy servant can serve in holiness.
Epiphanius, *Panarion* 48.  (56)

We no more do away with marriage when we reject second marriages, than we are against food when we fast quite often. Abolition is one thing, moderation another.
Tertullian, *On Monogamy* 15.  (57)

If even today the representative Spirit were to prescribe total, absolute virginity or continence, not allowing the seething heat of the flesh to foam down even in a single marriage, He would still not be introducing anything obviously new. When you consider this, you will not find it hard to convince yourself how much more fitting it is for the representative, administrating Spirit to proclaim a single marriage, for He could just as well have proclaimed that there should be no marriage at all. How much more readily should we believe Him since the advocating Spirit merely tempers absolute rejection, which coming from Him would have been quite proper also. You must only recognize what was Christ's will, and in this too you must recognize the representative Spirit as the administrating Advocate.

Tertullian, *On Monogamy* 3. (58)

The New Prophecy is rejected because Montanus, Maximilla, and Priscilla plainly teach more frequent fasting than marrying.

Tertullian, *On Fasting* 1. (59)

He is the man who taught the dissolution of marriages and prescribed laws on fasting.

Apollonius, quoted in Eusebius V.18.2. (60)

We do not reject the prophecy of Montanus proclaiming the future judgment. It promises great glory at the consummation of God's Kingdom. Montanus challenged his opponents and won himself followers.

Tertullian, *Praedestinatus* 26. (61)

A word of the New Prophecy belonging to our faith attests and proclaims that a picture of the City shall be visible for a sign before it actually appears. We confess that the coming royal rulership was promised to us anew for this earth and, what is more, before the advent of the heavenly Kingdom and quite different in its nature. After the resurrection it shall come for a thousand years in a state whose constitution is a work of God. It is the Jerusalem which shall come down from Heaven. The Apostle, too, describes this Jerusalem as our mother above and as the polity of our citizenship, which is that of a free city governed by its own laws. It testifies to the prophetic conviction that it is coming from the Heavens. It will definitely correspond to a heavenly city-state, come what may.

Tertullian, *Against Marcion* III.24. (62)

In the form of a woman clad in shining raiment, Christ came to me and put wisdom into me. He revealed to me that this place is holy and that the Jerusalem which comes from Heaven shall descend here.

Priscilla, or perhaps Maximilla or Quintilla, quoted in Epiphanius, *Panarion* 49.1. (63)

As the Spirit [the representative Advocate] teaches, God brought forth the Word just in the same way as the root brings forth the fruit, the spring the river, and the sun the ray.

Tertullian, *Against Praxeas* 8. (64)

The administrating advocating Spirit is rejected, not because Montanus, Priscilla, and Maximilla proclaim another God, not because they do away with Christ at all, or because they overthrow anything at all in the rule of faith and in the expectation.

Tertullian, *On Fasting* 1. (65)

Those who are called after the region of Phrygia [in Asia Minor] accept the whole of the old Scriptures; they read and confess the New Testament and proclaim the resurrection of the dead just as all true Christians do. Concerning the Father, the Son, and the Holy Spirit, they hold the same convictions as the holy Church everywhere.
Epiphanius, *Panarion* 48.1.                                    (66)

They acknowledge God to be the Father of the universe and the Creator of all things just as the whole Church does. They also acknowledge all the things which the Gospels testify concerning Christ.
Hippolytus, *Philosophumena* VIII.19.                          (67)

They accept the Law and the Prophets; they confess the Father and the Son and the Spirit; they expect the resurrection of the flesh in the same way as the whole Church everywhere proclaims it.
Philastrius, *Heresies* 49, quoting Hippolytus, *Syntagma*.  (68)

There in Pepuza in Phrygia they gather in the open to hold their symbolic celebrations, offering hospitality to each other, as those who are consecrated.
Epiphanius, *Panarion* 48.14.                                  (69)

The Spirit blesses and inspires those who are exultant and elated, who rejoice and take pride in Him. He makes them to be something through the immensity of the promises.
Eusebius V.16.9.                                               (70)

Virgins clad in white and carrying lamps entered their meetings. They strode from afar to bring prophetic truth to the people. They stirred up profound agitation in the

meeting by their enthusiasm, making them all weep. In repentance they all cried as if bewailing the dead, shedding tears. In their whole demeanor they lamented and bemoaned the life of men.
Epiphanius, *Panarion* 49.2. (71)

They are flesh, and yet they hate the flesh.
Priscilla, quoted in Tertullian, *On the Resurrection of the Flesh* 11. (72)

The true Church can forgive every sin.
The Paraclete speaking in the new prophets in Tertullian, *On Modesty* 21. (73)

Do not listen to me! Listen to Christ! ... The Lord has sent me, a staunch supporter, a revealer, an interpreter of this suffering and task and of this covenant and message of promise. Whether or not I want to, I am compelled to receive the knowledge of God.
Maximilla, quoted in Epiphanius, *Panarion* 48.12,13. (74)

Here is the knowledge of discipleship, and the teaching.
Epiphanius about Maximilla, in *Panarion* 48.13. (75)

Behold, man is like a lyre, and I sweep over him like a plectrum drawing forth sound. Man sleeps, but I keep watch and arouse. See, it is the Lord who throws men's hearts into ecstasy and who gives men heart.
Montanus, quoted in Epiphanius, *Panarion* 48.4. (76)

The Gospel is proclaimed by the holy prophetess Prisca to the effect that the holy servant knows how to administer a life of sanctification. She bears witness that he brings into harmony that which purifies. They see visions. They discern the importance of everything here below and determine the shape. They hear clear voices announcing salvation as well as those full of hidden mysteries.

Tertullian, *Exhortation to Chastity* 10.     (77)

What do you say of the one who is saved and who is above other men? The representative, administrating Spirit says that the righteous man will shine a hundred times more brightly than the sun, and once saved, even the smallest among you will shine a hundred times more brightly than the moon.

Epiphanius, *Panarion* 48.10.     (78)

I am chased like a wolf from the flock of sheep. I am not a wolf. Word am I, and Spirit, and Power.

Antimontanist quoting Maximilla. Anonymous in Eusebius V.16.17.     (79)

There shall be wars and revolutions.

Maximilla, quoted in Eusebius V.16.18.     (80)

Do not wish to die in bed, or in childbirth, or in enervating fevers. No, wish yourself a martyr's death! In this way He who suffered for you shall become great!

The Paraclete of the New Prophecy, in Tertullian, *On Flight in Persecution* 9; *On the Soul* 55.     (81)

Blushing for shame you will be dragged before the public. That is good for you, for he who is not publicly exposed like this before men will be publicly exposed before God. Do not be disquieted. It is righteousness which will exhibit you in the midst of all. How can you be thrown into confusion? You wear the crown of victory! Power streams forth when you are seen by men.

Tertullian, *On Flight in Persecution* 9. (82)

I the Lord, the Almighty God, make my dwelling in a man, and thus I speak!

Epiphanius, *Panarion* 48.11. (83)

Neither an angel nor an envoy but I, the Lord, God the Father, have come.

Epiphanius, *Panarion* 48.11. (84)

Not a messenger, not an elder, but I, the Lord, the God Father, have come.

Didymus, *On the Trinity* 41.1. (85)

I am the Father and the Son and the representative, administrating Spirit.

Didymus, *On the Trinity* III.41.1. Cf. Origen, *Against Celsus* VII.9. (86)

# ANNOTATIONS, EXPLANATIONS, AND SUPPLEMENTARY SOURCES

For the Introduction and Survey we have used standard superior figures for reference. For the annotations to the "Sources of the First Centuries" (pp. 335 ff.) we have followed the German edition in the use of figures in bold parentheses ( ) corresponding to the numbers placed at the end of the individual selections.

The main sections of our book are referred to by their initial letters:

Introduction and Survey: I.&S.
State, Society, and Martyrs: S.S.&M.
Christian Self-Portraits: C.S.P.
Confession of Faith and Scriptures: C.F.&S.
Lord's Sayings, The Teaching of the Twelve Apostles, and Letters: L.S.T.A.&L.
Meetings and Worship: M.&W.
Proclamation and Prophecy: P.&P.

# ANNOTATIONS TO
# INTRODUCTION AND SURVEY

1. In the Introduction and Survey at the beginning and in the annotations and explanations at the end of our book we have not attempted to go into scholarly discussion on theological opinions or on the results of earlier or later research. This would have to be done elsewhere. With this book we want to render simple and objective help to those who have earnest questions and concerns so that they might begin to grasp the Christ-witness in past centuries just as it was given to men in those times. Historical explanations and literary references are therefore reduced to the minimum necessary for proper understanding.

The conclusions and results of scholarship and research, however, especially in the last decades, have been fully taken into consideration. Without taking sides, we have tried to highlight all the trends which led from living faith to a practical life of love in trust and loyalty under Christ's direction. Among other factors that bear out the authenticity of these early Christian testimonies is their simultaneous quotation by many different ancient sources.

The bibliographical and reference material is intended as a help in following up all the testimonies which have made a significant impression on the reader. The following annotations will help him to explore our book from the most important points of view. The Topical Index and the Index of Names and Writings will also help in this. Above all however, the express purpose of this source book should be kept in mind: to point to faith in God, to the witness of the Living Christ, and to the working of the Holy Spirit among the gathered believers everywhere throughout the centuries.

2. The life-witness of the historical Jesus (to which the first three pages are meant to call attention) is seen in this paragraph in the light of the Lord's Prayer, p. 2, par. 1.

3. While the death of Jesus on the Cross and the goal and character of Christ's future remain the cornerstone of His way (pp. 2-3), the Sermon on the Mount teaches the new way of loving brotherhood as the realization of God's love in the present. In our book, several texts with their accompanying annotations go more specifically into the Sermon on the Mount. See Topical Index under Sermon on the Mount.

4. The commission with which Jesus charged His disciples and apostles is to be found in Matthew 10, Mark 6:2-11, and Luke 9:1-6. Throughout the centuries, that commission proved a very powerful challenge to men to go the way of Jesus, and in the primitive time of the Church it faced men with a momentous decision, as is borne out by the texts and annotations. See Topical Index under Apostles, Teachers, Prophets.

5. The witness of the first fellowship of disciples took shape in their avowal of the Cross, the resurrection, and the future Kingdom; it took shape in that, through love, power from the Holy Spirit overcame possessions and healed men (pp. 3-4). The Acts of the Apostles, especially chapters 2-4, contains the Biblical description of this decisive manifestation of the Church.

6. We are concerned here (pp. 5-6) with the life work of the apostle Paul, with the recognized leadership held by the primitive Church in Jerusalem and the fact that it was the Church at Antioch that in the beginning took the lead in the mission task. The Acts of the Apostles and the Letters of Paul, in fact the whole New Testament, are the authentic documents of the earliest Christian time.

The agreement between Jerusalem and Paul referred to here can be found in Acts 15. Compare Lev. 17, and the seven "Noachian Precepts," which according to the Talmud apply to people living before and outside Abraham everywhere, to the "sojourners living within the gates of Israel." These precepts are: obedience to authority; reverence for God's Name; abstinence from idolatry and fornication, murder and robbery; and prohibition of the consumption of blood.

7. The extinction of the first Jewish-Christian Church cannot then be considered a sign of weakness but must be seen as the catastrophe of the Cross suffered by the Church. The martyrdom of James is a vivid illustration of this. See Index of Names under James. Ignatius describes the Cross as judgment over the present world-age, judgment over the world-rule of Satan and his demons. See Topical Index under Cross.

According to Eusebius, Hegesippus (one of the earliest Christians after the apostles) sharply defines the beginning of the period covered by our book as decisive for the end of the earliest Christian period (Eusebius, *Church History* III.32.6-8; IV.22.4-6). According to Hegesippus, until the death of James the Church had remained pure and undefiled like a virgin. Only when none of the apostles remained did the false teachers throw off their masks and dare to contradict the proclamation of the truth. Compare annotation to our S.S.&M. (9) pp. 335-337.

8. Ignatius, *Letter to the Ephesians,* abbreviated in our L.S.T. A.&L. (56) pp. 196-199.

9. The same words are used in *Acts of Peter: Vercelli Acts* 38 (9): "This Cross alone is the Word stretched out." Here too the Spirit is called the proclaiming Power. The Spirit says of the Cross, "For what else is Christ but the Word! ... The

beams of the Cross are the resounding voice of God. . . . The
deadly nails mean the turning about and change of heart. . . .
The Word is the life-giving tree of the Cross," *Acts of Peter* 39
(10). The Cross is man's encounter with the Spirit, to be
perceived only through the Spirit, to be praised only with the
silence of man's voice. The Name of the Cross is the hidden
mystery, the unutterable grace, *Acts of Peter* 37 (8). "No redemption can be expected save through the despised and
taunted Nazarene, through Him who was crucified, who died
and rose again," *Acts of Peter* 7. Compare the adoration of
the Cross in *Acts of Andrew* 9, our P.&P. (19) pp. 268-269.
See indexes of names and topics.

The *Acts of John* 99 witnesses to the Cross which through
the Word joins all things unto itself, gives birth to all things,
and compacts all things into one. Also the mystery of the
dance in *Acts of John* (to be found in our M.&W. (40) pp.
255-256) is explained in the *Acts* themselves (101) as the
suffering of the Cross, as the wounding, the piercing and
hanging up, and the shedding of His blood. Compare the text
in our book (P.&P. (20) pp.269-270) about the piercing, the
blood, the wounding and the hanging, and the suffering and
death of the Word—also the calling upon the Crucified and
Risen One at the driving out of demons, as in *Acts of Thomas*
V.47. The strength of the Wooden Gallows is called the conquering force for all who put it on, the victorious power
which has settled on the wood of the Cross (*Acts of Thomas*
XIII.157). For the early Christians, the Cross is the only
power that gives salvation and healing. Compare all this with
the places listed in the indexes of names and topics.

10. The point here is that the believers are crucified with Christ
and raised with Him, as Paul testifies. Ignatius expresses this
in his *Letter to the Smyrnaeans* (in our book L.S.T.A.&L. (61)

pp. 201-203) and in the same passage he confesses that the blood of Christ is the foundation of love. To the Philadelphians the same Ignatius writes of partaking in the suffering and uniting with the blood, that is with the death, of Christ. In his *Letter to the Smyrnaeans,* he greets in the name of Jesus all who are gathered in the unity of God, in the unity which they have because they are rooted in His flesh and blood, in suffering and resurrection. This suffering together and dying together, stressed also in Ignatius' *Letter to Polycarp* (our L.S.T.A.&L. (62) pp. 203-204) is the same fellowship of the Cross witnessed to by all believers in Christ even today, except that in those times this fellowship of suffering was so much more real than today because of persecutions, martyrdom, and death. It is needful to mount upon the Cross with Jesus Christ, the true God (*Acts of Peter* 38, 39). See indexes of names and topics.

11. Origen, *Against Celsus* VI.34. Celsus explains that this belief of the Christians about receiving life and resurrection from the wooden Cross originates from the fact that their Master was nailed to the Cross and was a carpenter by trade. Celsus adds ironically, "If Christ had been thrown down a cliff or pushed into a pit, or strangled with a rope, ... then they would speak of a cliff of life or a pit of resurrection or a rope of immortality."

12. Lucian, *On the Death of Peregrinus* 11. Lucian, the cynical pagan poet, was also an enemy of the Christians in the second century.

13. Taken from the Syriac *Testament of Our Lord Jesus Christ* and the Arabic *Didascalia* (*Didascalia et Constitutiones Apostolorum,* ed. F. X. Funk, Paderborn, 1905, vol. 2), chapter

XXXIX, where it is introduced as *mystagogia Jesu Christi*. The Syriac *Testament* I.28 speaks of the Cross of Christ bringing victory over Death: the alarmed questions of the conquered Devil and the answer of those who are initiated, "Here is Christ, the Crucified!" Compare Ode of Solomon 22: the victorious battle of Christ against Death and the Devil who have to give up their own, our M.&W. (35) p. 249.

14. Ode of Solomon 22, our M.&W. (35) p. 249.

15. Like this in the oriental Liturgy of James, p. 33, the Liturgy of Mark, and the Abyssinian Liturgy, p. 218; similar in the so-called "Clementine Liturgy" in the *Apostolic Constitutions,* and also similar in the Syriac *Testament of Our Lord*. We owe these passages to G. P. Wetter (Upsala), who compiled them in his two significant books on ancient Christian liturgies. ⟨Wetter quotes F. E. Brightman, *Liturgies Eastern and West-ern,* and for such quotes page numbers are Brightman's.⟩ See bibliography and annotations 16, 18, and 23 below.

16. Quoted like this by Wetter from the Armenian Liturgy, p. 452 and many other places (e.g. in the *Apostolic Constitu-tions* VIII, Clem. Liturgy, after Psalm 118:26) and pointed out as extremely old. Wetter's work based on liturgical research provides us with excellent material on the original worship of Jesus and on the experience of His presence in the Church. However, he misses the main point, or at any rate he sadly plays it down; namely, that this faith in Christ's power present among them, faith in the power of the Cross, the resurrection, and the coming of Jesus, was possible only because the early Christians believed in the historical reality of the Christ Jesus, and because for them the Holy Spirit was a reality.

17. Compare Pliny's report to the Emperor Trajan, our S.S.& M. (11) pp. 63-65. The comparison on p. 9, between those tied

to the Cross (the Christians united with the Crucified One) and Ulysses, is included as coming from very early Christian times in Grisa's *Histoire de Rome et des Papes,* Paris, 1906, illustration 131. ⟨See W. Lowrie, *Art in the Early Church,* revised edition, N.Y., 1965, p. 75 and plate 23, illustrations a and b.⟩

18. Tertullian, *Apology* 39. On the basis of some of the oldest liturgies, Wetter proves that these gifts represented one of the most important aspects of the Lord's Supper and the Lovemeal in early Christian times. See in Brightman the Abyssianian Liturgy, pp.199 and 203; Coptic Liturgy, p.145; and others. "Bring your offering! Bring your offering! Bring your offering!" See also the Syriac Byzantine Liturgies, pp. 54, 89, 58, 97, 99, 444; the Nestorian Liturgy, ed. Eusèbe Rénaudot, vol. 2, p. 636; particularly the Roman Liturgy which ends with the words, "who [all believers] bring their gifts to Thee"; and many other places.

19. As it is described in the old manuscript Parasinus 974.

20. Hippolytus, *The Apostolic Tradition* 28 ⟨B. S. Easton, p. 52⟩.

21. Irenaeus, *Against Heresies* IV.17.4-5.

22. Origen, *Against Celsus* VIII.28,33,34.

23. See Wetter, *Altchristliche Liturgien,* vol. 2, pp. 101-102, for his evidence and conclusion.

24. A. Harnack, *The Mission and Expansion of Christianity in the First Three Centuries* ⟨after this referred to as Harnack ET (English Translation)⟩, vol. 1, pp. 401 ff. He emphasizes that according to the Old Testament this designation "the poor" was a name of distinction. Later it was applied to the narrow Jewish-Christian sect of the Ebionites, "those called after poverty."

25. Here (*To Donatus* 4) Cyprian glorifies the freely flowing Spirit which cannot be restrained by any barriers or limits, but flows perpetually in rich exuberance—only our hearts must thirst and be open for it. Compare our I.&S. at "33," p. 14.

26. Origen, *Homily XV on Genesis* VIII, quoted by A. Harnack, *Die Mission und Ausbreitung des Christentums in den ersten drei Jahrhunderten,* vol. 1, p. 220.

27. Macarius Magnes, *Apocriticus* III.17, Porphyry Fragment No. 95 in Harnack's edition. Compare Cyprian's witness after his conversion (*To Donatus* 4):

> Suddenly, in a wonderful way, that which had been doubtful became assured, that which had been closed lay open before me, that which had been dark became light; what had seemed difficult now turned out to be easy, what had seemed impossible, possible.

See our I.&S. at "25" and "33," pp. 13 and 14.

28. Macarius Magnes, *Apocriticus* IV.19, in *"Porphyrius gegen die Christen,* 15 Bücher." (Quoted by Harnack in "Zeugnisse, Fragmente und Referate," *Abhandlung der Preuss. Akad. der Wissenschaften,* No. 88, p. 97, 1916.) Nevertheless, Porphyry holds that the purpose of his own philosophizing is the healing of the soul. For the Christian experience compare Cyprian (*To Donatus* 3):

> When I was still languishing in darkness and black night and was tossed about on the open sea of this storm-wrenched world, ... I regarded it as unlikely, especially when I considered my own character at that time, for a man to be born again. ... I asked myself, how is such a tremendous transformation possible that all at once

man throws off everything which is innate and hardened or which has become deeply ingrained through prolonged habit?

29. Justin, *First Apology* 61.

30. See *Second Letter of Clement* 6.9, "If we do not keep our baptism pure and undefiled, how can we be confident of entering the Kingdom of God?"

31. In our book, L.S.T.A.& L. (54) pp. 181-189. In this context special note should be taken of what is said at the beginning of the *Didache* (see corresponding note) about the two ways leading to life and to death, about love to enemies, surrender of all possessions, and about a life in keeping with the Sermon on the Mount. For a significant description of early Christian baptism see our L.S.T.A.& L. (54) pp. 184-185. Compare Topical Index under Baptism. It may be that all of the *Didache* should be taken as baptismal instruction. As to the training for the new life during this period of instruction, it is worth noting that Origen (*Against Celsus* III.51) relates that:

> Individuals are taught as hearers, and only when they have given ample proof that they want to lead a good life are they introduced into the community. Some of the Christians are appointed to watch over the lives and appraise the conduct of those who want to join them. They refuse to receive into the community those who have become guilty of evil deeds, while they receive the others with great joy, making them better from day to day.

32. Harnack ET, vol. 1, p. 388, quotes Tertullian, *Apology* 18, "Men are made, not born Christians," and *On the Testimony*

*of the Soul* 1, "The Christian soul is always *made,* never naturally born." The children of Christian families are simply called "household members" or more exactly "domestic slaves" of the Church by Tertullian (*On the Soul* 51). Justin (*First Apology* 65, written about A.D. 150) says, "Only he who is convinced and has given his assent is to be baptized." But already at the time of Hippolytus, a leading figure in the years 217-235, infant baptism was taken for granted: the parents or other relatives speak for those who cannot speak for themselves (*The Apostolic Tradition* 21.4 ⟨Easton, p. 45⟩, from the year 218).

33. This contrast between the old and the new life was nowhere described in a more forceful, vivid, and intimate way than in Cyprian's *Letter to Donatus,* where he talks about the revolutionary change that took place in his own life. In paragraphs 3 to 5 Cyprian emphasized his search for that power which was to salvage him from the desperate filth of his earlier years.

Cyprian, *To Donatus* 4:
> With the help of the life-giving water of baptism the filth of former years was washed away. The light from above streamed into my reconciled and purified heart, after I had breathed in the Heavenly Spirit. Through the second birth I was transformed, made into a new man.

Cyprian, *To Donatus* 5:
> O mighty power of the Spirit, O wondrous strength by which one is torn away from the pernicious contact with the world, atoned and purified, freed from the danger of being defiled by the attacking Enemy, but still growing in strength and purified, able to command the whole army of the raging Adversary with imperial authority.

Compare with annotations 25 and 27 to our I.&S. p. 322.

34. Origen, *Against Celsus* III.55,56; Cyprian, *Epist.* 2; Tertullian, *Apology* 42.

35. See *The Teaching of the Twelve Apostles* 12.4; Clem. *Homilies* 8 ⟨quoted by Harnack ET, vol. 1, p. 175⟩.

36. *Didascalia* XIII ⟨see also English translation, R. H. Connolly, pp. 128-129⟩.

37. *Shepherd* of Hermas, 6.5-7, our P.&P. (33) pp. 278-294.

38. John 13:35.

39. The pagan Lucian (compare our I.&S. after "11," pp. 7-8), *Peregrinus* 13, describes here how the Christians helped prisoners.

40. E.g. Justin, *First Apology* 67.

41. Macarius Magnes, *Apocriticus* III.5, Porphyry Fragment No. 58 in Harnack's edition, p. 82. ⟨Harnack ET, vol. 2, pp. 74-75.⟩

42. E.g. *Didascalia* XV ⟨see also Connolly, p. 138⟩.

43. Julian, Sozomen, V.17 ⟨see also Harnack ET, vol. 1, p. 162⟩.

44. Tertullian, *To His Wife* II.4.

45. Bishop Cornelius in Eusebius VI.43. Harnack ⟨in the 1924 edition of *Mission und Ausbreitung*, p. 183⟩ calculated that the Church at Rome spent 240,000 marks ⟨$72,000⟩ annually on 1,500 poor and 100 Church officials, for relief alone 200,000 marks ⟨$60,000⟩ if you take the lowest cost of living as 150 marks ⟨$45.00⟩ per year. ⟨See Harnack ET, vol. 1, p. 157.⟩ In the preamble of his letter *To the Romans* Ignatius says that Rome "presided in works of love."

46. Tertullian, *To His Wife* II.4.

47. Harnack, *Texte und Untersuchungen* II, p. 24.

48. See annotations referred to in Topical Index under Deacons and Poverty. The brothers and sisters serving at table had the oversight of the gifts offered at the Lord's Supper and the Lovemeal, with the task of distributing them among the poor. In this way table service in the meetings and service to the poor of the city belonged together.

49. In Cyprian, *Letters* 76-79. Especially in *Letter* 62 ⟨Ante-Nicene Fathers, vol. 5, pp. 355-356⟩ he explains how the Christians all feel pain about the unfortunate situation of their brothers, whose imprisonment they consider their own. The duty of faith urges them to ransom their brothers, yes, they have to exert all their strength to give effective help to them, because in every suffering brother they see Christ himself. Therefore all of them contribute money to help their brothers, quickly, joyfully, and plentifully, ready at all times to do the good works of God according to the strength of their faith.

50. Tertullian, *To His Wife* II.4.

51. One could be in agreement that a Christian holds a high office empowered to pass judgment over the life and death or the civic rights of a person, only if at the same time the holder of that office does not condemn anyone, or penalize anyone, or cause anyone to be put into chains, thrown into prison, or tortured (Tertullian, *On Idolatry* 17).

52. Tertullian and other texts. See Topical Index under Government office. Tertullian, *On Idolatry* 12: "Faith does not fear hunger" (Harnack, *Texte und Untersuchungen* 42, 2 and 4, pp. 117 f.). According to Origen also, no Christian may exercise the power of the sword against anyone.

53. Origen (*Against Celsus* III.29-30) states that the Church of Jesus had a different *politeia* (polity) or a different conception of citizenship from that of the worshipers of demons. Everywhere, Christians were strangers among the populace, but even their most lowly, least worthy members were much wiser than the pagans. Because of their moral conduct, their overseers and councillors, even their less perfect ones, were far ahead of the councillors and rulers of the existing municipalities. See Topical Index under Politics.

54. Justin and Origen, our C.S.P. (7) and (8), p. 97.

55. Tertullian, *On Idolatry* 1.

56. See Tertullian, *Apology* 21. For the next lines, refer to Tertullian, *Apology* 30. There the Emperor is "second only to God, before and above all gods." ⟨See also Harnack ET, vol. I, p. 298.⟩

57. Eusebius III.37.3.

58. Tertullian, *On the Soul* 9. Irenaeus reports that he himself, in meetings of the Church, heard many brothers speak who possessed prophetic gifts: through the Spirit they talked in various tongues, they brought to light the hidden things of men and revealed the mysteries of God (Irenaeus, *Against Heresies* V.6.1). In the *Testament of Job,* pp. 48 ff., we read of a Christian woman who received a new heart and sent up a hymn of praise to God in angel-tongue and after the manner of angels (see M. R. James, "Apocrypha Anecdota" in *Texts and Studies,* vol. 5, p. 135).

59. Reported in *Apophthegmata Patrum*, Migne, *Patrologie Graeca* 65, p. 276, as an experience of Macarius of Egypt. In the next sentence of the text the description of forms taken by demons comes from Epiphanius, *Panarion* 80 and Timothy

of Constantinople, "De receptione haereticorum" (see Cotelier, *Monumenta Ecclesiae Graecae,* vol. 3, p. 401, Tradition of the Messalians).

60. Told by the Egyptian monk Serapion in *Apophthegmata Patrum,* 65, pp. 313 ff. Similarly in *Historia Lausiaca* 37 (ed. C. Butler, *Texts and Studies* 1-2, 1904, p. 109), and in Irenaeus, *Against Heresies* II.31.2, where he speaks of the raising of a dead man through the proclamation of the truth.

61. Clement of Alexandria, *What Rich Man Can Be Saved?* 42; Eusebius III.23.6-19.

62. *Mystagogia* in the *Testament of Our Lord; Acts of Peter* 39: I give thanks not with these lips nor with this word uttered with the skill of earthly nature; but I give thanks to Thee, O King, with that voice which is heard only in silence. It is not heard aloud. It does not come from any bodily organ. It does not enter any natural ear. It is not heard by anything corruptible. It does not belong to this world. It is not spoken on this earth. But I thank Thee, O Jesus Christ, with that voice which is the silence of the voice. It encounters the Spirit within me, the Spirit that loves Thee, speaks with Thee and sees Thee. Thou art perceived of the Spirit only.

63. *Acts of Peter* 2.

64. *Acts of Thomas* VI.51.

65. Origen, *On Prayer* 28.

66. 1 Cor. 12:28.

67. Clement of Alexandria; Pseudo-Clementine, *Two Letters Concerning Virginity* I.11; *Shepherd* of Hermas, our P.&P. (33) pp. 278-294. Therefore Tertullian considers teachers close

to martyrs, as Spirit-bearers (*On the Prescription of Heretics* 3 and 14).

68. Tertullian, *On Repentance* 10. Compare with *Shepherd* of Hermas, our P.&P. (33) pp. 278-294, and *Second Letter of Clement,* our P.&P. (32) pp. 274-278. Also Papias (see Topical Index) and Clement of Alexandria. According to all these, there are only two things called "Church" in the time of the first Christians (as Harnack among others established in spite of his view in opposition to that of Sohm): firstly, the Church of God, object of faith; secondly, the independently responsible, individual Church. The Church, living in God, takes shape on earth in such individual Churches according to the measure of their faith.

69. *First Letter of Clement* 48; *Barnabas* 4.10.

70. *The Teaching of the Twelve Apostles* 4.2; Justin, *First Apology* 67.

71. This form of the Confession of Faith, evidently the earliest, can be read from top to bottom as well as from left to right; we should note this in order to realize the significance of its individual parts and their mutual interaction. The simple Confession reads as follows:

I believe

| | | |
|---|---|---|
| in God | the Father | the All-Powerful |
| in Jesus Christ | the Son | our Lord |
| in the Holy Spirit | the Church | the Resurrection of the Flesh |

72. Origen, *Homily II.10 on Numbers*. Compare Harnack, *Über den privaten Gebrauch der heiligen Schriften in der alten Kirche*, 1912; Tatian, *Address to the Greeks* 29; Justin, *Dialogue with Trypho the Jew* 7,8; and Proclamation of Peter in Clement of Alexandria, *Miscellanies* VI.15. According to Tertullian (*Apology* 46), that which the Christians testify is proved to be true by the following: first, the antiquity of the Divine Writings and the evidence of faith found in them; second, the acknowledgment of Christ by the evil spirits, the vanquished demonic powers. In other words, faith in the truth of the ancient Bible and in His victorious power over the demons had a crucial and convincing significance for Tertullian.

73. See Tatian, our C.F.&S. (44) pp. 148-149. Tatian, *Address* 29: "While I was seriously pondering what the good brings about, there fell into my hands some barbarian writings older than Greek teaching and divine compared with Greek fallacy. They succeeded in convincing me." Tatian witnesses here in this passage to what is convincing in the impact of the Bible, which is referred to in our I.&S., p. 34. See Justin, our C.F.&S. (69), pp. 160-161; and Proclamation of Peter in Clement of Alexandria, *Miscellanies* VI.15: "When we opened the Books of the Prophets and recognized all that was written in them we came to have faith in God."

74. The Lord's Sayings, the words spoken by Jesus or claimed to have been spoken by Him, possessed singular authority in the early Christian communities, before the New Testament was given its final form and delimitation. In our L.S.T.A.&L. (pp. 171-180) and in the corresponding annotations (pp. 365-375) can be found all of the more than ninety significant Sayings of Jesus not contained in the New Testament, but yet regarded at that time as spoken by Jesus. Papias wrote

his five-volume *Sayings of the Lord Explained* most probably before the middle of the second century. He could
vouch for their authenticity, since he had learned and remembered from the elders of the early times everything he included
in his collection. Papias was one of the earliest Christian
witnesses; he had talked with the first elders, with those who
had still heard Andrew speak, or Peter, Philip, Thomas, James,
John, Matthew, or some other of the Lord's disciples, or the
old Church-leaders Aristion and John (Papias' preface in
Eusebius III.39.3 ff.). See Index of Names for the passages
from Papias. His ingenuous recounting of some of the oldest
memories merits our special attention.

75. See our C.F.&S. (77)-(79) pp. 163-164.

76. Lucian, *On the Death of Peregrinus* (e.g. ch. 11). See
Index of Names under Lucian. That women too could have
this gift of prophecy and fulfill the task of a prophet is borne
out by the Coptic version of the *Acts of Paul,* where two
prophetesses are mentioned. Even Origen still pointed out that
only one of the judges of Israel bore the name of prophet:
Deborah, a woman. "This grace is determined by purity of
mind alone, not by difference of sex" (Origen, *Homily V.2 on
Judges,* 11).

77. Origen, *Against Celsus* VII.9,11.

78. Origen, *First Principles* II.8.5. The multitude of believers
represents the Body of Christ. The apostles are the soul of
this Body. Therefore Origen calls the apostles "kings" (*Homily
XII.2 on Numbers* 10). Clement of Alexandria even calls them
"savers of mankind" (*Eclogae propheticae* 16). Compare
*Pistis Sophia* 7, where the apostles are exaggeratedly seen as
twelve savers of the treasure of light, those who save the
whole world.

79. Grenfell and Hunt, *Oxyrhynchus Papyri,* Part I, No. 5, pp. 8-9. As late as c. A.D. 200 Serapion of Antioch (in Eusebius V.19.2) wrote about the power of this prophetic order, or status, or rank, or manner of living in a clearly defined order.

80. Eusebius I.13. Abgar story.

81. Eusebius III.37.

82. Harnack, *History of Dogma* vol. 1, pp. 157-163. This fact is substantiated in our book by pp. 36-40 in I.& S., annotation 78 to I.& S. above, and by C.S.P. (3)-(4) pp. 95-96; for the apostles were the decisive instruments of Christ's Spirit and of His message.

83. See our L.S.T.A.&L. (54) p. 187, P.&P. (33) p. 293, and Topical Index under Apostles. Origen and Eusebius knew of apostles in the second century. In the *Acts of Paul* even a woman, Thecla, was called apostle.

84. See Origen, *Against Celsus* I.6; Irenaeus II.31.2; and Justin, *Second Apology* 6, *Dialogue with Trypho* 30,85. Compare our texts listed in the Topical Index under Demons. The existence and work of the demons described above (our I.& S. p. 40, par. 2) is gone into thoroughly by Tertullian (*Apology* 23-27, 37) and Tatian (*Address to the Greeks* 7-18).

85. Justin, *Second Apology* 6: "The Son of God became man to destroy the demons." Also Tertullian, *Apology* 23; Pseudo-Clementine, *Two Letters Concerning Virginity* I.12.

86. Cyprian, *To Donatus* 5. See Topical Index under Demons.

87. Tertullian, *Apology* 46. Compare Topical Index under Demons.

88. Tertullian, *Apology* 27; Tatian, *Address to the Greeks* 16.

89. Cyprian, *To Demetrianus* 15; see also *To Donatus* 5.

⟨89ᵃ. "Church" here in the sense of *Kirche* as against *Gemeinde.*⟩

90. Irenaeus, *To Florinus,* in Eusebius V.20.7.

91. Irenaeus III.3,4; Eusebius IV.14.7.

92. Irenaeus III.3,4; Eusebius III.28.6; IV.14.6.

93. Irenaeus IV.33.8.

94. Theodore of Mopsuestia, *Commentary on 1 Timothy,* H.B. Swete, 1882, pp. 121 ff. ⟨see Harnack ET, vol. 1, pp. 445-446⟩.

95. Tertullian, *On the Prescription of Heretics* 20; *On Modesty* 21. Even with the apostles, the authority to forgive sins is given only through the gift of the Holy Spirit, and it continues to be given by the Spirit only to whom He wills and when He wills. The prophecies and miracles of the apostles were proof of the Holy Spirit in them, who gave them authority to forgive sins. Only inspired men, men filled with the Spirit, can administer the forgiveness of sins, which God alone can give. Compare with Origen, *On Prayer* 28, and see Topical Index under Forgiveness.

96. In A.D. 375 a Roman presbyter published *Quaestiones Veteris et Novi Testamenti* (93, ch. 2, pp. 163 ff.) as well as a commentary on Paul's Letters. See Souter's edition, Vienna, 1908.

97. C. F. Arnold, *Die Geschichte der alten Kirche* §18, 6, p. 95; particularly in F. Wieland, *mensa und confessio: Studien über den Altar und altchristlichen Liturgie,* 1906; *Der vorirenäische Opferbegriff,* 1909; and *Altar und Altargrab der christlichen Kirche im vierten Jahrhundert,* 1912; Emil Dorsch, *Der Opfercharakter der heiligen Eucharistie,* 1909. The holy altar devel-

oped only in the course of the third century. Before that time, therefore, there was no church in the sense of a consecrated building. Tertullian, Hippolytus, Clement of Alexandria, Minucius Felix, Origen, and Cyprian were the first to mention rooms or buildings set aside for worship. In the second century, the Christians did not yet have common meeting rooms in the big cities, or consecrated, holy places for worship (Clement of Alexandria, *Miscellanies* VII.5; very clear in the *Acts of Justin Martyr*). In our book refer to S.S.&M. (15) p. 75 and annotation pp. 340-341.

98. Regarding this shift, the detailed documentation in Wetter's two books is instructive. See annotations 15 and 23 to our I.&S. pp. 320 and 321.

99. Tertullian, *On the Prescription of Heretics* 44; Eusebius IV.22.

100. The third canon of the important Synod of Arles states that "those who throw away their weapons in times of peace shall be excluded from communion." In contrast, the Emperor Constantine (*Vita Constantini* II.33) granted former soldiers a free and peaceful life if they chose to profess their religion rather than enjoy military rank.

101. Cf. Tertullian, *On the Prescription of Heretics* 20.

102. Irenaeus IV.33.1,8.

# ANNOTATIONS TO
## STATE, SOCIETY, AND MARTYRS

(1)-(7) The Roman Empire, as the clearest and most typical example of a State, shows that a unified State religion, however broad and tolerant the concept, will of necessity appear indispensable to the very existence of such a State. Therefore any religion that excludes or opposes the religious State-concept or the recognized State religions is an extremely dangerous attack on the State at its very core. The Roman emperor-cult was but the sum total, the visible culmination, of the State religion which pervaded all of Roman civilization. Consequently, on this point there could be no tolerance on the part of Rome until later a new religious concept of the State placed the institutional Church at the service of the State.

⟨(7) Suetonius, *Lives of the Twelve Caesars* III.36.⟩

(8) The main importance of this earliest report of an official Roman persecution lies in the fact that Tacitus, while openly acknowledging the judicial murder committed by Nero, charged Christians with hatred of the human race, an accusation which reflects the feeling against the Christians prevalent at that time.

(9) Next to the stoning of the first martyr, Stephen (Acts 7), the death of James was the most significant murder of a martyr-confessor committed by the Jews. Stephen, being of prophetic nature, saw Israel's history in purely prophetic terms and charged the Jews with the murder of the prophets and the Messiah; he was therefore regarded as an enemy of the Holy Place and of the Law. James, however, was highly honored even by the Jews because of his reputation for great righteousness in keeping the Law. Compare our I.&S. p. 6. It is very remarkable that Josephus (who was active from A.D.

56 and finished his history of the Jews in A.D. 77) stood up for James in this way, because Josephus was a friend of the Pharisees and combined a genuinely Jewish view of life with efforts to assimilate Roman and Greek culture.

Hegesippus gives the most detailed report of the fate of James in Book V of his *Memoirs* (in Eusebius, *Church History* II.23.3-19; IV.22.4; III.32.1-7; compare Clement of Alexandria, *Outlines* VII). A born Jew who had found faith, Hegesippus belonged to the first generation of Christians after the apostles. Hegesippus writes as follows:

James, the brother of the Lord, succeeded the apostles in the Church at Jerusalem. He was often found on his knees, praying for forgiveness for the people, so that his knees were calloused like a camel's from constantly bending them in prayer before God, asking forgiveness for the people. Because of his outstanding sense of justice he was called "the Just" or *Obdias* which means "protection of the people" and "righteousness." When asked what "the door of Jesus" meant, he answered, "He is the Healing Savior." Through this some of them came to believe that Jesus is the Christ.

Now when a number of the leaders also came to believe, a confusion arose among the Jews and scribes and Pharisees. They said there was a danger of the whole nation expecting Jesus as the Messiah. Therefore they met and addressed James, "We challenge you to restrain the people, for they are mistaken in thinking that Jesus is the Messiah. Make the facts about Jesus clear to the people! For all the people and all of us follow you. Place yourself upon the Temple parapet so that up there you can be seen by all and your words can be heard well by all the people."

Then these scribes and Pharisees made James stand on

the parapet and shouted to him, " O Just one, whom we all must follow: since the people in their error are following Jesus, who was shamefully executed, tell us what the 'door of Jesus' is."

He answered in a loud voice, "Why do you ask me about Jesus, the Son of Man! He is enthroned in Heaven at the right hand of the Great Power. He will come soon on the clouds of heaven!"

Then they climbed up and threw the Just one down. And they said to one another, "Let us stone James the Just." So they began to stone him, since he had not died of his fall. He had turned, gone on his knees, and was praying.

While they beat him down with stones, one of the priests called, "Stop! What are you doing? The Just one is praying for you!" And one of them, a fuller, took the wooden cudgel which he used for beating clothes and struck the Just one on the head.

After James the Just had suffered a martyr's death like the Lord and on the same accusation, Simeon, the son of the Lord's uncle Clopas, became overseer of the Church. He was elected by all because he was the Lord's cousin. This son of Clopas was also accused before Atticus, the provincial Governor, on the same charges and because he was of the house of David and a Christian. After being tortured for days, he too suffered martyrdom. All were amazed, even the Governor, how he could endure all this at the age of 120. He was sentenced to die on the cross.

See our I.&S. p. 6 and annotation 7, p. 317 for the testimony of Hegesippus that the martyrdom of James put an end to the pure Christianity of the earliest Church.

(10) On the charge of atheism, see our I.&S. p. 23 and Topical Index under Atheism. A similar report is contained in the book by Suetonius on Domitian ⟨*Lives of the Twelve Caesars* VIII.15⟩, written c. A.D. 130, where Suetonius speaks with contempt of Flavius Clemens' lack of energy.

(11) This authentic imperial document of the opposition to the Christians is elucidated by C. F. Arnold in *Studien zur plinianischen Christenverfolgung* 1888 and by T. Zahn in *Skizzen aus dem Leben der alten Kirche*, pp. 271 ff., "Die Anbetung Jesu." What is typical here is the evidence, given by Christians who deserted their faith, that Christ was worshiped like a god, that the Christians lived a resolutely moral life, that they refrained from quarreling about possessions, and that their Lovemeal was a harmless, ordinary meal. In particular, "the girls serving at table" clearly describes the nature of the *diakonia*. It is the same in the Gallic Acts of Martyrs (our S.S.&M. (16) pp. 77-82) where mention is made of brothers serving at table. Here again in criminal investigation the basic question is the worship of the State-constituted gods. Hence it is the stiff-necked, dogged refusal to meet this demand of the State that has to be punished.

(13)-(18) In the following twenty pages, 66-86, all Acts of Martyrs belonging to the period covered by this book are collected and condensed to the most important facts and testimonies. First see (9)-(11) above, pp. 62-65. The State record from Carthage (17) pp. 82-84, the most obviously authentic, is reproduced in its entirety. In the Acts of Rome (15) pp. 74-77, as in those of Pergamum in Asia Minor (14) pp. 71-74, official court minutes were evidently used, whereas the accounts of Vienne and Lyons (16) pp. 77-82, and of the martyrdom of Polycarp at Smyrna in Asia Minor (13) pp. 66-71, reflect the Churches' concept of martyrdom. The last account from Rome (18) pp. 84-86, from the pen of Justin Martyr, gives a particularly vivid sketch of contemporary morals and the ethical radicalism of the Christians.

All these testimonies show clearly that what distinguished the Christians of that time was the rightabout turn to justice, which takes place under the impress of approaching judgment and changes a man's whole being. The simple confession of being a Christian, the testifying to the name "Christian" (as the actual name of the newly made man), became at times a Confession of Faith in the invisible God as the Creator (who has no name as men have); in Jesus Christ as the Lord, the Savior, and the Proclaimer of Truth; and in the prophetic power of the Spirit as the defending Advocate. The martyrs testified that they served Christ with their whole lives, the Christ whom they were ordered to curse. Consequently, they refused to swear by the genius of the Emperor and were destroyed as "atheists." They called the "all-controlling gods" demons and confronted their nothingness with the Creator of all worlds. Through the testimony of the martyrs, the murderous judges of the State were unmasked as the tools of demons. The authorities were even described as possessed by them.

The other side of this is the worship of Jesus by the Christians and their martyrs from the very beginning: "We can worship no other." According to the martyrs, the grace of the salvation of all men lies in the fact that Jesus, the guiltless One, suffered for the guilty. The martyrs are accounted worthy of participation in this suffering. Christ triumphs in them. What happens here is like that which happened at the trial and execution of Jesus.

In the communion of His suffering, the community with God becomes visible. With their own eyes the believers see in and through the crucified martyr the One who was crucified for them. "This Meal is prepared for me too," cries out one of these voluntary martyr sisters in rapture, witnessing to the sacred character of the martyr's death: it is the bloody Supper of the Lord described in our I.&S. pp. 24-27. Faith in the resurrection, in the Kingdom already now established in Heaven, and in the promise of earth's final goal, was so strong that one of the martyrs had to declare, "I recognize no empire of this present age" (our S.S.&M. (17) p. 82). He recognizes only the one King, who is Lord of all lords.

That this period was marked by a powerful movement of the Spirit becomes clear in two ways: firstly, the centers of the Montanist movement, Asia Minor and Phrygia, Gaul, and Africa, are predominant in most of these first Acts of Martyrs, that is in four out of six, while the other two already show Rome's growing importance; secondly, one of the martyrs, Papylus, was obviously a prophet who had children of the Spirit everywhere as a result of his evangelistic journeys. Thus the letter of the Gauls to the Phrygians speaks in the language of this Montanist revival about the fire of the Spirit and about the Spirit as the defending Advocate.

A similar picture of a Spirit-filled revivalist movement is still to be found some twenty years later in the martyrdom of Perpetua and Felicitas in the year 203, where a strong witness is given to the power of the Holy Spirit, to the pouring out of the Spirit, to the prophecies and new visions and all the gifts of the Holy Spirit, as well as to personal instruction, guidance, and prompting by the Holy Spirit, and to the battle against the Devil himself.

(13) Polycarp's last prayer from this Act of Martyrs can be found at the end of our main section M.&W. p. 258. Who Polycarp was and the extent of his influence is evident from these passages. See Index of Names.

(15) For these early times it is very significant that Justin

categorically denies the statement of the City Prefect that all Christians meet in one and the same place. The God of the early Christians cannot be confined to any one place. Because He fills Heaven and earth He is glorified everywhere, which makes Justin go so far as to declare that he knows no other meeting place than his own home, and he mentions this only because the City Prefect asks him where he gathers his pupils.

(16) This evidence of slaves becoming informers and lying traitors against their Christian masters goes counter to the passage in our C.S.P. (39) p. 120. This contradiction shows that the situation was not the same everywhere or at all times. Further examples of these accusations of cannibalism and sexual immorality are contained in our S.S.&M. (19)-(27) pp. 101-109. They are refuted in our C.S.P. (38)-(40) pp. 116-121. See also Topical Index under Martyrdom.

(17) The fact that letters and writings of Paul, found in the satchel carried by a martyr, were taken as "incriminating evidence" is significant because it shows the recognition given to the New Testament.

(18) In Ptolemaeus we recognize the importance of Spirit-gifted teachers at that time, which is explained in the Introduction (see Topical Index under Teachers). For seducing his pupil to the Christian life, this teacher had to suffer the death penalty.

(19) Minucius Felix was a lawyer and as such had taken part himself in the unjust conviction of Christians before his conversion.

(25) These four lines, taken from Dr. R. C. Kukula, *Bibliothek der Kirchenväter,* Kempten and Munich, are strikingly typical of what Tatian says in chapters 31.7-35.3. In the same

context Tatian says, "Also the poor receive free instruction. All who want to listen, even old women and immature adolescents, persons of every age and race, they all come into their own."

(26) Recalling actual discussions at the end of the second century, the lawyer Marcus Minucius Felix, in about the year 200, puts into the mouth of the pagan Caecilius the extraordinarily typical vilifications of the Christians quoted above. There is no doubt, however, that similar abominations did in fact occur in the Gnostic circles which were harshly rejected by the Christians. See Introduction, p. 45, the texts listed under Gnosis in the Topical Index, and L. Fendt, *Gnostische Mysterien*, Munich: Chr. Kaiser, 1922.

(29) See the Index of Names for more information about the antichristian Celsus.

(27)-(30) In the passages (19)-(26) pp. 86-90, the slanderous charges of unchastity and cannibalism are clearly established historically. (The Christian refutations to these can be found in our C.S.P. (38)-(40) pp. 116-121.) Here, in passages (27)-(30), further reasons are given why the stance of the Christians provoked hatred among the pagans. Compare Topical Index under Martyrdom.

(31)-(34) These four examples show how aggressively the Christians defended themselves at that time against the monstrous charges leveled against them.

# ANNOTATIONS TO
# CHRISTIAN SELF-PORTRAITS

(1)-(15) In these texts, apostolic power identifies itself with the stupendous authority of the risen Christ over the demons. In the Introduction, pp. 3-4 and 37-41, this power is more fully described and substantiated by additional examples and proofs. The statement that demons are "outsiders from divine religion" (5) means that, though these spiritual beings actually belong to the Household of God, they became estranged from their divine Home by rebellion.

(6)-(23) The conduct of the first Christians described here can be understood only in the context of their full acceptance and affirmation of the Sermon on the Mount. ⟨See Eberhard Arnold, *Salt and Light: Talks and Writings on the Sermon on the Mount*, Rifton, N.Y.: The Plough Publishing House, 1967.⟩ One should therefore read this teaching of Jesus with these early Christian testimonies in mind in order to appreciate how Jesus defines the character of the comrades of the future Kingdom and of His disciples, who go on His way and who receive His life energy.

(19) In this instance castration was desired in an all-too-literal interpretation of Jesus' word on those who made themselves eunuchs for the sake of the Kingdom of God. Origen, however, did mutilate himself in his youth though in his later years he judged this act immature. Moreover, it was expressly condemned in important proclamations of the Church, such as *The Apostolic Tradition* (our C.S.P. (27) p. 108, par. 2).

(22)&(23) This evaluation of property, in wealth and in poverty, is in accordance with the Sermon on the Mount and was common to all first Christians.

(24) This classic early Christian self-portrait, seen together

with our passages (28) and (29) C.S.P. pp. 109-113, is fundamental in forming a picture of the attitude to life that Christians represented and strove for and to a great extent carried
out in actual practice.

Aristides shows in this famous and earliest Christian self-
portrait that the Spirit of the Sermon on the Mount is perfect
love and reveals the truth. Because love and truth embrace the
whole of their life from within, it is through the Christians that
good flows into the world. The Christians have the truth. To
know the truth one must read their writings.

(25) The way of the Christians as the way of love to God
and man, of worship without temples and sacrifices, of peace
and adoration is characterized here in the Sibylline Oracles,
which were originally completely pagan. Christians readily
drew upon and expanded these prophetic oracles of ecstatic
Greek women who, according to their own testimony, may
have originated in Babylon.

(26) Celsus, the most brilliant antagonist of Christianity at
that time, perhaps at any time, recognizes sharply and clearly
that the acceptance of small and wretched people is a peculi-
arity of Christendom. Celsus is often quoted in this book. See
Index of Names.

(27) In contrast to (26), the third-century *Apostolic Tradition* of Hippolytus (evidently quoting very old, original principles of Church life) shows the very decisive and clear-cut
nature of the conditions and requirements for acceptance into
the community of the Church. Again, these conditions and
requirements are in accord with a full acceptance, both literal
and spiritual, of the Sermon on the Mount of Jesus.

(30) (31) and (32) From the time of the Greek apologists,
the Logos becomes very prominent in Christian thought as the

Word of God, His reason, mind, and revelation. It is not by chance that in these texts Justin mentions the Logos in connection with Stoicism and popular Greek philosophy, with Heraclitus and Socrates even, and with Greek poets and thinkers in general. The idea of the seed of the Logos scattered everywhere is evident already in Philo and in Stoicism, where it is often very similar to the ideas of Plato.

In spite of the fact that the early apologists persistently maintained their belief that the Logos was fully manifest only in Christ, their conception of the Logos placed the Christian faith in extremely dubious proximity to Greek philosophy. To the Christians of Asia Minor the Logos and the Holy Spirit appear like the two hands of God the Creator and Law Giver, who thus becomes the Redeemer. Yet God remains above and beyond all metaphors. Through the Logos He embraces the whole world. For the creation of the world, the Logos proceeded from God, almost, as Justin saw it, as another God in number (Justin, *Dialogue with Trypho the Jew* 56). In Jesus the Logos becomes man. He comes into the flesh. The historical Jesus brings into history the event of salvation, the event of mankind's new creation, thereby annulling the history of sin. In Christ, the Logos is revealed as the subordinate God within God himself. For the Christians of Asia Minor, the Logos is almost interchangeable with the Spirit, proceeding from God as the ray proceeds from the sun. In the administration of God's Household, the Logos and the Spirit—in complete penetration of all areas of life—are made to dwell in the historical Son until by this means everything is fully in God once more. This example of the development of second-century Christian thinking had to be at least briefly outlined here to help the reader discern, also in this area, the transition from the primitive Christianity of the New Testament to the emerging institutional Church and her theology.

(33)&(34) The mystery of faith unfathomable to man, this completely new worship of God by the Christians, is Christ himself, the Christ who was shamefully executed and cursed for the sake of all men, who from death was brought to life again by God: Christ, the Crucified and Risen One!

(35)-(37) show how the death and resurrection of Jesus affected the dying and living of the Christians.

(36) For the elders in Irenaeus see Topical Index under Episcopate.

(38)-(40) are pertinent examples of the way the early Christians answered the heavy charges of unbridled sexual immorality and cannibalism. The charges are to be found in our passages S.S.&M. (19) and (26) pp. 86 and 88-90. See Topical Index under Martyrdom.

(39) In this text, as in general, Athenagoras shows a strong affinity with Tertullian. His almost Tolstoyan concept of marriage, his designation of second marriages as camouflaged adultery, his most rigorous concept of single marriage (the exclusiveness of marrying only one woman for the purpose of procreating children): all this was widespread among second-century Christians, especially through the influence of the Montanist revival movement. Athenagoras' description of the brotherly and sisterly kiss, an expression of inner fellowship among the first Christians, is an example of their "freedom of conduct," offensive to some and possible only through very strict discipline and strong moral determination.

(39) The assertion (p. 120) that the slaves of Christian households never imputed to Christians the serious accusation of licentiousness and murder, should be compared with our S.S.&M. (16) pp. 77-82.

(41)-(42) The demand that the State should convict Christians only on the basis of their actual conduct, only upon proof of offenses actually committed, comes to expression here as a vigorous testimony for a life grounded in the Sermon on the Mount, a life of nonresistance which surrenders all possessions and makes litigation impossible. It also leads to the assertion that ultimately their persecutors were aiming at the very life of the Christians and at their complete annihilation.

(43) and (45) The divine power revealed in the courage of the martyrs, evident even in women and children, points to the real presence of their General, Christ, under whose eyes alone they were able to put up such a fight.

(44) For Lucian see Index of Names.

(1)-(45) In summarizing what the early Christians have to say about their own stand in life, we are confronted with a vision which is as broad and lofty in concept as it is severe and deep in the responsibility it implies. Christians portray themselves as a continuously increasing body of people, a people gripped and directed by the infinite greatness of the Creator who made the universe, by the Word, Messiah, and Spirit sent forth by Him, a people who expect the complete transformation of all things from Him alone: for through Him they are already now translated into that Power which combines perfect love, kindliness, and readiness to suffer, with rigid moral discipline and single-minded firmness of faith.

# ANNOTATIONS TO
# CONFESSION OF FAITH AND SCRIPTURES

(1)-(5) pp. 127-131. The genesis of the Apostolic Confession of Faith, of which the most important examples are given here, is described in our I.&S. pp. 33-34. There, and in annotation 71 to our I.&S. p. 329, the oldest and shortest "Rule of Faith," the ninefold Confession, is represented and interpreted. It is the basis of the Egyptian texts, our C.F.&S. (1).

Baptism of faith is now generally recognized as the origin of the Confession of Faith. The most important witnesses are Ignatius (our L.S.T.A.&L. (58) pp. 199-200), Irenaeus (our C.F.&S. (4) pp. 129-130), and Tertullian (our C.F.&S. (3) pp. 128-129), who were supported later by Augustine. Origen too calls the main articles of faith expressed in the baptismal symbol the "Rule of Faith." This rule or plumb line, this canon or yardstick, means that the faith witnessed to here, the truth witnessed to here, is the power that shapes all thinking and all conduct. The whole of life is ruled by this foundation, this content of true life.

Such a radical and all-embracing concept can become reality only if the Holy Spirit imprints this testimony on the believing heart (our C.F.&S. (6) p. 131). Augustine bears witness to the attitude still prevailing in his own time, that the Confession of Faith was not to be written down, but must be imprinted on the heart and mind. He still transmits it to those about to be baptized, with the following words for their baptism: "Receive, O sons, the Rule of Faith, which is called the Symbol" (Address to the Catechumens About the *Symbolum,* op. VIII. 1593; Address 213 On the Tradition of the Symbol, op. VIII. 938; XI. 594).

Irenaeus calls the Rule of Faith the "Rule of Truth" in most instances (see *Against Heresies* I.9.4; I.22.1; III.2.1; III.15.1), but he also speaks of the "Body of Truth" (I.9.4). In his other work and in its title, *Demonstration of the Apostolic Proclamation,* chapters 3, 6, and 98, he also speaks of the "Canon of Faith," the "Proclamation of the Truth," and the "Apostolic Proclamation." Clement of Alexandria uses almost all of these expressions in his *Miscellanies* IV.15, where he also speaks of the "Canon of the Gospel," and in *Misc.* III.66, where he speaks of that "Rule of Life" which truly corresponds to the Gospel. All these expressions and definitions show that the Joyful News, expressed in the facts of the Creed, embraces the whole of life and becomes the norm which determines all conduct. Compare Theodor Zahn, *Glaubensregel und Taufbekenntnis,* Leipzig, 1881.

(2) p. 127. Introduced as "our faith in the great Christianity." This short version gives powerful expression to the fact that in the earliest times the Church of forgiveness was spiritual (pneumatic) in character, and her faith embraced the salvation of the entire world. The whole thought-structure of the *Epistle of the Apostles* can be understood as an extensive interpretation of this short confession.

The *Epistle of the Apostles* (*Epistula Apostolorum*) was probably written before A.D. 160. It witnesses to the way and to the work of Jesus during His lifetime and to the reality of His resurrection. When He returns the decisive sign of the Cross will go before Him (ch. 16). The believers brought to Christ are brothers and comrades who, after judgment has been executed by Christ, will in the flesh win the Kingdom in the time to come. The faith to which this letter bears witness means confessing the name of Jesus and, which is the same thing, fulfilling His commandments (ch. 27). Through this faith the believers are purified of evil and liberated from the powers now ruling in the present world-age. The signs of the end, the protection of the elect in the final world crisis, the poverty, and the reproof of wealth (see chs. 34-46) clearly show the eschatological and practical character of this epistle, which covers about fifty pages.

By all indications this writing came from the Johannine circles of Asia Minor. It claims authorship by the eleven apostles. The epistle became known only in 1919, published by C. Schmidt in *Texte und Untersuchungen* ⟨later by M.R. James, in *The Apocryphal New Testament,* 1924, pp. 485-503⟩.

(3) pp. 128-129. The development of the Apostolic Confession of Faith from the formula of baptism explained in the above annotation to (1)-(5), in the Introduction, pp. 33-34, and in annotation 71 to our I.&S. p. 329, becomes very clear in these texts. The Confession of Faith, like a military oath of allegiance or watchword (see also Topical Index under Fighting attitude), appears as the only prerequisite to the lively, intimate exchange among the Christians of the "Church privileges": the kiss of peace, the name "brother," and hospitality. See Introduction, pp. 15 and 48. The Confession of Faith was the distinguishing sign or token passed on by word of mouth, the secret password, as it were, for the unity of the Church.

In this presentation of the oath of allegiance, as in all of Tertullian's writings, the power of faith given by the Holy Spirit comes to the fore as a stance of faith given by the breath of the Spirit. In this whole context Tertullian's emphasis on the management of the divine Household or Economy of God corresponds to a view common among the Montanist circles to which he belonged. See Topical Index under Household of God. The New Testament witnesses to this Economy (Ephesians 1:10 and 3:9), which is also implied in John's Gospel by the designation of the Holy Spirit as the representative Advocate, or Counselor. The Christian circles in Asia Minor, strongly influenced by the Gospel of John, actively disseminated this idea about God. We find it in Ignatius, Justin, Irenaeus, and Tertullian, also in Origen, and later in Marcellus of Ancyra and others, particularly during the Arian and Nicene controversies. It is related to the Logos doctrine: See Topical Index and especially annotation to our C.S.P. (31) and (32) pp. 344-345.

Irenaeus (our C.F.&S. (43) pp. 147-148) sees the administration of God's Household in an arrangement and apportionment of steps by which man climbs upwards through the Spirit to the Son and through the Son to the Father, until the Son hands over His work to the Father, just as according to Justin (*Dialogue with Trypho the Jew* 45) the Son and the Spirit descend from God.

In this autonomous Household Plan of God, the oneness of God in Himself has distinct threefold being: the Creator steps out from Himself through the Logos-Word or through the Spirit, for the sake of creation; the new revelation of God is accomplished, the origin of a new mankind is won in the Word-become-man, in the Christ; the Holy Spirit, God's third revelation, is present in the Church; finally, the return of the Christ and the coming Kingdom will consummate this work for the earth, so that ultimately Logos and Spirit are completely one again in God—all this gives the central place to Jesus Christ.

The first man, called to likeness with God, fell into the hands of the spirit Prince of this world-age, under the dominion of death and sin. At this point the second Adam, Christ, steps into the breach: in death and through rising again He breaks the Dark Power and brings new life, even to the Underworld of the dead. God now reveals Himself to the world in His Son, crucified in the flesh and risen from the dead, and in His Spirit who administers everything. He reveals Himself for the new creation of the new man.

The Economy therefore is two things in one: it is the Household of God's threeness in oneness administered within God; at the same time it is His Household Plan of Salvation for the renewal of His creation and for man's true destiny. Hence God's Kingdom coming on earth has to have a place of moment in this Economy, as proven by "Traditions of the Elders" of Asia Minor, reported by Irenaeus (our C.F.&S. (43) pp. 147-148; compare our C.F.&S. (46) pp. 149-151).

In connection with this the word "Trinity" emerges for the first time, in Tertullian (*Against Praxeas* 2). Before him, about A.D. 180, Theophilus of Antioch, who already considered Paul's Letters as God's Word, speaks similarly of a "threeness" in *To Autolycus* II.15. Compare also Athenagoras, our C.F.&S. (8) pp. 131-133. For Tertullian, the Father, the Son, and the Spirit are a regulating, dispensing Threeness—not according to position and essential nature, but according to degree and function.

The Latin-African Tertullian is often quoted in this book because he stood up for the old Christian view of life and faith with particular clarity, decisiveness, and faithfulness. The son of an army officer and a jurist by profession, he became a Christian as late as A.D. 195. We should not forget, however, that he became a Montanist in A.D. 202 or 207 and as such represented a definite and distinct direction in Christian thinking during the last period of his life, until his death about the year 220. The strong and lasting influence of this acknowledged teacher and leader is all the more striking.

(4) pp. 129-130. Irenaeus, born between A.D. 115 and 140

in Asia Minor, was a pupil of Polycarp and of other disciples of John. He was an elder in Gaul and became overseer in Lyons. Apart from Tertullian and Hippolytus it was Irenaeus who, at the turn of the second century, represented the purest possible conception of earliest Christian life and faith, with emphasis on the Rule of Faith, the Old Testament, and a basic form of the New Testament. Therefore he stressed in this Confession of Faith that the Church, spread out over the whole earth, is based on the faith of the apostles and their pupils. Hence the twofold coming of the Lord and with it His future return for the restoration of the earth and the flesh, stand out clearly in his writings. In his main work against the Gnostics, his faithfulness to historical facts and his reliability are very marked. Compare with other significant extracts from the writings of Irenaeus listed in the Index of Names.

(5) pp. 130-131. This earliest Roman form of the Apostolic Confession of Faith is the basis of the Apostolic Creed still used in Churches today. It is the apex of the movement leading from the baptismal formula to the Confession of Faith, which is evident in our texts (1)-(4) pp. 127-130 and explained in the annotations above and in the Introduction, pp. 33-34, with annotation 71, p. 329. The sources of this version can be found in Marcellus of Ancyra (see A. and L. Hahn, *Bibliothek der Symbole*, § 17) and in the Psalter of Aethelstan (Hahn, § 18), as well as in three versions by Rufinus. See Index of Names and Writings. Perhaps in its earliest form the first article read, "I believe in the one God."

(6) p. 131. This powerful witness from early times confirms that the confession formula was passed on orally in the beginning. See Introduction, p. 33, and annotation to our C.F.&S. (1)-(5) p. 348.

(7)-(8) pp. 131-132. These freer presentations of the Creed again contain the earliest Christian confession to Christ as the Crucified, and to the Holy, the prophetic Spirit seen here as the ray of light emitted by God. The confession to the Logos as thought that shapes and power that creates, to the Oneness of God and to His Economy is explained in the annotation to our C.S.P. (31) and (32) pp. 344-345, which is about the Logos concept, and in the annotation to our C.F.& S. (3) pp. 350-352 concerning the Economy of God.

(9)-(18) pp. 133-137. That Christians were accused of atheism in spite of this powerful Confession of Faith in God can be explained only as a result of their total rejection of every representation of God in human form—their absolute refusal to deify man—even in religious rites and symbols. Here God is the totally different One. Here He is so far removed from the transitoriness of matter and of human culture and religion that the faith of the Christians seemed "god-less" to the more concrete religious feeling of the pagans. See Topical Index under Martyrdom, Idolatry, and Demons. Texts (9)-(18) contain the testimony of the second century to the first article of the Confession of Faith: faith in God, the Creator.

(9) p. 133. Concerning the early Christian insight that the pagan gods were demons and that the persecution of the Christians by the State was demonic in character, compare Topical Index under Demons and Martyrdom and annotation to our C.S.P. (31) and (32) pp. 344-345.

The writings of Justin Martyr, so characteristic of the early Christian apologists, are frequently drawn upon in our book because he stood very close to the faith of the Church and to the Old Testament. He was born in Samaria and after his conversion became an itinerant teacher wearing the philosopher's cloak; he finally settled in Rome where he suffered martyrdom in A.D. 165. Refer to Index of Names regarding Justin and his concern with Greek thinking, his stress on Socrates, his convictions, and his martyrdom.

(15)-(16) pp. 135-136. This testimony proclaiming God the Creator is directed against Gnostic doctrines. See Topical Index under Gnosis.

(18)-(35), pp. 137-144, contain the second-century confession to the article "Jesus the Christ" of the Apostolic Creed, in particular as it was expressed by the apologists.

(18) p. 137. See Topical Index under God, Jesus, Demons, and Household of God, and annotation to our C.F.&S. (3) pp. 350-352.

(20) pp. 138-139. See Topical Index under Future, Love, Jesus, and Demons.

(21) p. 139. Starting from the virgin birth, the piercing and death, and the resurrection of Jesus, the apostolic mission makes the Christian a descendant of Jesus Christ through the spiritual procreation of the Word. See Topical Index under Apostles and Authority.

(22)-(23) pp. 139-140. Concerning the Logos, see annotation to our C.S.P. (31) and (32) pp. 344-345, and Topical Index.

(24) p. 140. Through the birth of Christ and through His second coming, Heaven and earth shall be newly created. See Topical Index under God and Future.

(25) p. 140. In this text the oldest presbyters quoted by Iren-aeus (see Index of Names and Topical Index) are described as men who lived with John, the disciple of Jesus, and who saw and heard other apostles as well. Hence we are concerned with those who were elders and teachers of the Church already

during the first century. The age of Jesus alleged here contradicts the age given in the New Testament, to which Justin testifies (our P.&P. (15) p. 267).

(26) pp. 140-141. In this powerful witness Justin summarizes in a few words the mighty power of God against all evil; Christ, who was crucified and who will come again, wields this might over all the powers and authorities on earth.

(27)-(29) pp. 141-142. According to these texts, the miracles Christ did as Man and the authority of the Church already reveal now the power of Christ's future arrival. So much is the world affected by this power now that the main international centers of demonic corruption and all centers of governmental authority are already under its sway.

(30)-(33) pp. 142-143. To give a name to the expected second coming of Christ is, for the oppressed, rejected, and dispossessed Christians, to name as a mystery a fact that is all-decisive by virtue of the power of resurrection.

(34)-(38), pp. 143-146, contain the declaration of early Christian faith in the future Kingdom of Jesus. It will be a Kingdom of a thousand years' duration; the earth will be fertile; there will be unity and peace, also among animals; the city of Jerusalem will be the center of the people of Israel in enduring work of mind and hand. Yet all this is only an allegory of the eternal resurrection because only then will men live like angels.

(34)-(35) pp. 143-144. Concerning the first elders see Topical Index and annotation to our C.F.&S. (25) above.

(36) p. 144. Papias was overseer or bishop of the Church in Hierapolis in Phrygia about the year 140. He possessed a collection of the Lord's Sayings, and about the year 142 composed

his five books of *Sayings of the Lord Explained,* based on oral information received from the oldest Christians of that time. Because he must have been very old then, we should pay great attention to his reminiscences about the first elders and followers of the disciples of Jesus.

Papias was a hearer of John and a friend of Polycarp (see annotation to our C.F.&S. (73) p. 362). Also he belonged to the same influential Johannine circle of Phrygia and Asia Minor. This circle emphasized with particular vigor the belief in what is often called the millennium, the conviction that the Kingdom of Jesus Christ will come on the earth. Compare all Papias texts listed in the Index of Names.

Papias reports about the apostle John that he gave his Gospel to the Churches during his lifetime and that in addition to Stephen, Peter, and Paul there were only two martyrs among the apostles, namely James and John. John's martyrdom is also corroborated by the inclusion of the words "John and James, the apostles in Jerusalem" in the Syriac martyrology of A.D. 411 for December 27 and in the Armenian martyrology for December 28. ⟨See E. Hennecke, *New Testament Apocrypha,* after this referred to as Hennecke ET(English Translation), vol. 2, p. 53.⟩

(39)-(44), pp. 146-149: testimonies about resurrection and immortality, about Heaven and Paradise.

(39)-(42) pp. 146-147. In *On the Resurrection of the Dead* the apologist Athenagoras explains in terms of reason and logic the early Christian certainty that resurrection of the body is the final goal of man's destiny. Compare our C.F.&S. (37), pp. 144-145, where Justin declares that those are not Christians who do not believe in the resurrection but maintain that the souls of the deceased are received into Heaven, thereby rejecting the renewal of the body.

(44)-(57), pp. 148-156, show how the prophetic Spirit of both the Old Testament prophets and the Old Testament as a whole is cited as the revelation of God pointing to Christ and His future.

(45) p. 149. Here Moses as the first prophet is seen to have predicted the first and second advent of Christ. This is a remarkable example of the bold way in which the early Christians used the Old Testament. The same is true of our C.F.&S. (46).

(46) pp. 149-151. Concerning the elders who had still seen the apostles, see Topical Index and annotation to our C.F.&S. (25) pp. 355-356. The whole of Biblical history reveals God's justice and holiness, shows man's smallness, and points to forgiveness of sin and fulfillment in Christ. The last sentences are directed against Gnostic false teachings (see Topical Index under Gnosis).

(47) p. 151. The inspiration of the prophets works in such a way that, gripped by the Spirit, they become God's instruments and pronounce and represent His Word. In this way, revealing the things of the past, the present, and the future, they point to God and to God only.

(48) p. 152. Compare the annotation to our P.&P. (40), p. 407, concerning the Roman authorities' prohibition against reading prophetic books, such as Hystaspes, the Sibyl, and the Old Testament, and the threat of capital punishment for those who disobeyed. Justin maintains here that the Christians were not intimidated from reading these books by this demonic threat of the authorities. The last paragraph shows that the Christians of this period were using the Septuagint as their Bible, i.e. the Greek translation of the Old Testament which originated in Egypt. This is confirmed in our C.F.&S. (56) p. 156.

(49) pp. 152-153. The whole history of salvation of Jesus Christ is found in the predictions of the prophets. Compare annotations to our C.F.&S. (45) and (46).

(51) p. 153. The testimony to Christ is not based on the thoughts and words of men but on the prophetic Word of God, which lifts the prophet in ecstasy above his own way of thinking. That the Holy Spirit inspires him in what he says, that the Spirit thus uses him as a flute player uses his flute (our C.F.&S. (52) p. 154) corresponds to the Montanist concept of the prophetic Spirit. Compare with our P.&P. (55) p.303, (74) and (76) p. 307, and (83)-(86) p. 309, and Topical Index under Spirit and Prophets.

(52) p. 154. Justin emphasizes just as much that it is not Spirit-filled man who speaks through the prophets, but it is the Spirit of God, the Logos of God himself, who moves these men and speaks through them. Therefore He can sometimes speak in the first person as God or Christ. However, Justin does not maintain that when this happens human thinking is actually suspended by ecstasy. Compare with our C.F.&S. (51) p. 153 and the Montanist concept under Spirit and Prophets in the Topical Index.

(53)-(54) pp. 154-155. Examples of the Father and the Christ speaking in the first person through the words of the prophets. See our L.S.T.A.&L. (64) p. 213, with annotation p. 385; our P.&P. (74) p. 307, and (83)-(86) p. 309, with annotation p. 410.

(55) pp. 155-156. This is an example of the proclamation of the future through the prophetic Spirit in the Old Testament.

(56) p. 156. The Septuagint was the Bible used by the Christians at this time; see annotation to our C.F.&S. (48) above and Topical Index under Old Testament.

(57) p. 156. The unbelievable and impossible is foretold through prophecy. It happens and it is believed. That alone constitutes a living faith.

(57)-(67) pp. 156-159. The Scripture of the Old Testament is the basis of the proclamation of Christ in the first Church. The Christians are the true Israel, in the faith of Abraham and the patriarchs, in the trust they have in the Scriptures of the Law and the Prophets. See our I.& S. p. 27, with annotation 58, p. 327; I.& S. p. 34, with annotations 72-73, p. 330; and Topical Index under Old Testament and Jews.

(58) pp. 156-157. All Jewish writings, which are in fact Christian because they are Messianic, are understood and observed in their true significance only by the Christians. Compare Topical Index under Old Testament and Jews.

(60) p. 157. Justin's assertion that the various passages of the Scriptures do not teach human concepts but reveal the thoughts of God and His will shows, as do all the texts here, that faith in the unique inspiration of the Bible and the prophets is very old.

(61) p. 157. Trust in the Scriptures and the clarity arising from them are only strengthened by false prophecy's demonic mimicking.

(62) pp. 157-158. See annotation to (60) above, our I.& S. p. 27, with its annotation 58, p. 327, and I.& S. p. 34, with annotations 72 and 73, p. 330, regarding Theophilus' statement that the testimonies of all the prophets agree with each other, and that the Holy Writings of the Christians—the Old Testament of the Jews—are proved to be the oldest and truest of all and bear the Holy Spirit within them.

(63) p. 158. The Christians, then, are the bringers of truth and of God's reality.

(64) p. 158. See our C.F.&S. (45) p. 149, with annotation p. 358.

(65)-(66) pp. 158-159. The understanding of the Scriptures which point to Christ is given through grace. No contradictions in the Scriptures are recognized (compare annotation to (60) above). Justin testifies here also that he came to faith through the prophets of the Old Testament and through the witnesses to the Crucified. Compare with our C.F.&S. (69) pp. 160-161, our I.&S. p. 34, and annotation 73, p. 330.

(67) p. 159. The Word of God must not be falsified by words of men. Compare with our C.F.&S. (60), (62), (65), and (66).

(68)-(73) pp. 159-162. The Spirit of God at work in the Old Testament is alive now in the Church of Christ.

(68) p. 159. Precisely through those Christians who are the feeblest and most ingenuous, the Word speaks by the power of God!

(69) pp. 160-161. This is Justin's noteworthy account of his own conversion through the writings of the Old Testament and the living witnesses to Christ. Compare with our C.F.&S. (65)-(66) pp. 158-159, our I.&S. p. 34, including annotation 73, p. 330, Index of Names under Justin, and the Topical Index under Old Testament.

(70) p. 161. In this passage the prophets are described as those who, in the Spirit of God, speak out what the Holy Spirit says to them and what they have seen and heard. They need no proofs for their words. What they say is trustworthy. This

can be demonstrated by the effect of their words and their lives and by the attendant power of working miracles. The beginning and end of all things is revealed to them. Compare with our C.F.&S. (47)-(55) pp. 151-156, (62) pp. 157-158, including annotation p. 360 and Topical Index under Prophets.

(70)-(72) pp. 161-162. The varied and clearly differentiated gifts of grace and powers from God, which Solomon, Daniel, Moses, Elijah, Jeremiah, David, and the other prophets received, had to cease among the Jews after Christ's coming so that they might arise once more among the Christ-believers who have received the Spirit.

(73) p. 162. Papias (see annotation to our C.F.&S. (36) pp. 356-357 and Index of Names) testified that he listened to the first elders and thus investigated the words of the apostles practically at their very source. He learned the truth not through book knowledge but from the living word of living witnesses.

(73)-(81), pp. 162-167, show how the Gospel of Jesus Christ and the Memoirs of the Apostles were emerging as the authority for the New Testament.

(74) and (75) pp. 162-163. The Gospel giving bodily substance to the Word, the apostles constituting the body of elders in the Church, and the prophets of old foretelling the Good News, all belong together because they are bearers of the same Spirit in the unity of Jesus Christ and in the hope for His future.

(76) p. 163. The crucial testimony to the truth, "It is written," refers not only to the ancient records of the Old Testament, but as much, no, even more to the Gospel, to Jesus Christ, to the unassailable records of His Cross, His death, His resurrection, His faith. For in them is man justified, in them is given the advent of the Healing Savior, the Lord Jesus Christ, and

the fulfillment of the prophecies. All this together is the unity of God. God's records are His deeds.

(77)-(79) pp. 163-164. It is the "Memoirs of the Apostles" (the Gospels) which constitute the basis of the New Testament and the faith of earliest Christendom. One of the main sources of these memoirs is to be found in the Sayings of Jesus. See Topical Index under Lord's Sayings. It is emphasized that the Memoirs of the Apostles center on the person of Jesus and the initiation of His Meal of Remembrance. Characteristically, the meetings of the first two centuries (our C.F.&S. (78) p. 164) consisted chiefly of long, animated readings from the Memoirs of the Apostles and the Writings of the Prophets. Compare with our M.&W. (12) pp. 222-225, (13) pp. 225-226, our I.&S. pp. 34-35 and 46-47, and our C.F.&S. (81) pp. 165-167.

(80) pp. 164-165. These sources are to be found in Papias, quoted by Eusebius III.39; *Argumentum in Patr. Apost. opera,* and Zahn, *Forschungen* 6; ⟨ninth century Codex Vaticanus Alexandrinus 14⟩; and Andrew of Caesarea, *Preface to the Revelation* 34.12.

(80)-(81) pp. 164-167. Concerning the emergence of the New Testament at the end of our period, see also the annotation to (79) above, with references. In this earliest extant catalog of the New Testament writings, the conclusion is remarkable: whereas the forged Letters to the Laodiceans and Alexandrians attributed to Paul are thrown out, the Letter of Jude, two (not three) Letters of John and his Revelation, together with the *Revelation of Peter* and even the *Wisdom of Solomon,* are included in the New Testament canon. However, express mention is made that some Christians do not want the *Revelation of Peter* to be read in the Churches.

Here the *Shepherd* of Hermas (see Index of Names and our P.&P. (33) pp. 278-294) is dated between the years 140-

155. It is banished from the New Testament and must not be read aloud in the assemblies of the Church together with the writings of the prophets and apostles, though it should be read privately. Over against this it must be stated that the prophetic *Shepherd* of Hermas was acknowledged by the following ancient authorities as belonging to the Bible and that with some it continued to remain a part of the New Testament. Irenaeus (*Against Heresies* IV.20.2) quotes a passage from the *Shepherd,* First Command, as "Scripture." Compare Eusebius V.8.7. Also Tertullian (*On Prayer* 16) recognizes the authority of the *Shepherd* as Scripture whereas later, after becoming a Montanist, he emphasizes that the *Letter of Barnabas* carries greater authority in the Church than the *Shepherd* of Hermas (*On Modesty* 20). Clement of Alexandria too quotes Hermas as Scripture (*Misc.* II.9,12; IV.8; VI.15), and so do Origen (*First Principles* I.3.3 and IV.1.11) and Pseudo-Cyprian (*Against Dice-Throwers* 2-4). In the Codex Sinaiticus, the *Shepherd* is included among the New Testament writings. In (80), pp. 164-165, it is strongly emphasized that John's Revelation was divinely inspired. In the *Muratorian Canon* the new birth, the suffering and resurrection of Jesus, His life with the disciples, and the twofold coming of Christ—the second, future coming in kingly power—are strongly in evidence. About the apostle Paul there is the highly important statement that for him Christ is the crux of everything. Very significant is the testimony that there is only one Church spread over the whole earth.

The *Muratorian Canon,* written about A.D. 180, is of crucial importance because it contains the first definite though preliminary catalog of the New Testament writings and because it clearly demonstrates the emerging authority of the New Testament as Scripture, which was gradually to become preeminent in times to come. The *Canon* concludes the period which we hope to make more widely known through this book.

# ANNOTATIONS TO LORD'S SAYINGS,
# THE TEACHING OF THE TWELVE APOSTLES,
# AND LETTERS

(1)-(53) pp. 171-180. The text of Oxyrhynchus Papyrus 654, published by Grenfell and Hunt in 1904 as the result of their second discovery, begins with the words: "These are the sayings which Jesus speaks, the Living One and the Lord. . . . He said to them [to Thomas and another apostle], 'Whoever hears these sayings shall never taste death.' " ⟨Compare the close similarity of the beginning of the Coptic *Gospel according to Thomas*. See Index of Names and Writings.⟩ In a Coptic translation the Gospel of the Hebrews says, according to Cyril of Jerusalem, "The Power came into the world." Similarly, the Gospel of Peter 5.19 says that Jesus cried out on the Cross, "My Power! O Power!"

We can see from these examples that many of the scattered sayings of Jesus resemble those in the New Testament so closely that it would not be worth while to differentiate between them. For instance, Augustine (in *Against the Enemy of the Law and the Prophets* II.4.14) quotes the following as a Lord's Saying: "You have rejected the Living One who stands before your eyes, and you babble about the dead." In the Syriac *Teaching of the Apostles* (*Didascalia*) XIX ⟨see also Connolly, p. 164⟩ Jesus says, "Fear *me*, who can destroy body and soul in Hell." Ephraem reports this as a Lord's Saying: "The physician hurries to where the pains are." There are several extant sayings of the risen Jesus, differing slightly from those of the New Testament, in which He announces to His disciples and women followers that it is He himself whom they are seeing (account of the resurrection in the Coptic version ⟨of the

*Epistle of the Apostles* 9-12; see James, *The Apocryphal New Testament,* pp. 488-489)). The Lord's Sayings very similar to those contained in the New Testament were for the most part omitted from our collection, giving precedence to sayings of Jesus which sound unusual and surprising to anyone well acquainted with the New Testament.

The numerous sources given underneath each saying and in the annotations show the authority the Lord's Sayings commanded in the first Church communities. This has been demonstrated in the Introduction, pp. 34-35, with annotation 74, pp. 330-331. It is proved there and in the annotation to our C.F.&S. (77)-(79) p. 363 that the Sayings of Jesus, of which Papias owned a collection, constituted the basic source for the "Memoirs of the Apostles" and consequently determined the formation of the Gospels and the New Testament. Compare annotation to our C.F.&S. (36) pp. 356-357. A word by Aristides about the authority of the Lord's Sayings is contained in our C.F.&S. (24) p. 105: "They observe the words of their Christ with much care."

Four Lord's Sayings are to be found in our book in *The Teaching of the Twelve Apostles,* L.S.T.A.&L. (54) p. 181, in the *Second Letter of Clement,* P.&P. (32) p. 276, in the *Letter of Barnabas,* L.S.T.A.&L. (64) p. 209, and in M.&W. (1) p. 217. The *Letter of Barnabas* contains a fifth Saying of Jesus. It is quoted in the annotation to our L.S. (45) pp. 373-374. It can be seen in an example from Athenagoras (our C.S.P. (39) p. 118) how difficult it is to know today whether or not the first Christians considered a certain text to be a Saying of Jesus. He quotes what the Logos has spoken. It seems probable that this passage on the pure character of the kiss of fellowship had its origin in the Spirit-filled words spoken by a prophet in a Church meeting.

(1) The central, crucial place which in this Saying Jesus attests to be His is clearly evident also in the following Lord's Sayings: (3) p. 171, (15) p. 174, and (24)-(26) pp. 175-176; (30) and (32) pp. 176-177; (34)-(37) p. 178; (42) p. 179; (48) and (51) p. 180; and most of all (52)-(53) p. 180. The fire of judgment brought by Jesus comes to expression in Sayings (6) p. 172, (15) p. 174, (30) pp. 176-177, (36) and (37) p. 178, and (46) p. 179. The Kingdom of God manifest in Jesus is also testified to in Sayings (16) p. 174; (22) p. 175; (27), (30), and (31) pp. 176-177; (34) and (35) p. 178; and (52) and (53) p. 180.

(2) In his *Gospel Commentary* 15 ⟨see also J. H. Hill, *Dissertation on the Gospel Commentary of S. Ephraem the Syrian*, Edinburgh, 1896, p. 101⟩, Ephraem the Syrian has the following parallel Saying: "Where one is alone I am with him, and where two are, I shall be with them." He adds this Lord's Saying to it: "And when we are three we gather as in the Church." See also our M.&W. (1) p. 217.

(3) See also our L.S. (1) p. 171, with annotation. In this Saying Jesus declares that He is the only door through which one can enter into life. According to Lord's Saying (6) p. 172, this means the complete reversal of all things and, according to Saying (38) p. 178, this entering brings about the "confusion" leading to repentance. Another Lord's Saying quoted by Macarius of Egypt in his *Homily* 37.1 describes this decisive step as the way going from faith and expectation through love to life: "Come together seeking faith and expectation. From both is born love, the friend of God and the friend of man, that bears eternal life." This Saying of Jesus testifies that the power of love springs from faith and from the eschatology of faith.

(4) The rescue of what is lost comes to expression in different ways also in Sayings (20) p. 174, (38) p. 178, (42) p. 179, and (53) p. 180.

(5) ⟨See also J. A. Ropes, "Agrapha," in *Dictionary of the Bible,* ed. J. Hastings, 1907, vol. 5, p. 345.⟩ About this plea for the Holy Spirit and His working, compare Lord's Sayings (40) p. 178 and (49)-(51) p. 180.

(6) Also found in the mystagogy contained in the *Testament of Our Lord* I.28 and in Pseudo-Linus, *Martyrdom of Peter* 17. See annotations to Sayings (3) and (4) above.

(7)-(8) In the Teaching of Addaeus we find this related Saying of Jesus: "Whatever you say in words to the people, practice in deeds before all men."

(9) Jesus attests to the truth of the holy writings in the Old Testament. Compare with Lord's Sayings (13) p. 173, (23)-(25) p. 175, (33) p. 177, and above all Saying (51) p. 180 where Jesus declares that He is the Logos (Word) speaking in the Spirit-filled prophets. See Topical Index under Logos.

(10) Compare with Saying (15) p. 174 concerning blindness of heart, (21) pp. 174-175 concerning what is hidden from the eyes, and (45) p. 179 concerning the truth which does not lie openly on the surface. According to *Didascalia* XXVI ⟨Connolly, p. 224⟩, Jesus expressly said that the eyes that see and the ears that hear are blessed.

(11) In another Saying of Jesus the same thought is expressed much more forcefully: "If you have seen your brother, you have seen your God (your Lord)" (Clem. Alex., *Misc.* I.19.94 and II.15.70; Rufinus, *History of the Monks* 55; Tertullian, *On Prayer* 26).

(11)-(13) In connection with these Lord's Sayings, Justin (*Dialogue with Trypho* 96, 124) and Clem. *Hom.* (III.57, XI. 12, and XVIII.2) quote the words of Jesus in the Sermon on the Mount in the sense that we should be just as kind and merciful as our Heavenly Father is. In Clem. *Hom.* (VII.4, XI.4, and XII.32) the words of the Sermon on the Mount are condensed in one single sentence to guide the practical Christian: "What he wishes for himself he wishes also for his neighbor." In the Clementine *Homilies* (III.69.1) Jesus is quoted as saying:

> If you love your brothers you will take nothing away from them. You will share your possessions with them; you will feed the hungry [and help the thirsty, the naked, the sick, the prisoners, and the strangers]; and you will hate no man.

A Lord's Saying quoted in a Coptic Bible manuscript applies this love of Jesus also to animals:

> Man, why do you beat your animal? . . . Woe to you that you do not hear how it complains to the Creator in Heaven and how it cries for mercy. But a threefold woe to the man about whom it moans and laments in its pain! . . . Never beat it again, that you also may find mercy.

A unique word, compared with the parables and similes of Jesus!

(14) This Saying is also in Anastasius of Sinai. Compare with *The Teaching of the Twelve Apostles,* our L.S.T.A.&L. (54) p. 181, and *Shepherd* of Hermas, our P.&P. (33), Second Commandment, p. 280 (abbreviated in our text). In Epiphanius, *Panarion* 80.5, we find the Lord's Saying: "The laborer's simple food is sufficient for him." This refers to the worker laboring in the proclamation of the Gospel. Compare with Lord's Sayings (28) p. 176 and (47) p. 179.

(15) See also annotation to Lord's Saying (10) p. 368. This lament of Jesus is intensified in a Saying from *Acts of Peter* 10, quoting the Gospel of the Egyptians: "Those who are with me have not understood me."

(16) See annotation to Lord's Saying (1) above. ⟨See also *Gospel according to Thomas* 2.⟩

(17) This differs from the words of Jesus in the Sermon on the Mount only in saying that the city is fortified and cannot fall.

(18)-(19) The right evaluation of the great and the small!

(20) The Ethiopic text says, "He that is weak will give powerful strength." Compare the Lord's Saying in Origen's *Commentary XIII.2 on Matthew*: "I became weak for the sake of the weak." See annotation to (4) above and Saying (15) p. 174.

(21) Compare with annotation to Lord's Saying (10) p. 368. This testimony about the raising up of the dead is unique in its phrasing.

(22) See annotation to Saying (1) above. This badly mutilated text has been translated in many different ways. The present translation comes closest to the convictions of the early days of Christendom. It attests that the Kingdom will come upon this earth, it regards the creatures of this earth as the instruments of the Father who draws men into the Kingdom, and it emphasizes the working of the Kingdom within us and among us.

(23) Compare annotation to Lord's Saying (9) above. Freedom from the Law can be given only through the freedom of the Spirit binding men in a different way.

(24) Compare the parables of Jesus. ⟨See also *Gospel according to Thomas* 62.⟩

(25) Also in Origen, *Commentary on Matthew* XVII.31; IV. 150. This Saying significantly symbolizes the spiritual gift of discernment. See also annotation to (9) above.

(26) Similar to John 6:44 and 15:16.

(27) ⟨See also *Gospel according to Thomas* 27.⟩ Regarding abstention, two other Lord's Sayings should be compared. In the first, according to Jerome (*On Illustrious Men* 2, quoting from the Gospel of the Hebrews), after His resurrection Jesus asked the one who was fasting to eat his bread. In the second, Jesus said that one who fasts can do so only for the sake of his brothers, not for the sake of Jesus (*Didascalia* XXI ⟨Connolly, p. 183⟩). Compare Topical Index under Property. Concerning the Kingdom of God in this text, see annotation to Saying (1) above.

(28) Compare annotation to Lord's Saying (14) above. The obscure last lines might possibly mean that, stripped of the carnal body in judgment, the disciples will not be put to shame.

(29) This significant Saying begins with the words, "Jesus, on whom be peace, has said: ...." (See also Hennecke ET, vol. 1, p. 90, and his *Handbuch*, p. 17.)

(30) The demonic character of the present world-age and its end are confirmed in other Lord's Sayings. Theodorus Balsamon cites as a "word of the Gospel": "The shape of this world shall pass away." Ephraem quotes: "The world shall be built up by grace." Compare Sayings (31)-(35) pp. 177-178. For the central testimony that Jesus was given into death for the sins of men so that they should turn about and sin no more,

see also the Sayings of Jesus (20) p. 174; (36), (41), and (42) pp. 178-179.

According to two other Lord's Sayings, sinful speech could be found even in the prophets anointed with the Spirit. For the first see Jerome, *Against Pelagius* 3.2, quoting from the Gospel of the Nazaraeans. The second Saying states: "Everybody who believes and is baptized shall have his past sins forgiven" (*Didascalia* XX ⟨see also Connolly, p. 178⟩). See also Lord's Saying (53) p. 180. Saying (30) then is very characteristic.

(31) About Papias, see Index of Names. Compare the Lord's Saying connected with the Sermon on the Mount, quoted by Aphraates, which says that the humble shall possess the land and dwell on the earth for ever.

(32) See annotation to Saying (1) above. This Saying clearly refers first of all to the beginning and the end of creation.

(33) See annotations to Sayings (1), (9), and (32) above.

(34) Compare with Lord's Sayings (1) p. 171, (7) and (8) p. 172, and (30)-(33) pp. 176-177.

(35) Compare with Lord's Saying (1) p. 171, including annotation to (1) p. 367, and (30)-(34) pp. 176-178.

(36) can also be found in Clem. Alex., *What Rich Man Can Be Saved?* 40.

(37) was found at Akhmim in Egypt. Only those who hunger and thirst are able to believe. There is another Lord's Saying about the testing of man's life: "No one shall attain the Kingdom of Heaven without having been tested" (Syriac *Didascalia* ⟨V, see also Connolly, p. 38⟩; Tertullian, *On Baptism* 20.2, contains a similar Saying).

(38) Compare with annotation to Lord's Saying (3) above and Paul's words in 2 Cor. 2:16.

(39) ⟨See also Hennecke ET, vol. 2, p. 383.⟩ The raising up of the dead and the miracle of the feeding of the multitudes are mere pointers to the greater object, faith.

(40) This Saying begins with the words, "I and my disciples. . . ." See annotation to Saying (5) above.

(41) In connection with this significant Saying about the interrelation of all guilt, see *Didascalia* XXI ⟨see also Connolly, p. 184⟩, which expands the words of Jesus in the Sermon on the Mount: "Blessed are those who mourn over the corruption of the unbelievers."

(42) Compare annotation to Lord's Saying (4) above. The *Didascalia* XI ⟨see also Connolly, p. 118⟩ quotes a Saying "from the mouth of the Lord Jesus Christ" attesting that it is His will and the will of His Father that nobody shall perish, but all men shall believe and live.

(43) The Gospel of Thomas refers to the age of seven, as the age when children, although awakened to full awareness, are still completely children.

(44) The "Antichrist" Celsus (see Index of Names) aptly describes here the true situation of Christianity!

(45) In this venture of faith and courage the disciples take up their Cross "with joy and jubilation," according to a Lord's Saying in the *Didascalia* XIX ⟨see also Connolly, p. 163⟩. The Lord's Saying in the *Letter of Barnabas*, mentioned in the annotation to Lord's Sayings (1)-(53) pp. 365-366, expresses a similar thought: "Those who wish to see me and to take hold of my

Kingdom need to go through affliction and suffering in order to grasp me." See also Topical Index under Fighting attitude.

(46) The Talmud quotes another Saying of Jesus dealing with judgment: "What came from filth shall return to the place of filth." ⟨See also J. Jeremias, *Unknown Sayings of Jesus,* pp. 10-11.⟩

(47) With reference to the poverty of those who proclaim Jesus without receiving any salary or compensation, compare annotation to Lord's Saying (14) above.

(48) In the same context the Clementine *Homilies* continue: "Therefore you should not let yourselves be called 'leaders', but only 'appointed ones.'" See annotation to Lord's Saying (1) above, and compare with Sayings (52) and (53) p. 180.

(49) See also annotation to Saying (5) above.

(50) Here the Spirit carries Jesus up to Mount Tabor, traditionally the Mount of Transfiguration (Origen, *Commentary II.6 on John*). This Saying from the Gospel of the Hebrews is also quoted by Origen (*Homily XV. 4 on Jeremiah*) and by Jerome (commentaries *On Micah* 7.6, *On Isaiah* 40.9, and *On Ezekiel* 16.13).

(51) See annotations to Sayings (1), (5), and (9) above.

(52) Compare with Lord's Saying (13) p. 173, annotation to Saying (1) p. 367, and Topical Index under Authority. In this Saying the secret of the power and glory of Jesus is revealed by the mandate given to the apostles: it is the authority to rule as King given to Christ by the Father.

(53) Compare with Saying (52) p. 180, annotations to Sayings (1), (3), and (30) above, and Topical Index under Apostles

and Authority. In this Saying Jesus calls His disciples "faithful apostles," whose testimony will take away the excuse of the unbelievers so that they cannot say, "We did not hear it." The message of their apostolic mission is the Joyful News of the One God and of faith in Jesus, revealing the future and rescuing the believers.

(54) pp. 181-189. The *Didache* or *The Lord's Teaching by the Twelve Apostles to the Heathen* gives a comprehensive insight into the life of the Church at the end of the first century and the beginning of the second. The finding of this Lord's Teaching in a hospice at Constantinople (and its subsequent publication in 1883) was the most important of the many valuable discoveries of early Christian writings since the end of the last century. Because of its significance, it is the only text from the period covered by our book reproduced without omissions. See our I.&S. p. 14, with annotation 31, p. 323, and Index of Names and Writings under *Teaching of the Twelve Apostles*.

In its witness to the truth the *Didache* is marked by utmost plainness and simplicity—one reason why it must have been close to apostolic times. Its earliest version evidently originated in Syria or Palestine before the year A.D. 100. Clement of Alexandria (*Miscellanies* I.20.100) counted the *Didache* among the New Testament writings; compare Eusebius (*Church History* III.25.4).

The first part of the *Didache* (pp. 181-184), closely related to Jewish moral teaching, was used for baptismal instruction. Only after instruction in the two ways of death and of life (p. 181) should the step of baptism be undertaken. See Topical Index under Discipline, Baptism, and Sermon on the Mount, and our M.&W. (4) p. 218. The Lord's Sayings, being commands of Jesus, are neither to be shortened nor enlarged upon.

The demands made by Jesus in the Sermon on the Mount determine the character of this first section of the *Didache*. The community which Christians have in immortal treasures should apply all the more to transitory, material possessions, and Christians should claim nothing as their own (p. 183). True love has nothing to do with legal rights: "You shall love men more than your own life." This love, free of covetousness, consists in reverence for the dignity of life and brings forth purity, honesty, and humility.

The second part, written like a very early liturgy, provides instruction for baptism, fasting, and praying with the Lord's Prayer (pp. 184-185) and for the Lord's Supper (pp. 185-186). The instructions concerning prayer and fasting are not without a legalistic trait. Because baptism pertains only to the convinced and determined believer, there can be no question of baptizing children. As submersion into the Father, the Son, and the Holy Spirit, baptism consists in the immersion of the body in living, flowing water. At the same time it is the symbol of being penetrated and impregnated by the wind and water of the Holy Spirit, of being buried into Christ, of being purified in this bath belonging to the new birth. See Topical Index under Baptism and Confession of Faith. Still or warm water and the pouring of water over the head and body are conceded as exceptions.

What comes to expression in the Lord's Supper is this: the breaking of bread signifies above all the unity of the Church Body, and the cup signifies above all the vine of Christ's blood. Compare the vine of the Son of Man pointing to the Messiah in Psalm 80. The Holy Spirit is the true drink and the true food. Here we meet some of the oldest Christian prayers offering thanks and adoration to the Father and to the Son. Deliverance from evil and the imminence of the Kingdom stand out in those prayers: "May grace come!"

"May this world-age pass away!" "Our Lord comes!" See also annotation to our L.S.T.A.&L. (30) pp. 371-372.

The third part of the *Didache* (pp. 186-189) is concerned with the life of the Church. First the work of the apostles, prophets, and teachers is discussed. Their whole manner of life—their incessant traveling, their life of poverty, and their laboring in and through the Spirit—was of symbolic significance, pointing to the mystery of the Church without demanding that all the believers imitate their way of life. Regarding all the above, and concerning the provision of work, and the itinerant life, see our I.&S. p. 16, with annotation 35, p. 325, and Topical Index under Apostles, Prophets, and Teachers, especially I.&S. pp. 30-40.

The prophets were the chief priests. The overseers and servants (p. 188), who later were to become "bishops" and "deacons," were regarded merely as deputies of the prophets and teachers. In this period of transition they did not yet hold a position of leadership and control, but they were not to be ignored either. Baptism too was not given through the overseers but through the whole Church. In connection with the meetings on the Lord's Day (Sunday) the overseers are not even mentioned. When the same reverence is demanded for the one who proclaims the truth as for the Lord himself (p. 183), this is meant for the person of every Spirit-bearer, not for the place of meeting or for the office of the one who speaks. "The Lord himself is in the place where the Lordship of the Lord is proclaimed."

The meetings were to take place as often as possible (pp. 183, 184-186, and 188-189). See our I.&S. p. 33, with annotation 70, p. 329. The constructive discipline and the offering of prayers and gifts in the meetings were bound up with the breaking of bread and the personal confession of transgressions.

*The Lord's Teaching* (the *Didache*) has an apocalyptic end-ing (p. 189) closely akin to the eschatology of the New Testament. The very definite and fully determined expectation of the coming end brings about the strongest exertion of moral responsibility. During these latter days, yes, in this last hour, the lamps must be kept burning. The persecutions of the martyrs, the rise of false prophets, and the imminent approach of the great World-seducer are the most powerful incentive. Soon the outstretched arms of the Crucified will appear in the sky! Soon the trumpet blasts will sound! The resurrection is at hand! The Lord is coming! Compare with annotation to Lord's Saying (3) p. 367.

(55)-(64), pp. 189-213, contain all that is important in the letters of our period.

(55) pp. 189-196. This letter was addressed by the whole Church of Rome—not just by her bishop—to the Church at Corinth before the year A.D. 100, perhaps in A.D. 94. (The so-called *Second Letter of Clement*, written about A.D. 150, is in actual fact a Church sermon, the oldest handed down to us, and can be found in our section P.&P. (32) pp. 274-278.) Clement, who belonged to the generation immediately following the apostles, was one of the leading men of the Church at Rome; however, he is not mentioned by name in this letter.

The *First Letter of Clement* was read in Church meetings until the time of Eusebius in more places than just Rome and Corinth (see Eusebius, *Church History* III.16; III.38.1; IV.23.11). Both letters of Clement occasionally found a place in the New Testament, as in the Codex Alexandrinus and the Syriac version. The prestige of the *First Letter of Clement* stems from the power in this attempt to encompass the attitude of faith and life of early Christianity and the early Church.

The first, longer "half" of the *First Letter of Clement* (pp. 189-194) is built around a well-founded challenge to fight through without envy for a transforming repentance (p. 191). It was through jealousy that death came into the world in times of old, and it is jealousy that causes death now in the Church at Corinth (p. 191). Jealousy is overcome by the obedience of faith which comes to expression in hospitality (p. 190) and humility (pp. 191-192). It is God's goodness alone—the righteousness born purely out of faith in God, in His will, and in Christ— which creates that stance in life characterized by good acts (p. 194). The believer bears the Lord's sayings in his heart; he gazes upon the defenseless, bloody suffering of Christ, which through the removal of sin has brought healing and transformation to the whole world (pp. 190-191). Since the Holy Spirit has been poured out over all (p. 190), the Church now looks toward the speedy return of Christ in most intense expectation (p. 193). This letter bears witness to the resurrection of the dead in vivid pictures, the most powerful of which is the very ancient myth of the bird phoenix (pp. 193-194).

In the second, weaker "half" of the *First Letter of Clement* (pp. 194-196), the Old Testament order of the priesthood (Num. 16) is introduced now by the Church at Rome as a deliberate innovation for the Christian congregations (pp. 194-195). According to this concept, Christ, the only High Priest, is succeeded by the bishops as priests and by the deacons as Levites. Here too, the ominous word "laymen" is used for the first time (p. 195). (The word "clergy" was used for the first time in a clearly defined way in *Monogamy* 12 by Tertullian, who was, however, opposed to the whole concept.)

For all that, it is just this letter which proves that the office of an all-controlling episcopate existed neither in Rome nor in Corinth at that time. But in dealing with the Church quarrel at Corinth, this letter tries to make clear that unity in the One Christ, in the One Spirit, and in the One Body is based on love, discipline, repentance, and humility (pp. 195-

196) through the recognition of the designated office (p. 195).
Compare with our I.&S. pp. 47-49 and Topical Index under
Episcopate. After all, youthful spirits had rebelled against
approved elders in Corinth! See pp. 190, 191, and 196. Regarding the testimony on the authority of the Spirit and on
the mission and task of the apostles and the apostolic elders,
p. 195, compare the references listed in the index under Apostles and Elders. Regarding voluntary imprisonment for the
ransom of others, p. 196, see our I.&S. p. 17 at "39" and
Topical Index under Love.

(56)-(62) pp. 196-204. The seven *Letters of Ignatius* are of
as much consequence as the *First Letter of Clement* for the
development of the primitive Church toward ecclesiasticism,
and as regards the slowly emerging theology, they reveal considerably more than the *First Letter of Clement*; they also
bear the stamp of greater originality. Ignatius, Bishop of
Antioch in Syria, wrote his letters at the time he was being
escorted by ten soldiers to suffer the death of a martyr in
Rome early in the second century. His passionate, insistent
urge for martyrdom (pp. 197, 200, and 202) and his equally
ardent insistence on the unity of the Church (pp. 197, 198,
199, 201, and 203) are the keynote of these resounding letters.

Already at the time of Ignatius, the overseers and bishops
exercised a ruling leadership in the Churches of Antioch. This
evidently happened under the influence of the primitive Church
in Jerusalem. Compare with annotation 7 to our I.&S.,
p. 317 and annotation to our S.S.&M. (9) pp. 335-337. The
way Ignatius insists that the reality of the Church depends on
the presence of the bishop—not, as was the case later in the
Roman Catholic Church, in his capacity as successor to the
apostles but as the representative of God and Christ (see (60)
p. 201 and (61) p. 203)—and, further, the energetic way he

fights for subordination to the bishops prove that the exclusive predominance of the bishops had not yet come to full victory at that time, but that its way was being paved from Jerusalem by Ignatius and at the same time from Rome (see *First Letter of Clement*). Here occurs for the first time the expression "universal = catholic, Church = institutional Church," (61) p. 203. It was also in the letters of Ignatius that the followers of Christ called themselves "Christians" for the first time; compare Acts 26.

In his outlook Ignatius belonged to the Johannine circles of Asia Minor. He emphasized that salvation means redemption from mortality and corruption, and communion with Christ the Redeemer. He could say of Him, "God suffered." His adoration of Christ was central. See our I.&S. pp. 6-10 and 24-27; with annotations 7 and 8, p. 317, and 10, pp. 318-319; and Topical Index under Lord's Supper, Household of God; and Martyrdom.

(56) pp. 196-199. This letter contains the sum of the proclamation of the Gospel in those early days as Ignatius saw it: glorify Christ, you who were brought to life through the blood of God, the Christ, through Christ the only Physician, the God who came into the flesh, who in His suffering of death is true life! His Cross is the hoist, His Spirit the rope. In Him we must live and gather. All demonic powers dash against the unity of peace given in this faith because through it the old kingdom is overthrown and everything is brought into motion. Compare our I.&S. p. 7. The deeds of faith and love give proof of this victory, even in silence. See Topical Index under Prayer.

(57) p. 199. Jesus is the Word who broke God's silence as the revelation and the proclamation of truth. See Topical Index under Household of God and Logos.

(58) pp. 199-200. Faith is the flesh, love is the blood of Christ. Compare (56) p. 198. See Topical Index under Confession of Faith and Resurrection.

(59) pp. 200-201. Martyrdom is the blood-stained Lovemeal in the flesh as the bread and in the blood as the drink of Christ; it is the imitation of His divine suffering for us and of His resurrection. Compare this concept with our I.&S. pp. 24-26 and Topical Index under Lord's Supper and Martyrdom.

(60) p. 201. This pronouncement of the Spirit shows even by its form that Ignatius, this champion of the episcopate, was conscious of being a bearer of the prophetic Spirit. See our I.&S. p. 47 and Topical Index under Prophets and Spirit.

(61) pp. 201-203. This letter testifies that faith consists in being nailed to the Cross, that love consists in being firmly established in the blood of Christ. This leads to an extensive Confession of Faith, particularly of the second article. See Topical Index under Confession of Faith. Christ's real manhood, His bloody suffering, and His resurrection through the Father bring judgment also upon the demonic spiritual princes. Therefore one should shun the Gnostics. Ignatius characterizes the dangers of their teaching (pp. 202-203). See Topical Index under Gnosis. With reference to Ignatius' faith in the Old Testament of the Prophets and in the New Testament of the Gospel, in the Cross, and in the resurrection, see Topical Index.

(62) pp. 203-204. A characteristically rousing exhortation to serve the Church, which Ignatius addresses to the Bishop Polycarp.

(63) pp. 204-205. Concerning the significance of Polycarp, see the account of his martyrdom, our S.S.&M. (13) pp. 66-71, our M.&W. (42) p. 258, and Index of Names. Here, he gives

his witness to God and to the Christ who is risen, who will return, rule, and judge. This means the certainty of resurrection for all believers who fulfill the love-will of His Sermon on the Mount. Polycarp feels at a very humble distance from Paul; he gives witness to Paul's New Testament faith, the mother from whom hope and love are born. The guarantee of the future age was given by Christ. He suffered for our sins so that we should imitate His suffering in our own lives.

(64) pp. 205-213. The *Letter of Barnabas* was written from Egypt either shortly before A.D. 100 or more likely around 130, but certainly after the year 70. It was not written by the apostle Barnabas (who was Paul's helper), nor does the letter claim apostolic authorship. Clement of Alexandria mentions it seven times as an apostolic writing. Origen in his treatise *On First Principles* (as well as Rufinus in his Latin version of the same) considers the *Letter of Barnabas* part of the New Testament. In the Bible manuscript Codex Sinaiticus it follows the Revelation of John and precedes the *Shepherd* of Hermas. The *Letter of Barnabas* reduces the legal and cultic precepts of the Old Testament to moral and religious spiritualizations or allegories which for a great part have nothing to do with the real meaning of the corresponding passages in the Old Testament.

Because of the danger of Judaic legalism, cult, and ritual, the main body of the letter sets out to prove, in the name of perfect knowledge (the word "gnosis" emerges here already!), that the Judaic Old Testament Covenant with God had become ineffective and invalid. According to Barnabas, the Old Covenant should be understood in a purely spiritual sense: in actual fact it never belonged to the Jews but always and exclusively to the Christians, the people of redemption. The somewhat brief supplement about the two ways is very similar to the first part of the *Didache* and was therefore considerably shortened in our book on p. 213, par. 2.

The writer of this remarkable letter, antagonistic to what the Jews believed, can be regarded as a forerunner of the "Gnostic" Marcion. Marcion looked upon the God of the Jews as a subordinate creative and legalistic spirit whom he wanted to oust by means of his own understanding of Paul's beliefs. As a result, Paul's Letters and a mutilated Gospel were almost all that Marcion retained in his Bible. The New Testament came into being not least of all as the result of opposition to this canon of Marcion. See indexes of names and topics under Marcion, Gnosis, and New Testament.

The *Letter of Barnabas* was held in high esteem in early times; apart from the attempt to ward off the dangers of Judaism, this is explained by the deep testimonies (closely related to those of Paul) about sin and the atonement of the Christ contained in this letter. It gives full recognition to the prophets and their spiritual gifts (p. 205). The demands made by the prophets and by Jesus—doing justice to the oppressed and to the hungry through love—should take the place of Jewish fasting (p. 206).

A quotation from the *Book of Enoch* (p. 206) points to the stumbling block, the "scandal," of the last times and to the imminent coming of the Beloved. Therefore we are called upon to stand together as men of the Spirit against the Black Spirit (p. 207). Since the Old Covenant is shattered, we are challenged to be faithful to the calling and to forgiveness (pp. 207-208). Christ had to suffer in order to wash us and purify us from our sins with His atoning blood, and to invalidate death through His resurrection (p. 208). See Topical Index under Forgiveness, Cross, and Resurrection. The Son of God appeared in the flesh so that we would be able to endure the sight of

Him and so that the murderers of the prophets would˙ fulfill
the measure of their sin against Him (pp. 208-209).

Through the new creation which is transforming us, we have
come into the good land of the New Man, the Lord; we
have come to faith and life, to authority and rulership, and
into the future inheritance (p. 209). The accursed sacrificial
goat, the consecrated goat of the altar, the scarlet wool, all
these foreshadow the crucified Son of God who will come again
(pp. 210-211). The same is true of other Old Testament
symbols which foreshadow His Cross, His blood, His slaughter,
His forgiveness and purification, His rulership from the Tree
(p. 211), His baptism, His outstretched hands, His New Covenant, and His Seventh Day of creating the coming new world
(pp. 211-212).

The New Temple arises through forgiveness and renewal
in our inner being, by faith and promise, by the demands made
upon us, and by the Word of prophecy speaking through us.
Therefore we should not look at the man who proclaims the
Word, but only at the One who dwells in him and speaks
through him! See our P.&P. (74) p. 307 and Topical Index
under Spirit and Prophets. In this way we must become rich
in Spirit, rich in the holy, prophetic Spirit (p. 213). The love
which does what is good and the awareness that the coming
Lord is imminent prove their worth in true freedom, the
freedom to become through the Spirit our own counselors and
lawgivers.

(1)-(64) pp. 171-213. This collection of the extra-Biblical
Lord's Sayings and the earliest writings from the post-apostolic
period, along with the *Shepherd* of Hermas (our P.&P. (33)
pp. 278-294), the *Second Letter of Clement* (our P.&P. (32)
pp. 274-278), and several other texts contained in our section
P.&P., calls for a comparison with the New Testament. Anyone

who turns once more to the four Gospels, the Acts of the Apostles, the New Testament Letters, and the Revelation of John after having read the Apostolic Fathers and the New Testament Apocrypha, will feel that the same Spirit and the same force are at work in all. Yet outside the New Testament, misguided legalism and ecclesiasticism, dangerous adulteration with foreign elements, and debilitating humanization are gaining ground.

# ANNOTATIONS TO
# MEETINGS AND WORSHIP

(1)-(42) pp. 217-258. From the very beginning, through the presence of Christ and through the working of the Holy Spirit, the coming together in faith, the gathering of the community, had great importance among the Christians. See Topical Index under Meetings and our L.S.T.A.&L. (2) p. 171, with annotation p. 367.

The texts of this main section are grouped as follows: (1)-(3) pp. 217-218 are the starting point—the prerequisites of the meetings are the presence of God (1) p. 217, the conversion to Christ and the gifts of the Spirit in the Church (2) p. 217, and the expansion over all lands and races (3) pp. 217-218. The texts concerning the solemn gatherings follow: the bath of immersion (4)-(7) pp. 218-220; the Lord's Supper and the Lovemeal (8)-(12) pp. 220-225; and the appointment of services, with the solemn consecration, the laying on of hands, and the driving out of demons belonging to it (13)-(15) pp. 225-228. Further texts, (16)-(41) pp. 228-257, are concerned with the other meetings: their nascent liturgy (16)-(19) pp. 228-231, their pleas and prayers (18)-(25) pp. 228-239 and (42) p. 258, and their songs and hymns (26)-(41) pp. 239-257. In connection with all these texts, particularly (4)-(25), compare the *Didache*, our L.S.T.A.&L. (54) pp. 181-189, which belongs essentially in this context.

(4)-(7) pp. 218-220. Baptism requires previous instruction (4) p. 218 (compare with annotations to our L.S.T.A.&L. (30) pp. 371-372, and to (53) and (54) pp. 374-378), personal insight and conviction, free decision, conversion, and rebirth (5) pp. 218-220. Originally, forgiveness of sin, purification from all evil, illumination by the Holy Spirit, and moral regeneration had in actual experience to precede the bath of immersion, though during the act of baptism, too, all of these elements are experienced as the very essence and purpose of this act (5)-(7) pp. 218-220. In the final analysis, therefore, it is not a question of baptism as such; rather it is a question of having the faith that men who go through baptism are cleansed and healed through the blood of Christ's death (6) p. 220. The Confession of Faith which is spoken out at the immersion points clearly the way leading from the baptismal symbol to the Rule of Faith (5) pp. 218-220. Compare Topical Index under Baptism and Confession of Faith.

(8)-(12) pp. 220-225. The Lord's Supper is described in its essential character in these texts, supplemented by (18) pp. 228-229, (19) pp. 229-231, and (20) pp. 231-232. Compare Topical Index under Lord's Supper but in particular our I.&S. pp. 8-13 and the *Didache,* our L.S.T.A.&L. (54) pp. 185-186. The Lord's Supper, a Lovemeal, derives its name from pure love, from *agape* (8) pp. 220-221. Therefore the kiss of fellowship belongs to it. See (12) pp. 222-223, our C.F. &S. (39) p. 118 and annotation to our L.S.T.A.&L. (1)-(53) pp. 365-366.

This love finds its social expression in the offering of gifts (8) pp. 220-221, which the deacons who serve at table take to the absent poor for their support. See Topical Index under Deacons, Poverty, Love, and our M.&W. (8) pp. 220-221, (11) p. 222, and (12) pp. 223-224. The overseers look after the poor of the whole city (see (12) pp. 222-224). Compare this description of their service at the Lord's Supper with *The Teaching of the Twelve Apostles,* our L.S.T.A.&L. (54) p.188.

The discipline characteristic of the Lord's Supper (8) pp. 220-221, in the eating as well as in the fellowship of love, is assured by the fact that only the believers, only those who are reborn and baptized, are admitted (12) p. 223. This is confirmed in the *Didache* (our L.S.T.A.&L. (54) p. 186): only those made holy and consecrated by repentance and baptism can take part in the Meal.

Gratitude for this renewal comes to expression in a manner typical of this Meal in the offering of thanksgiving, which explains the name "Eucharist" ⟨literally, thanksgiving⟩; see (12) p. 223, (9) p. 221, and (11) p. 222. The thanksgiving culminates in prayer and adoration (8) p. 221 and (11)-(12) pp. 222-224. This adoration is founded on the remembrance of the suffering and death of Jesus (9) p. 221, on Jesus Christ himself who, as the Word become flesh and blood, is the Helper and Savior (9) p. 221 and (12) pp. 224-225.

By sharing in the Meal, the believers are strengthened in flesh and blood for the resurrection which is an essential object of faith (11) p. 222 and (12) p. 223. Bread and wine, and water too, give this strengthening as the flesh and blood of Christ (12) p. 223. For this, Jesus' words of institution are cited from the Memoirs of the Apostles, i.e. the Gospels (12) p. 223. Compare Topical Index under Apostles and New Testament. Long passages from these Memoirs of the Apostles and from the Old Testament, that is the writings of the prophets, are read aloud in these solemn gatherings; both are considered Holy Scriptures (8) p. 221 and (12) p. 223.

The celebration of the Lord's Supper, which in early apostolic times took place every day, is now repeated every Sunday. The choice of this day is based on the first day of creation and on the day Jesus rose from the dead (12) pp. 224-225. Here, too, see the corresponding passage in the *Didache,* our L.S.T.A.&L. (54) p. 188. According to this main section, there could have been no thought of celebrating Sunday as a day of rest from work. Justin knew of a similar meal celebrated in the pagan mystery-cult of Mithras and regarded this as a demonic counterfeit of the Lord's Supper (12) p. 224; see also Topical Index under Demons.

(13)-(14) pp. 225-226. The appointment of overseers, elders, deacons, serving widows, and readers took place also on a Sunday, in a particularly solemn gathering to which the kiss of peace, the offering of gifts, and thanksgiving also belonged. See Topical Index under Love, Lord's Supper, Prayer, and Meetings.

In the time of Hippolytus, who was influential from c. A.D. 200 until 235, the year when he was banished from Rome, the different Church offices and their hierarchy were already fixed (compare with our I.&S. pp. 31-33, 42-43, and 46-49, and consult the Topical Index under Church, Episcopate, Apostles, Prophets, and Teachers): only the overseer or bishop, still elected by all members of the Church, received the laying on of hands from one of the overseers as if from all believers; the elder to be appointed received the laying on of hands from the overseer and the elders; the deacon received it only from the elders; widows to be engaged in the service of the poor (see our I.&S. p. 18, with annotations 47 and 48, p. 326) were simply chosen and appointed by spoken words, and the reader just by handing him the Book, i.e., the Old Testament, as well as prophetic and New Testament writings.

The laying on of hands, often combined with anointing, was a call for the Spirit to descend. The spiritual power of leadership given to the overseers was the Holy Spirit of grace and counsel given by Jesus to the apostles, the founders of the Church (see Apostles in the Topical Index). The prayers spoken with the laying on of hands calling on the Father, the Son, and the Spirit define the power of the Spirit: it purifies, seals, and gives clarity of thought. Here the freedom of the Spirit as it was in the earliest times still comes to expression in the fact that martyr-confessors, voluntary virgins (both men and women), and Spirit-filled members who had received from the Spirit gifts of healing, teaching, prophecy, or speaking in tongues did not need the laying on of hands because they were consecrated directly by the Spirit Himself. See Topical Index under Martyrdom and Spirit and compare the relevant passages in our I.&S. pp. 25-27 and 28-40, in particular pp. 30-31.

(15) pp. 227-228. Concerning the expulsion of demons see the texts listed in the Topical Index under Demons, where the nature of filth, poison, and death, corruption and slander (the nature of "Satan") is also clearly revealed as demonic. The power of evil spirits must detach itself and depart from body and soul, thought and deed, from prayers and privations of fasting, from all natural activities and moral pursuits of all those who in baptism and Lovemeal are waiting for the Messiah-King Jesus. With His ban Jesus holds sway over all spirits. His goodness and His purity expose and convict the evil spirits and through faith rescue men from them. The ineffably great and only God makes even the highest spiritual powers submit to Him. All creation surrenders in adoration to Him and worships Him who is invoked in this prayer.

(16)-(41), pp. 228-257, take us into the very midst of the meetings of the second century.

(16), p. 228, shows us the solemn beauty of the simple candle-lit room and the solemn devotion brought about by the healing and salvation of the Father, the Logos, and the Spirit in the Light given to the apostles.

(17)-(19) pp. 228-231. The Christ, the Messiah, the only begotten Son of God, is glorified in the solemn antiphony of question and answer as the manifestation of the first creation, as the Ruler over all, the Victor over the last enemy: Death. He is worshiped and proclaimed as the healing Helper and liberating Redeemer, the One who died and rose again, the Giver of the Holy Spirit and of faith, the Logos, the Word from God, the One who unites the Church. The prayers (20)-(25), pp. 231-239, have the same content.

(19), pp. 229-231, contains the very ancient basis of present-day liturgical antiphony: "The Lord be with you," "And with thy spirit," "Lift up your hearts," "We lift them up to the Lord." In this text, too, appear the virgin birth, the stretching out of the arms on the Cross, and the coming down of the Holy Spirit on the Church.

(20)-(25), pp. 231-239, are some of the oldest prayers (to which should be added those contained in the *Didache*, our L.S.T.A.&L. (54) pp. 184-189, and also our M.&W. (42) p. 258), and they contain the same thoughts and facts as (16)-(19). With burning love and deep emotion the God-man is worshiped as the paradoxical mystery full of the power to work miracles and to reveal truth. With passionate trust Jesus is called upon as the Physician of the sick and the Hope of the poor, that He may raise up those who have fallen, liberate the captives, and feed the hungry. He lives among the saints as the Enlightening One who opens men's eyes. He is called upon in supplication for the conversion of those who have gone astray, for the forgiveness of sin, and for the strength to lead a good life. In the same way supplication is made that peace will come to the whole earth and that Jesus will humble the proud, guide the nations, and help governments and authorities to find grace and to exercise their power with nonviolence and kindness. The liturgical passage from the *First Letter of Clement,* (21) pp. 232-235 (see also our L.S.T.A.&L. (55) pp. 189-196), is a very relevant example of Church prayer at that time. These prayers bring to light the majesty of His rulership, the revelation of the hidden future, and the conquest and opening up of the Underworld to new life just as clearly as they speak of the Heart that died in love for us and that gathers the evil ones, the straying ones, the unhappy ones, and the lost ones to Himself. The factual core, the kernel, of these prayers born of deeply moved hearts is God's creation and His new creation: the death of Jesus on the Cross and His resurrection, His ascension to God, His future rule, and the indwelling of the Holy Spirit, which is expected to come now. All these facts are expressed in ever-changing phrases in these prayers. Compare the main section Confession of Faith and Scriptures, pp. 127-167.

(26)-(41) pp. 239-257. Here is a selection from the rich treasury of ancient Christian songs, hymns, and odes, of which the New Testament itself contains the most valuable and powerful, particularly in Luke and John (Revelation!), but also in Paul. The institutional Church preserved very few of these powerful and at the same time deeply fervent Church hymns of the first two centuries. From our own collection only the hymns (26)-(28), pp. 239-240, and (41), pp. 256-257, are recognized by the institutional Church. These in particular go back to a very early date.

(26) pp. 239-240. This morning hymn of praise uses an abundance of Biblical expressions, mainly from the New Testament. Of these, the "Immaculate Lamb who takes the sins of the world upon Himself" and the "great High Priest" stand out.

(26)-(27) pp. 239-240. The content of these hymns reflects the liturgies and prayers (16)-(25).

(27) p. 240. This is the oldest Christian evening hymn extant. ⟨See also A. Hamman, *Early Christian Prayers,* Chicago: Henry Regnery Co., 1961, p. 144.⟩

(28), p. 240, shows the paradox in the mystery of Christ (see also (20) pp. 231-232). Melito was Church overseer or Bishop of Sardis at the time of Marcus Aurelius. As early as A.D. 155 he spoke of the "Books of the Old Covenant," thus pointing to the Books of the New Testament. The fragments of Melito's writings show the line of development which leads from the Johannine circles in Asia Minor through Polycarp and Ignatius to the teachers who represented the double nature of Jesus, the God-man. Melito considered himself a prophet. He may be the author of the words about the Spirit of the Body of Christ (see our P.&P. (34) p. 294 and our I.&S. p. 37, with annotation 79, p. 332).

(29) p. 241. Many more hymns are preserved from the Gnostics, among whom Church singing reached its peak. We have included a characteristic example. For more about gnosis, refer to Topical Index. This is a genuine Gnostic hymn of the kind which was most decidedly rejected by the Christians of that period, both in the Church at large and in the Montanist communities: in it the Spirit is the primal element; the son of the Spirit pours forth chaos; the soul is the third element, hunted in the labyrinth, between light and chaotic misery; it cannot find the ascent until Jesus descends to it, unveiling the knowledge (gnosis) of the mystery, after speaking with the Father and striding through the aeons.

This brief example of Gnostic teaching is included here to demonstrate to what extent Gnostic circles did or did not concur with the confessed beliefs of the first Christians. Compare the main section Confession of Faith and Scriptures, pp. 127-167.

(30)-(39) pp. 241-255. The origin of the *Odes of Solomon,* also composed in the second century, is not so clear. Most scholars consider also these odes Gnostic; nevertheless, it seems likely that they were sung for the most part in awakened circles of the Church particularly among those of the Montanists, and some very significant features of the odes, stressed in the following annotations, speak for this.

As late as the fifth and sixth centuries the Monophysites cherished the *Odes of Solomon.* The Monophysites stood for the separation of Church and State and gave particular honor to the Spirit; they preserved many ancient Christian treasures. Kaspar von Schwenkfeld, an important sixteenth-century witness to the Holy Spirit and the Scriptures, lived from the spiritual wealth of these circles. These hymns may be a collection of songs which had sprung up in different communities, though to us they seem to be very uniform in character. In our selection we try to show that the Good News of Christ, given in the outpouring of the Holy Spirit, unfolds with tremendous force in these odes.

Through their publication in Syriac in 1909 the *Odes of Solomon* became known afresh. Their original language was Greek. Our German translation was based on that of H. Gressmann in E. Hennecke, *Neutestamentliche Apokryphen,* 1924. (For an English translation from the Syriac see R. Harris and A. Mingana, *The Odes and Psalms of Solomon,* London and New York: Longmans, Green and Co., 1920.) We want to draw attention mainly to the essence of faith to be found in these remarkable hymns.

The Spirit sweeps through these odes like a breath of wind sweeping the chords of a harp, like a great, broad river sweeping through the land (30) p. 242. The Spirit is the water of immortality, it is the sun above the earth, it is the breath we breathe, it is the circumcision of the heart (33) pp.

246-248. Joy in the Lord is a violent, vehement passion of love, compared to the relationship of bride and bridegroom and to the bridal bed (31) p. 243 and (39) p. 254. The psalm-singer's passionate joy in the Lord compels him to proclaim the coming of Him who blazed forth in radiance as the Son (31) p. 244 and (38) pp. 252-253. All are called to go out to meet Him, to stand before Him, to behold Him and to praise His love, to sing to His grace and to confess His power; for hate shall be rooted out from the earth (31) p. 245. The joy of grace and love belongs to the elect saints, for they received the epistle containing the Plan of Salvation, which hastened across the earth like an arrow and as if on a wheel. It is a "letter of testament" from the Ruler now revealed, the true Son of the Father. It bears the Name of the Father, the Son, and the Spirit (36) pp. 250-251.

The Lord revealed Himself in His kindness and came so near to us that He appeared like us in form, and we can thus "grasp Him" and "put Him on" (31) p. 243. To this end He gave Himself and blazed the way for the knowledge of His light so that He penetrates the created universe with this redemption (p. 244). The manifest plan and will of the Lord is His Word and His redemption, everlasting life and eternal perfection in grace and in freedom, in truth and in justice (32) pp. 245-246. This redemption must be taken hold of with courage (p. 246). It takes place through the Holy Spirit, filling men with His love and His knowledge and establishing them upon the rock of truth. It is like speaking waters coming from His fountains; it is the casting off of folly and the renewal in His raiment of light which is His immortality; it is the being caught up into Paradise where the bitterness of the trees is cast off and everything is filled with His fruits (33) pp. 247-248.

This redemption coming down from on high leads upward from the depths, captures the intermediate region, and subdues it by overcoming all dragons, by destroying all poisons and all enemies, by raising all the dead from their graves, by renewing the universe, and by establishing the Kingdom (35) p. 249 and (37) pp. 251-252. For this purpose a human virgin became a mother and bore the Son in revelation of the power and redemption (34) p. 248. He is Lord, the only hope, the only object of faith, who appears to the believer and gives him the shining scepter of His power (37) p. 252.

Then the great day breaks forth in brightness, then life is received through Christ, then the believers join together in the name of the Lord, shining in His light, and then the Healing Savior gives new life to the soul, He, the humiliated Son of the Most High who is exalted in perfection, the Logos Christ, who was before the beginning of the world and who gives life forever (38) pp. 252-253.

The stretching out of His hands on the outstretched wood of the Cross is the sign for those who implore Him so that they too approach the Lord with outstretched arms, for this is how He comes to those who love Him. This is how. He rose from the dead and is with them now, speaking through their mouths. This is how He overcame death in the utmost depths and created the Church of the Living among the dead, how His mercy took the deceased out of darkness into His redemption because they listened to His voice, believed in His Name, and became His own in freedom (39) pp. 253-255.

(40) pp. 255-256. This dance hymn from the *Acts of John* is put into the mouth of Jesus. The profound paradox of the redeeming Savior, who wounds by His wounds, brings new birth through His birth, who wants to be heard and eaten and sought and who effects His washing, whose grief pierces the

heart of everyone and whose unity unites all, who homeless and free from temples sanctifies everything, who is the door and the pathway of the striding dance—this profound paradox is frequently attributed to Gnostic influences. Compare Topical Index under Gnosis.

(41) pp. 256-257. This poetic doxology extols Jesus as King and the leader of youth, as Word and shepherd, pinion and steersman, as aeon and light, as milk and fountain of the Spirit, as the mighty Son, Bringer of Peace. It is believed to be an authentic poem by Clement of Alexandria.

(42) p. 258. Our survey of the meetings and sacred gatherings of early Christian times ends with Polycarp's Spirit-filled prayer at his martyrdom. Gathering round the martyrs was felt to be the very crowning of the solemn meetings held by the Christians. Polycarp's prayer to the Almighty God of all spirits, powers, and creations contains a clear Christian confession of Jesus Christ, of His cup and His resurrection, of His sacrifice and His eternal life. Through His High Priesthood and through His Holy Spirit the martyr is made worthy to share in Him; however, honor is due to Christ alone, through God and the Holy Spirit. This prayer, which conveys the sacred character of the meetings around those who suffered bloody martyrdom (see our I.&S. pp. 24-27), is included as a typical prayer of the Church in the second century.

# ANNOTATIONS TO
# PROCLAMATION AND PROPHECY

(1)-(86) pp. 261-309. In this last main section the entire content of early Christian homily speaks to us. The texts (1)-(31), pp. 261-274, contain various excerpts from Christian writings of the second century, which seen together give insight into proclamation in the Church and in mission at that time. Compare the beliefs expressed in this proclamation with those in the main section Confession of Faith and Scriptures, pp. 127-167. (32), pp. 274-278, brings us a classic example of early Church homily, the only one preserved from the middle of the second century. The long text which follows this sermon, (33) pp. 278-294, is an equally singular example of prophetic proclamation. The Roman prophet Hermas was humanly seen not one of the most striking figures among the prophets of that time. The impact he makes stems solely from his honesty and the Spirit in his words. Texts (34)-(86), pp. 294-309, are further examples of early Christian prophetic and apocalyptic writings, some basic testimonies about the nature of prophecy, and finally some texts showing the termination in Montanism of late second-century Christian prophecy.

(1)-(3) pp. 261-262. About the foundation of second-century proclamation in the Church and in the missionary outreach of the apostles, prophets, teachers, and evangelists.

(1) p. 261. A brief and striking summary of some of the fundamentals of Christian proclamation.

(2) p. 262. Christ's Kingship, His Rulership from the Tree, from the fact of the Cross. Compare Topical Index under Cross.

(4)-(7) pp. 262-264. Love to the brothers and to all men as a main article of the proclamation: the twofold service of love flowing from love to God—service to God and service to men.

(8)-(12) pp. 264-265. About community with God and with the Holy Spirit, about circumcision of the heart, about putting off the old man, and about personal salvation and conversion to Jesus in dying to the world. See Topical Index under Rebirth, Cross, and Spirit.

(13)-(17) pp. 265-268. The proclamation about Jesus, who was foretold by the prophets, sent to this earth by God, and sacrificed for us: the Redeemer and Proclaimer of truth by the power of God in word and deed. See Topical Index under Jesus. Christ is the core of this message.

(14) p. 266. The proclamation of complete redemption, justification, salvation, and healing through the vicarious suffering of Jesus. See Topical Index under Cross. Here, the Cross stands in the center throughout.

(15) p. 267. Compare this statement that Jesus was thirty years old with the contradictory statement made by the elders in Irenaeus (our C.F.&S. (25) p. 140). The earthly life and work of Jesus, His baptism by the Spirit, His living and dying for a mankind laden with guilt. See Topical Index under Jesus and Cross.

(17) pp. 267-268. Regarding the reference to the Memoirs of the Apostles, see Topical Index under New Testament. The life of Jesus as the conquering power over all forces of evil and as the revelation and glorification of God culminating in His death on the Cross and in His resurrection (see Topical Index under Demons). The goal of faith is victory in the world of spirits.

(18)-(29) pp. 268-274. Here the Cross of Christ is the core of the proclamation.

(18) p. 268. Concerning the emerging significance of the outstretched hands in early Christian proclamation, see Topical Index under Cross. The two peoples pointed to by the two outstretched arms are the Jews and the Gentiles, united, as in Paul (Eph. 2:14-18), by Christ, the one Head in the middle. The next piece, (19) pp. 268-269, shows that the arms stretched out to the right and to the left were felt to be the sign of triumphant victory over all hostile forces.

(19) pp. 268-269. ⟨See also James, *The Apocryphal New Testament*, pp. 359-360.⟩ Concerning this triumphant adoration of the Cross as the sign of complete victory, compare Topical Index under Cross and Prayer.

(20) pp. 269-270. The Cross extolled as the loving and victorious Logos (see Topical Index under Logos).

(21) p. 270. Gripped by the mystery of the Cross, the Christians of that time saw symbols and reproductions of this decisive sign of God everywhere.

(22)-(26) pp. 270-272. These Old Testament prophetic symbols foreshadowing the blood and Cross of Christ proclaim liberation and forgiveness to be the ceasing of sin, the destruction of deadly, venomous power, and the salvation through uniting with Christ the Crucified; this also applies to the water-grave of baptism. So those who believe in the Cross, those who believe in Christ, are freed from the power of demons and become God-fearing bearers of peace in this world.

(27) pp. 272-273. The prophetic prediction of His suffering and death proves that the Crucified is the one and only

Messiah. God foretells and in this way shows us what He himself does.

(28), p. 273, is a refutation of Gnostic teaching, according to which the suffering of Jesus was a mere semblance. Compare Topical Index under Gnosis. The followers of this false doctrine did not believe that the Son became man.

(29) pp. 273-274. The proclamation of Christ and the mystery of His Cross culminate in possession of the land in friendship and in brotherly life together. See annotation to P.&P. (30) below and Topical Index under Future. By placing together water, faith, and wood for man's escape from the coming judgment, it is pointed out that baptism and the Cross are intrinsically linked together by faith.

(30) p. 274. The possession of the Holy Land promised to all its heirs cannot here, in (29) and (30), be shifted to some unearthly life hereafter. Justin, like most Christians of his time, was a firm believer in the real, earthy nature of the coming Kingdom. Faith in the whole Word of God spoken by the prophets and apostles is counted as righteousness. So is faith in the restoration of all creation.

(31) p. 274. This picture of the future worship of God at Christ's return is in keeping with the picture we have of religious meetings held by Christians at that time. Compare Topical Index under Prayer, Lord's Supper, and Meetings.

(32) pp. 274-278. This oldest surviving Church address is very important. Taking the greatness of God and Christ as its starting point, it testifies to the salvation and enlightenment which Christ gives to the very people who were totally lost. As a result, works of pure and warm love burst forth, kindled and nourished by the prophetic proclamation of the coming

age, the age utterly opposed and hostile to the present world epoch.

In the same way as Christ himself was in the flesh, the human body shall partake in God's future age. It is for this very reason that the body is to be kept pure now and, in accordance with the Lord's Saying quoted here, sexuality is to be overcome, but of course this will not be fully realized until the future is consummated. The body must be kept pure as the temple of the Church because the Spirit and the Church of the Spirit became flesh in Christ. Also here the Church is confessed to as an object of faith: she existed as the Body of Christ before the creation of the universe and has always been present in the Spirit from the very beginning in the same way that Christ has.

This proclamation culminates in a powerful message of faith and in a prediction of the coming Day of Judgment when Christ himself will come again and appear in person.

(33) pp. 278-294. Hermas, a preacher of repentance impelled by eschatology, claimed to be a prophet in the sense of the early Christian prophets who along with the apostles and teachers maintained the spiritual leadership in those times. Quadratus and Ammia, Polycarp and Melito, were considered prophets in the same sense. Thus Justin, in his *Dialogue with Trypho* 82, says, "Even to this day the gifts of prophecy are alive among us: you can see among us both men and women who are endowed with gifts of grace." Eusebius (*Church History* V.7.4) quotes Irenaeus (*Against Heresies* II.32.4) as saying, "The prophets have visions, apparitions, or dreams and speak about the future in prophetic utterances. It is impossible to enumerate the gifts of grace." And in *Against Heresies* V.6.1 (Eusebius, V.7.6) Irenaeus also says that through the Spirit, brothers and sisters speak with all kinds

of tongues, bring men's secret thoughts to light, and reveal the mysteries of God.

As regards the origin of the *Shepherd* of Hermas—quite a lengthy book—it is probably correct to accept the date A.D. 140-155 indicated by the *Muratorian Fragment* (see our C.F.&S. (81) pp. 165-167 and annotation pp. 363-364). Origen and Eusebius, however, place it in the times of the apostles, and in the Codex Sinaiticus the *Shepherd* is even included among the New Testament writings. See also the annotation to our L.S.T.A.&L. (64) pp. 383-386. Some deduce from the *Shepherd* itself that it may have been written toward the end of the first century.

Hermas cannot be included among the Montanist prophets or among their opponents. Quite independent of both, Hermas is a prophetic voice calling to repentance within the Church at Rome, which already had become old and weak. A former house slave, Hermas had little schooling. His Greek style and his logic reveal the uneducated man. The rural images he uses indicate his farming activities. We hear about his business affairs and the loss of his fortune in his later years as a freedman. He shares openly his own sinful thoughts and the apostasy of his children. So honest is he that he even admits he can never be completely truthful.

This old and simple man stands before us, then, a true prophet, inwardly prompted to speak, inspired by God's power. He speaks publicly whenever God wills it while exposing as false prophets those who accept payment and wait to be consulted. Hermas demands repentance because the angel of repentance charged him to do so. Repentance brings life; it means to sin no more. Conversion as Hermas sees it means that Christ and the Holy Spirit dwell in every believer and overcome in him all evil spirits like ill-temper, malice, arrogance, and impure passions.

Although in the *Shepherd* of Hermas the idea of recompense for good works appears for the first time, the main concern of Hermas is the movement of the Spirit in men's hearts. The virgins of his last and longest parable are holy spirits to him, powers of the Son of God. They stand for faith, truth, love, patience, chastity, and self-control.

The Spirit, the Church, and the Son of God are inseparable for Hermas. He, too, believes that the Church was created before all other things. The Church appears as an elderly matron, as a pure bride, and as an immense building into which all believers are fitted as One Body and One Spirit. The whole point of repentance is for man to become useful to God, to fit into this building. The stones must be rigorously squared for this building. Wealth and possessions must be cut away as with a stonecutter's hammer; only the minimum necessities of life may be kept, for the Christian lives in a foreign country under a State constitution alien to him. He belongs to the coming order, quite different from the present one, and therefore cannot acquire fields, houses, and other possessions here.

The present world epoch is wintertime. Only the future age, which will be summertime, will let the fruits of faith appear. Now is the time for repentance for those who are totally or half dead, who seek first places in worldly business or in some ambition, or who have defiled themselves by sinning. Repentance gives rise to doing what is good, especially to the poor who lack even the bare necessities of life. Every man must be rescued from his distress. Whoever neglects to do this becomes guilty of his blood. The sinner in the flesh is sternly called to repentance. Hermas, too, gives a high place of honor to those who remain innocent and pure like virgins. They are considered "children." See Topical Index under Discipline.

The man who through faith has the Lord in his heart will

master all things and keep the hardest commands and be steadfast in great suffering. Forgiveness is promised to those who truly repent. We are to focus our vision on the future world-age and the return of the Lord.

Anyone who can find his way into this little book with its revelations, stories, commands, and parables will feel a living contact with the life of the Church as it was at that time. For all its emphasis on the sublime angels of God and on the demonic angels of darkness, the Son of God himself remains God's Truth in this prophetic testimony. He remains the one Rock established before creation. He remains the only Foundation. He is the Gateway now opened wide to give all men entry into the Kingdom of God. He alone is the Master Builder of the tower. He alone determines the time of its completion. See Index of Names and annotation to our P.&P. (1)-(86) p. 399.

(34) p. 294. Perhaps by Melito, Bishop of Sardis, who knew himself to be a prophet. He wrote a book *On the Church* (which has not survived) and was opposed to the Montanists. About Melito, see our M.&W. (28) p. 240 with annotation p. 394, and for an alternative translation see Introduction p. 37 and annotations 78 and 79 belonging to it, pp. 331-332.

(35)-(41) pp. 294-295. Characteristic examples of prophecy and apocalypticism from the time covered by this book.

(36) pp. 295-297. In the Latin Bible this little book is included as chapters one and two of the Jewish Fourth Book of Ezra (or Esdras). Originally written in Greek, these two chapters contain announcements of punishment for the Jews and promises of glory for the Christians, drawing extensively on the Old Testament Prophets. The burning hope of prophetic Christianity and the dedicated love to one's neighbor find

powerful expression in this captivating book. Here, too, the mother is the Church. ⟨In E.J. Goodspeed's translation of *The Apocrypha* it appears as The Second Book of Esdras.⟩

(37) p. 297. Originally in Greek, this book is preserved as the fifteenth and sixteenth chapters of the Fourth Book of Ezra. It portrays the catastrophes caused by wars and natural forces at the end of the world, and the persecution of the martyrs. Most likely, these chapters were written later than the Fifth Book. Typical of the last phase of Church prophecy is the merging of Jewish and primitive Christian apocalypticism.

(39)-(41) pp. 298-300. About the Sibylline books see Index of Names and Writings.

(40) pp. 298-299. Prophecies like these, disseminated widely in the Christian circles of that time, provoked the Roman authority's ban on the reading, spreading, or interpretation of prophetic books. It was this kind of prophecy which to a large extent gave rise to the hatred and persecution meted out to Christians by the Roman State. Compare our C.F.&S. (48) p. 152, including annotation p. 358, and Topical Index under Martyrdom and Roman State and Law.

(42)-(45) pp. 300-301. Here the Montanists stand up for the true significance and task of the New Prophecy: it is the work of the Spirit, the representative Advocate, the Paraclete, promised in John's Gospel. Concerning the faith of the first Christians in the prophetic power of the Holy Spirit, see especially our I.&S. pp. 36-37 with annotations 76 to 79, pp. 331-332; our C.F.&S. (44)-(57) and (70) pp. 148-156 and p. 161 with their annotations pp. 358 and 361-362; and annotation to our P.&P. (33) above; see also Topical Index under Prophets.

(43) p. 300. Compare Topical Index under Household of God.

(48) pp. 301-302. Concerning this presentation of the House-hold of God, the Economy and administration of His divine Plan, see our P.&P. (46) p. 301 and Topical Index.

(49) p. 302. The Spirit, then, never gives the light of know-ledge and understanding without His power. He Himself makes enlightened men capable.

(51)-(54) pp. 302-303. The Spirit of this prophecy insists upon martyrdom which knows of no flight and can never draw the sword.

(55)-(60) pp. 303-304. Purity and sanctity of life, stressed here in sexual continence and fasting, are testified to as decisive qualities of the Holy Spirit.

(61)-(63) pp. 304-305. Montanist prophecy of the future. God's Day of Judgment was proclaimed to be so close at hand that Maximilla, who was called a prophetess, said, "After me there will be no other prophet, but the end" (Epiphanius, *Panarion* 48.2).

(63) p. 305. The Greek word describing the action of putting wisdom into the prophetess denotes something violent, as if something were thrown, flung, pushed, or thrust in. In this passage from Epiphanius the Montanists are called after the region of Phrygia in Asia Minor or after the prophetess Pris-cilla. They held their celebrations in the town of Pepuza. It was there that they waited together for Christ to come.

(64)-(68), pp. 305-306, show that the Montanists were fully in agreement with the Confession of Faith generally adhered to by Christians of that time. Compare our P.&P. (83)-(86) p. 309. This is also confirmed by their opponent Hippolytus in his *Philosophumena* VIII.19: "In agreement with the Church they acknowledge God . . . and all the things which the Gospels testify concerning Christ."

(67) p. 306. In the *Doctrina patrum de incarnatione verbi, Nova collectio VII*, the following words are quoted in connection with Montanus as a piece used by his singers or in his odes: "The Messiah [Christ] has one and the same nature and one and the same power both before and after He became flesh so that He can never become different and never do unlike or different things." Here it is proclaimed that Jesus Christ is the same yesterday, today, and in all ages to come. This fact indicates that the Monophysites and the songs known as the *Odes of Solomon* may well be largely Montanist. See these in the Index of Names and Writings.

(69)-(73) pp. 306-307. The inner life and the festive joyfulness of Montanist communities in contrast to the Gnostic freedom of the flesh. The Montanists evidently practiced community of goods and celebrated the Lord's Supper as a Lovemeal, even sending their gifts to members who were far away.

(74)-(86) pp. 307-309. The most important prophetic utterances of the Montanist revival movement.

(76) p. 307. "I hasten to the spot and urge on; I burst upon, flood, impel, shake, strike, and arouse." When Epiphanius adds, "It is the Lord who sets men's hearts beside themselves," he is obviously still quoting Montanus, a fact disputed by some scholars.

(79) p. 308. Eusebius mentions expressly that it was the Spirit who spoke through Maximilla here. Maximilla, then, does not speak for herself or about herself, but it is the Spirit who is the speaker through her.

(80) p. 308. This prophetic prediction corresponds to the Biblical prophecies about the end of our age in Matthew 24, Revelation of John, and other places.

(81) p. 308. See preceding annotation. Tertullian affirms emphatically that it is the representative Advocate, the Spirit of Christ, who gives this admonition.

(82) p. 309. Compare our (51) pp. 302-303 of this main section. Here Tertullian speaks explicitly about the Spirit whose counsel we ask as to what is more than the mere word. It is perfect love that drives out fear. The Spirit gives counsel by inciting to martyrdom; almost all the sayings of the Spirit do this.

(83)-(86) p. 309. In the man who is prophetically gripped by the Holy Spirit, God himself speaks and acts in His own Person, the only first Person, as the Father, the Son, and the Spirit. See P.&P. (64)-(68) pp. 305-306 and Topical Index under Confession of Faith, especially C.F.&S. (51)-(54) pp. 153-155, with their annotations p. 359. Because the Montanists believed "in blind trust" that the Spirit Himself, the defending Advocate of John's Gospel, had "entered" into their prophets and prophetesses (as Hippolytus points out in his *Philosophumena* VIII.19), they could—and even had to—recognize that God spoke through them in the first person, in the same way as He spoke in the prophets of the Old Testament.

# INDEXES AND SELECTED
# BIBLIOGRAPHIES

# TOPICAL INDEX

Altar, churches with altars: I.&S. at "97" p. 49 with ann. 97,
pp. 333-334; S.S.&M. (15) pp. 74-77; C.S.P. (25) pp. 106-
107; C.F.&S. (17) pp. 136-137; ann. to L.S.T.A.&L. (54)
p. 377; L.S.T.A.&L. (64) p. 212; M.&W. (40) p. 255

Angels: I.&S. p. 27 with ann. 58, p. 327; C.F.&S. (11) p. 134;
C.F.&S. (15) p. 135; P.&P. (33) pp. 280-294

Apostles: I.&S. at "4" p. 3 with ann. 4, p. 316; I.&S. at "34"
p. 15; I.&S. p. 31; ann. 95 to I.&S. p. 333; C.S.P. (2) p. 95;
C.F.&S. (21) p. 139; C.F.&S. (25) p. 140; C.F.&S. (55)
p. 155; C.F.&S. (75)-(81) pp. 162-167; L.S.T.A.&L. (54)
pp. 181, 187; L.S.T.A.&L. (48) p. 180; L.S.T.A.&L. (52)-
(53) p. 180; L.S.T.A.&L. (55) p. 195; M.&W. (3) pp.
217-218; M.&W. (13) pp. 225-226; M.&W. (16) p. 228;
P.&P. (1)-(3) pp. 261-262

Asia Minor and Phrygia (*see* Index of Names under John):
S.S.&M. (12) p. 66; S.S.&M. (11) p. 63; ann. to S.S.&M.
(13)-(18) pp. 338, 340; S.S.&M. (13) pp. 66, 67, 71; S.S.
&M. (14) pp. 71, 73; ann. to L.S.T.A.&L. (56)-(62) p.
381; P.&P. (63) p. 305 with ann. (63) p. 408

Atheism: I.&S. pp. 22-23; S.S.&M. (4) p. 60; S.S.&M. (10)
pp. 62-63; ann. to S.S.&M. (13)-(18) p. 339; S.S.&M.
(13) p. 68; C.F.&S. (7) p. 131; C.F.&S. (8) pp. 131-132;
C.F.&S. (9) p. 133; C.F.&S. (11) pp. 133-134; C.F.&S.
(13) p. 134

Authority: I.&S. pp. 3-5, 29, 31, 36-41, 47; C.S.P. (1)-(5) pp. 95-96; C.F.&S. (55) pp. 155-156; C.F.&S. (70) p. 161; L.S.T.A.&L. (26) p. 176; L.S.T.A.&L. (39) p. 178; L.S. T.A.&L. (44) p. 179; L.S.T.A.&L. (48), (49), (52), and (53) p. 180; L.S.T.A.&L. (55) pp. 194-195; L.S.T.A.&L. (64) pp. 209-210; M.&W. (2) p. 217; M.&W. (14) and (15) pp. 226-228; M.&W. (13) pp. 225-226; M.&W. (36) pp. 249-251; P.&P. (17) pp. 267-268; P.&P. (42) p. 300; P.&P. (44) pp. 300-301; P.&P. (46) p. 301; P.&P. (49) and (50) p. 302; P.&P. (55) and (56) p. 303; P.&P. (74) p. 307; P.&P. (82)-(86) p. 309

Baptism: I.&S. p. 10; I.&S. pp. 13-15 with ann. 28-33, pp. 322-324; I.&S. p. 49; C.S.P. (27) pp. 108-109; C.F.&S. (1)-(5) pp. 127-131; L.S.T.A.&L. (54) pp. 184-185; L.S.T. A.&L. (64) pp. 210-211; M.&W. (4)-(7) pp. 218-220; M.&W. (12) pp. 222-223; M.&W. (15) p. 227; M.&W. (40) pp. 255-256; ann. to P.&P. (22)-(26) p. 401; P.&P. (25) p. 272; P.&P. (29) pp. 273-274

Bloodshed: *see* Peace

Brotherhood: *see* Church

Christ: *see* Jesus

Christians: S.S.&M. (13)-(18) pp. 66-86 with ann. (13)-(18) p. 339; ann. to L.S.T.A.&L. (56)-(62) p. 381

Church, community, and brotherhood: I.&S. pp. 18, 20, 21-22, 25-27; I.&S. at "68" and "69" pp. 30-33 with ann. 68, p. 329; I.&S. pp. 44-45, 47-53, with ann. 97, pp. 333-334 and ann. 100, p. 334; C.S.P. (24) pp. 104-106; C.S.P. (28) pp. 109-110; C.S.P. (29) pp. 111-113; C.F.&S. (2) and (3) pp. 127-128; C.F.&S. (81) pp. 166-167; L.S.T.A.&L. (2) p. 171 with ann. (2) p. 367; L.S.T.A.&L. (54) pp. 185-189; L.S.T.A.&L. (55) pp. 189-196; L.S.T.A.&L. (56)-(62) pp. 196-204; M.&W. (19) pp. 229-231; M.&W. (39)

p. 253-255; M.&W. (40) pp. 255-256; P.&P. (18) p. 268; P.&P. (32) pp. 276-277; P.&P. (33) pp. 278-294; P.&P. (34) p. 294; P.&P. (36) pp. 296-297

Church buildings: *see* Altars, churches with altars

Confession of Faith: I.&S. pp. 33-34 with ann. 71, p. 329; I. &S. pp. 43, 46; ann. to S.S.&M. (13)-(18) p. 339; C.F.&S. (1)-(8) pp. 127-132 with ann. pp. 348-354; L.S.T.A.&L. (54) pp. 184-185; L.S.T.A.&L. (58) pp. 199-200; L.S.T. A.&L. (61) pp. 201-203; M.&W. (5) pp. 218-220; M.&W. (16) p. 228; M.&W. (17)-(25) pp. 228-239; M.&W. (26)-(27) pp. 239-240; M.&W. (36) pp. 249-251; P.&P. (64)-(68) pp. 305-306; P.&P. (83)-(86) p. 309

Cross: I.&S. pp. 2-4 with ann. 3 and 5, p. 316 and ann. 7, p. 317; I.&S. pp. 7-9 with ann. 9-17, pp. 317-321; I.&S. p.41; ann. to S.S.&M. (13)-(18) pp. 339-340; S.S.&M. (16) p. 80; S.S.&M. (22) p. 88; C.S.P. (5) p. 96; C.S.P. (34) p. 115; C.S.P. (35) p. 116; C.F.&S. (21) p. 139; C.F.&S. (26)-(28) pp. 140-141; C.F.&S. (30) p. 142; C.F.&S. (32) pp. 142-143; C.F.&S. (49) pp. 152-153; C.F.&S. (59) p. 157; C.F.&S. (65) p. 158; C.F.&S. (76) p. 163; L.S.T.A. &L. (55) pp. 190-192; L.S.T.A.&L. (56) pp. 196-199; L. S.T.A.&L. (58) pp. 199-200; L.S.T.A.&L. (59) pp. 200-201; L.S.T.A.&L. (61) p. 202; ann. to L.S.T.A.&L. (56)-(62) pp. 381-382; L.S.T.A.&L. (63) pp. 204-205; L.S.T.A. &L. (64) pp. 205-213, esp. pp. 208-211; M.&W. (6) p. 220; M.&W. (9) p. 221; M.&W. (12) p. 223; M.&W. (17)-(20) pp. 228-232; M.&W. (23) pp. 236-237; M.&W. (25) p. 238; M.&W. (39) p. 253; M.&W. (40) p. 255; M.&W. (42) p. 258; P.&P. (14), (15), and (17) pp. 266-268; P.&P. (18)-(29) pp. 268-274

Deacons and widows: I.&S. at "45" p. 18 with ann. 45 and 48, pp. 325, 326; S.S.&M. (11) p. 64; S.S.&M. (16) p. 78;

L.S.T.A.&L. (54) p. 188; ann. to L.S.T.A.&L. (55) p. 379; ann. to M.&W. (8)-(12) p. 388; M.&W. (12) pp. 223-224; M.&W. (13) pp. 225-226

Demons: I.&S. at "8," "9," "10," "13," and "14" pp. 7-9 with ann. 9, p. 318 and ann. 13, pp. 319-320; I.&S. at "33" pp. 14-15 with ann. 33, p. 324; I.&S. at "59" p. 27 with ann. 59, pp. 327-328; ann. 72 to I.&S. p. 330; I.&S. at "84" to "89" pp. 39-41 with ann. 84 and 85, p. 332; ann. to S.S.&M. (13)-(18) pp. 339-340; C.S.P. (3)-(5) pp. 95-96; C.S.P. (27) pp. 108-109; C.S.P. (30) pp. 113-114; C.F.&S. (9) p. 133; C.F.&S. (19) p. 138; C.F.&S. (26) p. 140; C.F.&S. (29) pp. 141-142; C.F.&S. (32) p. 143; ann. to C.F.&S. (9) p. 354; ann. to C.F.&S. (9)-(18) p. 354; C.F.&S. (48) p. 152; C.F.&S. (61) p. 157; L.S.T.A.&L. (30) pp. 176-177; L.S.T.A.&L. (64) p. 207; L.S.T.A.&L. (56) pp. 196-199; M.&W. (12) p. 224; M.&W. (15) pp. 227-228; M.&W. (35) p. 249; M.&W. (37) pp. 251-252; M.&W. (39) pp. 253-254; P.&P. (17) pp. 267-268; P.&P. (19) p. 269; P.&P. (22)-(24) and (26) pp. 270-272; P.&P. (33) pp. 281-285, 292-293; P.&P. (40) pp. 298-299; P.&P. (53) p. 303

Diaconate: *see* Deacons

Discipline: I.&S. pp. 17-18, 22; I.&S. pp. 29, 39, 50-51; S.S.&M. (11) pp. 63-64; S.S.&M. (18) pp. 84-86; S.S.&M. (22) p. 87; C.S.P. (14) p. 100; C.S.P. (19) p. 101; C.S.P. (21) p. 102; C.S.P. (24) pp. 103-106; C.S.P. (27) and (28) pp. 108-110; C.S.P. (29) pp. 111-113; C.S.P. (30) pp. 113-114; C.S.P. (38)-(41) pp. 116-121; C.F.&S. (46) pp. 149-151; C.F.&S. (81) p. 165; ann. to L.S.T.A.&L. (7)-(8) p. 368; L.S.T.A.&L. (30) pp. 176-177; L.S.T.A.&L. (34) p. 178; ann. to L.S.T.A.&L. (37) p. 372; L.S.T.A.&L. (41) pp. 178-179; L.S.T.A.&L. (54) pp. 181-183; L.S.T.A.&L. (55) pp. 190-191; L.S.T.A.&L. (64) pp. 212-213; M.&W. (5)-(7) pp. 218-220; M.&W. (8)

pp. 220-221; M.&W. (12) p. 223; M.&W. (13) p. 226; M.&W. (15) p. 227; M.&W. (20), (21), and (22) pp. 232, 234-236; M.&W. (36) pp. 249-250; P.&P. (32) pp. 274-278; P.&P. (33) pp. 280-282, 284-285, 287-288, 293-294; P.&P. (55)-(60) pp. 303-304; P.&P. (69)-(73) pp. 306-307

Ebionites ("the poor"): ann. 24 to I.&S. p. 321: *see* Topical Index under Property; Index of Names and Writings under Gospel Editions

Ecstasy: *see* Spirit

Elders: *see* Episcopate

Episcopate, overseers, and elders: I.&S. pp. 47-49 with ann. 95, p. 333; C.S.P. (29) p. 111; C.S.P. (36) p. 116; C.F. &S. (24) and (25) p. 140; C.F.&S. (34) pp. 143-144; C. F.&S. (43) pp. 147-148; C.F.&S. (46) pp. 149-151; C.F. &S. (67) p. 159; C.F.&S. (73) p. 162; L.S.T.A.&L. (55) pp. 194-196; L.S.T.A.&L. (56) p. 197; L.S.T.A.&L. (54) pp. 186-188; L.S.T.A.&L. (59) p. 200; L.S.T.A.&L. (61) and (62) pp. 203-204; ann. to L.S.T.A.&L. (56)-(62) pp. 380-381; M.&W. (12)-(13) pp. 222-226

Eschatology: *see* Future

Ethics: *see* Discipline

Evangelists: *see* Apostles; Prophets; Teachers

Faith: I.&S. at "27" pp. 13-14 with ann. 27 and 30, pp. 322, 323; I.&S. at "72" pp. 33-34 with ann. 72 and 73, p. 330; I.&S. pp. 9-10; ann. to S.S.&M. (9) pp. 336-337; C.S.P. (25) pp. 106-107; C.S.P. (31) p. 114; C.S.P. (33)-(34) p. 115 with ann. p. 346; C.F.&S. (1)-(5) pp. 127-131; C. F.&S. (18) p. 137; C.F.&S. (57) p. 156; C.F.&S. (58)-(67) pp. 156-159; C.F.&S. (76) p. 163; C.F.&S. (81) p. 165; L.S.T.A.&L. (3) p. 171; L.S.T.A.&L. (30) pp. 176-177; L.S.T.A.&L. (37) and (39) p. 178; ann. to L.S.T.A. &L. (42) p. 373; L.S.T.A.&L. (53) p. 180; L.S.T.A.&L.

(55) pp. 189-195, esp. p. 195; L.S.T.A.&L. (56) pp. 196-199; L.S.T.A.&L. (58) pp. 199-200; L.S.T.A.&L. (61) pp. 201-203; L.S.T.A.&L. (63) pp. 204-205; L.S.T.A.&L. (64) p. 211; M.&W. (6) p. 220; ann. to M.&W. (1)-(42) p. 387; M.&W. (11)-(12) pp. 222-223; M.&W. (15) p. 227; M.&W. (37) pp. 251-252; M.&W. (39) p. 253; P. &P. (29) pp. 273-274; P.&P. (31) p. 274; P.&P. (32) pp. 274-278; P.&P. (33) pp. 278-294

Fasting: *see* Discipline

Fighting attitude: I.&S. pp. 9-10, 15; I.&S. pp. 24-26, 35-36; C.S.P. (3) p. 95; C.S.P. (43) pp. 122-123; L.S.T.A.&L. (44) p. 179

Forgiveness: I.&S. pp. 13-14 with ann. 28 and 30, pp. 322-323; I.&S. pp. 28-29; I.&S. pp. 48-49 with ann. 95, p. 333; C.S.P. (26) p. 107; C.F.&S. (2) p. 127; C.F.&S. (46) pp. 150-151; L.S.T.A.&L. (30) pp. 176-177; L.S.T.A.&L. (40)-(42) pp. 178-179; L.S.T.A.&L. (53) p. 180; L.S.T.A.&L. (64) pp. 207-213; M.&W. (4)-(7) pp. 218-220; M.&W. (20)-(25) pp. 231-239; P.&P. (14) p. 266; P.&P. (22)-(25) pp. 270-272; P.&P. (29) pp. 273-274; P.&P. (33) pp. 280, 285, 288, 292-294; P.&P. (73) p. 307

Freedom: *see* Spirit

Future: I.&S. pp. 1-5 with ann. 3 and 5, p. 316; I.&S. pp.7-9, 21, 36, 42, 50; S.S.&M. (15) pp. 76-77; S.S.&M. (16) pp. 77, 82; ann. to S.S.&M. (9) p. 337; ann. to S.S.&M. (13)-(18) p. 340; C.S.P. (24) pp. 103, 105; C.F.&S. (20) pp. 138-139; C.F.&S. (24) p. 140; C.F.&S. (26)-(45) pp. 140-149; C.F.&S. (47) and (48) pp. 151-152; C.F.&S. (50) p. 153; C.F.&S. (52) p. 154; C.F.&S. (55) pp. 155-156; C.F.&S. (62) pp. 157-158; C.F.&S. (81) p. 165; L.S.T.A. &L. (1) p. 171; ann. to L.S.T.A.&L. (3) p. 367; L.S.T. A.&L. (16) p. 174; L.S.T.A.&L. (22) p. 175; L.S.T.A.&L.

(27)-(33) pp. 176-177; L.S.T.A.&L. (34)-(37) p. 178; ann. to L.S.T.A.&L. (30) pp. 371-372; ann. to L.S.T.A.&L. (45) pp. 373-374; L.S.T.A.&L. (52)-(53) p. 180; L.S.T. A.&L. (54) pp. 185-186, 189; L.S.T.A.&L. (55) pp. 192-193; L.S.T.A.&L. (63) pp. 204-205; L.S.T.A.&L. (64) pp. 205-207, 209-212; M.&W. (22) and (23) pp. 235-237 with ann. (20)-(25) pp. 392-393; M.&W. (32) p. 245; M.&W. (35), (36), and (37) pp. 249-252; P.&P. (2) p. 262; P.&P. (27) pp. 272-273; P.&P. (29)-(31) pp. 273-274; P.&P. (32) pp. 275-278; P.&P. (33) pp. 279, 285-287, 289, 294, with ann. (33) pp. 403, 405-406; P.&P. (36)-(41) pp. 295-300; P.&P. (61)-(63) pp. 304-305; P.&P. (68) p. 306; P.&P. (78) and (80) p. 308

Gnosis: I.&S. p. 45; C.S.P. (12) and (13) pp. 98-100; ann. to C.F.&S. (4) p. 353; C.F.&S. (15) p. 135; C.F.&S. (46) p. 151; L.S.T.A.&L. (61) pp. 201-203; ann. to L.S.T.A. &L. (64) pp. 383-384; M.&W. (29) p. 241 with ann. (29)-(40) pp. 394-398; P.&P. (28) p. 273 with ann. (28) p. 402

God the Creator: I.&S. pp. 33-34; S.S.&M. (3) p. 59; ann. to S.S.&M. (13)-(18) p. 339; S.S.&M. (15) pp. 74-75 with ann. (15) p. 341; C.S.P. (13) p. 99; C.S.P. (20) p. 102; C.S.P. (24) p. 103; C.S.P. (31) p. 114; C.S.P. (39) p. 119; C.F.&S. (1)-(5) pp. 127-131; C.F.&S. (7) and (8) pp. 131-132; C.F.&S. (11)-(19) pp. 133-138; C.F.&S. (40) p. 147; C.F.&S. (46) pp. 149-151; C.F.&S. (47) p. 151; C.F.&S. (48) p. 152; C.F.&S. (52) and (53) p. 154; C.F. &S. (59) and (60) p. 157; C.F.&S. (64) p. 158; C.F.&S. (67) p. 159; C.F.&S. (68) and (69) pp. 159-161; C.F.&S. (76) p. 163; L.S.T.A.&L. (22) p. 175; ann to L.S.T.A.&L. (11) p. 368; ann. to L.S.T.A.&L. (11)-(13) p. 369; L.S. T.A.&L. (26) and (28) p. 176; L.S.T.A.&L. (32) p. 177; L.S.T.A.&L. (63) pp. 204-205; M.&W. (1) p. 217; M.

&W. (12) p. 223; M.&W. (15)-(27) pp. 227-240; M.&W. (42) p. 258; P.&P. (32) pp. 274-278; ann. to P.&P. (33) p. 404; P.&P. (83)-(86) p. 309

Gospels: *see* New Testament

Government office: I.&S. pp. 19, 21-22, with ann. 51-53, pp. 326-327; I.&S. pp. 23-24 with ann. 56, p. 327; S.S.&M. (4) p. 60; S.S.&M. (26) p. 89; C.S.P. (8) p. 97; C.S.P. (9) and (10) pp. 97-98; C.S.P. (27) p. 108; C.S.P. (39) p. 119; P.&P. (33) pp. 285-286; P.&P. (53) p. 303

Great Commission of Jesus: *see* Apostles

Guilt: I.&S. pp. 13-14 with ann. 28, pp. 322-323 and ann. 33, p. 324; C.S.P. (37) p. 116; C.F.&S. (58) p. 156; L.S.T.A. &L. (30) pp. 176-177; L.S.T.A.&L. (41) pp. 178-179; L.S.T.A.&L. (64) pp. 205-213, esp. pp. 207-211; P.&P. (22)-(25) pp. 270-272

Healing of the sick: *see* Demons and I.&S. pp. 39-40

Hospitality: *see* Love

Household of God, Economy, Trinity: C.F.&S. (3) pp. 128-129; C.F.&S. (7)-(8) pp. 131-132 with ann. (7)-(8) p. 354; L.S.T.A.&L. (56)-(62) pp. 196-204; L.S.T.A.&L. (57) p. 199; M.&W. (36) pp. 249-251; P.&P. (42) and (43) p. 300; P.&P. (48) pp. 301-302

Idolatry: I.&S. p. 23; S.S.&M. (4) p. 60; S.S.&M. (10) p. 63; S.S.&M. (8)-(18) pp. 61-86; S.S.&M. (13) p. 67; S.S.&M. (30) p. 90; C.S.P. (24) pp. 103-104; C.S.P. (27) p. 108; C.F.&S. (7) and (8) pp. 131-132; C.F.&S. (11) pp. 133-134; C.F.&S. (13) p. 134; ann. to C.F.&S. (9)-(18) p. 354

Jerusalem: *see* Primitive Church

Jesus (*see also* Lord's Sayings; Faith): I.&S. pp. 1-4 with ann. 2-4, p. 316; S.S.&M. (8) p. 61; ann to S.S.&M. (9) pp. 335-337; S.S.&M. (11) pp. 63-65; ann to S.S.&M. (13)-(18) p. 339; S.S.&M. (13) pp. 70-71; S.S.&M. (14) p. 72;

S.S.&M. (15) pp. 74-75; S.S.&M. (21) p. 87; C.S.P. (3)-
(5) pp. 95-96; C.S.P. (31) p. 114; C.S.P. (32) pp. 114-
115; C.F.&S. (1)-(5) pp. 127-131; C.F.&S. (7)-(9) and
(11) pp. 131-134; C.F.&S. (46) pp. 149-151; C.F.&S. (49)
pp. 152-153; C.F.&S. (52) p. 154; C.F.&S. (54) pp. 154-
155; C.F.&S. (55) pp. 155-156; C.F.&S. (59) p. 157; C.F.
&S. (63) p. 158; C.F.&S. (69) pp. 160-161; C.F.&S. (76)-
(77) pp. 163-164; C.F.&S. (79)-(81) pp. 164-167; L.S.T.'
A.&L. (56)-(62) pp. 196-204; L.S.T.A.&L. (63) pp. 204-
205 with ann. (63) pp. 382-383; L.S.T.A.&L. (64) pp. 205-
213, esp. 206-212; M.&W. (2) p. 217; M.&W. (9) p. 221;
M.&W. (12) p. 223; M.&W. (15) pp. 227-228; M.&W.
(16)-(24) pp. 228-237; M.&W. (26) and (27) pp. 239-
240; M.&W. (28) and (29) pp. 240-241; ann. to M.&W.
(30)-(39) pp. 396-397; M.&W. (31) pp. 243-245; M.&W.
(34) p. 248; M.&W. (36) pp. 249-251; M.&W. (37) pp.
251-252; M.&W. (38) pp. 252-253; M.&W. (39) pp. 253-
255; M.&W. (41) and (42) pp. 256-258; P.&P. (2) p.
262; P.&P. (13)-(17) pp. 265-268; P.&P. (18)-(29) pp.
268-274; P.&P. (31) and (32) pp. 274-278; P.&P. (33)
pp. 278-294; P.&P. (67) p. 306; P.&P. (86) p. 309
Jews and Jewish Christians: I.&S. pp. 3-7 with ann. 5-7, pp.
316-317; S.S.&M. (9)-(10) pp. 62-63; S.S.&M. (20)-(22)
pp. 86-88; C.S.P. (12) pp. 98-99; C.S.P. (28) p. 110; C.
S.P. (33) p. 115; C.F.&S. (37) pp. 144-145; C.F.&S. (48)
p. 152; C.F.&S. (54)-(56) pp. 154-156; C.F.&S. (70) p.
161; ann. to L.S.T.A.&L. (54) p. 375; L.S.T.A.&L. (64)
pp. 205-213; P.&P. (36) pp. 295-297
Judgment: I.&S. p. 36; I.&S. pp. 40-41; I.&S. pp. 6-7 with
ann. 7, p. 317; L.S.T.A.&L. (1) p. 171; ann. to L.S.T.A.
&L. (28) p. 371; L.S.T.A.&L. (35) and (36) p. 178; L.S.
T.A.&L. (46) p. 179
Kingdom: *see* Future; Church; Life hereafter

Law: *see* Discipline

Laying on of hands: M.&W. (13)-(14) pp. 225-226

Letters: L.S.T.A.&L. (55)-(64) pp. 189-213

Life hereafter: I.&S. pp. 50-51; C.S.P. (28) p. 110; C.S.P. (44) p. 123; L.S.T.A.&L. (28)-(30) pp. 176-177; L.S.T. A.&L. (32) p. 177; L.S.T.A.&L. (35) p. 178; M.&W. (33) pp. 247-248; M.&W. (38) pp. 252-253; M.&W. (39) pp. 253-255

Liturgy: I.&S. pp. 8-10 with ann. 13, 15, 16, and 18, pp. 319-321; L.S.T.A.&L. (54) pp. 184-186 with ann. (54) pp. 376, 377-378; M.&W. (16)-(19) and (21) pp. 228-231, 232-235, with ann. (16)-(19) pp. 391-392

Logos: C.S.P. (30) pp. 113-114; C.S.P. (31) p. 114; C.S.P. (32) pp. 114-115 with full annotation (30)-(32) pp. 344-345; C.F.&S. (3) pp. 128-129 with ann. (3) p. 351; C.F. &S. (8) pp. 131-132; ann. to C.F.&S. (7)-(8) p. 354; C.F. &S. (9) p. 133; C.F.&S. (52) cf. (51) pp. 153-154; C.F. &S. (70) p. 161; C.F.&S. (77) pp. 163-164; ann. to L.S.T. A.&L. (1)-(53) p. 366; L.S.T.A.&L. (51) p. 180; L.S.T. A.&L. (57) p. 199; M.&W. (9) p. 221; M.&W. (12) p. 223; M.&W. (16)-(19) pp. 228-231; M.&W. (38) pp. 252-253; M.&W. (41) pp. 256-257; P.&P. (17) pp. 267-268; P.&P. (20) pp. 269-270

Lord's Sayings: I.&S. pp. 34-35 with ann. 74, pp. 330-331; C.S.P. (24) p. 105; C.S.P. (39) p. 118; ann. to C.F.&S. (36) pp. 356-357; L.S.T.A.&L. (1)-(53) pp. 171-180; ann. to L.S.T.A.&L. (1)-(53) pp. 365-375; ann. to C.F.&S. (77)-(79) p. 363; L.S.T.A.&L. (54) p. 181 with ann. (54) p. 375; M.&W. (1) p. 217

Lord's Supper, Lovemeal: I.&S. at "17" to "23" pp. 10-11 with ann. 17-23, pp. 320-321; I.&S. pp. 49-50 with ann. 98, p. 334; S.S.&M. (11) p. 64; ann. to S.S.&M. (13)-(18) pp. 339-340; C.S.P. (29) pp. 111-113; C.F.&S. (79) p. 164;

L.S.T.A.&L. (54) pp. 185-186 with ann. (54) pp. 376-377; L.S.T.A.&L. (59) pp. 200-201 with ann. to (59) p. 382; L. S.T.A.&L. (61) pp. 202-203; L.S.T.A.&L. (64) pp. 207-209; M.&W. (8)-(12) pp. 220-225; M.&W. (13) pp. 225-226; M.&W. (15) p. 227; M.&W. (40) pp. 255-256; M. &W. (42) p. 258; P.&P. (31) p. 274; P.&P. (69)-(73) pp. 306-307 with ann. p. 409

Love: I.&S. pp. 3, 4, with ann. 5, p. 316; I.&S. pp. 11, 16-19, with ann. 39 and 45, p. 325; I.&S. p. 53; ann. 49 to I.&S. p. 326; C.S.P. (24) pp. 103-106; C.S.P. (25) pp. 106-107; C.S.P. (28) pp. 109-110; C.S.P. (29) pp. 111-113; C.S.P. (39) p. 118; C.F.&S. (18) p. 137; C.F.&S. (20) pp. 138-139; C.F.&S. (81) p. 166; ann. to L.S.T.A.&L. (3) p. 367; L.S.T.A.&L. (11)-(13) p. 173; L.S.T.A.&L. (55) pp. 190, 194-196; L.S.T.A.&L. (56) pp. 196-199; L.S.T.A. &L. (61) pp. 201-203; L.S.T.A.&L. (63) pp. 204-205; L.S. T.A.&L. (64) pp. 207-209; M.&W. (8)-(12) pp. 220-225 with ann. (8)-(12) p. 388; M.&W. (13) and (14) pp. 225-226; M.&W. (38) and (39) pp. 252-255; P.&P. (4)-(7) pp. 262-264; P.&P. (32) pp. 274-278; P.&P. (33) pp. 279-283

Lovemeal: *see* Lord's Supper

Marriage: *see* Discipline

Martyrdom, slander, and persecution: I.&S. pp. 6-7 with ann. 7, p. 317; I.&S. pp. 24-26; S.S.&M. (4) p. 60; S.S.&M. (8)-(18) pp. 61-86 with all the ann., esp. (9) pp. 335-337; S.S.&M. (19)-(27) pp. 86-90; C.S.P. (1) and (2) p. 95; C.S.P. (12) pp. 98-99; C.S.P. (13) pp. 99-100; C.S.P. (28) pp. 109-110; C.S.P. (29) and (30) pp. 112-114; C.S.P. (35)-(37) p. 116; C.S.P. (38) and (39) pp. 116-120; C.S.P. (41)-(43) pp. 121-123; C.S.P. (45) p. 123; C.F.&S. (31) p. 142; C.F.&S. (55) pp. 155-156; L.S.T.A.&L. (44) p. 179; L.S.T.A.&L. (54) p. 189; L.S.T.A.&L. (55) pp. 194-

196; L.S.T.A.&L. (57) p. 199; esp. L.S.T.A.&L. (59) pp. 200-201; L.S.T.A.&L. (62) pp. 203-204; ann. to M.&W. (13)-(14) pp. 390-391; M.&W. (42) p. 258; P.&P. (51)-(54) pp. 302-303; P.&P. (82) p. 309

Meetings: I.&S. pp. 8-12; I.&S. pp. 26-28, 30-33; I.&S. p. 42; I.&S. pp. 49-50; S.S.&M. (11) pp. 64-65; S.S.&M. (15) p. 75; S.S.&M. (26) pp. 88-90; C.S.P. (25) pp. 106-107; C.S.P. (29) pp. 111-113; C.F.&S. (71) and (73) p. 162; C.F.&S. (79) p. 164; ann. to L.S.T.A.&L. (2) p. 367; L.S.T.A.&L. (54) pp. 183, 184-186, 188, 189; L.S.T.A.&L. (55) p. 195; L.S.T.A.&L. (56) p. 197; L.S.T.A.&L. (57) p. 199; L.S.T.A.&L. (60) p. 201; L.S.T.A.&L. (61) pp. 202-203; M.&W. (1) and (2) p. 217; M.&W. (5) p. 218; M.&W. (8) and (9) pp. 220-221; M.&W. (10)-(14) pp. 220-226; M.&W. (16)-(19) pp. 228-231; M.&W. (21) pp. 232-235; M.&W. (26)-(28) pp. 239-240; P.&P. (4) pp. 262-263; P.&P. (32) pp. 274-278; P.&P. (55) and (56) p. 303; P.&P. (69) p. 306; P.&P. (71) pp. 306-307; P.&P. (73) p. 307; P.&P. (79) p. 308

Military, the: *see* Peace

Military service: *see* Peace; Government office

Mission and propaganda: *see* Apostles

Monasticism: *see* Sermon on the Mount

Montanist movement: *see* Prophets; Spirit

Morals: *see* Discipline

Mythras, cult of: *see* Paganism

New Testament: ann. 6 to I.&S. pp. 316-317; I.&S. pp. 3-8; I.&S. p. 29; I.&S. pp. 34-35 with ann. 74, pp. 330-331; I.&S. pp. 43, 46-47; S.S.&M. (17) p. 83; S.S.&M. (22) p. 87; C.S.P. (24) p. 103; C.S.P. (29) p. 111; ann. to C.F.&S. (3) pp. 350-351; C.F.&S. (15) p. 135; C.F.&S. (73)-(81) pp. 162-167 with ann. (73)-(81) pp. 362-364; ann. to L.S.

T.A.&L. (1)-(53) pp. 365-366; ann. to L.S.T.A.&L. (54) and (55) pp. 375-376, 377-378; L.S.T.A.&L. (61) p. 203; ann. to L.S.T.A.&L. (64) p. 383; ann. to L.S.T.A.&L. (1)-(64) pp. 385-386; M.&W. (8) p. 221; M.&W. (12) pp. 223-224; M.&W. (13) p. 226; ann. to M.&W. (26)-(41) p. 393; M.&W. (36) pp. 250-251; P.&P. (17) p. 268; ann. to P.&P. (18) p. 401; P.&P. (30) p. 274; P.&P. (32) p. 277; ann. to P.&P. (33) p. 404; ann. to P.&P. (42)-(45) p. 407

Old Testament: I.&S. at "72" and "73" p. 34 with ann. 72 and 73, p. 330; C.S.P. (24) pp. 105-106; C.S.P. (29) p. 111; C.F.&S. (3)-(4) pp. 128-130; C.F.&S. (8) p. 132; C.F.&S. (15) p. 135; C.F.&S. (16) pp. 135-136; C.F.&S. (30)-(37) pp. 142-145; C.F.&S. (38) pp. 145-146; C.F.&S. (44)-(67) pp. 148-159; C.F.&S. (48) p. 152; C.F.&S. (56) p. 156; C.F.&S. (74) p. 162; C.F.&S. (75) pp. 162-163; L.S.T.A.&L. (9) p. 172; L.S.T.A.&L. (13) p. 173; L.S. T.A.&L. (23) and (25) p. 175; L.S.T.A.&L. (33) p. 177; L.S.T.A.&L. (51) p. 180; ann. to L.S.T.A.&L. (23) p. 370; L.S.T.A.&L. (61) pp. 201-203; L.S.T.A.&L. (64) pp. 205-213; M.&W. (8) pp. 220-221; M.&W. (12) p. 224; M. &W. (13) p. 226; P.&P. (13), (15), and (17) pp. 265-266, 267, 268; P.&P. (21)-(27) pp. 270-273; P.&P. (30) p. 274; P.&P. (32) and (36) pp. 277, 295-296

Paganism: I.&S. pp. 21-25 with ann. 53, p. 327; C.S.P. (30) pp. 113-114; C.S.P. (32) pp. 114-115; M.&W. (12) p. 224: *see* Idolatry; Martyrdom; Roman State and law

Peace, bloodshed, and military service: I.&S. at "52" to "56" pp. 19, 21-24, with ann. 52, p. 326; I.&S. at "100" p. 52 with ann. 100, p. 334; C.S.P. (7) and (8) p. 97; C.S.P. (27) p. 108; C.S.P. (38) pp. 116-117; C.S.P. (39) pp. 119-120; C.S.P. (40) pp. 120-121; C.F.&S. (35) p. 144; C.F.&S.

(55) pp. 155-156; L.S.T.A.&L. (31) p. 177; M.&W. (20)-(25) pp. 231-239; P.&P. (25) and (26) p. 272; P.&P. (29) pp. 273-274; P.&P. (53) p. 303

Pharisees: *see* Jews

Phrygia: *see* Asia Minor

Places of meeting: *see* Meetings; Altars, churches with altars

Politics: I.&S. pp. 19-26 with ann. 51-53, pp. 326-327; S.S. &M. (5) p. 60; S.S.&M. (13)-(18) pp. 67-86; S.S.&M. (26) pp. 88-89; C.S.P. (28) pp. 109-110; C.S.P. (29) p. 111; P.&P. (33) pp. 285-287 with ann. (33) p. 405; P.&P. (40) pp. 298-299

Poverty: *see* Property

Prayer: I.&S. at "62" p. 28 with ann. 62, p. 328; S.S.&M. (13) pp. 68, 70; S.S.&M. (14) pp. 73-74; C.S.P. (13) p. 100; C.S.P. (24) pp. 104-105; C.S.P. (29) p. 111; C.S.P. (32) pp. 114-115; L.S.T.A.&L. (54) pp. 185-189; L.S.T. A.&L. (56) pp. 196-199; M.&W. (8)-(12) pp. 220-224; M.&W. (13) and (14) pp. 225-226; M.&W. (17)-(27) pp. 228-240; M.&W. (31) and (42) pp. 244-245, 258

Presence of the Lord and the Spirit: I.&S. pp. 8-10; I.&S. pp. 27-28; C.S.P. (45) p. 123; L.S.T.A.&L. (1)-(3) and (7) pp. 171, 172; ann. to M.&W. (1)-(42) p. 387; M.&W. (17)-(25) pp. 228-239

Primitive Church: I.&S. pp. 3-4, 5-6, with ann. 5 and 6, pp. 316-317; ann. to L.S.T.A.&L. (54) p. 375; ann. to L.S.T. A.&L. (56)-(62) pp. 380-381

Prisoners, help for: *see* Love

Proclamation: I.&S. pp. 3-5, 7, 8, 10, 15, 25-27, 29, 30, 33-38; S.S.&M. (13) pp. 69-70; S.S.&M. (14) pp. 72-74; S.S. &M. (15) pp. 75-76; S.S.&M. (20) pp. 86-87; S.S.&M. (34) p. 92; C.S.P. (2) and (3) p. 95; C.S.P. (26) p. 107; C.F.&S. (18) p. 137; C.F.&S. (19) pp. 137-138; C.F.&S. (21) p. 139; C.F.&S. (66) p. 159; C.F.&S. (69) and (70) pp. 160-161; C.F.&S. (71)-(73) p. 162; C.F.&S. (76) p. 163; L.S.T.A.&L. (25) p. 175; L.S.T.A.&L. (47) and (48) pp. 179-180; L.S.T.A.&L. (52) and (53) p. 180; M. &W. (2) p. 217; M.&W. (4) p. 218; M.&W. (16) and (17) p. 228; P.&P. (1)-(86) pp. 261-309, esp. (1)-(31) pp. 261-274: *see* Apostles; Prophets; Teachers; Authority

Property, poverty, work, and economy: I.&S. at "21" to "24" pp. 11-12 with ann. 24, p. 321; I.&S. at "35" to "51" pp. 15-19 with ann. 39-45, p. 325 and ann. 48, 49, and 51, p. 326; I.&S. pp. 51-52; C.S.P. (15) and (16) pp. 100-101; C.S.P. (22) and (23) pp. 102-103; C.S.P. (29) pp. 111-113; C.S. P. (42) pp. 121-122; L.S.T.A.&L. (12)-(14) p. 173; L.S. T.A.&L. (28) p. 176; L.S.T.A.&L. (47) p. 179; L.S.T.A. &L. (54) pp. 181-184; M.&W. (8) pp. 220-221; M.&W. (11) p. 222; M.&W. (12) p. 224 with ann. (8)-(12) p. 388; P.&P. (33) pp. 278-294; ann. to P.&P. (69)-(73) p. 409

Prophets, Christian, and evangelists: I.&S. p. 27 with ann. 58, p. 327; I.&S. at "66" p. 30; I.&S. pp. 35-38 with ann. 76-79, pp. 331-332; I.&S. pp. 42-44, 47-48; S.S.&M. (9) p. 62 with ann. (9) p. 335; S.S.&M. (13)-(18) pp. 66-86; C.F. &S. (47)-(55) pp. 151-156 with ann. to C.F.&S. (52) p. 359; C.F.&S. (57) and (58) pp. 156-157; C.F.&S. (61)-(65) pp. 157-159; C.F.&S. (69) pp. 160-161; C.F.&S. (70) p. 161; C.F.&S. (72) p. 162; C.F.&S. (75) and (76) pp. 162-163; C.F.&S. (78) p. 164; ann. to L.S.T.A.&L. (1)-(53) pp. 365-366; L.S.T.A.&L. (54) pp. 186-188; L.S.T. A.&L. (60) p. 201; L.S.T.A.&L. (64) pp. 205-207, 208-209, 211; M.&W. (13) pp. 225-226; M.&W. (39) pp. 253-255; P.&P. (1)-(3) pp. 261-262 with ann. (1)-(3) p. 399; P.&P. (33) esp. pp. 283-284 with ann. (33) pp. 403-404; P.&P. (34) p. 294; ann. to P.&P. (36), (37), and (40) pp. 406-407; P.&P. (42)-(86) pp. 300-309 with ann. (83)-(86) p. 410

Rebirth, conversion, and repentance: I.&S. pp. 12-14 with ann. 25, 27, and 28, pp. 322-323; ann. 32 and 33 to I.&S. pp. 323-324; I.&S. pp. 27-29; S.S.&M. (13) p. 69 with ann. (13)-(18) pp. 339-340; C.S.P. (3) p. 95; C.F.&S. (6) p. 131; C.F.&S. (58) p. 156; C.F.&S. (69) pp. 160-161; L.S.T.A.&L. (3), (4), and (6) pp. 171-172; L.S.T.A.&L. (38) p. 178; L.S.T.A.&L. (54) pp. 184-186; L.S.T.A.&L. (64) pp. 210-211, 212; M.&W. (2) p. 217; M.&W. (5)-(7) pp. 218-220; M.&W. (12) pp. 222-223; M.&W. (20) and (21) pp. 232-233; M.&W. (31) and (33) pp. 243, 246-248; M.&W. (36) pp. 249-250; M.&W. (39) pp. 253-255; M.&W. (40) pp. 255-256; P.&P. (8)-(12) pp. 264-265; P.&P. (14) p. 266; P.&P. (22)-(25) pp. 270-272; P.&P. (32) pp. 274-275; P.&P. (33) pp. 278-283, 285, 288-289, 291-294, with ann. (33) pp. 403-406; P.&P. (49) p. 302; P.&P. (55) p. 303; P.&P. (70), (71), and (76) pp. 306-307

Resurrection: I.&S. p. 3 with ann. 5, p. 316; I.&S. at "10" p. 7 with ann. 10, pp. 318-319; I.&S. at "13" to "16" pp. 8-9 with ann. 13-16, pp. 319-320; C.S.P. (4) p. 96; C.S.P. (34) p. 115; C.S.P. (35)-(37) p. 116 with ann. (35)-(37) p. 346; C.F.&S. (1) p.127; C.F.&S. (21) p. 139; C.F.&S. (27) p. 141; ann. to C.F.&S. (30)-(33) p. 356; C.F.&S. (37) pp. 144-145; C.F.&S. (49) pp. 152-153; C.F.&S. (76) p. 163; ann. to L.S.T.A.&L. (1)-(53) pp. 365-366; L.S.T.A.&L. (21) pp. 174-175; ann. to L.S.T.A.&L (27) p.371; L.S.T.A.&L. (55) pp. 193-194; L.S.T.A.&L. (56) p. 199; L.S.T.A.&L. (58) pp. 199-200; L.S.T.A.&L. (61) pp. 201-203; L.S.T.A.&L. (63) pp. 204-205; M.&W. (11) p. 222; M.&W. (35) p. 249; M.&W. (17)-(24) pp. 228-237; M. &W. (37) pp. 251-252; M.&W. (39) p. 254; M.&W. (42) p. 258

Revolution: *see* Politics

Roman State and law: S.S.&M. pp. 59-92, esp. (1)-(19) pp. 59-86, S.S.&M. (23) p. 88, and S.S.&M. (26)-(28) pp. 88-90; C.S.P. (29) pp. 112-113; C.F.&S. (48) p. 152; P.&P. (40) p. 299

Rome: I.&S. p. 18 with ann. 45, p. 325; I.&S. pp. 42, 43, 48; S.S.&M. (15) p.75; L.S.T.A.&L. (55) p. 189; L.S.T.A.&L. (59) pp. 200-201; ann. to M.&W. (13)-(14) p. 390; ann. to P.&P. (33) pp. 403-404

Sacrilege: *see* Atheism; Roman State and law

Sadducees: *see* Jews

Sect: *see* Church, community, and brotherhood

Septuagint: *see* Old Testament

Sermon on the Mount: I.&S. at "3" p. 3 with ann. 3, p. 316; I.&S. at "31" p. 14 with ann. 31, p. 323; I.&S. pp. 51-52; C.S.P. (8)-(24) pp. 97-106; C.S.P. (27) pp. 108-109; C.S.P. (39) p. 119; C.S.P. (42) p.121; L.S.T.A.&L. (54) pp. 181-184; L.S.T.A.&L. (63) pp. 204-205

Silent worship: *see* Prayer

Sin: *see* Guilt; Forgiveness

Slavery: I.&S. p. 22; S.S.&M. (13) p. 67; S.S.&M. (16) pp. 77-82; C.S.P. (21) p. 102; C.S.P. (24) p. 104; C.S.P. (27) pp. 108-109; C.S.P. (39) p. 120; ann. to P.&P. (33) p. 404

Songs, hymns, and odes: I.&S. at "58" p. 27 with ann. 58, p. 327; I.&S. pp. 10, 27; C.S.P. (25) pp. 106-107; M.&W. (26)-(41) pp. 239-257; ann. to P.&P. (67) p. 409; ann. to M.&W. (26)-(41) pp. 393-398

Spirit: I.&S. at "5" p. 3 with ann. 5, p. 316 and ann. 9, pp. 317-318; I.&S. at "16" p. 9 with ann. 16, p. 320; I.&S. at "25" pp. 12-13 with ann. 25, p. 322; ann. 33 to I.&S. p. 324; I.&S. p. 17; I.&S. pp. 42-43; I.&S. pp. 36-38; I.&S. at "58" and "59" p. 27 with ann. 58, p. 327; I.&S. at "72" pp. 33-34 with ann. 71 and 72, pp. 329-330; I.&S. pp. 40-

41; I.&S. at "95" p. 48 with ann. 95, p. 333; S.S.&M. (15) pp. 74-75; S.S.&M. (16) pp. 77-78; C.S.P. (27) p. 109; C.S.P. (21) p. 102; C.F.&S. (3) pp. 128-129; C.F.&S. (6)-(8) pp. 131-132; C.F.&S. (11) pp. 133-134; C.F.&S. (14) pp. 134-135; C.F.&S. (47) p. 151; C.F.&S. (48) p. 152; C.F.&S. (50) p. 153; C.F.&S. (51) and (52) pp. 153-154; ann. to C.F.&S. (51) and (52) p.359; C.F.&S. (54) and (55) pp. 154-156 with ann. (55) p. 359; C.F.&S. (57) p. 156; C.F.&S. (59) p. 157; C.F.&S. (62) p.157; C.F.&S. (69) p. 160; C.F.&S. (70) p. 161; C.F.&S. (71)-(72) p. 162; C.F.&S. (74) p. 162; C.F.&S. (81) p. 165; L.S.T. A.&L. (5) p. 172; ann. to L.S.T.A.&L. (23) and (25) pp. 370, 371; L.S.T.A.&L. (30) and (40) pp. 176-177, 178; L.S.T.A.&L. (49)-(51) p. 180; L.S.T.A.&L. (54) pp. 184-189; L.S.T.A.&L. (55) pp. 189-190; L.S.T.A.&L. (60) p. 201; L.S.T.A.&L. (64) pp. 207, 211; ann. to M.&W. (1)-(42) p. 387; M.&W. (2) p. 217; M.&W. (5)-(7) pp. 218-220; M.&W. (13) and (14) pp. 225-226; M.&W. (16)-(25) pp. 228-239; M.&W. (26) and (27) pp. 239-240; M.&W. (30)-(39) pp. 241-255 with ann. (30)-(39) pp. 395-396, especially (30) pp. 241-243, (33) pp. 246-248, (36) pp. 249-251, and (39) pp. 253-254; M.&W. (40)-(42) pp. 255, 257, 258; P.&P. (8) and (9) p. 264; P.&P (15) p. 267; P.&P. (19) pp. 268-269; P.&P. (32) pp. 276-277 with ann. (32) p. 403; P.&P. (33) pp. 278-294 with ann. (33) pp. 403-406; P.&P. (34) p. 294; P.&P. (35) and (36) pp. 294-297; P.&P. (42)-(86) pp. 300-309 with ann. (42)-(45) p. 407, (49)-(60) and (63) p. 408, (76) p. 409, and (82) and (83)-(86) p. 410

State religion: *see* Jews; Roman State and law
Stoicism: *see* Paganism
Subversion: *see* Politics
Sunday: *see* Meetings

Synods: *see* Church, community, and brotherhood

Teachers: I.&S. pp. 30-35; S.S.&M. (13) p. 69; S.S.&M. (18) pp. 84-86; C.S.P. (27) pp. 108-109; L.S.T.A.&L. (54) pp. 186-188; M.&W. (13) pp. 225-226; ann. to P.&P. (1)-(3) p. 399

Treason, high treason: *see* Roman State and law

Truth: *see* Faith; Confession of Faith

Unchastity: *see* Martyrdom, slander, and persecution

Virginity: *see* Discipline

Women: ann. 76 to I.&S. p. 331; ann. 83, p. 332; S.S.&M. (25) p. 88; S.S.&M. (33) p. 91; C.S.P. (21) p. 102; C.S.P. (43) pp. 122-123

Work and economy: *see* Property

# INDEX OF NAMES AND WRITINGS
# WITH DATES

Abgar story: ann. 80 to I.&S. p. 332. After 200 the Abgar story emerges, which tells of King Abgar of Edessa's correspondence with Jesus and missionary work by the apostle Thaddaeus.

Abraham (Gen. 11:26 - 25:10): C.F.&S. (16) p. 135; C.F. &S. (37) p. 145; C.F.&S. (59) p. 157; C.F.&S. (76) p. 163; P.&P. (3) p. 262

Acts: *see under the various proper names*

Adam (Gen. 1:26 - 3:20): C.F.&S. (38) p. 146

Addaeus or Addai, an apostle near the Tigris around the year 100: I.&S. p. 38. *Lehre des Addäus oder Addai*, published by Lagarde, 1856 ⟨English translation by G. Philips, *The Doctrine of Addai, the Apostle*, London, 1876⟩: ann. to L.S. T.A.&L. (7)-(8) p. 368

Agathonica, died c. A.D. 165 in Asia Minor: S.S.&M. (14) pp. 73-74. Voluntary martyr.

Ananos, family of high priests in Jerusalem during the first century: S.S.&M. (9) p. 62

Andrew and *Acts of Andrew*, anti-Jewish apocryphal writing about the activities of the apostle Andrew, composed around 200: ann. 9 to I.&S. p. 318; ann. 74 to I.&S. p. 331; C.F. &S. (73) p. 162; C.F.&S. (81) p. 165; P.&P. (19) pp. 268-269

Aphraates, Persian, Syrian bishop, wrote about 340 homilies: ann. to L.S.T.A.&L. (31) p. 372

Apollonius, a martyr after 180: P.&P. (60) p. 304

*Apophthegmata Patrum*, spiritual maxims of the Fathers: ann. 59 and 60 to I.&S. pp. 327-328

Aristides, his *Apology* written about A.D. 137: C.S.P. (24) pp. 103-106; C.F.&S. (21) p. 139; ann. to L.S.T.A.&L. (1)-(53) p. 366

Aristion, with the apostle John in Asia Minor, around the year 70: ann. 74 to I.&S. p. 331

Athenagoras, wrote in defense of the Christians in the year 177: S.S.&M. (3) p. 59; S.S.&M. (6) p. 61; S.S.&M. (24) p. 88; C.S.P. (6) pp. 96-97; C.S.P. (39) p. 120; C.S.P. (42) p. 122; C.F.&S. (8) p. 132; C.F.&S. (13) p. 134; C.F.&S. (14) p. 135; C.F.&S. (39) p. 146; C.F.&S. (40)-(42) p. 147; C.F.&S. (51) p. 153; ann. to L.S.T.A.&L. (1)-(53) p. 366

Augustine of Hippo, born A.D. 354, baptized in the year 387, died in A.D. 430: ann. to C.F.&S. (1)-(5) p. 348; ann. to L.S.T.A.&L. (1)-(53) p. 365

*Barnabas, Letter of*, written between A.D. 70 and 130 in Egypt: ann. 69 to I.&S. p. 329; ann. to L.S.T.A.&L. (1)-(53) p. 366; ann. to L.S.T.A.&L. (45) pp. 373-374; L.S.T.A.&L. (64) pp. 205-213 with ann. (64) pp. 383-385; L.S.T.A.&L. (32) p. 177

Basil, born A.D. 330 in Athens, died as Bishop of Caesarea in 379: M.&W. (27) p. 240

Blandina and Biblis, martyred in the south of France, A.D. 177: S.S.&M. (16) pp. 77-82

Carpus, martyred at Pergamum, Asia Minor, c. A.D. 165-170: S.S.&M. (14) pp. 71-74

Celsus, wrote the antichristian book *The True Word* about the year 178: I.&S. p. 15; I.&S. p. 36; I.&S. p. 49; ann. 11 to I.&S. p. 319; S.S.&M. (5) p. 60; S.S.&M. (29) p. 90; C.S.P. (8) p. 97; C.S.P. (26) p. 107; L.S.T.A.&L. (44) p. 179; P.&P. (86) p. 309

Church Orders, for instance *Didache* (*see The Teaching of the Twelve Apostles*) around A.D. 100; *Apostolic Church Order,* original version around A.D. 160, latest version around 310 adapting and combining the Syriac *Didascalia* or *Teaching of the Apostles* (*see* index) which was in use around the year 250, and the *Roman Church Order* and *Egyptian Church Order* around 218 or 230 (*see* Hippolytus) ; also *Apostolic Constitutions* in eight books, written around the year 370: C.S.P. (27) p. 109; L.S.T.A.&L. (14) p. 173; L.S.T.A.&L. (20) p. 174; L.S.T.A.&L. (25) p. 175; M.&W. (26) pp. 239-240; M.&W. (13) p. 226

Cicero, Roman orator and author, died in 43 B.C.: S.S.&M. (1) p. 59

Clement, principal of the school in Alexandria, born A.D. 150, died after 200, chief writings around 195: ann. 61, 67, and 68 to I.&S. pp. 328-329; ann. 73 to I.&S. p. 330; ann 78 to I.&S. p. 331; ann. 97 to I.&S. p. 334; ann. to S.S.&M. (9) p. 336; C.S.P. (18) p. 101; C.S.P. (21) p. 102; C.S.P. (36) p. 116; ann. to C.F.&S. (1)-(5) p. 349; L.S.T.A.&L. (4) p. 171; L.S.T.A.&L. (16) and (18) p. 174; L.S.T.A.&L. (24) and (25) p. 175; L.S.T.A.&L. (41) and (42) p. 179; L.S.T.A.&L. (53) p. 180; ann. to L.S.T.A.&L. (11) p. 368; ann. to L.S.T.A.&L. (36) p. 372; ann. to L.S.T.A.&L. (54) p. 375; ann. to L.S.T.A.&L. (64) p. 383; M.&W. (41) p. 257

*Clement, First Letter of,* letter from the Church at Rome, before the year 100: ann. 69 to I.&S. p. 329; L.S.T.A.&L. (55) pp. 189-196 with ann. (55) pp. 378-380; M.&W. (21) pp. 232-235 with ann. (20)-(25) pp. 392-393

*Clement, Second Letter of,* in fact the oldest Christian Church sermon, from the middle of the second century at the latest, written in Rome or Corinth: ann. 30 to I.&S. p. 323; ann.

68 to I.&S. p. 329; P.&P. (32) pp. 274-278 with ann. (32) pp. 402-403

Clementine *Homilies* (20) and *Recognitions* (12), revision of the romance-like story of Clement ⟨of Rome⟩, written between A.D. 225 and 300: ann. 35 to I.&S. p. 325; C.F.&S. (20) p. 139; L.S.T.A.&L. (3) p. 171; L.S.T.A.&L. (8) and (9) p. 172; L.S.T.A.&L. (12) p. 173; L.S.T.A.&L. (24) and (25) p. 175; L.S.T.A.&L. (33) p. 177; L.S.T. A.&L. (45) and (47) p. 179; L.S.T.A.&L. (48) p. 180; ann. to L.S.T.A.&L. (11)-(13) p. 369

Constantine the Great, Emperor A.D. 324-327: ann. 100 to I.&S. p. 334

Cyprian of Carthage, wrote *To Donatus* in A.D. 246 and *To Demetrianus* in 252, martyred in A.D. 258: ann. 25 to I.&S. p. 322; ann. 27 to I.&S. p. 322; ann. 33 and 34 to I.&S. pp. 324-325; ann. 49 to I.&S. p. 326; ann. 86, 89, and 97 to I.&S. pp. 332-333

Cyprian, Pseudo, second half of the third century: L.S.T. A.&L. (49) and (51) p. 180

Cyril, Bishop of Jerusalem A.D. 351-386: ann. to L.S.T.A.&L. (1)-(53) p. 365

Daniel, Book of, Old Testament apocalyptic prophecy: C.F. &S. (28) p. 141; C.F.&S. (70) p. 161

David (1 Sam. 16 to 2 Sam. 24:1; 1 Chron. 2-29): C.F.&S. (46) p. 149; C.F.&S. (58) p. 156; C.F.&S. (70) p. 161

*Didache*: see *Teaching of the Twelve Apostles*

*Didascalia apostolorum,* Syriac *Teaching of the Apostles,* completed around the year A.D. 250: ann. 36 and 42 to I.&S. p. 325; ann. to L.S.T.A.&L. (1)-(53) p. 365; L.S.T.A.&L. (8) p. 172; ann. to L.S.T.A.&L. (10) p. 368; L.S.T.A.&L. (14) p. 173; L.S.T.A.&L. (25) p. 175; ann. to L.S.T.A.&L. (27) and (30) pp. 371-372; L.S.T.A.&L. (32) p. 177; ann.

to L.S.T.A.&L. (37) p. 372; ann. to L.S.T.A.&L. (41), (42), and (45) p. 373

Didymus the Blind, of Alexandria, died c. A.D. 395: L.S.T. A.&L. (1) p. 171; P.&P. (45) p. 301; P.&P. (85) and (86) p. 309

Dio Cassius, pagan historian after A.D. 200: S.S.&M. (10) p. 63

*Diognetus, Letter to*, written end of the second or beginning of the third century: C.S.P. (20) p. 102; C.S.P. (23) p. 103; C.S.P. (28) p. 110; C.S.P. (33) p. 115; C.S.P. (45) p. 123; C.F.&S. (18) p. 137; M.&W. (16) p. 228; P.&P. (1) p. 261; P.&P. (14) p. 266

Doctrine of the Fathers on the Incarnation of the Word, *Doctrina Patrum*, late writing with parts from the third century: ann. to P.&P. (67) p. 409

Domitian, Emperor A.D. 81-96: S.S.&M. (10) pp. 62-63

Ebionites: *see* Gospel of the Ebionites

Elijah (1 Kings 17-19; 2 Kings 1-2): C.F.&S. (61) p. 157; C.F.&S. (70) p. 161

*Enoch, Book of*, this version translated into Greek in Egypt possibly during the first century (quoted in Jude 14-15); drawn on in the *Letter of Barnabas* and several early Christian apocalypses; belongs to the Old Testament of the Ethiopic Church, where it precedes the Book of Job; often read by the first Christians ⟨see R. H. Charles, *Apocrypha and Pseudepigrapha*, vol. 2, pp. 188-281⟩: L.S.T.A.&L. (64) p. 206 with ann. (64) p. 384

Ephraem the Syrian, deacon at Edessa, about A.D. 373: ann. to L.S.T.A.&L. (1)-(53) p. 365; ann. to L.S.T.A.&L. (2) p. 367; ann. to L.S.T.A.&L. (30) p. 371

Epiphanius, born in Palestine, leading Bishop of Cyprus, died a monk in Egypt A.D. 403, almost one hundred years old: ann. 59 to I.&S. p. 327; ann. to L.S.T.A.&L. (14) p. 369;

P.&P. (47) p. 301; P.&P. (50) p. 302; P.&P. (56) p. 303; ann. to P.&P. (61)-(63) p. 408; P.&P. (63) p. 305; P.&P. (66) and (69) p. 306; P.&P. (71) p. 307; P.&P. (74),(75), and (76) p. 307; P.&P. (78) p. 308; P.&P. (83) and (84) p. 309

*Epistle of the Apostles* (*Epistula Apostolorum*), written c. A.D. 160 probably in Asia Minor: C.F.&S. (2) p. 127 with ann. (2) pp. 349-350; P.&P. (38) p. 297

Eusebius, born c. A.D. 264, Bishop of Caesarea from about 314-340; first leading Church historian: ann. 45 to I.&S. p. 325; ann. 57 to I.&S. p. 327; ann. 74, 79, 80, 81, and 83 to I.&S. pp. 331, 332; I.&S. p. 38; ann. 90, 91, 92, and 99 to I.&S. pp. 333, 334; ann. to S.S.&M. (9) p. 336; C.F.&S. (34) and (36) pp. 143-144; L.S.T.A.&L. (26) p. 176; ann. to L.S.T.A.&L. (54) p. 375; ann. to L.S.T.A.&L. (55) p. 378; P.&P. (50) p. 302; P.&P. (60) p. 304; P.&P. (70) p. 306; P.&P. (79) and (80) p. 308

Ezekiel, Old Testament prophet among the Jews exiled in Babylon: C.F.&S. (37) p. 145

Ezra, Books of, Fifth Book from the second century, Sixth Book from the third century: P.&P. (36) and (37) pp. 295-297 with ann. (36)-(37) pp. 406-407

Festus, procurator in Judea A.D. 60-62: S.S.&M. (9) p. 62

Flavius Clemens and Flavia Domitilla, martyred in A.D. 95: S.S.&M. (10) p. 63

Germanicus, martyr at Smyrna, Phrygia, in Asia Minor, A.D. 156: S.S.&M. (13) p. 67

Gospel Editions, for example Gospel of the Hebrews which originated as the Gospel of the Twelve around the years 70-125 among the Jewish-Christians who spoke Greek but were inwardly not hellenized (*see also* Gospel of the Ebionites): M.&W. (17) p. 228; L.S.T.A.&L. (7) p. 172; L.S.T.A.&L. (11) and (13) p. 173; L.S.T.A.&L. (16) and (20) p. 174;

L.S.T.A.&L. (22) and (24) p. 175; L.S.T.A.&L. (43) p. 179; L.S.T.A.&L. (52) p. 180; ann. to L.S.T.A.&L. (1)-(53) pp. 365-366; ann. to L.S.T.A.&L. (2) p. 367; ann. to L.S.T.A.&L. (11)-(13) p. 369; ann. to L.S.T.A.&L. (15) and (20) p. 370; ann. to L.S.T.A.&L. (27) and (30) pp. 371-372; ann. to L.S.T.A.&L. (43) p. 373; ann. to L.S.T. A.&L. (50) p. 374

Gospel of the Ebionites, Gospel used by the Jewish-Christian sect of the Ebionites in the second century: L.S.T.A.&L. (3) p. 171; L.S.T.A.&L. (8) and (9) p. 172; L.S.T.A.&L. (11) p. 173; L.S.T.A.&L. (24) p. 175

Gregory of Nyssa, bishop from A.D. 371 until his death in 395: L.S.T.A.&L. (5) p. 172

Hadrian, Emperor A.D. 113-138: S.S.&M. (12) p. 66

Hegesippus, of Jewish origin, in Rome from A.D. 150 to 177; wrote five books of *Memoirs*: ann to S.S.&M. (9) pp. 336-337

Heraclitus of Ephesus, around 500 B.C., one of the earliest and profoundest Greek philosophers: C.S.P. (30) p. 113

Hermas, *Shepherd* of, around A.D. 140: I.&S. p. 16 with ann. 37, p. 325; ann. 67 to I.&S. p. 328; C.F.&S. (81) p. 167 with ann. (80)-(81) pp. 363-364; ann. to L.S.T.A.&L. (14) p. 369; ann. to L.S.T.A.&L. (64) p. 383; P.&P. (33) pp. 278-294 with ann. (33) pp. 403-406

Hilary of Poitiers, bishop there from about A.D. 350-366; follower of Origen: C.F.&S. (6) p. 131

Hippolytus, rival Bishop of Rome from A.D. 202 to 235: ann. 32 to I.&S. p. 324; ann. 97 to I.&S. p. 334; C.S.P. (27) p. 109 with ann. (27) p. 344; ann. to C.F.&S. (4) p. 353; C.F.&S. (80) p. 165; L.S.T.A.&L. (43) and (46) p. 179; M.&W. (13) p. 226; M.&W. (19) p. 231; P.&P. (67) and (68) p. 306

Hystaspes, a pagan prophet known only by name: C.F.&S. (48) p. 152

Ignatius, overseer of the Church at Antioch; martyred in the year 107 or 115: ann. 7 and 8 to I.&S. p. 317; ann. 10 to I.&S. pp. 318-319; ann. 45 to I.&S. p. 325; C.S.P. (1) p. 95; ann. to C.F.&S. (1)-(5) p. 348; C.F.&S. (75) and (76) p. 163; L.S.T.A.&L. (56)-(62) pp. 196-204 with ann. pp. 380-381

Inscription, also on the Indian gateway: *see* Manuscripts

Irenaeus, born in Asia Minor, Bishop of Lyons, died after A.D. 180: ann. 21 to I.&S. p. 321; ann. 58 to I.&S. p. 327; ann. 84 to I.&S. p. 332; ann. 90, 91, 92, and 93 to I.&S. p. 333; I.&S. p. 53 with ann. 102, p. 334; ann. to C.S.P. (36) p. 346; C.F.&S. (4) p. 130; ann. to C.F.&S. (1)-(5) pp. 348-349; ann. to C.F.&S. (3) pp. 351, 352; ann. to C.F.&S. (4) pp. 352-353; C.F.&S. (15) p. 135; C.F.&S. (25) p. 140; C.F.&S. (34) and (35) p. 144; C.F.&S. (43) p. 148; C.F.&S. (46) p. 151; C.F.&S. (67) p. 159; C.F.&S. (80) p. 165 with ann. to (80)-(81) p. 364; L.S.T.A.&L. (31) p. 177; L.S.T.A.&L. (63) p. 205; P.&P. (18) p. 268; ann. to P.&P. (15) p. 400; ann. to P.&P. (33) pp. 403-404

Isaac (Gen. 17:17-35): C.F.&S. (16) p. 135; C.F.&S. (37) p. 145; C.F.&S. (59) p. 157; C.F.&S. (76) p. 163; P.&P. (3) p. 262

Isaiah, the great prophetic book of the Old Testament, written c. 700 B.C.: C.F.&S. (37) and (38) p. 145; C.F.&S. (51) p. 153 and (53) p. 154; C.F.&S. (58) p. 156; C.F.&S. (70) p. 161; P.&P. (6) and (7) p. 263

Jacob, also called Israel, son of Isaac (Gen. 25:22-49): C.F. &S. (16) p. 135; C.F.&S. (30) p. 142; C.F.&S. (37) p. 145; C.F.&S. (59) p. 157; C.F.&S. (76) p. 163; P.&P. (3) p. 262; P.&P. (13) p. 265

James, brother of Jesus; martyred in Jerusalem in A.D. 63, 61, or 66: I.&S. p. 6; ann. 7 to I.&S. p. 317; S.S.&M. (9) p. 62 with ann. (9) pp. 335-337; ann. to C.F.&S. (36) p. 357 (the apostle?); C.F.&S. (73) p. 162

Jeremiah, the Old Testament prophet about 600 B.C.: C.F.&S. (51) p. 153; C.F.&S. (70) p. 161

Jerome, c. A.D. 340-420: L.S.T.A.&L. (11) p. 173; L.S.T.A. &L. (30) pp. 176-177; L.S.T.A.&L. (38) p. 178; L.S.T. A.&L. (50) p. 180; ann. to L.S.T.A.&L. (27) and (30) pp. 371, 372; ann. to L.S.T.A.&L. (50) p. 374; P.&P. (4) pp. 262-263

Jesus Christ: *see* Topical Index

John, the apostle and elder, active mainly in Ephesus and Asia Minor until after A.D. 100: ann. 74 to I.&S. p. 331; I.&S. p. 28; I.&S. p. 45; ann. to C.S.P. (30)-(32) pp. 344-345; ann. to C.F.&S. (3) pp. 350-351; C.F.&S. (25) p. 140; C. F.&S. (34) pp. 143-144; C.F.&S. (38) p. 146; ann. to C.F.&S. (36) p. 357; C.F.&S. (73) p. 162; C.F.&S. (80) and (81) pp. 164-167; ann. to L.S.T.A.&L. (56)-(62) p. 381; ann. to P.&P. (42)-(45) p. 407; P.&P. (4) pp. 262-263

*John, Acts of,* earliest of the apocryphal Acts of the Apostles, written in the middle of the second century: ann. 9 to I.&S. p. 318; L.S.T.A.&L. (30) pp. 176-177; M.&W. (14) p. 226; M.&W. (15) pp. 227-228; M.&W. (40) pp. 255-256; P.&P. (20) pp. 269-270

Josephus, active and writing between the years A.D. 63 and 95: S.S.&M. (9) p. 62

Julian the Apostate, Caesar from A.D. 355-360, Emperor from A.D. 361-363: I.&S. p. 17 with ann. 43, p. 325

Justin, died c. A.D. 165 at Rome (about his life see ann. to C. F.&S. (9) pp. 354-355): ann. 29 to I.&S. p. 323; ann. 32 to I.&S. p. 324; ann. 40 to I.&S. p. 325; ann. 54 to I.&S.

p. 327; ann. 72 to I.&S. p. 330; I.&S. p. 34 with ann. 73, p. 330; ann. 84 and 85 to I.&S. p. 332; ann. 97 to I.&S. p. 334; S.S.&M. (4) p. 60; S.S.&M. (15) pp. 74-77; S.S. &M. (18) p. 86; S.S.&M. (20)-(23) pp. 86-88; S.S.&M. (34) p. 92; C.S.P. (2)-(5) pp. 95-96; C.S.P. (7) and (9) pp. 97-98; C.S.P. (11)-(17) pp. 98-101; C.S.P. (19) p. 101; C.S.P. (30)-(32) pp. 113-115; C.S.P. (34) p.115; C.S.P. (35) and (37) p. 116; C.S.P. (41) p. 121; ann. to C.F.&S. (3) p. 351; C.F.&S. (7) p. 131; C.F.&S. (9), (11), and (12) pp. 133-134; C.F.&S. (16) p. 136; C.F.&S. (19) p. 138; C.F.&S. (22)-(24) pp. 139-140; ann. to C.F.&S. (25) p. 356; C.F.&S. (26)-(33) pp. 141-143; C.F.&S. (37) p. 145; C.F.&S. (38) p. 146; C.F.&S. (45) p. 149; C.F. &S. (48)-(50) pp. 152-153; C.F.&S. (52)-(61) pp. 154-157 with ann. (52) p. 359; C.F.&S. (63)-(66) pp. 158-159 with ann. (65)-(66) p. 361; C.F.&S. (68)-(72) pp. 159-162 with ann. (69) p. 361; C.F.&S. (77)-(79) p. 164; ann. to C.F.&S. (39)-(42) p. 357; ann. to C.F.&S. (48) p. 358; L.S.T.A.&L. (34) and (36) p. 178; ann. to L.S.T.A.&L. (11)-(13) p. 369; M.&W. (2) p. 217; M.&W. (5)-(7) p. 220; M.&W. (9)-(12) pp. 221-225 with ann. (8)-(12) pp. 389-390; P.&P. (2) and (3) p. 262; P.&P. (5) p. 263; P.&P. (7) and (9) p. 264; P.&P. (11)-(13) pp. 265-266; P.&P. (15)-(17) pp. 267-268; P.&P. (21)-(31) pp. 270-274; ann. to P.&P. (30) and (33) pp. 402, 403

Justin, Pseudo: P.&P. (55) p. 303

Lucian, satirical writer from Samosata, A.D. 166-182: I.&S. pp. 7-8 with ann. 12, p. 319; ann. 39 to I.&S. p. 325; I.&S. p. 36 with ann. 76, p. 331; C.S.P. (44) p. 123

Lucius, martyred A.D. 150 at Rome: S.S.&M. (18) p. 86

Luke, writer of the Gospel and the Acts of the Apostles between A.D. 75 and 93: C.F.&S. (81) pp. 165, 166; ann. to M.&W. (26)-(41) p. 393

Macarius Magnes, with his fragments from Porphyry; died A.D. 391 : I.& S. p. 13 with ann. 27 and 28, p. 322; ann. 41 to I.& S. p. 325; ann. 59 to I.& S. p. 327; L.S.T.A.& L. (35) p. 178; ann. to L.S.T.A.& L. (3) p. 367

Manuscripts, rare, mostly originating from earliest times, e.g. Oxyr. Papyrus, Grenfell and Hunt, 1897, written perhaps about A.D. 200: L.S.T.A.& L. (2) p. 171; L.S.T.A.& L. (5) and (10) p. 172; L.S.T.A.& L. (15)-(17) and (19) p. 174; L.S.T.A.& L. (21)-(23) p. 175; L.S.T.A.& L. (27)-(30) pp. 176-177; L.S.T.A.& L. (37), (39), and (40) p. 178; ann. to L.S.T.A.& L. (1)-(53) p. 365; ann. to L.S.T.A.& L. (37) p. 372; ann. to L.S.T.A.& L. (54) p. 375; M.& W. (17) and (18) pp. 228-229; M.& W. (27) p. 240; P.& P. (34) p. 294

Marcellus of Ancyra, bishop, died c. A.D. 373: ann. to C. F.& S. (3) and (5) pp. 351, 353

Marcian, jurist, shortly after A.D. 200: S.S.& M. (28) p. 90

Marcion, from Sinope (Asia Minor), in Rome between A.D. 139-160: C.F.& S. (81) p. 166; L.S.T.A.& L. (5) p. 172; ann. to L.S.T.A.& L. (64) p. 384

Marcus Aurelius, Caesar from A.D. 147, Emperor from 161-180: S.S.& M. (26) p. 89; ann. to M.& W. (28) p. 394

Mark, author of the Gospel of Mark, between the years A.D. 64 and 75: C.F.& S. (80) p. 164

Mary, mother of Jesus: C.F.& S. (3) pp. 128, 129; C.F.& S. (4) and (5) p. 130; C.F.& S. (21) p. 139; C.F.& S. (24) p. 140; M.& W. (19) p. 230; M.& W. (34) p. 248; P.& P. (13) p. 265

Matthew, author of the Gospel, written in Aramaic about the year 62: ann. 74 to I.& S. p. 331; C.F.& S. (73) p. 162; C. F.& S. (80) p. 164; ann. to P.& P. (80) p. 410

Matthias, Traditions of, ascribed to the apostle appointed

later, Acts 1:26; considered authoritative by the Gnostics: L.S.T.A.&L. (41) p. 179

Maximilla, Montanist prophetess, died in A.D. 179: P.&P. (59) p. 304; ann. to P.&P. (61)-(63) p. 408; P.&P. (63) and (65) p. 305; P.&P. (74) and (75) p. 307; P.&P. (79) and (80) p. 308 with ann. to (79) p. 409

Melito, Bishop of Sardis, was active c. A.D. 165-170: I.&S. p. 37 with ann. 79, p. 332; M.&W. (28) p. 240 with ann. (28) p. 394; ann. to P.&P. (33) and (34) pp. 403, 406

Memoirs of the Apostles: *see* Topical Index under New Testament

Methodius, Bishop of Tyre, martyred around 311: C.F.&S. (80) p. 165

Minucius Felix, wrote his dialogue *Octavius* around A.D. 175 or 235: ann. 97 to I.&S. p. 334; S.S.&M. (19) p. 86; S.S.&M. (26) p. 90; C.S.P. (22) p. 103; C.S.P. (38) p. 117; C.S.P. (43) p. 123; C.F.&S. (10) p. 133; C.F.&S. (17) p. 137

Montanus, prophetic leader of the Montanist revival movement, active from A.D. 156 to about 180: I.&S. pp. 42-43; P.&P. (45) p. 301; P.&P. (59) and (61) p. 304; P.&P. (65) p. 305; ann. to P.&P. (67) p. 409; P.&P. (76) p. 307

Moses, led the people of Israel out of Egypt (see the Pentateuch): C.S.P. (34) p. 115; C.F.&S. (16) p. 136; C.F.&S. (32) pp. 142-143; C.F.&S. (34) pp. 143-144; C.F.&S. (45) p. 149; C.F.&S. (51) p. 153; C.F.&S. (58) pp. 156-157; C.F.&S. (64) p. 158; C.F.&S. (70) p. 161; L.S.T.A.&L. (64) pp. 209, 211

*Muratorian Canon,* of the New Testament, between the years 180 and 195 at Rome: I.&S. pp. 46-47; C.F.&S. (81) pp. 165-167 with ann. (80)-(81) pp. 363-364; ann. to P.&P. (33) p. 404

Musonius, Stoic moralist and philosopher active around A.D. 60-90: C.S.P. (30) p. 113

Nathan, prophet at the time of David (2 Sam. 7-12; 1 Chron. 29): C.F.&S. (46) p. 149

Nero, Emperor A.D. 54-68: S.S.&M. (8) and (9) pp. 61-62; compare P.&P. (40) pp. 298-299

Odes of Solomon, from the original Greek text; collection of Christian hymns from the second century; Gnostic and Montanist in character: I.&S. p. 8 with ann. 13 and 14, p. 320; M.&W. (30)-(39) pp. 241-255 with ann. (30)-(39) pp. 395-397; ann. to P.&P. (67) p. 409

Origen, of Alexandria, lived about A.D. 183-252: ann. 11 to I.&S. p. 319; ann. 22 to I.&S. p. 321; I.&S. p. 13; ann. 34 to I.&S. p.325; ann. 53 and 54 to I.&S. p. 327; ann. 65 to I.&S. p. 328; I.&S. p. 34 with ann. 72, p. 330; I.&S. pp. 36-37 with ann. 76-78, p. 331; I.&S. p. 38 with ann. 83 and 84, p. 332; ann. 95 to I.&S. p. 333; ann. 97 to I.&S. p. 334; S.S.&M. (5) p. 60; S.S.&M. (29) p. 90; C.S.P. (8) p. 97; C.S.P. (26) p. 107; ann. to C.F.&S. (1)-(5) p. 348; ann. to C.F.&S. (3) p. 351; ann. to C.F.&S. (80)-(81) p. 364; L.S.T.A.&L. (1) p. 171; L.S.T.A.&L. (13) p. 173; L.S.T.A.&L. (18) p. 174; L.S.T.A.&L. (44) p. 179; L.S.T.A.&L. (50) p. 180; ann. to L.S.T.A.&L. (20) p. 370; ann. to L.S.T.A.&L. (25) p. 371; ann. to L.S.T.A.&L. (50) p. 374; ann. to L.S.T.A.&L. (64) p. 383; P.&P. (86) p. 309; ann. to P.&P. (33) p. 404

Paeon, voluntary martyr c. A.D. 163 in Rome, at the martyrdom of Justin, the Christian woman Charito, Chariton, Hierax, Euelpistus, and Liberian: S.S.&M. (15) pp. 74-77

Papias, Bishop of Hierapolis, wrote in his old age, around A.D. 142, five explanatory writings about the Lord's Sayings: ann. 68 to I.&S. p. 329; ann. 74 to I.&S. pp. 330-331; C.F.&S. (36) p. 144 with ann. (36) pp. 356-357; C.F.&S. (67)

p. 159; C.F.&S. (73) p. 162 with ann. (73) p. 362; C.F. &S. (80) pp. 164-165 with ann. (80) p. 363; ann. to L.S.T. A.&L. (1)-(53) p. 366; L.S.T.A.&L. (31) p. 177

Papylus, evangelical prophet, martyred at Pergamum, Asia Minor, around the year 165: S.S.&M. (14) pp. 71-74

Papyrus: *see* Manuscripts

Paul, the Apostle to the Gentiles, became a Christian c. A.D. 35 and was executed in Rome c. A.D. 67 (see the New Testament for the Letters of Paul and the Acts of the Apostles): I.&S. pp. 5-7 with ann. 6, pp. 316-317 and 10, p. 318; I.&S. pp. 38, 43. (*Acts of "Paul"* written around A.D. 150 to 160 by a presbyter in Asia Minor, who was removed from office as a result, although, as he said, he had done it out of love for Paul; reported by Tertullian, *On Baptism* 17.) Ann. 66 to I.&S. p. 328; ann. 76 to I.&S. p. 331; ann. 83 to I.&S. p. 332; ann. 96 to I.&S. p. 333; S.S.&M. (17) p. 83; ann. to C.F.&S. (3) pp. 350-351, 352; ann. to C.F.&S. (36) p. 357; C.F.&S. (43) p. 148; C.F.&S. (81) pp. 165-167 with ann. (80)-(81) pp. 363, 364; L.S.T.A.&L. (39) p. 178 with ann. (38) and (39) p. 373; L.S.T.A.&L. (63) p. 204 with ann. (63) p. 383; ann. to L.S.T.A.&L. (64) pp. 383-384; ann. to M.&W. (26)-(41) p. 393; ann. to P.&P. (18) p. 401

Peter, the leading apostle of Jesus Christ in the first Church, executed around the year 67 at Rome; Letters of Peter in the New Testament; Proclamations of "Peter" (Kerygmata Petrou) in the *Pseudo-Clementines* I, from Palestine, written between A.D. 116 and 150; Proclamation of "Peter" (Kerygma Petrou) from Egypt written between A.D. 125 and 130; *Acts of "Peter"* from the *Pseudo-Clementines* II, written in Antioch in Syria around A.D. 200; *Vercelli Acts of "Peter"* written around A.D. 250; *Apocalypse (Revelation) of "Peter"* written about the years 100-135: I.&S.

pp. 3-5 with ann. 5, p. 316; ann. 9 and 10 to I.&S. pp. 317-319; ann. 62 and 63 to I.&S. p. 328; ann. 72-74 to I.&S. pp. 330-331; I.&S. p. 34; ann. to C.F.&S. (36) p. 357; C.F.&S. (73) p. 162; C.F.&S. (80) and (81) pp. 164-167 with ann. (80)-(81) p. 363; L.S.T.A.&L. (6) p. 172; ann. to L.S.T.A.&L. (15) p. 370; L.S.T.A.&L. (37) p. 178; L.S.T.A.&L. (53) p. 180; P.&P. (35) p. 295

Philip, one of the twelve disciples, who is said to have had two prophetic daughters. The *Acts of Philip* and *Deeds of Philip* are of a later date, the latter from the fourth century: ann. 74 to I.&S. p. 331; C.F.&S. (73) p. 162; L.S.T.A.&L. (6) p. 172

Philo, Alexandrian Jewish philosopher influenced by Greek thought; Jewish ambassador, loyal in upholding Mosaic Law and in making pilgrimages to Jerusalem, active around the years A.D. 35-40: ann. to C.S.P. (30), (31), and (32) p. 345

Pius, overseer of the Church at Rome c. A.D. 140-155: C.F. &S. (81) p. 167

Plato, the Greek philosopher, lived c. 427-347 B.C.: C.S.P. (32) pp. 114-115; C.F.&S. (69) p. 160

Pliny, the Younger, Governor of Bithynia, Asia Minor, during the years A.D. 111-113: S.S.&M. (11) pp. 63-65 with ann. (11) p. 338

Polycarp, Bishop of Smyrna, born in A.D. 69, executed on Feb. 23, 155: S.S.&M. (13) pp. 66-71; ann. to C.F.&S. (4) pp. 352-353; ann. to C.F.&S. (36) p. 357; L.S.T.A.&L. (62) and (63) pp. 203-205 with ann. (62) and (63) pp. 382-383; ann. to M.&W. (28) p. 394; M.&W. (42) p. 258 with ann. (42) p. 398; ann. to P.&P. (33) p. 403

Porphyry, wrote against the Christians in A.D. 268: I.&S. pp. 13-14 with ann. 27 and 28, p. 322; ann. 41 to I.&S. p. 325

Pothinus, overseer in Lyons, martyred at the age of 90 in A.D. 177: S.S.&M. (16) p. 79

Prisca, Priscilla, Montanist prophetess c. A.D. 170: P.&P. (59) p. 304; P.&P. (63) p. 305 with ann. (63) p. 408; P.&P. (65) p. 305; P.&P.(72) p. 307; P.&P. (77) p. 308

Pseudo-Cyprian: *see* Cyprian, Pseudo

Pseudo-Justin: *see* Justin, Pseudo

Ptolemaeus, "teacher" in the Church at Rome, martyred in A.D. 150: S.S.&M. (18) pp. 85-86

Pythagoras, the Greek philosopher, lived about 577-496 B.C.: C.F.&S. (69) p. 160

Quadratus, disciple of the apostles, and prophet; his Apology addressed to Hadrian in Athens around the year 125: ann. to P.&P. (33) p. 403

*Quaestiones Veteris et Novi Testamenti* (Questions Concerning the Old and New Testaments) by a presbyter at Rome in the year A.D. 375: I.&S. p. 49 with ann. 96, p. 333

Quintilla, Montanist prophetess, c. A.D. 160 170: P.&P. (63) p. 305

Quintus, martyred at Smyrna in A.D. 156 at the martyrdom of Polycarp and Germanicus: S.S.&M. (13) pp. 66-71

Rufinus, hermit, lived about A.D. 345-410: ann. to C.F.&S. (5) p. 353; ann. to L.S.T.A.&L. (64) p. 383

Rusticus, Prefect of the City of Rome c. A.D. 160-170: S.S. &M. (15) pp. 74-77

Sanctus, deacon martyred in the south of France: S.S.&M. (16) pp. 78-79

Saturninus, Proconsul at Carthage in the year A.D. 180: S.S. &M. (17) pp. 82-84

Saul, first King of Israel and Judah, reigned for twenty-two years before the year 1000 B.C. (1 Sam. 9-31; 1 Chron. 10): C.F.&S. (46) p. 149

Schwenkfeld, Kaspar von, lived from 1489 to 1561: ann. to M.&W. (30)-(39) p. 395

Serapion, Bishop of Antioch in A.D. 190-211: I.&S. p. 37 with ann. 79, p. 332

Serapion, the Egyptian at Thmuis, writer of the *Apophtheg-mata,* died about A.D. 358: ann. 60 to I.&S. p. 328

Severus, Septimius, Emperor A.D. 193-211: S.S.&M. (28) p. 90

*Shepherd*: *see* Hermas

Sibyl, *Sibylline Oracles,* ancient Greek prophetesses originating in Babylon, of whom already Heraclitus says that "they were driven by God to speak with raving mouths"; used as mouth-pieces before 500 B.C., later by the Romans, by the Jews, and by the Christians: C.S.P. (25) pp. 106-107 with ann. to (25) p. 344; C.F.&S. (47) p. 151; ann. to C.F.&S. (48) p. 358; P.&P. (39)-(41) pp. 298-300

Socrates, the Greek philosopher, lived from about 470 B.C. until his execution c. 400: C.S.P. (31) p. 114 with ann. (30), (31), and (32) p. 345; C.F.&S. (9) p. 133 with ann. (9) p. 355

Solomon, third King of Israel, reigned for 60 years around the year 1000 B.C. or soon after (1 Kings 1-11; 2 Chron. 1-9): C.F.&S. (46) pp. 149-150; C.F.&S. (70) p. 161; C.F.&S. (81) p. 167 with ann. (80)-(81) p. 363. The *Wisdom of "Solomon"* written about 50 or 100 years before Christ by a hellenized Jew. For the Christian "Odes of Solomon," *see* Odes: ann. to P.&P. (67) p. 409

Speratus, martyred with Secunda, Nartzalus, Cittinus, Donata, and Vestia (Hestia), Veturius, Felix, Aquilinus, Laetantius, Januaria, and Generosa, at Carthage on July 17, 180: S.S. &M. (17) pp. 82-84

Stephen, the leading prophetic deacon in the first Church at Jerusalem (Acts 6 and 7); martyred around the year A.D. 34: ann. to S.S.&M. (9) p. 335; ann. to C.F.&S. (36) p. 357

Suetonius, Roman historian, died A.D. 140: S.S.&M. (7) p. 61

⟨with ann. (7) p. 335⟩; ann. to S.S.&M. (10) p. 338

Tacitus, wrote his history, the *Annals,* in the years A.D. 115-117: S.S.&M. (8) p. 62 with ann. (8) p. 335

Talmud, Jewish books interpreting the Law for the life of the people; the first part Mishna written around A.D. 220; the second, the Aramaic Gemara finished around A.D. 350: ann. to L.S.T.A.&L. (46) p. 374

Tatian, born in Assyria, became a Christian around A.D. 150, and separated himself from the emerging institutional Church in A.D. 172: I.&S. p. 34 with ann. 72 and 73, p. 330; ann. 84 and 88 to I.&S. p. 332; S.S.&M. (25) p. 88; S.S.&M. (33) p. 91; C.S.P. (10) p. 98; C.F.&S. (44) pp. 148-149; P.&P. (8) and (10) p. 264

*Teaching of the Twelve Apostles, Didache,* written between the years A.D. 80 and A.D. 200 from Palestine: I.&S. p. 14 with ann. 31, p. 323 (note particularly) and ann. 35 p. 325; ann. 70 to I.&S. p. 329; I.&S. p. 51; ann. to L.S.T.A.&L. (1)-(53) p. 366; ann. to L.S.T.A.&L. (14) p. 369; L.S.T.A.&L. (54) pp. 181-189 with ann. (54) pp. 375-378; ann. to L.S.T.A.&L. (64) pp. 383-384; ann. to M.&W. (1)-(42) p. 387 and to (8)-(12) pp. 388-389; ann. to M.&W. (20)-(25) p. 392

Tertullian, Quintus Septimius Florens, lived around A.D. 153-222: ann. 32 to I.&S. pp. 323-324; ann. 34 and 44 to I.&S. p. 325; ann. 46, 50, 51, and 52 to I.&S. p. 326; ann. 55, 56, and 58 to I.&S. p. 327; I.&S. p. 27; ann. 67 and 68 to I.&S. pp. 328-329; ann. 72 to I.&S. p. 330; ann. 84, 85, 87, and 88 to I.&S. p. 332; I.&S. p. 48 with ann. 95 and 97, pp. 333, 334; ann. 99 and 101 to I.&S. p. 334; I.&S. p. 38; I.&S. pp. 50, 52; S.S.&M. (4) p. 60; S.S.&M. (27) p. 90; S.S.&M. (30), (31), and (32) pp. 90-91; C.S.P. (29) p. 113; ann. to C.S.P. (39) p. 346; ann. to C.F.&S. (1)-(5) p. 348; C.F.&S. (3) p. 129 with ann. (3) p. 350-352; Tertullian's life p. 352;

ann. to C.F.&S. (4) p. 353; ann. to (80)-(81) p. 364; ann. to L.S.T.A.&L. (11) p. 368;  ann. to L.S.T.A.&L. (37) p. 372; ann. to L.S.T.A.&L. (55) p. 379; M.&W. (3) p. 218; M.&W. (8) p. 221; P.&P. (42)-(44) and (46) pp. 300-301; P.&P. (48) and (49) p. 302; P.&P. (51)-(54) p. 303;  P.&P. (57)-(59) and (61) pp. 303-304;  P.&P. (62), (64), and (65) p. 305; P.&P. (72) and (73) p. 307; P.&P. (77) and (81) p. 308; (82) p. 309 with ann. (81) and (82) p. 410

*Testament of our Lord Jesus Christ,* title given to the first two books of the Syriac Book of Law translated from the Greek original into Syriac in A.D. 687; contains an eschatology or apocalypse from the mouth of Jesus and an expansion of *The Apostolic Tradition* by Hippolytus: ann. 62 to I.&S. p. 328; ann. to L.S.T.A.&L. (6) p. 368

Thaddaeus: *see* Addaeus

Thecla, called a prophetess or an apostle in the *Acts of Paul* (*see Acts of Paul,* c. A.D. 150, under Paul): ann. 83 to I.&S. p. 332

Theodore of Mopsuestia, A.D. 350-428, Bishop in Cilicia: I.&S. pp. 47-48 with ann. 94, p. 333

Theophilus, Bishop of Antioch, wrote his *Apology* and *To Autolycus* around A.D. 183: C.S.P. (40) p. 121; ann. to C.F.&S. (3) p. 352; C.F.&S. (47) p. 151; C.F.&S. (62) p. 158; P.&P. (6) p. 263

Thomas, the apostle, known from the New Testament, the "Israelite philosopher" who is said to have extended his missionary journeys as far as India: ann. 74 to I.&S. p. 331; C.F.&S. (73) p. 162; ann. to L.S.T.A.&L. (1)-(53) p. 365. *Acts of "Thomas,"* written A.D. 160-200, not without Gnostic influence: ann. 9 to I.&S. p. 318; ann. 64 to I.&S. p. 328; M.&W. (20) p. 232; M.&W. (22)-(25) pp. 235-239. Gospel of "Thomas" (Infancy Gospel): ann. to L.S.T.

A.&L. (43) p. 373. ⟨The Coptic *Gospel according to Thomas* discovered at Nag Hamâdi, Egypt, in 1945 (since the publishing of *Die ersten Christen*) has been used to augment the citations. The numbers used are those of the Brill edition by A. Guillaumont, H.-Ch. Puech, and others. It contains Sayings of Jesus, collected about A.D. 140, based on very early sources but showing Gnostic influence: ann. to L.S.T. A.&L. (1)-(53) p. 365; L.S.T.A.&L. (2) p. 171; L.S.T.A. &L. (15) and (17) p. 174; ann. to L.S.T.A.&L. (16) p. 370; L.S.T.A.&L. (21) p. 175; ann. to L.S.T.A.&L. (24) and (27) p. 371; L.S.T.A.&L. (28) p. 176⟩

Tiberius, Roman Emperor during the years A.D. 14-37: S.S.&M. (7) p. 61

Trajan, Roman Emperor during the years A.D. 98-117: S.S.&M. (11) pp. 63-65

Urbicus, City Prefect of Rome in the year A.D. 150: S.S.&M. (18) pp. 84-86

Vettius Epagathus, martyred with Blandina, Biblis, and Sanctus in the south of France, A.D. 177: S.S.&M. (16) p. 77

Zechariah, the prophet and author of the Old Testament book called after him, written during the reign of Darius Hystaspes, in Persia, 522-485 B.C.: C.F.&S. (58) p. 156

Zechariah, father of the prophet John the Baptist (Luke 1:5-25,39,67-80): S.S.&M. (16) p. 78

# SELECTED BIBLIOGRAPHY, GERMAN EDITION

From the wealth of literature thankfully used for this book, from all the text editions, translations, versions, and explanations of early Christianity, only some reference books can be listed here. In these, the reader who wants to explore further will meet the many works which make up the material and form the foundation of our book *The Early Christians* and which introduce him to the rest of the literature used.

Aall, A. *Der Logos.* Leipzig, 1896-1899.

Achelis, H. *Das Christentum in den ersten drei Jahrhunderten.* 2 vols. Leipzig: Quelle und Meyer, 1912 –.

———(trans. and ed.). *Die Syrische Didaskalia.* Leipzig: Joh. Flemming, 1904.

———. *Hippolytstudien.* Leipzig, 1897.

Archambault, G. *Dialogue avec Tryphon.* Greek text. Paris, 1909.

Arnold, C.F. *Die Geschichte der alten Kirche.* Leipzig: Quelle und Meyer, 1919.

———. *Zeittafeln und Überblicke zur Kirchengeschichte.* Weingarten's edition completely revised. Leipzig: Hinrichs, 1905.

———. *Studien zur plinianischen Christenverfolgung.* 1888.

———. *Die neronische Christenverfolgung.* 1888.

Arnold, Eberhard. *Innenland: Ein Wegweiser in die Seele der Bibel.* Sannerz and Leipzig, 1923. Especially the chapters "Der Geist" and "Das Wort."

Arnold, Gottfried. *Unparteiische Kirchen- und Ketzer-Historie.* Frankfurt, 1729. Schaffhausen, 1741.

Bardenhewer, O. *Geschichte der altkirchlichen Literatur.* 1902 and 1913, 1914.

——. *Patrologie.* Freiburg, 1910.

Bardenhewer, O; Schermann; and Weymann. *Bibliothek der Kirchenväter.* Kempten and Munich: Kösel, 1911 –, and also their old first edition, 1869-1888. Especially:

Bardenhewer, O; Schermann; and Weymann. *Frühchristliche Apologeten und Märtyrerakten.* 2 vols. 1914.

Zeller. *Die apostolischen Väter.* 1918.

Häuser. *Justinus Dialog. Pseudo-Justinus Mahnrede.* 1917.

Klebba. *Irenäus.* 2 vols. 1912.

Bigelmair, and Pfättisch, L. *Eusebius von Cäsarea.* 1913.

Stiefenhofer. *Macarius, des Ägypter Schriften.* 1913.

Preysing. *Hippolytus von Rom.* 1922.

Kellner. *Tertullians ausgewählte Schriften.* Vol. 1, 1912. Vol. 2, 1915.

Koetschau. *Origenes.* 1926.

Baer. *Cyprianus sämtliche Schriften.* 1918.

Bonwetsch, N. and Achelis, H. *Hippolyts Werke.* 1897-1916.

——. *Die Prophetie im apostolischen und nachapostolischen Zeitalter.* 1884.

Bonwetsch, N. *Geschichte des Montanismus.* 1881.

——. *Texte zur Geschichte des Montanismus.* 1914.

Bousset, W. *Hauptprobleme der Gnosis.* 1907.

Bratke, E. *Wegweiser zur Quellen- und Literaturkunde der Kirchengeschichte.* 1890.

Cavallera, F. *Indices zur Series Graeca.* Paris, 1912.

Christ, W.v. *Geschichte der griechischen Literatur.* Revised by W. Schmidt and O. Stählin. Vol. 2, from 100-530. Munich: Chr. Kaiser, 1913.

Deissmann, A. *Licht vom Osten: Das Neue Testament und die neutestamentlichen Texte der hellenischrömischen Welt.* Tübingen, 1923.

Delitzsch, F. and Schnedermann, G. *Jüdische Theologie auf Grund des Talmud.* 1897.

Dobschütz, E. v. *Das apostolische Zeitalter.* 1904, 1905.

―――. *Probleme des apostolischen Zeitaltars.* Leipzig, 1904.

―――. *Die urchristlichen Gemeinden.* 1902.

Dölger, F. J. *Das Fischsymbol in frühchristlicher Zeit.* Rome, 1910.

Dorsch, E. *Der Opfercharakter der heiligen Eucharistie.* 1909.

Ehrhard, A. *Die altchristliche Literatur und ihre Erforschung von 1884-1900. Erste Abteilung: Die vornicäische Literatur.* Freiburg in Breisgau, 1900.

Erbes, C. *Ursprung und Umfang der Petrusakten.* 1911.

Faye, E. d. *Introduction à l'étude du gnosticisme.* Paris, 1903.

Ficker, J. *Studien über christliche Denkmäler.* 1902 –. (Earlier *Archäologische Studien,* 1895-1899.)

Funk, F. X. *Didascalia et constitutiones Apostolorum.* Paderborn, 1905.

―――. *Doctrina Duodecim Apostolorum.* Tübingen, 1887.

―――(ed. with Latin version). *Canones Apostolorum.* Tübingen, 1877.

―――. *Patres apostolici.* Tübingen, 1901. Revised by F. Diekamp, 1913.

―――(ed.). *Opera Patrum Apostolicorum.* Vols. 1 and 2. Tübingen, 1871.

Gebhardt, O. v. *Acta martyrum: Ausgewählte Märtyrerakten.* Berlin, 1902.

Gebhardt, O. v; Harnack; and Zahn. *Patres apostolici.* 1875, 1876, 1877, and 1878.

Gebhardt, O. v. and Harnack. *Texte und Untersuchungen zur*

*Geschichte der altchristlichen Literatur.* 1883–. For example: *Tatiani oratio ad Graecos.* Revised by Eduard Schwartz. Leipzig, 1888 and 1891.

Geffcken, J. *Christliche Apokryphen.* 1908.

Gersdorf. *Recognitiones clement.* 1838.

Goltz, E. v. d. *Tischgebete und Abendmahlsgebete.* 1905.

Goodspeed, E. J. *Die ältesten Apologeten.* Göttingen, 1915.

———. *Index patristicus.* 1907.

———. *Index apologeticus.* 1912.

Grapin, E. *Eusèbe: Hist. eccl.* Vols. 9 and 10. Paris, 1913.

Hahn, A. and L. *Bibliothek der Symbole und Glaubensregeln der alten Kirche.* Breslau, 1897.

Harnack, A. *Hermae Pastor Graece.* With a Latin version, revised and elucidated by Oscar v. Gebhardt and others. Leipzig, 1877.

———. *Die Mission und Ausbreitung des Christentums in den ersten drei Jahrhunderten.* Leipzig: Hinrichs, 1923, 1924.

———. *Geschichte der altchristlichen Literatur bis Eusebius. Die Überlieferung und der Bestand.* Leipzig, 1893.

———. *Lehrbuch der Dogmengeschichte.* Vol. 1. 1894-1897.

———. *Grundriss der Dogmengeschichte.* 1898.

———. *Entstehung und Entwicklung der Kirchenverfassung.* 1910.

———. *Analecta.* 1905.

———. *Militia Christi.* 1905.

———. *Tertullians Bibliothek christlicher Schriften.* 1914.

———. *Tatians Rede an die Griechen.* Translated into German. Giessen, 1884.

———. *Das Neue Testament um das Jahr 200.* Freiburg, 1889.

———. *Die Entstehung des Neuen Testaments.* 1914.

———. *Über den privaten Gebrauch der heiligen Schriften in der alten Kirche.* 1912.

――――. *Der Vorwurf des Atheismus in den ersten drei Jahrhunderten.* 1903.

――――. *Chronologie der altchristlichen Literatur.* Leipzig, 1894, 1897.

Heinrici, F. G. *Das Urchristentum.* Göttingen, 1902.

Hemmer, Oger, and Laurent. *Les pères apostoliques.* Paris, 1907.

Hennecke, E. *Neutestamentliche Apokryphen.* 2nd ed. Tübingen: Mohr (Siebeck), 1924.

――――. *Handbuch zu den neutestamentlichen Apokryphen.* Tübingen: Mohr (Siebeck), 1904.

――――. *Die Apologie des Aristides: Recension und Reconstruction des Textes.* Texte und Untersuchungen (IV, 3). Leipzig, 1893.

Herzog, J. J., and Hauck, A. *Realencyclopädie für protestantische Theologie und Kirche.* Leipzig, 1896-1906. Many articles.

Heussi. *Kompendium der Kirchengeschichte.* Tübingen: Mohr (Siebeck), 1909 –.

Hilgenfeld, A. (ed.). *Ignatii Antiocheni et Polycarpi Smyrnaei: Epistolae et Martyria.* Berlin, 1902.

――――. *Novum Testamentum extra canonem receptum.* 1866, 1876-1884.

――――. *Ketzergeschichte des Urchristentums.* Leipzig, 1884.

Heikel, J. A. *Eusebius Werke.* Leipzig, 1902.

Hoennicke, G. *Das Judenchristentum im ersten und zweiten Jahrhundert.* 1908.

Holl, K. *Tertullian als Schriftsteller.* 1897.

James. *Apokrypha anecdota.* 1893, 1897.

Jordan, H. *Geschichte der altchristlichen Literatur.* 1911.

Kattenbusch, F. *Das apostolische Symbol.* Leipzig, 1891-1900.

Kautzsch, E. *Die Apokryphen und Pseudepigraphen des Alten Testaments.* Tübingen: Mohr (Siebeck), 1900.

Keim, Th. *Celsus: Wahres Wort.* 1873.

Kittel, Rud. *Die Oden Salomos.*

Klein. *Aus der Schatzkammer heiliger Väter.* Berlin: Deutsche Evangelische Buch- und Traktat-Gesellschaft.

Klosterman, E. *Eusebius Werke.* Leipzig, 1906.

Knopf, R. *Einführung in das Neue Testament: Bibelkunde des N. T. Geschichte und Religion des Urchristentums.* 1919. Weinel und Lietzmann, 1923.

————. *Das nachapostolische Zeitalter: Geschichte der christlichen Gemeinden vom Beginn der Flavierdynastie bis zum Ende Hadrians.* Tübingen, 1905.

————. *Ausgewählte Märtyrerakten.* Tübingen and Leipzig, 1901.

————. *Der erste Clemensbrief.* Analytical edition. 1899.

Kötschau. *Origenes gegen Celsus.* 1899.

Krüger, G. *Geschichte der altchristlichen Literatur in den ersten drei Jahrhunderten.* Freiburg and Leipzig, 1895.

————. *Sammlung ausgewählter kirchen- und dogmengeschichtlicher Quellenschriften.* Tübingen, 1891. 1904.

————. *Justin: Apologie.* 1915.

Kunze, J. *Glaubensregel, heilige Schrift und Taufbekenntnis.* Leipzig, 1899.

Lagarde de. *Homilie clement.* 1865.

Lietzmann, H. *Liturgische Texte zur Geschichte der orientalischen Taufe und Messe im zweiten und vierten Jahrhundert.* 1909.

————. *Handbuch zum Neuen Testament.*

————. *Kleine Texte für theologische und philologische Vorlesungen und Übungen.* 1902 –.

Lipsius, R. A. *Die apokryphen Apostelgeschichten und Apostellegenden.* Brunswick, 1883-1890.

Lipsius, R. A. and Bonnet, N. *Acta apostolorum apocrypha.* 1891 –.

————. *Zur Quellenkritik des Epiphanios.* Vienna, 1865.

Loofs, F. *Leitfaden der Dogmengeschichte.* Halle: Niemeyer, 1906.

Maranus and Prudentius. *Die griechischen Apologeten.* Paris, 1742. Venice, 1747.

Mehlhorn. *Aus den Quellen der Kirchengeschichte.* Book 1, up to Constantine. Berlin: Reimer, 1894.

Migne, J. P. *Patrologiae cursus completus, series graeca.* Paris, 1857-1866.

————. *Patrologiae cursus completus, series latina.* Paris, 1844-1855.

Oehler, F. (ed.). *Tertulliani opera.* Leipzig, 1853-54.

Otto, J. C. Th. v. *Corpus Apologetarum Christianorum saeculi secundi.* Jena, 1847, 1857, 1861, 1877, and 1879.

Overbeck, F. "Über die Anfänge der patristischen Literatur." *Histor. Zeitschrift.* Edited by v. Sybel. 1882.

Pfättisch, J. M. *Justinus des Philosophen und Märtyrers Apologieen,* Münster, 1912.

Patigny. *Textes et documents.* Paris, 1904.

Pearson, J. B. *Conspectus auctorum. . . . Patrologiae graeco-latinae.* 1882.

Peter, H. *Die geschichtliche Literatur über die römische Kaiserzeit bis Theodosius I und ihre Quellen.* 1897.

Pfleiderer, O. *Das Urchristentum: seine Schriften und Lehren.* Berlin, 1902.

Preuschen, E. *Antilegomena: Die Reste der ausserkanonischen Evangelien.* Giessen: Töpelmann, 1905.

————. *Zwei gnostische Hymnen.* Giessen, 1904.

Preussische Akademie der Wissenschaften. *Die griechischen christlichen Schriftsteller der ersten drei Jahrhunderte.* Leipzig: Kirchenväter-Kommission, 1897 –.

Probst, F. *Lehre und Gebet in den ersten drei Jahrhunderten.* 1871.

Puech, A. *Les apologistes grecs du 2 siècle de notre ère.* 1912.

Rauschen, G. *Grundriss der Patrologie.* 1910, 1913.

————. *Florilegium patristicum.* Bonn, 1904 to 1911.

Reifferscheid, and Wissowa, G. *Tertulliani opera.* Vienna, 1890 –.

Rinn and Jüngst. *Kirchengeschichtliches Lesebuch.* Large edition. Tübingen: Mohr (Siebeck), 1906.

Ritschl, A. *Die Entstehung der altkatholischen Kirche.* Bonn, 1857.

Robinson, J. A. (ed.). *Texts and Studies: Contributions to Biblical and Patristic Literature.* Cambridge: University Press, 1891-1909.

Rolffs, E. *Urkunden aus dem antimontanistischen Kampfe.* 1895.

Ruinart. *Acta primorum martyrum sincera et selecta.* Paris, 1689. Regensburg, 1854.

Schanz, M. *Geschichte der römischen Literatur.* 1905.

Scheel, O. *Die Kirche im Urchristentum.* 1912.

Schermann, Th. *Die allgemeine Kirchenordnung frühchristlicher Liturgien und kirchlicher Überlieferung.* 1914, 1916.

Schmidtke, A. *Neue Fragmente und Untersuchungen zu den judenchristlichen Evangelien.* 1911.

Schwartz, E. and Mommsen, T. *Eusebius von Cäsarea: Eccles. historia.* Greek and Latin. Leipzig, 1903-1909.

Schwartz, E. *Über die pseudo-apostolischen Kirchenordnungen.* Strasbourg, 1910.

Schultze, V. *Archäologie der altchristlichen Kunst.* 1895.

Seeberg, R. *Lehrbuch der Dogmengeschichte.* Leipzig: Deichert, 1913.

Sievers, E. *Tatian.* Latin and Old German. 1892.

Soden, H. v. *Mysterium und sacramentum in den ersten zwei Jahrhunderten der Kirche.* 1911.

Sohm, R. *Kirchenrecht.* Vol. 1. 1892.

————. *Wesen und Ursprung des Katholizismus.* 1912.

Stählin, O. *Clemens von Alexandria.* 1905-1909.

Stieren, A. *Apparatus ad Opera Sancti Irenaei Episcopi Lugdunensis.* Leipzig: T. O. Weigel, 1853.

————. *Irenaei contra omnes haereses libri quinque.* 1853-1858.

————. *Epiphan. Sancti Irenaei Episcopi Lugdunensis.* Leipzig, 1851.

Teuffel. *Geschichte der römischen Literatur.* 1913.

Tischendorf. *Evangelia apocrypha.* 1876.

Troeltsch, E. *Die Soziallehren der christlichen Kirchen.* Tübingen: J. C. Mohr (Siebeck), 1919.

Voigt, H. G. *Eine verschollene Urkunde des antimontanistischen Kampfes.* Leipzig, 1891.

Waltzing, J. P. Louvain, 1902, 1906, 1907. *Minucius Felix: Dialogue Octavius.* In Bibliotheka Teubneriana. Leipzig, 1912.

————. *Studia Minuciana.* Paris, 1906.

Weinel, H. *Die Wirkungen des Geistes und der Geister.* Freiburg, 1899.

Weiss, J. *Das Urchristentum.* 1914.

Weizsäcker, C. *Das apostolische Zeitalter der christlichen Kirche.* Tübingen and Leipzig: J. C. Mohr (Siebeck), 1902.

Wendland, P. *Hippolytus Werke.* Published for the Kirchenväterkommission der preussischen Akademie der Wissenschaft. Leipzig, 1916.

————. *Die hellenistisch-römische Kultur in ihren Beziehungen zu Judentum und Christentum.* 1907.

————. "Die urchristlichen Literaturformen." In *Handkommentar zum Neuen Testament.* Lietzmann. 1912.

Wernle, P. *Die Anfänge unserer Religion.* Tübingen and Leipzig, 1904.

Wetter. *Altchristliche Liturgien.* 2 vols. Göttingen: Vandenhoeck und Ruprecht, 1921, 1922.

Wieland, F. *Mensa und confessio.* 1906.

Wiener Akademie der Wissenschaften. *Corpus scriptorum ecclesiasticorum latinorum.* Vienna, 1866 –.

Wobbermin, G. *Altchristliche liturgische Stücke.* 1899.

Zahn, Th. *Ignatii et Polycarpi Epistulae. Martyria Fragmenta.* Edited and elucidated. In Patrum Apostolicorum Opera, vol. 2, Leipzig, 1876.

————. *Skizzen aus dem Leben der alten Kirche.* Leipzig: A. Deichert, 1908.

————. *Geschichte des neutestamentlichen Kanons.* Erlangen, 1888-1889, 1890, 1892, 1893.

————. *Einleitung in das Neue Testament.*

————. *Acta Joannis.* Revised with the use of T. von Tischendorf's bequest. Erlangen, 1880.

————. *Das Evangelium des Petrus.*

————. *Das apostolische Symbolum: Eine Skizze seiner Geschichte und eine Prüfung seines Inhalts.*

————. *Forschungen zur Geschichte des neutestamentlichen Kanons und der altchristlichen Literatur.* Erlangen and Leipzig, 1881-1908. Subdivisions cover: Tatians Diatessaren, Supplementum Clementinum, Analecta zur Geschichte und Literatur im zweiten Jahrhundert, Apostel und Apostelschüler in der Provinz Asien, Brüder und Vettern Jesu.

# SELECTED BIBLIOGRAPHY,
# ENGLISH EDITION

This bibliography is to indicate some source books and provide further reading for the English reader.

Altaner, B. *Patrology*. Translated by H. C. Graef. 2nd ed. New York: Herder and Herder, 1961.

Arnold, E. *Salt and Light: Talks and Writings on the Sermon on the Mount*. Rifton, N. Y.: The Plough Publishing House, 1967.

Baillie, J.; McNeill, J. T.; and Dusen, H. P. van. *Library of Christian Classics*. Vols. 1 and 2. Philadelphia: The Westminster Press.

Bainton, R. H. *Christian Attitudes to War and Peace*. Nashville, Tenn.: Abingdon Press, 1960.

———. *Early Christianity*. Princeton, N.J.: D. Van Nostrand Company, Inc., 1960.

Brightman, F. E. *Liturgies Eastern and Western*. 2 vols. Oxford, 1906.

Canfield, L. H. *The Early Persecutions of the Christians*. New York, 1913.

Chadwick, H. (trans. and ed.). *Origen: Contra Celsum*. Cambridge: University Press, 1965.

——— and Oulton, J. E. L. (ed.). *Alexandrian Christianity*. The Library of Christian Classics, vol. 2. Philadelphia: The Westminster Press, 1953.

Charles, R. H. *Apocrypha and Pseudepigrapha*. 2 vols. Oxford, 1913.

Connolly, R. H. (trans.). *Didascalia apostolorum*. Oxford, 1929.

Crafer, T. W. *The Apocriticus of Macarius Magnes*. London: S. P. C. K., 1919.

Deissmann, A. *Light from the Ancient East*. Translated by L. R. Strachan. London: Hodder and Stoughton, 1910.

De Soyres, J. *Montanism and the Primitive Church: A Study in the Ecclesiastical History of the Second Century.* Cambridge: Deighton, Bell and Co., 1878. Reprint, Lexington, Ky.: American Theological Library Association, 1965.

Dunkerley, R. *Beyond the Gospels.* Baltimore, Md.: Penguin Books Inc., 1957.

Easton, B. S. (trans. and ed.). *The Apostolic Tradition of Hippolytus.* Cambridge: University Press, 1934. Reprint, U. S. A.: Archon Books, 1962.

Falls, T. B. (trans.). *Saint Justin Martyr: The First Apology, The Second Apology, Dialogue with Trypho, Exhortation to the Greeks, Discourse to the Greeks, The Monarchy or The Rule of God.* The Fathers of the Church, vol. 6. Edited by L. Schopp. Washington, D. C.: Catholic University of America Press, 1948.

Frend, W. H. C. *Martyrdom and Persecution in the Early Church: A Study of a Conflict from the Maccabees to Donatus.* Garden City, N.Y.: Anchor Books, Doubleday and Company, Inc., 1967.

Glover, R. T. (trans.). *Tertullian: Apology, De spectaculis.* Rendall, G. H. (trans.). *Minucius Felix.* Loeb Classical Library. Cambridge, Mass.: Harvard University Press, 1960.

Goodspeed, E. J. (trans.). *The Apostolic Fathers: An American Translation.* London: Independent Press Ltd., 1950. Copyright by Harper & Brothers, U. S. A.

Grant, R. M. *The Apostolic Fathers: A New Translation and Commentary.* 6 vols. Camden, N. J.: Thomas Nelson & Sons, 1968.

———(ed.). *Second-Century Christianity: A Collection of Fragments.* London: S. P. C. K., 1957.

Guillaumont, A.; Puech, H.-Ch.; Quispel, G.; Till, W.; and †Yassah 'Abd Al Masih; (trans. and ed.). *The Gospel according to Thomas.* New York: Harper & Brothers, 1959.

Harmon, A. M. (trans. and ed.). *Lucian.* Vol. 5. Cambridge: Loeb Classical Library.

Harnack, A. *The Constitution and Law of the Church in the First Two Centuries.* London, 1910.

———. *History of Dogma.* Vol. 1. Translation by Neil Buchanan of *Lehrbuch der Dogmengeschichte.* New York: Russell & Russell, 1958.

———. *The Mission and Expansion of Christianity in the First Three Centuries.* Vol. 1. Translated and edited by James Moffat. New York: Harper & Brothers, 1962.

———. *The Origin of the New Testament.* English translation, 1925.

———. *Outlines of the History of Dogma.* Boston: The Beacon Press, 1957.

Hennecke, E. *New Testament Apocrypha.* English translation edited by R. McL. Wilson. 2 vols. Philadelphia: Westminster Press, 1963 and 1965.

James, M. R. (trans.). *The Apocryphal New Testament: Being the Apocryphal Gospels, Acts, Epistles, and Apocalypses.* Oxford: Clarendon Press, 1953.

Jeremias, J. *Unknown Sayings of Jesus.* London: S. P. C. K., 1958.

Kelly, J. N. D. *Early Christian Creeds.* London: Longmans, Green and Co., 1950.

Krüger, G. *History of Early Christian Literature in the First Three Centuries.* Translated by C. R. Gillet. New York, 1897.

Labriolle, P. de. *La Crise Montaniste.* Paris, 1913.

———. *Les Sources de l'histoire du Montanisme.* Fribourg, Switzerland, 1913.

Lawlor, H. J., and Oulton, J. E. L. (trans. and ed.). *Eusebius, Bishop of Caesarea: Ecclesiastical History and the Martyrs of Palestine.* 2 vols. London: S. P. C. K., 1954.

Lightfoot, J. B. (trans. and ed.). *The Apostolic Fathers.* 5 vols. London, 1889-1890. One-vol. edition by J. Harmer, London, 1893.

Owen, E. C. E. *Some Authentic Acts of Early Martyrs.* Oxford: Clarendon Press, 1927.

Quasten, J. *Patrology.* Vols. 1 and 2. Westminster, Md.: The Newman Press, 1951, 1953.

────── and Plumpe, J. C. (ed.). *Ancient Christian Writers: The Works of the Fathers in Translation.* Vols. 1, 6, and 13. Westminster, Md.: The Newman Press, 1946, 1948, and 1951.

Richardson, C. C. (ed.). *Early Christian Fathers.* The Library of Christian Classics, vol. 1. Philadelphia: The Westminster Press, 1953.

Roberts, A. and Donaldson, J. (ed.). *The Ante-Nicene Fathers: Translations of the Writings of the Fathers down to A. D. 325.* American edition, edited by A. C. Coxe, 1896 ff. 10 vols. Reprint Grand Rapids, Mich.: Wm. B. Eerdmans Pub. Co., 1952.

Robinson, J. A. (trans.). *St. Irenaeus: The Demonstrations of the Apostolic Teaching.* London: S. P. C. K., 1920.

────── (ed.). *Texts and Studies: Contributions to Biblical and Patristic Literature.* Cambridge: University Press, 1891-1909. For example: *The Apology of Aristides On Behalf of the Christians.* Translated and edited by J. R. Harris. 1891.

Stevenson, J. (ed.). *A New Eusebius: Documents illustrative of the history of the Church to A. D. 337.* London: S. P. C. K., 1957.

Terry, M. S. (trans.). *The Sibylline Oracles.* 2nd ed. New York, 1899.

Troeltsch, E. *The Social Teaching of the Christian Churches.* Translated by Olive Wyon. 2 vols. New York: Harper and Row, 1960.

Weiss, J. *Earliest Christianity: A History of the Period A.D. 30-150.* Translated by F. C. Grant. Vol. 1. New York: Harper and Brothers, 1959.

Workman, H. B. *Persecution in the Early Church: A Chapter in the History of Renunciation.* London: Charles H. Kelly, 1906.

Zahn, Th. *Introduction to the New Testament.* English translation. Edinburgh, 1909.

# THE SYMBOLS USED IN THIS BOOK

The following early Christian symbols appear in gold on a red background immediately preceding each major section of this volume.

 The Cross with alpha and omega:
Jesus, "the first and the last,
the beginning and the end"

 The Cross and flames:
martyrdom of the believers

 A fish swimming in water:
the Christian who lives
in the water of baptism

 The open vessel: faith
Above it the Cross combined
with a Christ monogram (chrismon)

 Early catacomb sign combining:
the sun symbolizing Christ,
a chrismon, alpha and omega—
all in threes for the Trinity

 Catacomb sign of a woman:
the Church in prayer
Chrismon: earliest known
symbol for Christ

The Cross and the sun
with rays streaming outward:
Jesus the Christ

Each of the following illuminated letters contains an early
Christian symbol corresponding with a dominant theme in the
portion of the Introduction and Survey which it precedes.

A ship with the Cross for its mast:
the Church

The fish outline: Christ
The wheat and the grapes:
the Lord's Supper

The deer drinking from a pool:
Christian baptism

The Cross and flames:
martyrdom of the believers

The dove and the serpent:
the fight between
Good and Evil

The three fish:
the Holy Trinity

The original cover was designed by Rudolf Koch. The wood-cut "Light-Struggle of the Early Christians" is by Daniel Greiner. The book owes the indexes and the work entailed to Else von Hollander in Sannerz.